# Motion Picture Directors:

## A Bibliography of Magazine and Periodical Articles, 1900-1972

compiled by
MEL SCHUSTER

The Scarecrow Press, Inc.
Metuchen, N. J.      1973

Library of Congress Cataloging in Publication Data

Schuster, Mel.
    Motion picture directors.

    1. Moving-picture producers and directors--
Biography--Bibliography.  I.  Title.
Z5784.M9S34      016.79143'0233'0922        73-780
ISBN 0-8108-0590-1

# ACKNOWLEDGMENTS

Much of the material referred to in this volume was located and viewed through the impressive cooperation of numerous persons including private collectors, publication editors and staffs, and magazine/book retailers. Sincere gratitude is extended to all those who took time to grant requests for assistance: to the various Manhattan and Brooklyn branch library staffs for helpful guidance, especially the Lincoln Center branch where much of this work was done; to Rod Bladel, Theatre Collection, Lincoln Center Library, whose interest in this project from the beginning and continuing through the completion, often served as needed encouragement; to Richard Trupp and Caroline Underwood, friends who provided valuable research assistance; to Robert F. Gray, actor and fellow film lover, for providing extremely useful material; to Ernest D. Burns, proprietor of Cinemabilia, for patience with my difficult requests, and cooperation which contributed no small amount toward the completeness of coverage attained.

Correspondence with magazine editors and staffs resulted in an amazing degree of cooperation. The majority of my requests were positively acknowledged: material was supplied; I was allowed to actually view magazines in their offices; avenues of search were suggested which led to missing issues. The list of contributors is long, but it also will reflect the remarkable cooperation granted this project from the magazine staffs. Their assistance filled in gaps within the run of a magazine, allowing for a high degree of completeness throughout this volume.

My sincere thanks to: William Como, After Dark; Peter Sainsbury, Afterimage; Sarajane Johnson, American Film Institute Publications; George Stover, Black Oracle; Calvin Beck, Castle of Frankenstein; Gary Crowdus, Cineaste; Frederick S. Clarke, Cinefantastique; Janey Place, Cinema (BH); Richard Dyer MacCann, Cinema Journal; Paula G. Putney, Contempora; Ben Hamilton, CTVD; Richard Corliss, Film Comment; Leonard Maltin, Film Fan Monthly; Anthony Macklin, Film Heritage; Thomas R. Atkins, The Film

Journal; William Sloan, Film Library Quarterly; Suni Mallow;
Filmmaker's Newsletter; Murray Summers, Filmograph;
Charles Phillips Reilly, Films In Review; June Carlsen, For
Monsters Only; Mike Barrier, Funnyworld; Gary J. Svehla,
Gore Creatures; Greg Shoemaker, Japanese Fantasy Film
Journal; Don Shay, Kaleidoscope; Boone Mancall, Making
Films in New York; Mark Frank, Photon, Marie Ricci,
Show; Mrs. Esme J. Dick, Sightlines; Peter Lebensold,
Take One; Barry Tanenbaum, Todays Filmmaker; James F.
Haughton, TV Guide.

# TABLE OF CONTENTS

# INTRODUCTION

This bibliography is a research guide to articles appearing in English language magazines and periodicals from 1900 through October 1972, devoted to motion picture directors, filmmakers, and animators.

Over two thousand three hundred directors, filmmakers* and animators (hereafter referred to collectively as directors) are represented herein, appearing either in the bulk of the book, or in the listing of directors on whom no material was found.

The material sought was biographical or career-oriented in nature. No reviews of individual works are included unless the review was expanded to include critical or analytical conclusions about the artist and/or work which might have research value beyond the review of a given work. In some cases the material referred to is brief. In that this was often the only information discovered about some directors, it was decided these notes should be included. There are also references to brief quotes which were considered of possible value to the researcher.

## Publications Covered

Mass fame is a comparatively new reward to directors; the bulk of the literature on their art exists in film magazines. However, a large majority of these magazines have not been documented by such bibliographic services as Readers' Guide or Biography Index which deal primarily with magazines less specific in content.

Two bibliographies of current film magazines were used as guides for this research:

---

*"Filmmakers" enjoys a variety of appearances: film makers, FilmMakers, film-makers, filmmakers. Throughout this work it has been standardized as "filmmakers."

1. Reilly, Adam. Current Film Periodicals in English; An Annotated Bibliography. Revised January 1970. Privately Published, 1970.

2. Reilly, Adam. Current Film Periodicals in English. Revised edition January 1972. New York: The Educational Film Library Association, 1972.

Pursuing those publications applicable to the needs of this work resulted in a total of 340* magazines researched (see Appendix I). In the case of film/theatre/entertainment publications not elsewhere documented, a concentrated effort was made to actually view or in some other reliable way become informed of the contents of every single issue during the run of a given magazine. In spite of stringent pursuits, there are a few missing issues here and there, primarily in the English publications not so easily accessible in the United States; most notably the first year of Films & Filming and a here-and-there issue of Brighton Film Review. In spite of scattered, small gaps, the 100 per cent completeness of coverage given to all publications is in the high majority.

It should be noted that the world of newspapers is vast, and worthy of a separate treatment. Except for special supplements, newspapers are not included. The New York Times is a valuable source, and an occasional article is quoted. However, no concentrated effort was made to include it, except in that the Biographical Edition, now in its third year, was documented. These are loose pages, usually accessible on open shelves and readily reproduced for personal use. Most newspapers do interviews, personality portraits and obituaries. It thus seemed subjective to include The New York Times. However, The New York Times does its own documentation which is available in most large libraries.

As to the coverage of "general" magazines, this information was obtained from existing bibliographic sources (below) and reflects the duration of coverage given by those

---

*This figure is modest in that the bibliographic works examined reflect a vast number of publications not applicable to the interests of this book. Thus the researcher may know that if a magazine is examined by (e.g.) Readers' Guide, but is not listed in this volume, there has been no literature on directors done by that publication.

sources (in most cases that coverage has been quite thorough).

Biography Index: A Cumulative Index to Biographical Material in Books and Magazines. New York: H. W. Wilson Co., 1946-1971.

The Dramatic Index. Boston: F. W. Faxon Co., Inc., 1909-1949.

International Index to Periodicals. New York: H. W. Wilson Co., 1931-1963.

Miles, Mildred Lynn. Index to Playboy: Belles-Lettres, Articles and Humor, December 1953-December 1969. Metuchen, N. J.: Scarecrow Press, 1970.

The New York Times Obituaries Index. New York: New York Times, 1958-1968.

Readers' Guide to Periodical Literature. New York: H. W. Wilson Co., 1900-1971.

Schuster, Mel. Motion Picture Performers: A Bibliography of Magazine and Periodical Articles, 1900-1969. Metuchen, N. J.: Scarecrow Press, 1971.

Social Sciences and Humanities Index. New York: H. W. Wilson Co., 1965-1971.

Although inclusion of references already available in other bibliographic sources may seem redundant, it should serve as a convenient, time-saving device to the researcher whose necessity to wade through all those volumes is now obviated. Furthermore, it is conceivable that a library may not own the complete run of a given bibliographic publication, or indeed subscribe to it at all.

Abbreviated references to publications have been kept to a minimum. A complete list of publications covered appears as Appendix I, which will help clarify any questions.

How to Read the Entries

As much information as possible has been given in each entry. Some entries are less than complete, e. g., no issue number, no page number, no date. However, where available, complete data has been shown.

EXAMPLE

Moskowitz, G.  Robert Aldrich in Berlin.  Sight & Sound 27-
  4:177 Spg '58

(An article by G. Moskowitz entitled "Robert Aldrich in Berlin"
can be found on page 177 of Sight & Sound, vol. 27, issue no. 4,
dated Spring 1958. )

Although there are occasional variations, in every case
there is enough information to lead the researcher to the de-
sired article.  (See Appendix II for Key to Abbreviations used
within the entries. )

## Where to Find Sought-After Material

"The library" should be the logical answer to this problem, but it is quite frequently not the solution.  Even the spectacular collection at New York's Lincoln Center Library does
not subscribe to all film publications, and there are frequent
missing issues in the runs of those to which they do subscribe.  However, "the library" (and, if possible, the
Lincoln Center Library) is the prime source.

Film magazines do not lose their value with age.
Quite the reverse is true; their value may increase alarm-
ingly with age!  Many back issues of a magazine are available directly from the publisher.  Adam Reilly's work (already referred to) often quotes prices of back issues, or a
note to the publisher will elicit this information.  Various
retail sources (walk-in and mail order) devoted to film,
both active and nostalgic, are stocked with back issues,
most notably Cinemabilia in New York City, and Larry Edmonds Book Shop in Los Angeles.  When all else fails, a
modest fee will place an ad in a film magazine which may
provide contact.  Film buffs often exhibit a family interest
in the needs of other buffs.

## Directors Covered in This Work

Establishing criteria for inclusion became a problem
which was here questionably solved.  The director's art has
grown informally, resulting in a vast number of participants.
Obviously it was meaningless to research the thousands who

have one or two films to their credit, but who achieved no lasting (or even temporary) success or glory as a director. The problem became even more complex in the case of "occasional" directors who enjoyed fame in other professional areas, e.g., writers, cinematographers, artists, photographers, choreographers, and especially actors/actresses who seem to be increasingly interested in giving directing a try. A tremendous amount of material exists on such occasional and diverse film directors as Marc Chagall, Salvador Dalí, Man Ray, Howard Hughes, Harry Houdini, Goeran Gentele, Marcel Duchamp, José Quintero, Clifford Odets, Frank O'Connor, Ben Hecht, Kate Millett, Lillian Gish, Charles Laughton, Norman Mailer, Dalton Trumbo, Romain Gary, Jean Genet, Noel Coward, Jerome Robbins, and others; to include such people would disproportionately increase the amount of work, the size, and, no doubt, the price of the finished product.

It has been reasoned that these people (to date, or possibly will never) represent mirimal participation in the director's art (which does not reflect qualitatively on their temporary involvement) and therefore are eliminated from coverage herein. Admittedly a few found their way in on the subjective grounds of their primary film-involvement, though not necessarily as a director (e.g., producers Carl Foreman and Mack Sennett, novelist Alain Robbe-Grillet, humorist Woody Allen, cinematographer Karl Freund, et al.).

A few individuals presented less difficult decision-making: those who enjoy fame both as a director and in another profession, e.g., Charles Chaplin, Orson Welles, Jacques-Yves Cousteau, Jean Cocteau. They are included since their participation as directors was adjudged unquestionably solid. There were borderline cases who are included because their interest in directing has been long-ranged and continual in spite of possible greater fame as actors: Dick Powell, Gene Kelly, Ida Lupino, Cornel Wilde, John Cassavetes, José Ferrer, etc. Those researchers interested in articles which may exist on the directing careers of the vast number of actors who have directed one or a few films are referred to the companion volume, Motion Picture Performers: A Bibliography of Magazine and Periodical Articles, 1900-1969, compiled by Mel Schuster, Scarecrow Press, 1969, and First Supplement (in preparation).

The list of directors grew naturally from those masses of magazines gone through. This list was then augmented by tallying the year-to-year output of all directors whose credits are listed in Film Daily Annuals dating back to 1918. All directors on whom material had not already been found, and with at least five pictures to their credit were then added to the to-be-researched list. This was an arbitrary number, but was selected as representative of the duration of the individual's involvement with direction. As Film Daily reflects films released in the United States, the director list was further deepened by absorbing the sources listed below, which attempted to internationalize this work, as well as umbrella those directors working outside the mainstream of commercial film.

Anderson, Joseph L. and Richie, Donald. The Japanese Film; Art and Industry. Rutland, Vermont: Charles E. Tuttle Company, 1929 S/R 1959.

Barnouw, Erik and Krishnawamy, S. Indian Film. New York: Columbia University Press, 1963.

Bucher, Felix in collaboration with Leonhard H. Gmur. Screen Series: Germany; An Illustrated Guide. London: A. Zwemmer, Ltd.; New York: A. S. Barnes & Co., 1970.

Cowie, Peter in collaboration with Arne Svensson. Screen Series: Sweden 1; An Illustrated Guide. London: A. Zwemmer, Ltd.; New York: A. S. Barnes & Co., 1970.

Directors Guild of America, Inc. Directory of Members: 1971-1972. Hollywood; Chicago; New York: Directors Guild of America, Inc., 1971.

Gifford, Denis. British Cinema: An Illustrated Guide. London: A. Zwemmer, Ltd.; New York: A. S. Barnes & Co., 1968.

Grove, Martin A. and Ruben, William S. The Celluloid Love Feast; The Story of Erotic Movies. New York: Lancer Books, 1971.

Hibbin, Nina. Screen Series: Eastern Europe; An Illustrated Guide. London: A. Zwemmer, Ltd.; New York, A. S. Barnes & Co., 1969.

Jarratt, Vernon. The Italian Cinema. London: Falcon Press, 1951.

Levin, G. Roy. Documentary Explorations. Garden City, N. Y.: Doubleday & Co., 1971.

Leyda, Jay. Kino; A History of the Russian and Soviet Film. New York: Macmillan Co., 1960.

Martin, Marcel. France; An Illustrated Guide. London: A. Zwemmer, Ltd.; New York: A. S. Barnes & Co., 1971.

Renan, Sheldon. An Introduction to the American Underground Film. New York: E. P. Dutton & Co., 1967.

Svensson, Arne.  Screen Series: Japan; An Illustrated Guide. London:  A.  Zwemmer,  Ltd. ; New York: A.  S. Barnes  &  Co. ,  1971.

WID's  Films  and  Film  Folk,  Inc.   Film Daily Year Book of Motion  Pictures.   New York:  WID's  Films  and  Film Folk,  Inc. ,  1920-1970.

Willis,  John.   Screen World 1971.   Volume 22.   New  York: Crown  Publishers,  Inc. ,  1971.

Unfortunately no reference aids were located to mirror such industries existing or emerging in Africa, Australia, South America, Spain, China, and others.  Nevertheless, when magazine articles were found which spotlighted these localities, representative directors were abstracted and added to the list in an endeavor to secure the international coverage of this work.

The resulting list of directors, more than 2300, was then applied to the bibliographic sources previously detailed, to complete the coverage on each director.

# DIRECTORS ON WHOM NO MATERIAL WAS FOUND

Abbe, Derwin M.
Abrahams, Derwin
Abramson, Hans
Abramson, Ivan
Abuladze, Tengiz
Acres, Birt
Adlophson, Edvin
Adreon, Franklin
Aimanov, Shaken
Albicocco, Jean-Gabriel
Alessandrini, Goffredo
Algar, James Nelson
Allégret, Marc
Allégret, Yves
Allen, Irving
Allen, Irwin
Allen, Lewis
Alov, Alexander
Amadia, Silvio
Ambrosio, Arturo
Amy, George
Andrews, Del
Anthony, Joseph
Apostolof, Stephen
Argyle, John
Arnold, Jack
Arthuys, Philippe
Asher, Robert
Asher, William
Ashley, Helmut
Atamanov, Lev
Audry, Jacqueline
Auer, John H.
Averback, Hy
Axel, Gabriel
Axelman, Torbjörn
Aylott, Dave

Babaja, Ante
Baker, Fred
Baker, Robert S.
Band, Albert
Barabáš, Stanislav
Bare, Richard
Barsha, Leon
Bartlett, Richard
Barton, Charles
Barua, Pramathesh Chandra
Batley, Ernest G.
Batley, Ethyle
Batory, Jan
Bauer, Branko
Bava, Mario
Becker, Jean
Bellamy, Earl
Benazeraf, José
Bencivenga, Edoardo
Bennett, Chester
Bennett, Hugh
Berke, William
Bernds, Edward
Bernhard, Jack
Berthomieu, Andre
Bertram, William
Bhatvadekar, Harischandra S.
Bielik, Pal'o
Billimoria, Fali
Binney, Joseph
Binyon, Claude
Björkman, Stig
Blache, Herbert
Blaier, Andrei
Blair, George
Blakeley, John E.
Blier, Bertrand
Bočan, Hynek

Boese, Carl
Boetticher, Oscar Jr.
Boisrond, Michel
Boisset, Yves
Bonnardot, Jean-Claude
Booth, Walter R.
Borghesio, Carlo
Bose, Debaki Kumar
Bose, Nitin
Bossak, Jerzy
Bostan, Elisabeta
Bostan, Ion
Boyadgieva, Lada
Bracken, Bertram
Bradbury, Robert N.
Bragaglia, Carlo L.
Bramble, A. V.
Brannon, Fred C.
Bratu, Lucian
Braun, Harald
Brdečka, Jiři
Brignone, Guido
Brooks, Thor
Brown, Harry Joe
Brunius, John W.
Bryce, Alex
Brynych, Zbyněk
Buchvarova, Radka
Burnley, Fred
Burton, David
Butler, Alexander
Bykov, Rolan

Čalinescu, Bob
Čalinescu, Paul
Calotescu, Virgil
Calvert, Charles Co.
Camerini, Mario
Campanile, Pasquale Festa
Campbell, Ivar
Cannon, Raymond
Carow, Heiner
Carpenter, Horace B.
Carr, Thomas
Carruth, Milton
Caserini, Mario
Cawston, Richard

Cazaneuve, Paul
Ceder, Ralph
Chaudet, Louis
Chautard, Emile
Chenal, Pierre
Chkheidze, Revaz
Chmielewski, Tadeusz
Ciampi, Yves
Ciulei, Liviu
Clemens, William
Cloche, Maurice
Cocea, Dinu-Constantin
Cohn, Bennett
Coleby, A. E.
Coleman, C. C. Jr.
Collins, Alf
Collins, Arthur G.
Collins, Edwin J.
Colmes, Walter
Comencini, Luigi
Conrad, William
Conyers, D'arcy
Cooper, Arthur Melbourne
Cooper, George A.
Corrigan, Lloyd
Costa, Mario
Cowen, William
Cravenne, Marcel
Csőke, József
Curren, W. Hughes
Cutts, J. Graham

Dalrymple, Ian
Danielsson, Tage
Daquin, Louis
Das Gupta, Hari
Daumery, John
Davis, Redd
Davovski, Dako
Dearholt, Ashton
De Broca, Philippe
de Chalonge, Christian
Decoin, Henri
De Courville, Albert
de Givray, Claude
De Kowa, Viktor
De Lacey, Robert

Delannoy, Jean
de la Pattelliere, Denys
del Colle, Ubaldo
de Liguoro, Guiseppe
Delluc, Louis
DeLouche, Dominique
Deray, Jacques
Derbenev, Vadim
de Riso, Camillo
de Robertis, Francesco
Dewever, Jean
Dewhurst, George
di Cocco, Francesco
Dierge, Samuel
Dierker, Hugh
Dillon, John Francis
Dinov, Todor
Djordjević, Puriša
Dolin, Boris
Domnick, Hans
Domnick, Ottomar
Donev, Donyu
Doukov, Stoyan
Drach, Michel
Driefuss, Arthur
Dunlap, Scott
Durand, Jean
Durning, Bernard

Earle, William P. S.
Edgren, Gustaf
Edwards, Henry
Elliott, Grace
Elton, Arthur
Engel, Erich
Engels, Erich
Ensminger, Robert
Eustache, Jean

Falck, Åke
Faye, Randall
Fehér, Imre
Fescourt, Henri
Filgate, Terry
Finney, Edward

Fitzgerald, Dallas M.
Fitzhamon, Lewin
Flynn, Emmett
Fogwell, Reginald
Ford, Philip
Forde, Eugene (Gene)
Forde, Walter
Förnbacher, Helmut
Forst, Willi
Fosco, Piero
Foss, Keneim
Foster, Lewis R.
Fox, Finis
Fox, Wallace
Francisci, Pietro
Frank, Melvin
Franz, J. J.
Freda, Riccardo
Freeland, Thornton
Fregonese, Hugo
Friedman, Seymour
Froelich, Carl
Frölich, Gustav

Gad, William
Gaidai, Leonid
Gaisseau, Pierre-Dominique
Gallagher, Donald
Gallen, Henrik
Gallone, Carmine
Gamlin, Yvgve
Ganev, Hristo
Ganguly, Dhiren
Gannaway, Albert C.
Ganzer, Alvin
Garson, Harry
Gasnier, Louis J.
Gass, Karl
Georgi, Katja
Gering, Marion
Geronimi, Clyde
Gerrard, Gene
Gerron, Kurt
Gertler, Viktor
Gibson, Tom
Giersz, Witold

Gilles, Guy
Gilmore, Stuart
Giovanni, José
Girard, Bernard
Gliese, Rochus
Goldberger, Kurt
Golden, Sidney M.
Goodwins, Leslie
Gordon, Michael
Graham, William
Grauman, Walter E.
Grayson, Godfrey
Grede, Kjell
Greville, Edmond T.
Grgić, Zlatko
Grigoriev, Roman
Grigorov, Roumen
Grimault, Paul
Grissell, Wallace A.
Gross, Jerry
Gruel, Henri
Grune, Karl
Guazzoni, Enrico
Guiol, Fred
Günther, Egon

Haas, Charles
Hadžić, Fadil
Haggar, William
Haldane, Bert
Hall, Ken G.
Halldoff, Jan
Halperin, Victor H.
Hamilton, William
Hampton, Benjamin B.
Hanbury, W. Victor
Hand, David
Hanžeković, Fedor
Harlow, John
Hart, Harvey
Hartford, David M.
Haskin, Byron
Haynes, H. Manning
Heerman, Victor
Heffron, Thomas
Heifitz, Yosif
Heisler, Stuart

Hellberg, Martin
Hellbom, Olle
Hellstrom, Gunnar
Hepworth, Cecil M.
Herman, Jean
Herskó, János
Heynowski, Walter
Hibbs, Jesse
Higgin, Howard
Hilbard, John
Hill, Sinclair
Hines, Charles
Hiscott, Leslie
Hively, Jack
Hladnic, Boštjan
Hoffman, Herman
Hoffman, Renaud
Hole, William J. Jr.
Homoki Nagy, István
Honda, Ishiro
Hopper, E. Mason
Hopper, Jerry
Horikawa, Hiromichi
Horner, Robert J.
Hoyt, Harry O.
Hughes, Harry
Huisken, Joop
Hunebelle, Andre
Hurst, Paul
Huth, Harold
Hutton, Brian G.

Iacob, Mihai
Ichac, Marcel
Ilieşu, Mirel
Iliu, Victor
Inagaki, Hiroshi
Irani, Ardeshia M.
Ishmukhamedon, Elyar
Ito, Daisuke
Ivanov-Vano, Ivan

Jaccard, Jacques
Jacoby, Georg
Jakubisko, Juraj
Jakubowska, Wanda

James, Allan
Jasný, Vojtěch
Jason, William
Jaworski, Tadeusz
Jay, Antony
Joannon, Léo
Johnson, Raymond K.
Jones, Harmon
Junge, Winfried
Juráček, Pavel
Juran, Nathan
Jutriša, Vladimir

Kachyňa, Karel
Kadijević, Djordje
Kahn, Richard
Kalik, Moisei
Kane, Joseph
Karabasz, Kazimierz
Karasik, Yuli
Kardos, Leslie
Katzin, Lee H.
Keays, Vernon
Keleti, Márton
Keller, Harry
Kellino, Roy
Kellino, Will P.
Kenton, Erle C.
Khitruk, Fedor
Khutsiev, Marlen
Kidawa, Janusz
Killy, Edward
King, Burton
King, George
Kirkland, David
Kjellgren, Lars-Eric
Kjellin, Alf
Klein, Gerhard
Klercker, Georg Af
Kline, Benjamin
Kluba, Henryk
Knight, Castleton
Knopf, Edwin H.
Koenig, Wolf
Kolar, Boris

Kollányi, Ágoston
Konwicki, Tadeusz
Kopalin, Ilya
Korabov, Nicolai
Korber, Serge
Kostelac, Nikola
Kovachev, Hristo
Kowalski, Bernard
Krejčik, Jiří
Krish, John
Krška, Václav
Kulidjanov, Lev
Kulik, Buzz
Kunert, Joachim
Kuney, Jack
Kurahara, Koreyoshi
Kyrou, Ado


Lacombe, Georges
Laemmle, Edward
LaJournade, Jean-Pierre
Lamprecht, Gerhard
Landers, Lew
Landres, Paul
Lane, Lupino
Lapoujade, Robert
Lautner, Georges
Laven, Arnold
Lawrence, Quentin
Le Borg, Reginald
Le Chanois, Jean-Paul
Lederman, D. Ross
Lee, Norman
Leeds, Herbert I.
Legg, Stuart
Leiterman, Douglas
Leni, Paul A.
Lesaint, Edward J.
Lesiewicz, Witold
Leszczyński, Witold
Levering, Joseph
Liebeneiner, Wolfgang
Lilley, Edward C.
Lindgren, Lars Magnus
Lingen, Theo
Lipský, Oldřich

Lisakovitch, Viktor
Lods, Jean
Lomnicki, Jan
Longford, Raymond
Lord, Del
Lotar, Éli
Luby, S. Roy
Lüders, Günther
Luntz, Édouard
Luske, Hamilton
Lynn, Robert

McCarey, Raymond
McCarthy, Henry
McCarthy, John P.
McCarthy, Michael
McDonald, Frank
MacDougall, Ranald
MacFadden, Hamilton
McGann, William H.
McGowan, Dorrell
McGowan, Stuart
Mack, Max
McLaglen, Andrew
Magnusson, Charles
Maigne, Charles
Majewski, Janusz
Makarczyński, Tadeusz
Makhnach, Leonid
Malins, Geoffrey H.
Maloney, Leo
Marcellini, Romolo
Marcus, Manole
Máriássy, Félix
Marinovich, Anton
Marks, Aleksandar
Marmstedt, Lorens
Martin, Charles
Martinek, H. Oceano
Martinson, Leslie H.
Martoglio, Nino
Máša, Antonín
Mason, Herbert
Mason, Noel
Matsuyama, Zenzo
Mattison, Frank S.
May, Joe

Medveczky, Diourka
Meehan, J. Leo
Meins, Gus
Meisel, Kurt
Mendes, Lothar
Mesaros, Titus
Messter, Oskar
Metzner, Ernö
Meyer, Sidney
Mihu, Iulian
Miller, Frank
Miller, Robert Ellis
Miner, Allen H.
Misumi, Kenji
Mitchell, Bruce
Mitchell, Oswald
Mitrović, Žika
Mitta, Alexander
Modi, Sohrab
Molander, Olof
Monakhov, Vladimir
Monicelli, Mario
Moore, Michael
Morante, Milburn
Morey, Edward Jr.
Morgan, Sidney
Morgan, William
Morris, Ernest
Morris, Howard
Morse, Terry
Mortimer, Edmund
Moullet, Luc
Mundrov, Dutcho
Munteanu, Francisc
Monteanu, Stefan
Murayama, Shinji
Muressan, Mircea
Murphy, Dudley
Murphy, Ralph
Mycroft, Walter Charles

Nakahira, Ko
Nash, Percy
Naumov, Vladimir
Nazarro, Ray
Negroni, Baldassare
Neill, Roy William

Neilson, James
Neitz, Alvin J.
Nelson, Jack
Nelson, Sam
Nepp, József
Neuman, Kurt
Newall, Guy
Newfield, Sam
Newland, John
Newman, Widgey R.
Newmeyer, Fred
Nicolaescu, Sergiu
Nichols, George Jr.
Nosseck, Max
Noy, Wilfred

O'Connell, Jack
O'Connor, William
Oertel, Curt
Okeyev, Tolomush
Olin, Stig
Omegna, Rodolfo
Ophuls, Marcel
Orlebeck, Lester
Ormond, Ron
Osco, Bill
Osten, Franz
Ostermayr, Peter
Oury, Gerald
Oxilia, Nino

Pagliero, Marcel
Panijel, Jacques
Parkinson, H. B.
Paris, Jerry
Pasquali, Ernesto
Passendorfer, Jerzy
Paton, Stuart
Paul, Fred
Paul, Val
Paviot, Paul
Peerce, Larry
Pembroke, Scott
Petelska, Ewa
Petelski, Czeslaw
Petrie, Daniel

Pfleghar, Michael
Phalke, Dadasaheb
Phillips, Bertram
Pick, Lupu
Piel, Harry
Pincus, Ed
Pintilie, Lucian
Pirosh, Robert
Piskov, Hristo
Plumb, Hay
Pogačić, Vladimir
Pojar, Břetislav
Pollard, Bud
Pollock, George
Popescu-Gopo, Ion
Popović, Mihailo-Mika
Poppe, Nils
Pronin, V. M.
Prosperi, Franco

Rabenalt, Arthur Maria
Radev, Vulo
Rafkin, Alan
Raizman, Yuli
Rakonjac, Kokan
Ranódy, László
Rapper, Irving
Rätz, Günter
Rawlins, John
Ray, Albert
Ray, Bernard B.
Raymaker, Herman C.
Raymond, Charles
Reinl, Harald
Reisch, Günter
Reisner, Charles F.
Reitherman, Wolfgang
Rényi, Tamás
Reynaud, Émile
Reynolds, Lynn F.
Riazanov, Eldar
Rich, David Lowell
Ridgwell, George
Riemann, Johannes
Rignelli, Gennaro
Rippert, Otto
Risi, Dino

Robbins, Jesse
Robert, Yves
Roberts, Ralph Arthur
Roberts, Stephen
Robison, Arthur
Rockwell, Theodore
Rogell, Albert
Rooke, Arthur H.
Roosling, Gösta
Rosen, Phil
Rosenberg, Stuart
Rosmer, Milton
Ross, Nat
Roullet, Serge
Rouquier, Georges
Rouse, Russell
Rowland, William
Różewicz, Stanislaw
Ruben, J. Walter
Rücker, Günther
Ruspoli, Mario
Russell, William D.
Ruttmann, Walter
Ryan, Frank
Rybkowski, Jan
Rychmann, Ladislav
Rye, Stellan

Sabel, Virgilio
Sagal, Boris
Saizescu, George
Salce, Luciano
Salkow, Sidney
Saltikov, Alexei
Samuelson, George Berthold
Santley, Joseph
Săucan, Mircea
Sautet, Claude
Schaaf, Johannes
Schaeffer, Armand
Schertzinger, Victor
Scheumann, Gerhard
Schmidt, Jan
Schneiderov, Vladimir
Schünzel, Reinhold
Schuster, Harold

Scola, Ettore
Scott, Sherman
Searle, Francis
Seeling, Charles R.
Segel, Yakov
Seiler, Lewis
Seitz, Franz
Sekely, Steve
Sekigawa, Hideo
Selman, David
Shah, Chandulal J.
Shane, Maxwell
Shariliev, Borislav
Sharlandgiev, Ljubomir
Shaw, Harold M.
Sheldon, Forrest
Shengelaya, Eldar
Shepitko, Larissa
Sher, Jack
Sherman, George
Sherman, Vincent
Shibuya, Minoru
Sholen, Lee
Shonteff, Lindsay
Shores, Lynn
Sibianu, Gheorghe
Simon, Jean-Daniel
Škanata, Krsto
Skuibin, Vladimir
Ślesicki, Wladyslaw
Slijepčević, Vladan
Smart, Ralph
Smith, George Albert
Smith, Herbert
Smith, Noel
Solan, Peter
Soltntseva, Yulia
Sremec, Rudolf
Stein, Paul L.
Steinhoff, Hans
Stekel, Leonard
Steklý, Karel
Stevens, Robert
Stewart, Peter
Štiglic, France
Stiopul, Savel
Stoloff, Benjamin

Stolper, Alexander
Stork, Henri
Stoyanov, Yuli
Strayer, Frank
Štrbac, Milenko
Summers, Jeremy
Summers, Walter
Švankmajer, Jan
Swift, David
Szczechura, Daniel
Szemes, Marianne
Szemes, Mihály

Takács, Gábor
Talankin, Igor
Tallas, Gregg C.
Tanaka, Kinuyo
Tanaka, Tokuzo
Tansey, Robert Emmett
Tarkovsky, Andrei
Tasaka, Tomotaka
Taylor, S. E. V.
Tennyson, Penrose
Terwilliger, George
Tewksbury, Peter
Thiel, William (Wilhelm)
Thorndike, Andrew
Thorndike, Annelie
Thornton, F. Martin
Tichawsky, Heinz
Timár, István
Tinling, James
Tokar, Norman
Topaldgikov, Stefan
Topouzanov, Hristo
Tosheva, Nevena
Tourjansky, Victor
Toyoda, Shiro
Trenker, Luis
Tronson, Robert
Týrlova, Hermína

Uchida, Tomu
Ucicky, Gustav
Uher, Štefan
Urayama, Kirio

Urson, Frank

Varéla, José
Várkonyi, Zoltán
Varnel, Marcel
Varnel, Max
Vas, Judit
Vávra, Otakar
Vergano, Aldo
Vergez, Gérard
Verhoeven, Paul
Verneuil, Henri
Vierny, Sacha
Vilardebo, Carlos
Vitandis, Gheorghe
Vláčil, František
Vogeler, Volker
Vohrer, Alfred
Von Czerépy, Arzen
Von Harbou, Thea
Von Wagenheim, Gustav
Vulchanov, Rangel

Wadia, Homi
Waggner, George
Walker, Norman
Wallace, C. R.
Wallén, Sigurd
Warren, Charles Marquis
Watson, Robert
Watt, Nate
Webb, Harry
Webb, Kenneth
Wegener, Paul
Weidenmann, Alfred
Weight, Harmon
Werker, Alfred L.
West, Roland
West, Walter
Weston, Charles H.
Weston, Sam
Wheeler, René
Whelan, Tim
Whitman, Philip H.
Whitney, William
Wiene, Robert

Wilder, W. Lee
Williamson, James A.
Wilson, Frank
Wilson, Georges
Wilson, Rex
Windemere, Fred
Winston, Ron
Woodruff, Frank
Woods, Arthur
Worne, Duke
Worthington, William
Wright, Mack V.


Yamamoto, Kajiro
Yamamoto, Satsuo
Yanchev, Vladimir
Yankov, Yanko
Yarborough, Jean
Yarmatov, Kamil
York, Eugen
Yorkin, Bud
Yoseliani, Otari
Yoshimura, Kozaburo
Young, Harold M.
Young, James


Žalakevičius [Zhalakyavichus],
    Vitautus
Zaninović, Stejpan
Zarkhi, Alexander
Zecca, Ferdinand
Zeisler, Alfred
Zguridi, Alexander
Zhandov, Zahari
Zheljazkova, Binka
Zils, Paul

# BIBLIOGRAPHY OF DIRECTORS

ABALON, ROGELIO
    Yoshiyama, T.  Philippines' Abalon.  CTVD 2-4:2 Sum
     '64

ABBAS, K. A.
    Mirror of India.  Theatre Arts 32:51 F '48

ABBOTT, George
    Biographical sketch.  Theatre Arts 11:530 Jl '27
    The Broadway playwright in Hollywood.  Theatre 49:42
     My '29
    Eustis, M.  Interview.  Theatre Arts 20:120 F '36
    Nathan, G. J.  Director of public works.  Newsweek
     10:30 N 1 '37
    New play in Manhattan.  Time 30:30 N 1 '37
    Nathan, G. J.  Plays produced by him.  Newsweek 11:24
     My 2 '38
    Biography.  Current Biography '40
    Who's who among the producers.  Theatre Arts 26:620
     O '42
    Kutner, N.  If you were George Abbott's daughter.  Good
     Housekeeping 117:31 Jl '43
    Director's lot.  N. Y. Times Mag p19 Ap 15 '51
    New musical in Manhattan.  Time 63:66 My 24 '54
    Musicals take over.  Theatre Arts 38:20 Jl '54
    Millstein G.  Mr. Abbott: one-man theatre.  N. Y. Times
     Mag p19 O 3 '54
    Zolotow, M.  Broadway's most successful penny pincher.
     Sat Evening Post 227:32 Ja 29 '55
    Prideaux, T.  Perennial hatcher of hits and talents.  Life
     48:61 Ja 18 '60
    Dean of repairmen.  Newsweek 55:79 My 16 '60
    Fuller, J. G.  Trade winds.  Sat R 46:10 D 6 '63
    Funny thing happened on the way to the printer; excerpts
     from Mister Abbott.  Time 82:84 D 6 '63
    Call him Mister.  Newsweek 62:91 D 9 '63
    Prideaux, T.  Round-up for Abbott.  Life 55:112 D 13 '63
    Mister Abbott; excerpt.  Theatre Arts 48:27 Ja '64
    Biography. Current Biography 26:3 O '65

Same.   Current Biography Yearbook '65
Salute of the week.   Cue 39-2:1 Ja 10 '70

ACKLAND, RODNEY
   Hast, N.   Story of.   Theatre World 31:8 Ja '39
   Ackland, R.   The bubble-reputation.   Sight & Sound
      12-45:8 Sum '43

ADACHI, MASAO
   Listing of films.   Film Culture 37:7 Sum '65

ADAMS, CLEVE FRANKLIN
   Obit. N.Y. Times p19 D 30 '49
      Wilson Library B 24:407 F '50

ADOLFI, JOHN
   Oscar, J.   The most important man.   Photoplay 7-3:125
      F '15

ALBERTS, ULVIS
   Alberts, U.   The wedding was beautiful, the people were
      crying....   Todays Filmmaker 2-1:42 Ag '72

ALDRICH, ROBERT
   Sex and violence justified by Robert Aldrich.   America
      92:583 Mr 5 '55
   Fenin, G. N.   Interview.   Film Culture 2-4(10):8 '56
   Knight, A.   Aldrich against the army.   Sat R 39:25
      S 1 '56
   Personality of the month.   Films & Filming 3-3:3 D '56
   Moskowitz, G.   Robert Aldrich in Berlin.   Sight & Sound
      27-4:177 Spg '58
   Aldrich, R.   Learning from my mistakes.   Films & Film-
      ing 6-9:9 Je '60
   Jarvie, I.   Hysteria and authoritarianism in the films of
      Robert Aldrich.   Film Culture 22-23:95 '61
   Meehan, T.   The last days of The last days.   Show 2-5:
      79 My '62
   Aldrich: censor in Sodom; interview.   Movie 6:19 Ja '63
   Fenin, G.   The face of '63--United States.   Films &
      Filming 9-6:55 Mr '63
   Mayersberg, P.   Robert Aldrich.   Movie 8:4 Ap '63
   Interview; filmog.   Movie 8:8 Ap '63
   Sarris, A.   Third line; filmog.   Film Culture 28:18 Spg
      '63
   Hollywood--still an empty tomb; interview.   Cinema (BH)
      1-3:4 '63
   Eyles, A.   The private war of Robert Aldrich.   Films &

Filming 13-12:4 S '67

Greenberg, J.   Interview.   Sight & Sound 38-1:8 Win
'68/69

Morgenstern, J.   Letting George do it.   Newsweek 72:90
D 23 '68

Aldrich, R.   Why I bought my own studio.   Action 4-1:7
Ja/F '69

Let's bring back 1909!   Sat R 52:10 S 13 '69

Aldrich, R.   Impressions of Russia.   Action 6-4:11 Jl/Ag
'71

American directors visit Moscow.   Making Films 5-4:30
Ag '71

Silver, A. Interview; filmog.   Film Comment 8-1:14 Spg '72

Interview; filmog; biblio.   Dialogue On Film 2:entire issue '72


ALEA, THOMAS GUITIERREZ
Douglas, M. E.   The Cuban cinema; filmog.   Take One
1-12:6 Jl/Ag '68
Engel, A.   Solidarity and violence.   Sight & Sound 38-4:
196 Aut '69


ALEXANDROV, GRIGORY V.
His home life.   Life 11:118 D 1 '41
Alexandrov, G. V.   Potemkin and after.   Films & Filming
3-7:10 Ap '57


ALEXEIEFF, ALEXANDER
Etchings for the movies.   Living Age 347:174 O '34
Granja, V.   Alexander Alexeieff.   CTVD 4-1:6 Win '66
Alexeieff, A.   The fleeting art.   CTVD 4-1:6 Win '66
Animation quartet.   International Film G 3:175 '66
Filmography.   Film Culture 48/49:48 Win/Spg '70
Granja, V.   Biographical note; filmog.   CTVD 31:28 Win
'71/72


ALLEN, RON
Allen, R.   The commercial director.   Action 4-1:26 Ja/F
'69


ALLEN, WOODY
Pushing back.   Newsweek 60:87 Ag 20 '62
His own Boswell.   Time 81:78 F 15 '63
Mee, C. L.   On stage.   Horizon 5:46 My '63
Zinsser, W. K.   Bright new comic clowns toward success.
Sat Evening Post 236:26 S 21 '63
Stang, J.   Verbal cartoons.   N. Y. Times Mag p120 N 3
'63
Kolowrat, E.   Loser on Top. Senior Scholastic 83:23 N 22 '63

Six quitters.   Esquire 62:102 S '64

Miller, E.   Tallest dwarf in the world.   Seventeen 25:159
My '66

Biography.   Current Biography 27:3 D '66

Same.   Current Biography Yearbook 1966:3 '67

Woody, Woody, everywhere.   Time 89:90 Ap 14 '67

Interview.   Playboy 14-5:63 My '67

Reddy, J.   Woody Allen's bed of neuroses.   Readers
Digest 91:113 Jl '67

Higgins, R.   He has more hangups than a pop-poster joint.
TV Guide 16-47:43 N 33 '68

Allen, W.   How Bogart made me the superb lover I am
today.   Life 66:64 Mr 21 '69

Bester, A.   Conversation with Woody Allen.   Holiday 45:
71 My '69

Tornabene, L.   Walking with Woody Allen.   McCalls 96:
44 Je '69

Salute of the week.   Cue 38-37:1 S 13 '69

What directors are saying.   Action 6-4:20 Jl/Ag '71

The professional director speaks.   Making Films 5-4:40
Ag '71

Wolf, W.   The intellectual schnook makes good.   Cue 41-
21:2 My 20 '72

Allen, W.   Everything you've always wanted to know about
sex you'll find in my new movie.   Playboy 19-9:115
S '72


ALLIO, RENE
Two arts in one; conversation.   Cahiers (Eng) 6:25 D '66
Zavriew, A.   Rene Allio.   Film 54:36 Spg '69


ALMENDROS, NESTOR
Listing of films.   Film Culture 37:7 Sum '65


ALMOND, PAUL
Nolan, J. E.   Letter.   Films In Review 21-10:651 D '70


ALTMAN, ROBERT
Creation in chaos.   Time 96:62 Jl 13 '70
What directors are saying.   Action 5-4:30 Jl/Ag '70
What directors are saying.   Action 5-6:22 N/D '70
AuWerter, R.   A conversation.   Action 6-1:2 Ja/F '71
On the scene.   Playboy 18-4:198 Ap '71
Harmetz, A.   15th man who asked to direct M*A*S*H
(and did) makes a peculiar western.   N. Y. Times Mag
p11 Je 20 '71
Atlas, J. & Guerin, A.   Robert Altman, Julie Christie

and Warren Beatty make the western real. Show 2-6:
18 Ag '71

Cutts, J.   M*A*S*H, McCloud and McCabe;
interview.   Films & Filming 18-2:40 N '71

What directors are saying.   Action 7-1:36 Ja/F '72

Williams, J.   The Altman images.   Films Illustrated
1-10:36 Ap '72

Eyles, A.   Biographical note; filmog.   Focus On Film
9:9 Spg '72

Dawson, J.   Altman's images.   Sight & Sound 41-2:68
Spg '72

O'Brien, G.   Robert Altman, F*K*N genius.   Interview
25:30 S '72

Johnson, D.   Robert Altman's Images a very strange
picture.   Show 2-7:46 O '72


ALVAREZ, SANTIAGO
Douglas, M. E.   The Cuban cinema; filmog.   Take One
1-12:6 Jl/Ag '68

Engel, A.   Solidarity and violence.   Sight & Sound 38-4:
196 Aut '69


AMATO, GIUSEPPE
Obit.   Film Review p45 '64/65


AMYES, JULIAN
Filmography.   Film 14:8 N/D '57

British feature directors; an index to their work.
Sight & Sound 27-6:289 Aut '58


ANDERSON, LINDSAY
Anderson, L.   Needed: a sense of real purpose.   Film
15:12 Ja/F '58

The critical issue: a discussion between Paul Rotha,
Basil Wright, Lindsay Anderson, Penelope Houston.
Sight & Sound 27-6:270 Aut '58

Anderson, L.   Three to cheer for.   International Film
A 2:79 '58

Anderson, L.   Sport, life and art.   Films & Filming
9-5:15 F '63

Desert island films.   Films & Filming 9-11:11 Ag '63

Cowie, P.   An interview.   Film Q 17-4:12 Sum '64

Gray, P.   Class theatre, class film; interview.   Tulane
Drama R 11:122 Fall '66

Robinson, D.   On shooting If...   Sight & Sound 37-3:130
Sum '68

Kael, P.   Current cinema.   New Yorker 45:152 Mr 15 '69

Gladwell, D.   Editing Anderson's If...   Screen 10-1:24
    Mr/Ap '69
Guy, V.   Lindsay Anderson; interview.   Play & Players
    17-3:48 D '69
What directors are saying.   Action 5-2:16 Mr/Ap '70
What directors are saying.   Action 5-6:22 N/D '70
Director of the year; filmog.   International Film G p9 '70
British cinema filmography.   Film 65:10 Spg '72
O'Brien, G. & Morrissy, P.   Interview.   Interview 2-1:
    12 n. d.
(Anderson was a frequent contributor to Sight & Sound
    during the 1950's. For listings of his writings on other
    directors, see: FORD, JOHN; JENNINGS, HUMPHREY)

ANDERSON, MADELINE
    I am somebody; interview.   Film Library Q 5-1:39 Win
    '71/72

ANDERSON, MICHAEL
    Filmography.   Film 14:8 N/D '57
    Anderson, M.   Director's choice: gimmicks, the story
        and the public. International Film A 1:139 '57
    British feature directors; an index to their work.   Sight &
        Sound 27-6:289 Aut '58

ANDERSON, SYLVIA
    Women on Women on films.   Take One 3-2:10 N/D '70

ANDREWS, BERT
    Schroeder, W.   The odyssey of a filmmaker; interview.
        Filmmakers Newsletter 5-1:28 O '71

ANGER, KENNETH
    Kelman, K.   Thanatos in chrome: filmog.   Film Culture
        31:6 Win '63/64
    Listing of films.   Film Culture 37:7 Sum '65
    Interview.   Film Culture 40:68 Spg '66
    Alexander, T. K.   San Francisco's hipster cinema.   Film
        Culture 44:70 Spg '67
    Lipton, L.   Interview.   Filmmakers Newsletter 1-1:2 N
        '67
    Rayns, T.   Lucifer: a Kenneth Anger kompendium. Cinema
        (Lon) 4:22 O '69
    Sitney, P. A.   Avant garde film.   Afterimage 2:22 Aut
        '70
    Interview.   Take One 1-6:12 n. d.

ANKER, MARSHALL
    Survey among unsuccessful applicants for the Ford Found-
        ation film grants.    Film Comment 2-3:10
        Sum '64

ANNAKIN, KEN
    Filmography.    Film 14:8 N/D '57
    Annakin, K.    ...and what it wants are comedies.    Film
        15:7 Ja/F '58
    British feature directors; an index to their work.    Sight &
        Sound  27-6:290 Aut '58
    Annakin, K.    In the vast outdoors.    Films & Filming 6-
        10:15 Jl '60
    The screen answers back.    Films & Filming 8-8:12 My
        '62

ANTONIONI, MICHELANGELO
    New names.    Sight & Sound 25-3:119 Win '55/56
    Antonioni, M.    There must be a reason for every film.
        Films & Filming 5-7:11 Ap '59
    Kaplan, N.    Antonioni's La notte.    Sight & Sound 29-4:
        179 Aut '60
    Manceaux, M., Roud, R., Houston, P.    Antonioni; inter-
        view.    Sight & Sound 30-1:4 Win '60/61
    Kauffman, S.    Arrival of an artist.    New Republic 144:
        26 Ap 10 '61
    Pepper, C. F.    Rebirth in Italy: three great movie di-
        rectors.    Newsweek 58:66 Jl 10 '61
    Antonioni, M.    Reflections on a film actor.    Film Culture
        22-23:66 '61
    Lane, J. F.    A diary.    Films & Filming 8-6:11 Mr '62
    Parkin, R. W.    Letter.    Film Journal (Aus) 19:59 Ap '62
    Antonioni, M.    Making a film is my way of life.    Film
        Culture  24:43 Spg '62
    A talk with Antonioni on his work; filmog.    Film Culture
        24:45 Spg '62
    Cameron, I.    Antonioni.    Film Q 16-1:entire issue Fall
        '62
    Alpert, H.    Talk with Antonioni.    Sat R 45:27 O 27 '62
    Momento mori.    Time 81:89 Ja 11 '63
    Lane, J. F.    The face of '63--Italy.    Films & Filming
        9-7:11 Ap '63
    Gerard, L. N.    Antonioni.    Films In Review 14-4:253
        Ap '63
    Moore, R. J.    Hollywood myth has fallen.    Popular Photo
        93:94 Jl '63
    Beckley, P. V.    Two on the aisle.    Sat R 47:36 F 8 '64

Manceaux, M.   In the red desert.   Sight & Sound 33:119
   Sum '64
Davis, M. S.   Most controversial director.   N. Y. Times
   Mag p34 N 15 '64
Biography.   Current Biography 25:3 D '64
   Same.   Current Biography Yearbook 1964:8 '64
Reality and cinema verite.   Atlas 9:122 F '65
Jean-Luc Godard interviews Michelangelo Antonioni. Movie
   12:31 Spg '65
Hartog, S.   Interview.   International Film G 2:37 '65
Paolucci, A.   Italian film.   Massachusetts R 7:556 Sum
   '66
Antonioni talks about his work.   Life 62:66 Ja 27 '67
Antonioni's hypnotic eye on a frantic world.   Life 62:62B
   Ja 27 '67
Barzini, L.   Adventurous Antonioni.   Holiday 41:99 Ap
   '67
Garis, R.   Watching Antonioni.   Commentary 43:86 Ap
   '67
Kinder, M.   Antonioni in transit.   Sight & Sound 36-3:132
   Sum '67
Warshow, P.   Reply with rejoinder to Garis.   Commen-
   tary 44:14 Ag '67
Shaw, E.   Antonioni says New York is too vertical for
   filmmaking.   Making Films 1-4:20 O '67
Interview.   Playboy 14-11:77 N '67
Samuels, C. T.   Blow up; sorting things out.   American
   Scholar   37:120 Win '67
Slover, G.   Blow up: medium, message, mythes and
   make-believe.   Massachusetts R 9:753 Aut '68
Kinder, M.   Zabriskie point.   Sight & Sound 38-1:26 Win
   '68/69
Joseph, R.   Billboards, beards and beads.   Cinema (BH)
   4-4:2 D '68
Biography.   British Book Year 1968:138 '68
Director of the year; filmog.   International Film G 5:9
   '68
Bosworth, P.   Antonioni discovers America.   Holiday 45:
   64 Mr '69
Roud, R.   Memories of Resnais.   Sight & Sound 38-3:124
   Sum '69
Fondiller, H. V.   Antonioni: from super 8 to panovision.
   Popular Photo 65:122 S '69
What directors are saying.   Action 4-5:32 S/O '69
Hamilton, J.   Antonioni's America.   Look 33:36 N 18 '69
What directors are saying.   Action 5-1:28 Ja/F '70
Kauffmann, S.   Films.   New Republic 162:20 Mr 14 '70

Samuels, C. T. Interview. Vogue 155:96 Mr 15 '70
Samuels, C. T. Interview. Film Heritage 5-3:1 Spg '70
Antonioni: what's the point? Discussion with John Simon,
Joseph Gelmis, Martin Last, Harrison Starr and Al
Lees. Film Heritage 5-3:26 Spg '70
Gow, G. Antonioni men. Films & Filming 16-9:41 Je
'70
Tudor, A. The road to Death Valley. Cinema (Lon)
6/7:22 Ag '70
Let's talk about Zabriskie Point. Esquire 74:68 Ag '70
Hernacki, T. Michelangelo Antonioni and the imagery of
disintegration. Film Heritage 5-3:13 Aut '70
Gindoff, B. Thalberg didn't look happy. Film Q 24-1:3
Fall '70
Robinson, W. R. The movies as a revolutionary moral
force (L'Avventura). Contempora 2-1:26 F '72

APFEL, OSCAR
Montanye, L. Interview. Motion Pic Classic 6:55 Ag
'18
Obit. N. Y. Times p23 Mr 23 '38

ARCHAINBAUD, GEORGE
Obit. N. Y. Times p21 F 21 '59

ARLISS, LESLIE
British feature directors; an index to their work.
Sight & Sound 27-6:290 Aut '58

ARMSTRONG, BERYL
Armstrong, B. Filming a football match. Movie Maker
6-3:148 Mr '72

ARMSTRONG, MICHAEL
British cinema filmography. Film 65:10 Spg '72

ARZNER, DOROTHY
St. Johns, I. Sketch. Photoplay 31:40 Mr '27
Tildesley, R. M. Dorothy Arzner; director. Womans J
14:25 F '29
Cruikshank, H. Sketch. Motion Pic Classic 30:33 S '29
St. Johns, A. R. Get me Dorothy Arzner. Silver
Screen 4-2:22 D '33
They stand out from the crowd. Lit Digest 118:12 N 3
'34
Biographical sketch. Time 28:32 O 12 '36
Sketch. Movie Classic 11:64 D '36

Sketch.   Motion Pic 53:22 Ap '37

Tildesley, A. L.   She stepped down to step up.   Independent Woman 32:402 N '53

Feldman, J. & H.   Women directors.   Films In Review 1-8:9 N '50

Pyros, J.   Notes on women directors.   Take One 3-2:7 N/D '70


ASCH, TIMOTHY

Asch, T.   Ethnographic filming and the Yanomamo Indians.   Sightlines 5-3:7 Ja/F '72


ASHBY, HAL

Ashby, H.   Breaking out of the cutting room.   Action 5-5:7 S/O '70


ASHUR, GERI

Kaplan, D.   Selected short subjects.   Women & Film 2:37 '72


ASQUITH, ANTHONY

Asquith, A.   Wanted -- a genius.   Sight & Sound 7-25:5 Spg '38

Asquith, A.   Note on Americanization.   Film 5:12 S/O '55

Filmography.   Film 14:8 N/D '57

Massie, P.   What Asquith did for me.   Films & Filming 4-5:11 F '58

British feature directors; an index to their work.   Sight & Sound 27-6:290 Aut '58

Asquith, A.   The play's the thing.   Films & Filming 5-5:13 F '59

The screen answers back.   Films & Filming 8-8:12 My '62

Desert island films.   Films & Filming 9-11:11 Ag '63

Cowie, P.   This England.   Films & Filming 10-1:13 O '63

Balcon, M.   Anthony Asquith.   Sight & Sound 37-2:77 Spg '68

Obit.   British Book Year 1969:566 '69
    N. Y. Times p32 F 22 '68
    Screen World 21:231 '70
    Sight & Sound 37:77 Spg '68


ASTRUC, ALEXANDRE

Spotlights five young Frenchmen who are giving French cinema a new look.   Films & Filming 5-3:18 D '58

ATWOOD, HARRY
Who's who in filmmaking; filmog.   Sightlines 2-3:4 Ja/F
'69

AUBERT, CLAUDE BERNARD
(See:  BERNARD-AUBERT, CLAUDE)

AUGUST, EDWIN
Obit.   Screen World 16:219 '65

AULT, WILLIAM
Listing of films.   Film Culture 37:7 Sum '65

AUSLENDER, LELAND
Auslender, L.   Distortion techniques used in filming The
birth of Aphrodite.   American Cinematographer 52-9:
868 S '71

AUTANT-LARA, CLAUDE
Claude Autant-Lara.   Film 17:12 S/O '58
6 films 6 faces.   Unifrance 50:24 Jl/S '59
Durgnat, R.   The rebel with kid gloves.   Films & Filming 7-1:11 O '60

AVAKIAN, ARAM
Meryman, R.   Cinematic assault.   Life 67:65 N 7 '69
Keneas, A.   Independent.   Newsweek 75:100 Mr 16 '70
On the scene.   Playboy 17-8:149 Ag '70

AVERY, CHARLES
Biographical note.   Photoplay 9-4:42 Mr '16

AVERY, TEX
Adamson, J.   Interview.   Take One 2-9:10 Ja/F '70

AVILDSEN, JOHN
What directors are saying.   Action 6-3:28 My/Je '71
The professional director speaks.   Making Films 5-4:40
Ag '71

AXELROD, GEORGE
Hit in a hurry; how Seven year itch happened.   Theatre
Arts 38:33 Ja '54
Candidates for prizes.   Vogue 123:135 My 1 '54
That third act, playwright's terror.   N. Y. Times Mag
p26 Mr 25 '56
Zolotow, M.   Will failure spur George Axelrod?   Theatre

Arts 40:31 Mr '56
George Axelrod.   Esquire 60:32 Jl '63
Hamilton, J.   Virna Lisi: experiment in star making.
Look 29:60 My 18 '65
Milne, T.   The difference of George Axelrod.   Sight &
Sound 37-4:164 Aut '68
Hanhardt, J.   George Axelrod and The manchurian candi-
date; filmog.   Film Comment 6-4:8 Win '70/71

BABAJA, ANTE
Biographical note. International Film G 6:190 '69

BACHER, WILLIAM A.
Obit. Screen World 17:233 '66

BACON, DOUGLAS
Obit. N. Y. Times p27 Ja 24 '52

BACON, LLOYD
Lloyd Bacon ... Warner Brothers' ace. Cue 2-23:3
Ap 6 '35
Biographical note; filmog. Movies & People 2:39 '40
Parsons, L. Cosmopolitan's citation for the best direc-
tion of the month. Cosmop 126:12 My '49
Obit. Newsweek 46:78 N 28 '55
N. Y. Times p35 N 16 '55
Screen World 7:221 '56
Time 66:100 N 28 '55

BACSO, PETER
Biographical note. International Film G 8:175 '71

BADGER, CLARENCE
Biographical note. Photoplay 9-4:42 Mr '16
Obit. N. Y. Times p25 Je 20 '64

BAILLIE, BRUCE
Baille, B. Letter to Jonas Mekas. Film Culture 29:76
Sum '63
Survey among unsuccessful applicants for the Ford Found-
ation film grants. Film Comment 2-3:10 Sum '64
Polt, H. The films of Bruce Baillie. Film Comment
2-4:50 Fall '64
Listing of films. Film Culture 37:7 Sum '65
Alexander, T. K. San Francisco's hipster cinema. Film
Culture 44:70 Spg '67
Whitehall, R. An interview with Bruce Baillie. Film
Culture 47:16 Sum '69
Weiner, P. New American cinema; filmog. Film 58:22
Spg '70
Interview; filmog. Film Comment 7-1:25 Spg '71
Barrios, G. Interview. Interview 1-9:22 n. d.

BAKER, GEORGE D.
  Obit.  N. Y. Times p13 Ja 29 '49

BAKER, ROY
  Filmography.  Film 14:8 N/D '57
  British feature directors: an index to their work.  Sight
    & Sound 27-6:290 Aut '58
  British cinema filmog.  Film 65:10 Spg '72

BAKSHI, RALPH
  Barrier, M.  The filming of Fritz the cat (Part 1).
    Funnyworld 14:4 Spg '72
  Fathering Fritz; Ralph Bakshi talks.  Interview 22:34
    Je '72

BALABAN, BURT
  Obit.  N. Y. Times p45 O 15 '65

BALAZS, BELA
  Hungarian letter.  Dial 74:387 Ap '23
  Movies for the middle class.  Living Age 339:294 N '30

BALCON, MICHAEL
  Gibbs, P.  A case for the independent producer.  World
    R p40 Mr '48
  Balcon, M.  The feature carries on the documentary
    tradition.  Q Film Radio TV 6-4:351 Sum '51
  Balcon, M.  Greetings to Film.  Film 1:6 O '54
  Tynan, K.  Tight little studio.  Harper 211:52 Ag '55
  Balcon, M.  An author in the studio.  Films & Fiming
    3-10:7 Jl '57
  Balcon, M.  The secret of Earling comedy.  International
    Film A 1:62 '57
  Balcon, M.  The money in films.  Films & Filming
    9-10:9 Jl '63
  Houston, P.  Survivor: interview with Sir Michael Balcon.
    Sight & Sound 32-1:15 Win '62/63
  Balcon, M.  Anthony Asquith.  Sight & Sound 37-2:77
    Spg '68
  Balcon, M.  One professional survivor to another.  Silent
    Pic 2:8 Spg '69

BALLIN, HUGO
  Macgowan, K.  Director of stage scenery.  Motion Pic
    Classic  8:16 Mr '19
  Scenic background.  Mentor 9:22 Jl '21
  Matzen, M.  Sketch.  Motion Pic Classic 23:30 Ag '23

Sketch.   Motion Pic 32:55 N '26
Puts over a hoax on Academy.   Newsweek 3:22 Je 9 '34
Offended painter works.   Lit Digest 117:26 Je 16 '34
Thunder on the right.   American Mag Art 27:390 Jl '34
Artist can sell his hoaxes but not really serious works of
    art.   Newsweek 7:28 F 1 '36
Obit.   N. Y. Times p35 N 28 '56

BALSER, ROBERT
    Granja, V.   An American in Lisbon; interview; filmog.
      CTVD 5-2:8 Fall '67

BALSHOFER, FRED J.
    Mitchell, G. J.   Fred J. Balshofer.   Films In Review
      16-7:459 Ag/S '65

BANKS, MONTY
    Spensley, D.   Sketch.   Photoplay 32:67 Ag '27
    Shelton, G.   Sketch.   Motion Pic 34:66 D '27
    Obit.   N. Y. Times p25 Ja 9 '50
      Screen World 2:233 '51
      Time 55:76 Ja 16 '50
    Will.   N. Y. Times p10 F 25 '50

BARAK, DAN
    Survey among unsuccessful applicants for the Ford Found-
      ation film grants.   Film Comment 2-3:10 Sum '64

BARATIER, JACQUES
    Biographical note.   Unifrance 45:10 D '57
    Sadoul, G.   Notes on a new generation.   Sight & Sound
      23-3/4:111 Sum/Aut '59
    Meeting La nouvelle vague; conversation.   Films & Film-
      ing 6-1:7 O '59

BARDEM, JUAN ANTONIO
    New names.   Sight & Sound 25-4:212 Spg '56
    Bardem, J. A.   Spanish highway.   Films & Filming
      3-9:6 Je '57
    Cobos, J.   The face of '63--Spain.   Films & Filming
      10-1:39 O '63

BARKER, REGINALD
    Biographical note.   Photoplay 9-4:42 Mr '16

BARMA, CLAUDE
    Biographical note.   Unifrance 48:14 O '58

BARNET, BORIS
   Kusmina, E.   A tribute to Boris Barnet.   Film Comment
      5-1:33 Fall '68

BARRETO, LIMA
   On the Brazilian screen.   Americas 5:13 Je '53

BARRETO, LUIS CARLOS
   Viany, A.   Who's who in the Cinema Novo.   CTVD
      5-4:26 Sum '68

BARRON, ARTHUR
   Barron, A.   Towards new goals in documentary.   Film
      Library Q 2-1:19 Win '68/69
   Rosenberg, B. & Howten, F. W.   The self-discovery of
      a documentary filmmaker; interview.   Film Comment
      6-1:6 Spg '70
   Barron, A.   Network television and the personal docu-
      mentary.   Film Comment 6-1:16 Spg '70
   Barron, A.   The intensification of reality.   Film Com-
      ment 6-1:20 Spg '70
   Arthur Barron filmography.   Film Comment 6-1:24 Spg
      '70
   Rosenthal, A.   Interview.   Film Library Q 4-1:21 Win
      '70/71
   Orville and Wilbur: production report.   Filmmakers News-
      letter 5-7:21 My '72

BARSKAYA, MARGARITA
   Feldman, J. & H.   Women directors.   Films In Review
      1-8:9 N '50

BARTLETT, HALL
   Knight, A.   Film producer.   Scholastic 66:6 Ap 6 '55
   Bartlett, H.   I did it my way.   Action 6-4:12 Jl/Ag '71

BARTOSCH, BERTHOLD
   Knight, D.   Berthold Bartosch.   Film 23:26 Ja/F '60
   Alexeieff, A.   Berthold Bartosch.   CTVD 6-2:2 Win
      '68/69

BASS, SAUL
   People in print.   Print 15:4 My '61
   Man with a golden arm.   Time 79:46 Mr 16 '62
   A conversation with Saul Bass.   Cinema (BH) 4-3:30
      Fall '68
   Aison, E.   The designer as filmmaker.   Print 23:90 Ja '69

BATCHELOR, JOY
Halas and Batchelor; profile of a partnership.   Film 4:15
Mr '55
Filmography.   International Film G 1:165 '64
Halas and Batchelor.   International Film G 2:175 '65

BAUM, RALPH
Ralph Baum speaks of his films.   Unifrance 21:18 N '52

BAUMAN, SCHAMYL
Obit.   Screen World 18:232 '67

BAXTER, JOHN
Anstey, E.   Work of John Baxter.   Spectator 168:419
My 1 '42
British feature directors; an index to their work.   Sight &
Sound 27-6:290 Aut '58

BEATTIE, PAUL
Listing of films.   Film Culture 37:7 Sum '65

BEAUDINE, WILLIAM (BILL) Sr.
Oldtime.   Time 62:90 Jl 13 '53
Scheuer, P. K.   60 years in films.   Action 4-4:16 Jl/Ag
'69
Obit.   Classic Film Collector (reprint from Variety)
27:60 Spg/Sum '70
Film Review p22 '70/71
N. Y. Times p47 Mr 19 '70
Newsweek 75:56 Mr 30 '70
Screen World 22:235 '71

BEAUMONT, HARRY
Interview.   Motion Pic 9:102 Mr '15
How he became a photoplayer.   Motion Pic 9:95 Je '15
Sketch.   Motion Pic 10:113 D '15
A pioneer harks back.   Lions Roar 3-5:no p     D'44

BECKER, HAROLD
Kevles, B. L.   Interview.   Film Culture 38:29 Fall '65

BECKER, JACQUES
Grunberg, I.   Film directors in France.   Life & Letters
56:153 F '48
Lisbona, J.   Microscope director.   Films & Filming
3-3:6 D '56
Moskowitz, G.   A visit to Jacques Becker and Modigliani.

Sight & Sound 27-3:112 Win '57/58
Jacques Becker and Montparnasse 19.    Film 17:13 S/O
  '58
Lennon, P.   Jacques Becker; letter.    Films In Review
  11-4:247 Ap '60
Klava, I.   Jacques Becker: 15 September '06 - 20 Feb-
  ruary '60.   Film Journal (Aus) 16:95 Ag '60
Obit.   Sight & Sound 29:96 Spg '60
Guillermo, G. P.   Jacques Becker: two films.    Sight &
  Sound 38-3:142 Sum '69


BECKERMAN, HOWARD
What they say.   Making Films 4-3:47 Je '70


BEIER, CARL JR.
A new way of looking at things.   Hollywood Q 2-1:1 O '46


BELL, MONTA
Tully, J.   Sketch.   Classic 20:23 N '24
Winship, F.   Sketch.   Photoplay 28:68 Jl '25
Dodge, H. J.   Sketch.   Motion Pic Classic 26:25 Ja '28
Movies and talkies.   No. American 226:429 O '28
Director.   Theatre Arts 13:645 S '29
Cruikshank, H.   Sketch.   Motion Pic Classic 30:330 '29
Obit.   N. Y. Times p28 F 5 '58


BELLOCCHIO, MARCO
Chiaretti, T.   Clear and explicit.   Atlas 12:56 Ag '66
Thomsen, C. B.   Bellocchio.   Sight & Sound 37:14 Win
  '67/68
Kael, P.   Current cinema.   New Yorker 43:90 Ja 13 '68
Morgenstern, J.   Welcome Bellocchio.   Newsweek 71:84
  Ja 22 '68
Kauffmann, S.   Grace and disgrace.   New Republic 158:
  26 F 3 '68
Rapf, M.   Evil-sweet from Italy.   Life 64:8 Mr 1 '68
Lane, J. F.   Italy's angry young directors.   Films &
  Filming 15-1:75 O '68
What directors are saying.   Action 4-6:28 N/D '69
Interview.   Cineaste 4-1:24 Sum '70
Macklin, F. A.   The art of Marco Bellocchio.   Film
  Heritage 7-1:33 Fall '71
Interview.   Film Society R 7-5:33 Ja '72


BELSON, JORDAN
Callenbach, E.   Phenomena and Samadhi.   Film Q 21:48
  Spg '68

Eliscu, L.   Jordan Belson makes movies.   Show 1-1:57
   Ja '70
Youngblood, G.   The cosmic cinema of Jordan Belson.
   Film Culture 48/49:13 Win/Spg '70

BENE, CARMELO
   The baroque cinema of Carmelo Bene.   Films & Filming
   16-12:38 S '70

BENEDEK, LASLO
   Directing Death of a salesman for the screen.   Theatre
   Arts 36:36 Ja '52
   Benedek, L.   Play into picture.   Sight & Sound 22-2:82
   O/D '52
   Koval, F.   Benedek in Hamburg.   Sight & Sound 24-3:118
   Ja/Mr '55
   Nolan, J. E.   Films on TV; listing of TV work.   Films
   In Review 20-1:42 Ja '69

BENNETT, COMPTON
   British feature directors; an index to their work.   Sight
   & Sound 27-6:291 Aut '58

BENNETT, SPENCER GORDON
   Geltzer, G.   40 years of cliffhanging.   Films In Review
   8-2:60 F '57
   Danard, D.   Bennett's serials.   Films In Review 14-8:
   509 O '63
   Shipley, G.   King of the serial directors.   Views & Re-
   views 1-2:5 Fall '69
   Shipley, G.   Spencer Gordon Bennett; filmog.   Classic
   Film Collector 29:53 Win '70
   Malcomson, R. M.   The sound serial.   Views & Reviews
   3-1:13 Sum '71
   Tuska, J.   Interview.   Those Enduring Matinee Idols
   2-7:240 Je/Jl '72
   Fernett, G.   Spencer Gordon Bennett biography off the
   press.   Classic Film Collector 36:63 Fall '72

BENNETT, WHITMAN
   Smith, F. J.   Interview.   Motion Pic Classic 11:19 S '20
   Obit.   N. Y. Times p47 Ap 19 '68

BENOIT-LEVY, JEAN
   Biography.   Current Biography 8:5 O '47
      Same.   Current Biography Yearbook 1947:46 '48
   Biography.   Current Biography Jl '48

Tribute to Mr. Benoit-Levy.   U. N.  Bulletin 7:153 Ag 1 '49
Obit.   Chemistry & Industry 32:1023 Ag 8 '59
   Current Biography 20:3 N '59
   Current Biography Yearbook 1959:34 '60
   Screen World 11:215 '60
   Sight & Sound 28-3/4:186 Sum/Aut '59
   Time 74:80 Ag 17 '59

## BERGENSTRAHLE, JOHAN
What directors are saying.   Action 6-4:20 Jl/Ag '71
The professional director speaks.   Making Films 5-4:40
   Ag '71
Peary, G.  Interview.   Cineaste 5-2:21 Spg '72
Filmmaking in Sweden.   Interview 1-7:26 n. d.

## BERGER, HENRI DIAMANT
Henri Diamant Berger discusses Mon cur chez les riches.
   Unifrance 21:19 N '52

## BERGER, LUDWIG
Hall, G.  Sketch.   Motion Pic Classic 28:26 Ja '29

## BERGMAN, INGMAR
Bergman, I.  I am a conjurer.   Films & Filming 2-12:
   14 S '56
Bergman, I.  Dreams and shadows.   Films & Filming
   3-1:15 O '56
Ulrichsen, E.  Ingmar Bergman and the Devils.   Sight &
   Sound 27-5:224 Sum '58
Sylvester, D.  Films of Ingmar Bergman.   New States-
   man 56:518 O 18 '58
Personality of the month.   Films & Filming 5-1:5 O '58
Weightman, J. B.  Bergman, an uncertain talent.   20th
   Century 164:566 D '58
Alpert, H.  Other Bergman.   Sat R 42:34 Mr 21 '59
Stanbrook, A.  An aspect of Bergman.   Film 20:10 Mr/
   Ap '59
Genet.  Letter from Paris.   New Yorker 35:102 Je 13 '59
Archer, E.  The rack of life.   Film Q 12-4:3 Sum '59
Bergman and Wilder.   Sight & Sound 28-3/4:134 Sum/Aut
   '59
Bergman, I.  Each film is my last.   Films & Filming
   5-10:8 Jl '59
Alpert, H.  Show of magic.   Sat R 42:23 Ag 29 '59
Balliett, W.  Current cinema.   New Yorker 35:76 S 5 '59
Hatch, R.  Films.   Nation 189:180 S 26 '59
Oldin, G.  Ingmar Bergman.   American Scandinavian 47:
   250 S '59

Moonman, E. Summer with Bergman. Film 21:18 S/O '59

Kauffmann, S. Not quite mesmerized. New Republic 141:21 O 12 '59

Talk with the director. Newsweek 54:116 N 23 '59

Jarvie, I. Notes on the films of Ingmar Bergman; filmog. Film Journal (Aus) 14:9 N '59

Wiskari, W. Another Bergman gains renown. N. Y. Times Mag p26 D 20 '59

Holland, N. N. Brace of Bergmans. Hudson R 12:570 Win '59/60

Baffling movie master. Life 48:59 F 22 '60

Croce, A. Bergman legend. Commonweal 71:647 Mr 11 '60

I am a conjurer. Time 75:60 Mr 14 '60

Birch, W. Letter response to Jarvie. Film Journal (Aus) 15:62 Mr '60

Biography. Current Biography 21:4 Ap '60

Same. Current Biography Yearbook 1960:28 '61

Becker, J. Bergman on Victor Sjostrom. Sight & Sound 29-2:96 Spg '60

Alpert, H. Bergman as writer. Sat R 43:22 Ag 27 '60

Dymling, C. A. Rebel with a cause. Sat R 43:23 Ag 27 '60

Gow, G. Working with Bergman. Films & Filming 6-11:7 Ag '60

Jarvie, I. Letter reply to Birch. Film Journal (Aus) 16:95 Ag '60

Barkun, M. Letter. Films In Review 11-7:441 Ag/S '60

Ross, W. Strange vision of Ingmar Bergman. Coronet 48:57 O '60

Biography. Colliers Year book 1960:720 '60

Johnson, W. Movie viewer. Modern Photo 25:28 F '61

Newman, G. Bergman and the Whigs. Film 28:32 Mr/Ap '61

Nilmeyer, G. Bergman: image and meaning. National R 10:257 Ap 22 '61

Bergman touch. Newsweek 57:67 My 8 '61

Vermilye, J. An Ingmar Bergman index; filmog. Films In Review 12-5:280 My '61

Fleisher, F. Ingmar Bergman. Contemporary R 200:436 Ag/S '61

Bergman, I. Away with improvisation--this is creation. Films & Filming 7-12:13 S '61

Duprey, R. A. Bergman and Fellini; explorers of the modern spirit. Catholic World 194:13 O '61

Russell, F. Beginners' Bergman. National R 11:311 N 4 '61

Dienstfey, H.   Success of Ingmar Bergman.   Commentary
32:391 N '61
Alpert, H.   Style is the director.   Sat R 44:39 D 23 '61
Roemer, M.   Bergman's bag of tricks.   Reporter 26:37
F 15 '62
Bergman's bag of tricks; discussion.   Reporter 26:11 Mr
15 '62
Dienstfey, H.   Success of Ingmar Bergman; discussion.
Commentary 33:348 Ap '62
Jansen, B.   Bergman on opera; interview.   Opera News
26:12 My 5 '62
Rose, S. C.   Bergman's testament.   Christian Century
79:1198 O 3 '62
Early Bergman.   Time 81:42 Ja 25 '63
Jarvie, I.   The recent films of Ingmar Bergman.   Film
Journal (Aus) 22:14 O '63
Hedlund, O.   Ingmar Bergman the listener.   Sat R 47:47
F 29 '64
How Sweden's film god brings in the kronor.   Business
Week p128 F 29 '64
Abraham, H. H. L.   Alienation in Ingmar Bergman.
Commonweal 80:290 My 29 '64
Interview.   Playboy 11:61 Je '64
Steene, B.   Archetypal patterns in four Ingmar Bergman
plays.   Scandinavian Studies 37:58 F '65
Steene, B.   The isolated hero of Ingmar Bergman.   Film
Comment 3-2:69 Spg '65
Fleisher, F.   Ants in a snakeskin.   Sight & Sound 34:176
Aut '65
Sjoman, V.   From L136: a diary of Ingmar Bergman's
Winter light.   Literary R 9:257 Win '65/66
Note.   International Film G 2:41 '65
Godard, J-L.   Bergmanorama.   Cahiers (Eng) 1:56 Ja '66
Munk, E.   Each film is my last.   Tulane Drama R 11:94
Fall '66
Loney, G.   Bergman in the theatre.   Modern Drama
9:170 S '66
Schickel, R.   Scandinavian screen.   Holiday 40:156 N '66
Furhammar, L.   Arts as therapy.   Atlas 13:52 F '67
Bergman, I.   The serpent's skin.   Cahiers (Eng) 11:24
S '67
Comolli, J-L.   The phantom of personality.   Cahiers
(Eng) 11:30 S '67
Newman, E.   My need to express myself in a film; inter-
view.   Film Comment 4-2/3:58 Fall/Win '67
Gilliatt, P.   Current cinema.   New Yorker 44:163 Ap 20
'68

Quotemanship.  Action 3-3:20 Jl/Ag '68

Ingmar Bergman.  Take One 2-1:16 S/O '68

Bjorkman, S. ; Manns, T. ; Sima, J.  Interview.  Movie 16:2 Win '68/69

Kael, P.  Current cinema.  New Yorker 44:56 D 28 '68

Heroic despair.  Time 93:68 Ja 10 '69

Grazzini, G.  Whirlpool of horror.  Atlas 17:58 Ja '69

Riffe, E.  Through a filmmaker darkly.  Take One 2-3:11 Ja/F '69

Lothwall, L-O.  Moment of agony; interview.  Films & Filming 15-5:4 F '69

Cantor, J.  Ingmar Bergman at fifty.  Atlantic 223:150 Mr '69

Lauder, R. E.  Bergman's Shame and Sartre's Stare. Catholic World 209:247 S '69

Harcourt, P.  The interplay of forces large and small. Cinema (BH) 6-2:32 F '70

Gibson, A.  Creative response to the films of Ingmar Bergman.  Catholic World 211:43 Ap '70

Gilliatt, P.  Current cinema.  New Yorker 46:103 Je 13 '70

Riffe, E.  An improbable interview.  Making Films 4-3: 12 Je '70

Rosen, R.  The relationship of Ingmar Bergman to E. T. A. Hoffman.  Film Comment 6-1:27 Spg '70

Greenberg, H. R.  Rags of time.  American Imago 27:62 Spg '70

My three powerful commandments.  Film Comment 6-2:9 Sum '70

Bergman, I.  The snakeskin.  Film Comment 6-2:14 Sum '70

Biography; filmog.  Film Comment 6-2:16 Sum '70

Young, V.  Cinema borealis.  Hudson R 23:252 Sum '70

Steene, B.  Images and words in Ingmar Bergman's films.  Cinema J 10-1:23 Fall '70

Bergman tells how he directs his actors.  Making Films 4-5:16 O '70

Cowie, P.  Ingmar Bergman; filmog.  Focus On Film 5:11 Win '70

Beauman, S.  Sweden's wary genius.  Show 2-4:38 Je '71

What directors are saying.  Action 604:20 Jl/Ag '71

Robinson, W. R.  The movies as a revolutionary moral force (Hour of the wolf).  Contempora 1-6:15 My/Ag '71

The professional director speaks.  Making Films 5-4:40 Ag '71

Elsaesser, T.  Cinema in Huis Clos:Bergman.  Monogram 2:8 Sum '71

Always my own experience; filmog.   Films Illustrated
1-4:23 O '71
Carduner, A.   Nobody has any fun in Bergman's films.
Film Society R 7-5:27 Ja '72
Ingrid Thulin comments on Ingmar Bergman. Dialogue On
Film 3:16 '72
Flatley, G.   Liv and Ingmar remain ... such good friends.
N. Y. Times Bio Ed Ap 9 '72
Bergman, I.   Film and creativity.   American Cinema-
tographer 53-4:378 Ap '72
Simon, J. Ingmar Bergman.   Film Comment 8-3:37S/O '72

BERKELEY, BUSBY
Berkeley, B. Beauty on Broadway. Lions Roar 1-5:no p# Ja '42
Tried and tested.   Lions Roar 2-2:no p   N '42
Cort, R. F.   Berkeley and Santell; letter.   Films In Re-
view 8-6:301 Je/Jl '57
Johnson, A.   Conversation with Roger Edens.   Sight &
Sound 27-4:179 Spg '58
Sarris, A.   Likable but elusive; filmog.   Film Culture
28:35 Spg '63
Gill, B.   Current cinema.   New Yorker 41:110 D 4 '65
One hundred lighted violins.   Newsweek 66:104 D 13 '65
Jenkinson, P.   The great Busby.   Film 45:30 Spg '66
Comolli, J-L.   Dancing images.   Cahiers (Eng) 2:22 '66
Brion, P. & Gilson, R.   A style of spectacle.   Cahiers
(Eng) 2:26 '66
Crandall, R.   Filmography.   Cahiers (Eng) 2:38 '66
Bevis, D. L.   A Berkeley evening.   Films In Review
18-6:380 Je/Jl '67
Roman, R. C.   Busby Berkeley.   Dance 42:34 F '68
Where are they now?   Newsweek 71:24 Ap 8 '68
Murray, W.   Return of Busby Berkeley.   N. Y. Times
Mag p26 Mr 2 '69
Busby Berkeley and his gorgeous girls.   Vogue 155:203
My '70
What directors are saying.   Action 5-3:30 My/Je '70
Gorton, D.   Busby and Ruby.   Newsweek 76:63 Ag 3 '70
Winge, H.   Busby Berkeley's girls glitter again.   Life
70-6:42 F 19 '71
Biography.   Current Biography 32:3 Ap '71
Fernett, G.   Hollywood dance directors were more than
Busby Berkeley.   Classic Film Collector 35:IX Sum '72
Lyons, D.   Interview.   Interview 2-2:4 n. d.

BERKOVIC, ZVONIMIR
Biographical note.   International Film G 6:190 '69

BERLANGA, LUIS G.
New names.   Sight & Sound 25-4:213 Spg '56
Cobos, J.   Spanish fighter.   Films & Filming 4-5:12
F '58
Berlanga, L.   The day I refused to work.   Films & Film-
ing 8-3:9 D '61
Cobos, J.   The face of '63--Spain.   Films & Filming
10-1:39 O '63

BERLIN, ABBY
Obit.   Screen World 17:233 '66

BERMAN, DONALD STUART
Listing of films.   Film Culture 37:7 Sum '65

BERNARD-AUBERT, CLAUDE
Biographical note.   Unifrance 45:10 D '57
Sadoul, G.   Notes on a new generation.   Sight & Sound
28-3/4:111 Sum/Aut '59

BERNHARDT, CURTIS (Kurt)
Parsons, L. O.   Cosmopolitan's citation for the best direction of the month.   Cosmop 120:68 Je '46

BERRI, CLAUDE
Nathan, P.   Rights and permissions.   Publisher W 195:45
Mr 24 '69
Berkvist, R.   First you live it, then you film it.   N. Y.
Times Bio Ed Ja 18 '70
What directors are saying.   Action 5-3:30 My/Je '70

BERRY, JOHN
Parsons, L. O.   Cosmopolitan's citation for the best di-
rection of the month.   Cosmop 120:45 F '46
Films on TV; filmog.   Films In Review 22-2:95 F '71

BERTOLUCCI, BERNARDO
Kael, P.   Starburst by a gifted twenty-two year-old.   Life
59:12 Ag 13 '65
Bragin, J.   A conversation with Bernardo Bertolucci.
Film Q 20-1:39 Fall '66
Bertolucci, B.   Versus Godard.   Cahiers (Eng) 10:16
My '67
Kael, P.   Current cinema.   New Yorker 43:94 Ja 13 '68
Goldin, M.   Bertolucci on The conformist; interview.
Sight & Sound 40-2:64 Spg '71
Kreitzman, R.   Bernardo Bertolucci, an Italian young

master.    Film 61:4 Spg '71
Vogel, A.    Interview; filmog.    Film Comment 7-3:25
    Fall '71
Purdon, N.    Bernardo Bertolucci.    Cinema (Lon) 8:6 '71
Director of the year; filmog.    International Film G p11
    '72
Colaciello, R.    Interview.    Interview 1-11:19 n. d.

BERTUCELLI, JEAN-LOUIS
    Ramparts of clay; interview.    Cineaste 4-4:1 Spg '71
    Ramparts of clay; interview.    Film Library Q 4-4:36
        Fall '71
    O'Brien, G.    Interview.    Interview 2-1:26 n. d.

BEYER, ED
    The world is full of sound.    Making Films 4-3:45 Je '70

BEYER, FRANK
    Bean, R.    The face of '63--Germany.    Films & Filming
        9-9:41 Je '63

BIBERMAN, HERBERT
    Biberman, H.    American people and freedom of the
        screen.    Film Comment 3-4:67 Fall '65
    Obit.    N. Y. Times Bio Ed Jl 1 '71

BIELINSKA, HALINA
    The Polish cinema.    Film 31:26 Spg '62

BILLINGTON, KEVIN
    Arkadin.    Film clips.    Sight & Sound 36-4:207 Aut '67
    Robinson, D.    Case histories of the next renascence.
        Sight & Sound 38:37 Win '68
    The crisis we deserve.    Sight & Sound 39-4:172 Aut '70
    British cinema filmography.    Film 65:10 Spg '72

BINKEY, GEORGE
    Listing of films.    Film Culture 37:7 Sum '65

BIRDWELL, RUSSELL
    Reporter's adventures.    Newsweek 13:40 F 20 '39
    Biography.    Current Biography Jl '46
    Rally round the flack boys.    Time 72:74 N 17 '58
    Angles; interview.    Cinema (BH) 4-2:12 Sum '68

BIRT, DANIEL
    Filmography.    Film 14:8 N/D '57

BISHOP, TERRY (Terence)
  Filmography.  Film 14:8 N/D '57
  British feature directors; an index to their work.
    Sight & Sound 27-6:291 Aut '58

BJERRE, JENS
  Bjerre, J.  Filming the African native.  Sight & Sound
    16-64:148 Win '47/48

BLACHÉ, ALICE GUY
  Ford, C.  The first female producer.  Films In Review
    15-3:141 Mr '64
  Smith, F. L.  Alice Guy Blache.  Films In Review 15-4:
    254 Ap '64
  Blache, A. G.  Letter.  Films In Review 15-5:317 My
    '64
  Lacassin, F.  Out of oblivion.  Sight & Sound 40-3:151
    Sum '71
  Peary, G.  Czarina of the silent screen.  Velvet Light
    Trap 6:3 Fall '72

BLACK, NOEL
  Schrader, P.  They're young, they're in love, they kill
    people.  Cinema (BH) 5-2:28 Sum '69
  Diehl, D.  A talk with Noel Black.  Action 4-5:14 S/O
    '69
  What directors are saying.  Action 6-1:30 Ja/F '71

BLACKTON, JAMES STUART
  Work of.  Blue Book 19:243 Je '14
  Sketch.  N. Y.  Dramatic Mirror 76:26 Jl 15 '16
  Haskins, H.  Work of.  Motion Pic Classic 7:16 S '18
  Biographical sketch.  Current Biography 2:84 '41
  Obit.  Current Biography '41
    N. Y. Times p17 Ag 14 '41

BLAND, EDWARD
  Bland, E.  On The cry of jazz.  Film Culture 21:28
    Sum '60

BLANK, LES
  Cooper, K. & Kriss, E.  Filming the blues; the films of
    Les Blank.  Filmmakers Newsletter 5-8:21 Je '72

BLASETTI, ALESSANDRO
  The big screens.  Sight & Sound 24-4:209 Spg '55

BLIN, ROGER
    Gray, P.  Growing apart; interview.  Tulane Drama R
        11:115 Fall '66

BLUE, JAMES
    Batten, M.  Interview with James Blue.  Film Comment
        1-5:3 Sum '63
    Blue, J.  Thoughts on cinema verite and a discussion with
        the Maysles Brothers.  Film Comment 2-4:22 Fall '64
    Blue, J.  One man's truth; an interview with Richard
        Leacock.  Film Comment 3-2:15 Spg '65
    (James Blue was a frequent contributor to Film Culture)

BLYSTONE, JOHN G.
    Obit.  N. Y. Times p32 Ag 7 '38

BOBKER, LEE
    Bobker, L.  Don't blame the client.  Making Films 2-3:
        38 Je '68
    Bobker, L.  The documentary style.  Making Films 3-2:
        14 Ap '69
    Bobker, L.  Producers shooting abroad require informa-
        tion, language, tact and minimum New York crew.
        Making Films 3-3:37 Ag '69
    Bobker, L.  New men, machines, technique.... Making
        Films 3-6:6 D '69

BOENISH, CARL
    Boenish, C.  Masters of the sky.  American Cinema-
        tographer 52-8:774 Ag '71

BOETTICHER, BUDD
    The director and the public; a symposium.  Film Culture
        1-2:15 Mr/Ap '55
    Sarris, A.  Esoterica; filmog.  Film Culture 28:22 Spg
        '63
    Coonradt, P.  Boetticher returns.  Cinema (BH) 4-4:11D
        '68
    Wicking, C.  Budd Boetticher.  Screen 10-4/5:9 Jl/O
        '69
    Schrader, P.  Budd Boetticher; a case study in criticism.
        Cinema (BH) 6-2:23 Fall '70
    What directors are saying.  Action 6-1:30 Ja/F '71

BOGDANOVICH, PETER
    Talkies.  Esquire 58:33 Ag '62
    Bogdanovich, P.  Bogie in excelsis.  Esquire 62:108 S '64

Bogdanovich, P.  Go-go and hurry; it's later than you
  think.  Esquire 63:86 F '65
Bogdanovich, P.  Sonny and Cher; they're what's happen-
  ing, baby.  Sat Evening Post 239:46 Ap 23 '66
Bogdanovich, P.  Th' respawnsibility of bein' J...Jimmy
  Stewart.  Gosh!  Esquire 66:104 Jl '66
Godard in Hollywood.  Take One 1-10:13 Je '68
Bogdanovich, P.  Targets.  Sight & Sound 39-1:55 Win
  '69/70
What directors are saying.  Action 6-3:28 My/Je '71
The professional director speaks.  Making Films 5-4:40
  Ag '71
Bogdanovich:  director still fan.  N.Y. Times Bio Ed O
  27 '71
Salute of the week.  Cue 40-45:1 N 6 '71
Harmetz, A.  Peter still looks forward to his Citizen
  Kane.  N.Y. Times Bio Ed N 14 '71
Patterson, R.  Directed by John Ford: producing a com-
  pilation documentary.  American Cinematographer
  52-11:1138 N '71
Chase, D.  On location in Texas: Peter Bogdanovich and
  The last picture show.  Show 2-9:18 N '71
What directors are saying.  Action 6-6:22 N/D '71
O'Brien, G. & Feiden, R.  Interview.  Interview 20:28
  Mr '72
Castell, D.  I have always been a self-confessed oppor-
  tunist.  Films Illustrated 1-10:15 Ap '72
What directors are saying.  Action 7-3:28 My/Je '72
Smith, L.  Showing up.  Show 2-4:10 Je '72
Gow, G.  Without a dinosaur; interview; filmog.  Films &
  Filming 18-9:18 Je '72
(Peter Bogdanovich was a frequent contributor to
  various publications.  For his interviews with other
  directors, see: FORD, JOHN; HAWKS, HOWARD;
  LEWIS, JERRY; LUMET, SIDNEY; SIEGEL, DONALD;
  TASHLIN, FRANK; von STERNBERG, JOSEF)

BOGEAUS, BENEDICT E.
  Story of.  Colliers 117:63 My 18 '46
  Marshall, J.  Nothing to it; making movies is as easy
    as building a skyscraper.  Colliers 117:65 My 18 '46
  Obit.  N.Y. Times p88 Ag 25 '68

BOGIN, MIKHAIL
  A Russian six.  Films & Filming 13-12:27 S '67

BOIGELOT, JACQUES
Focus on a director. International Film G 9:60 '72

BOLESLAWSKI, RICHARD
Lessons in acting. Theatre Arts 11:121 F '29; 13:498 Jl
'29; 15:608 Jl '31; 16:121 F '32; 16:294 Ap '32; 16:477
Je '32
Richard Boleslawski, the soldier-director. Cue 3-30:3
My 25 '35
Obit. N.Y. Times p17 Ja 18 '37
Sketch. Motion Pic 53:20 Mr '37

BOLOGNINI, MAURO
Paolucci, A. Italian film. Massachusetts R 7:556 Sum
'66

BOLOTOWSKY, ILYA
Survey among unsuccessful applicants for the Ford Found-
ation film grants. Film Comment 2-3:10 Sum '64
Campbell, L. Squaring the circle and vice-versa. Art
N 68:38 F '70

BONDARCHUK, SERGEI
Director of the year; filmog. International Film G 6:9
'69
Gillett, J. Thinking big. Sight & Sound 39-3:135 Sum
'70
Lind, J. The road to Waterloo; filmog (as actor and
director). Focus On Film 4:24 S/O '70
The coming of the Russians. Action 6-2:4 Mr/Ap '71
The Russians are here. Making Films 5-3:10 Je '71

BOORMAN, JOHN
Miller, E. Dave Clark Five make a movie! Seventeen
24:90 Jl '65
Farber, S. Writer in American films; interview. Film
Q 21:3 Sum '68
Strick, P. White man's burden. Sight & Sound 38-3:121
Sum '69
Brown, J. L. Islands of the mind. Sight & Sound
39-1:20 Win '69/70
Putney, P. G. Wilderness world of Deliverance. Con-
tempora 1-6:30 My/Ag '71
The crisis we deserve. Sight & Sound 39-4:172 Aut '70
Gow, G. Playboy in a monastery; interview; filmog.
Films & Filming 18-5:18 F '72
British cinema filmography. Film 65:10 Spg '72

McGillivray, D.  Biographical note; filmog.  Focus On
   Film 11:13 Aut '72

BOROWCZYK, WALERIAN
   Animation quartet.  International Film G 3:175 '66
   Strick, P.  The theatre of Walerian Borowczyk.  Sight &
      Sound 38-4:166 Aut '69

BORZAGE, FRANK
   Haskins, H.  Sketch.  Motion Pic Classic 11:18 S '20
   Evans, D.  Sketch.  Photoplay 18:42 S '20
   Sketch.  Motion Pic 32:108 D '26
   Tully, V.  Interview.  Vanity Fair 27:50 F '27
   Cruikshank, H.  Sketch.  Motion Pic Classic 30:35 D '29
   Bahn, C. B.  Borzage and Calvacade.  Cinema Digest
      1-8:4 Ag 22 '32
   What's wrong with the movies?  Motion Pic 46:42 S '33
   Biographical note; filmog.  Movies & People 2:39 '40
   Frank Borzage: easy does it.  Lions Roar 1-2:no p    O
      '41
   Dudley, F.  A director confides about the players.
      Silver Screen 16-5:54 Mr. '46
   Parsons, L. O.  Cosmopolitan's citation for the best di-
      rector of the month.  Cosmop 121:73 O '46
   Biography.  Current Biography 7:9 D '46
      Same.  Current Biography Yearbook 1946:63 '47
   Obit.  British Book Year 1963:865 '63
      Current Biography 23:9 S '62
      Current Biography Yearbook 1962:45 '63
      Illustrated London N 240:1057 Je 30 '62
      N. Y. Times p32 Je 20 '62
      Newsweek 60:55 Jl 2 '62
      Screen World 14:221 '63
      Time 79:29 Je 29 '62
   Bease, A.  Frank Borzage.  Film Journal (Aus) 21:111
      Ap '63
   Sarris, A.  Second line; filmog.  Film Culture 28:11
      Spg '63
   Belton, J.  Souls made great by love and adversity.
      Monogram 4:20 '72
   Camper, F.  Disputed passage.  Cinema (Lon) 9:10 n. d.

BOSTROM, THOR
   Bostrom, T.  Directions.  Todays Filmmaker 1-1:14 Ap
      '71

BÖTTCHER, JÜRGEN
    Bean, R.  The face of '63--Germany.  Films & Filming
      9-9:41 Je '63

BOULTENHOUSE, CHARLES
    Tyler, P.  Two down and one to go?  Film Culture 21:33
      Sum '60
    Boultenhouse, C.  The camera as God.  Film Culture
      29:20 Sum '63
    Survey among unsuccessful applicants for the Ford Found-
      ation film grants.  Film Comment 2-3:10 Sum '64
    Markopoulos, G.  Three filmmakers.  Film Culture 35:
      23 Win '64/65
    Listing of films.  Film Culture 37:7 Sum '65

BOULTING, JOHN
    Gibbs, P.  Charter films is an interesting company.
      World R p57 Je '47
    Filmography.  Film 14:8 N/D '57
    British feature directors; an index to their work.  Sight
      & Sound 27-6:291 Aut '58
    Conrad, D.  What makes the British laugh?  interview.
      Films & Filming 5-5:7 F '59
    Watts, S.  The Boulting twins.  Films In Review 11-2:
      119 F '60
    Cowie, P.  The face of '63--Great Britain.  Films &
      Filming 9-5:19 F '63
    Sheed, W.  Pitfalls of pratfalls; Boulting Brothers come-
      dies.  Commonweal 78:402 Jl 5 '63

BOULTING, ROY
    Gibbs, P.  Charter films is an interesting company.
      World R p57 Je '47
    Filmography.  Film 14:8 N/D '57
    British feature directors; an index to their work.  Sight
      & Sound 27-6:291 Aut '58
    Conrad, D.  What makes the British laugh?  interview.
      Films & Filming 5-5:7 F '59
    Watts, S.  The Boulting twins.  Films In Review 11-2:
      119 F '60
    Cowie, P.  The face of '63--Great Britain.  Films &
      Filming 9-5:19 F '63
    Sheed, W.  Pitfalls of pratfalls; Boulting Brothers
      comedies.  Commonweal 78:402 Jl 5 '63
    Hamilton, J.  Hayley Mills; interview.  Look 32:102 My
      28 '68
    British cinema filmography.  Film 65:10 Spg '72

BOURGUIGNON, SERGE
> Graham, P. The face of '63--France. Films & Filming 9-8:13 My '63
> Zeitlin, D. Good drizzle after a big sizzle. Life 58:45 F 26 '65
> The reward; interview. Cinema (BH) 2-5:6 Mr/Ap '65

BOURSEILLER, ANTOINE
> Two arts in one; conversation. Cahiers (Eng) 6:25 D '66

BOX, MURIEL
> Filmography. Film 14:8 N/D '57
> British feature directors; an index to their work. Sight & Sound 27-6:291 Aut '58

BOZZETTO, BRUNO
> Granja, V. Animation is a wider liberty; interview. CTVD 4-4:10 Win '66/67
> Bozzetto, B. My superman brother VIP. CTVD 5-1:9 Spg '67

BRABIN, CHARLES J.
> Obit. N.Y. Times p35 N 6 '57
> Screen World 9:221 '58

BRADLEY, DAVID
> Bradley, D. Making films on small budgets. Film 6:12 D '55

BRAHM, JOHN
> Nolan, J. E. John Brahm; filmog. Films In Review 17-1:58 Ja '66

BRAKHAGE, STAN
> Tyler, P. Stan Brakhage. Film Culture 4-18:23 '58
> Brakhage, S. The silent sound sense. Film Culture 21:65 Sum '60
> Callenbach, E. Films of Stan Brakhage. Film Q 14-3: 47 Spg '61
> Sutherland, D. A note on Stan Brakhage. Film Culture 24:84 Spg '62
> Brakhage, S. Province and providential; letter. Film Culture 24:91 Spg '62
> Mekas, J. Notes on the new American cinema. Film Culture 24:6 Spg '62
> Brakhage, S. Notes. Film Culture 25:72 Sum '62
> Filmography. Film Culture 29:75 Sum '63

Brakhage, S.   Letters.   Film Culture 29:76 Sum '63
Sitney, P. A.   Metaphors on Brakhage; interview.   Film
   Culture 30:entire issue Fall '63
Survey among unsuccessful applicants for the Ford Found-
   ation film grants.   Film Comment 2-3:10 Sum '64
Letter from Brakhage on splicing.   Film Culture 35:51
   Win '64/65
Listing of films.   Film Culture 37:7 Sum '65
Hill, J.   Brakhage and Rilke.   Film Culture 37:13 Sum
   '65
Hill, J. & Davenport, G.   Two essays on Brakhage and
   his songs.   Film Culture 40:8 Spg '66
Stan Brakhage letters.   Film Culture 40:72 Spg '66
Brakhage, S.   A moving picture giving and taking book.
   Film Culture 41:39 Sum '66
Weiner, P.   New American cinema; filmog.   Film 58:22
   Spg '70
Brakhage, S.   In defense of the "amateur" filmmaker.
   Filmmakers Newsletter 4-9/10:20 Jl/Ag '70
Sitney, P. A.   Avant garde film.   Afterimage 2:9 Aut '70
Sainer, A.   Stan Brakhage; the courage of perception.
   Vogue 156:298 S 1 '70
Taped interview.   Take One 3-1:6 S/O '70
Lee, D.   Discovering Stan Brakhage.   Film Library Q
   4-3:23 Sum '71
Smith, K.   Transferring personal vision into rhythmic
   structure.   Film Library Q 4-3:43 Sum '71

BRANAMAN, ROBERT
   Listing of films.   Film Culture 37:7 Sum '65

BRASON, JOHN
   British cinema filmography.   Film 65:10 Spg '72

BRAULT, MICHEL
   Biographical note; filmog.   Cahiers (Eng) 4:42 '66

BREER, ROBERT
   Mekas, J.   Notes on the new American cinema.   Film
      Culture 24:6 Spg '62
   Cote, G. L.   Interview; filmog.   Film Culture 27:17 Win
      '62/63
   Breer, R.   A statement.   Film Culture 29:73 Sum '63
   Survey among unsuccessful applicants for the Ford Found-
      ation film grants.   Film Culture 2-3:10 Sum '64
   Listing of films.   Film Culture 37:7 Sum '65
   Robert Breer on his work.   Film Culture 42:112 Fall '66

Mancia, A. & Van Dyke, W.    Four artists as filmmakers.
    Art In America 55:64 Ja '67
Rosenstein, H.    Motionless motion.    Art N 66:37 N '67
Weiner, P.    New American cinema; filmog.    Film 58:22
    Spg '70
Tomkins, C.    Onward and upward with the arts.    New
    Yorker 46:84 O 3 '70

## BRENON, HERBERT

Craig, J.    The face that drives.    Photoplay 8-6:111 N '15
Sketch. N. Y.    Dramatic Mirror 76:26 Jl 15 '16
The king of Jamaica.    Photoplay 10-2:135 Jl '16
Smith, A.    Visit to his studio.    Dramatic Mirror 77:15
    Ag 25 '17
Bartlett, R.    Brenon, the man.    Photoplay 13-4:75 Mr '18
Bartlett, R.    Seventy-two reels of hard luck.    Photoplay
    15-1:55 D '18
Jameson, C.    Interview.    Motion Pic Classic 8:47 Mr '19
Smith, F. J.    Interview.    Motion Pic Classic 12:43 My
    '21
Must actors have temperament?    Motion Pic 31:52 F '26
Thorp, D.    Interview.    Motion Pic Classic 25:28 Je '27
Leamy, H.    Guiding the stars; interview.    Colliers 80:19
    O 8 '27
Cruikshank, H.    Interview.    Motion Pic Classic 28:33 N
    '28
Geltzer, G.    Herbert Brenon.    Films In Review 6-3:116
    Mr '55
Marvin, E. C.    Herbert Brenon; letter.    Films In Review
    6-5:254 My '55
Obit.    Screen World 10:221 '59

## BRESSANE, JULIO

Round table on the cinema nova.    Cinema (Lon) 5:15 F '70

## BRESSON, ROBERT

Lambert, G.    Notes on Robert Bresson.    Sight & Sound
    23-1:35 Jl/S '53
Monod, R.    Working with Bresson.    Sight & Sound 27-1:30
    Sum '57
Green, H.    Movies.    Reporter 17:41 N 28 '57
Interview.    Unifrance 45:3 D '57
Gow, G.    The quest for realism; discussion.    Films &
    Filming 4-3:13 D '57
Baxter, B.    Robert Bresson.    Film 17:9 S/O '58
Ford, C.    Robert Bresson.    Films In Review 10-2:65 F
    '59

6 films 6 faces. Unifrance 50:25 Jl/S '59
Roud, R. French outsider with the inside look. Films &
    Filming 6-7:9 Ap '60
Greene, M. Robert Bresson. Film Q 13-3:4 Spg '60
The French film; a discussion. Film 26:10 N/D '60
Cameron, I. Interview. Movie 7:28 F/Mr '63
Robert Bresson. Film 35:6 Spg '63
Graham, P. The face of '63--France. Films & Filming
    9-8:13 My '63
Jacob, G. Au Hasard, Balthazer. Sight & Sound 36-1:7
    Win '66/67
Godard, J-L & Delahaye, M. Interview. Cahiers (Eng)
    8:5 F '67
Michelson, A. Etc. in a Christian framework. Com-
    monweal 89:318 N 29 '68
Roud, R. Memories of Resnais. Sight & Sound 38-3:124
    Sum '69
Skoller, D. S. Praxis as a cinematic principle in films
    by Robert Bresson. Cinema J 9-1:13 Fall '69
Rhode, E. Dostoevsky and Bresson. Sight & Sound
    39-2:82 Spg '70
Biography. Current Biography 32:11 Ja '71
Zeman, M. The suicide of Robert Bresson. Cinema
    (BH) 6-3:37 Spg '71
Prokosch, M. Bresson's stylistics revisited. Film Q
    25-2:30 Win '71/72
Roud, R. The early work of Robert Bresson. Film Cul-
    ture 20:44 n. d.

BRETHERTON, HOWARD
    Obit. Classic Film Collector 24:14 Sum '69 (reprint
    from Variety)

BRIDGES, JAMES
    What directors are saying. Action 5-6:22 N/D '70
    A self interview. Action 6-1:5 Ja/F '71

BRISKIN, SAMUEL J.
    Obit. Screen World 21:232 '70

BROMLEY, ALAN
    Filmography. Film 14:8 N/D '57

BROOK, PETER
    Like the North Pole. Time 54:81 N 21 '49
    Griffin, J. He directed the new version of Faust.
    Theatre Arts 37:71 D '53

Filmography.   Film 14:8 N/D '57
Keep 'em still; summary of remarks.   Musical America
   79:11 Je '59
Brook, P.   The French game gave me my freedom.   Films
   & Filming 7-1:7 O '60
Personality of the month.   Films & Filming 8-4:7 Ja '61
Biography.   Current Biography 22:9 My '61
   Same.   Current Biography Yearbook 1961:74 '62
Peter Brook putting into question.   Film 29:17 Sum '61
Search for a hunger.   Mademoiselle 54:94 N '61
Brien, A.   Openings.   Theatre Arts 47:57 Ja '63
Houston, P. & Milne, T.   Interview.   Sight & Sound 32-
   3:108 Sum '63
Strick, P.   Lord of the flies and Peter Brook.   Film
   37:15 Aut '63
Reeves, G.   Shakespeare on three screens; interview.
   Sight & Sound 34-2:66 Spg '65
Gilliatt, P.   Peter Brook: a natural saboteur of order.
   Vogue 147:102 Ja 1 '66
Reddy, J.   Marat/Sade.   Look 30:110 F 22 '66
Knight, A.   Filming Marat/Sade.   Sat R 49:43 Jl 30 '66
Reeves, G.   Finding Shakespeare on film.   Tulane Drama
   R 11:117 Fall '66
Ronan, M.   Lively arts; interview.   Senior Scholastic
   90:21 Mr 31 '67
Taylor, J. R.   Peter Brook, or the limitations of in-
   telligence.   Sight & Sound 36-2:80 Spg '67
Deadly, holy, rough, immediate.   Time 92:94 N 8 '68
Marowitz, C.   From prodigy to professional as written,
   directed and acted by Peter Brook.   N. Y. Times Mag
   p62 N 24 '68
Immediate theater; excerpt from The empty space.
   Atlantic 222:82 N '68
Ansorge, P.   Peter Brook; interview.   Plays & Players
   18-1:18 O '70
Lewis, A.   Peter Brook's theater is a 'living event. '
   N. Y. Times Bio Ed Ja 15 '71
Salute of the week.   Cue 40-7:1 F 13 '71
British cinema filmography.   Film 65:10 Spg '72

BROOKS, CONRAD
   Gow, G.   Up from the underground.   Films & Filming
      17-11:24 Ag '71

BROOKS, DAVID
   Listing of films.   Film Culture 37:7 Sum '65

BROOKS, MEL
>2, 000 year old man.   Newsweek 66:88 O 4 '65
>Interview.   Playboy 13-10:71 O '66
>Producers.   Time 91:78 Ja 26 '68
>Kael, P.   Current cinema.   New Yorker 44:140 Mr 23 '68
>Robbins, F.   What makes Mel Brooks run?   Show 1-13:
>      13 S 17 '70
>What directors are saying.   Action 6-1:30 Ja/F '71
>Confessions of an auteur.   Action 6-6:14 N/D '71

BROOKS, RICHARD
>Brooks, R.   A novel isn't a movie.   Films In Review
>      3-2:55 F '52
>Vidor, K. & Brooks, R.   Two story conferences.   Sight
>      & Sound 22-2:85 O/D '52
>Personality of the month.   Films & Filming 2-8:3 My '56
>Brooks, R.   On filming Karamazov.   Films In Review
>      9-2:49 F '58
>Brooks, R.   Dostoievsky, love and American cinema.
>      Films & Filming 4-7:11 Ap '58
>Johnson, A.   Richard Brooks.   Sight & Sound 29-4:174
>      Aut '60
>Sarris, A.   Minor disappointments; filmog.   Film Culture
>      28:41 Spg '63
>Joyce, P.   Richard Brooks and Lord Jim.   Film 42:27
>      Win '64
>Lord Jim interview.   Cinema (BH) 2-5:4 Mr/Ap '65
>Richard Brooks.   Movie 12:2 Spg '65
>Mayersberg, P.   Conservative idealist.   Movie 12:10
>      Spg '65
>Vallance, T.   Filmography.   Movie 12:17 Spg '65
>Director of the year; filmog.   International Film G 3:23
>      '66
>In cold blood; interview.   Cahiers (Eng) 5:63 '66
>Jacobs, J.   In hot water.   Reporter 38:38 Ja 11 '68
>Should directors produce?   Action 3-4:10 Jl/Ag '68
>What directors are saying.   Action 5-2:16 Mr/Ap '70
>Simons, D.   From a troubled beginning to The happy
>      ending; filmog.   Show 1-13:42 S 17 '70
>Filmography.   Film Culture 6-4:101 Win '70/71

BROUGHTON, JAMES
>Playground; dance drama of our precarious times.   The-
>      atre Arts 30:450 Ag '46
>Gelffing, F.   Quandary and statement.   Poetry 77:359
>      Mr '51
>Edinburgh's documentary festival.   Sat R 34:60 O 13 '51

Broughton, J.   Film as a way of seeing; filmog.   Film
   Culture 29:19 Sum '63
Survey among unsuccessful applicants for the Ford Found-
   ation film grants.   Film Comment 2-3:10 Sum '64

BROWER, OTTO
   Condon, F.   Let Otto do it.   Colliers 105:19 Mr 30 '40
   Obit.   N. Y. Times p13 Ja 26 '46

BROWN, BARRY
   Fondiller, H. V.   Biography of a 120-second thriller.
      Popular Photo 58:112 My '66

BROWN, BERT
   Survey among unsuccessful applicants for the Ford Found-
      ation film grants.   Film Comment 2-3:10 Sum '64

BROWN, BRUCE
   Clark, P. S.   Bruce Brown:  home movies for the mil-
      lions.   Todays Filmmaker 1-3:46 F '72

BROWN, CLARENCE
   Manners, D.   Sketch.   Motion Pic Classic 27:26 Ap '28
   Tully, J.   Estimate.   Vanity Fair 30:79 Ap '28
   Gwin, J.   Clarence Brown tells about the players. Silver
      Screen 5-2:26 D '34
   Men behind megaphones.   Cue 4-10:3 Ja 4 '36
   Gwin, J.   The inside "low down. "  Silver Screen 6-7:35
      My '36
   Norberg, G.   Work of.   Motion Pic 51:58 Je '36
   Home of.   Photoplay 51:34 N '37
   Squire, G.   Not done with mirrors.   Silver Screen 8-5:51
      Mr '38
   Biographical note; filmog.   Movies & People 2:39 '40
   Brown, C.   Bringing Saroyan to the screen.   Lions Roar
      2-4:no p   Ap '43
   Hands across the screen.   Lions Roar 3-4:no p     Jl '44
   MGM's directors range from pioneers to newcomers.
      Lions Roar 3-4:no p     Jl '44
   Parsons, L. O.   Cosmopolitan's citation for the best di-
      rection of the month.   Cosmop 123:54 O '47
   Brown, C.   The producer must be boss.   Films In Re-
      view 2-2:1 F '51

BROWN, DANIEL
   Survey among unsuccessful applicants for the Ford Found-
      ation film grants.   Film Comment 2-3:10 Sum '64

BROWN, KARL
What libraries are doing in the audio visual field.
  Library J 72:39 Ja 1 '47
Your record is overdue.   Sat R 30:49 O 25 '47
Movie-go-round.   Sat R 35:40 My 10 '52

BROWN, MELVILLE
Obit.   N.Y. Times p21 F 1 '38

BROWN, ROLAND
Miller, D.   Notes on a blighted career; filmog.
  Focus On Film 7:43 n. d.
Letters.   Focus On Film 8:56 n. d.
Obit.   Screen World 15:219 '64

BROWNING, TOD
Dickey, J.   Sketch.   Motion Pic Classic 27:33 Mr '28
Geltzer, G.   Tod Browning.   Films In Review 4-8:410
  O '53
Obit.   N.Y. Times p47 O 10 '62
  Screen World 14:221 '63
Guy, R.   Horror: the Browning version.   Cinema (BH)
  1-4:26 Je/Jl '63
Dracula.   Famous Monsters 49:4 n. d.

BRUCE, MURRAY
Profile.   Making Films 2-5:38 O '68

BRUCKMAN, CLYDE
Everson, W. K.   Clyde Bruckman; letter.   Films In Review 6-2:91 F '55

BRUNEL, ADRIAN
Brunel, A.   Making films on small budgets.   Film 6:18
  D '55

BRUNER, RICHARD
Bruner, R.   Exciting?   Dramatic??   Filmstrips???
  Film Library Q 3-2:19 Spg '70

BRUNIUS, JACQUES
Robinson, D.   Jacques Brunius.   Sight & Sound 36-3:118
  Sum '67

BRUSATI, FRANCO
Disorder; interview.   Cinema (BH) 1-4:14 Je/Jl '63

BRYAN, JULIAN
  Hyatt, H.  Julian Bryan, internationalist.  Film Library
    Q 4-1:33 Win '70/71

BRYANT, BAIRD
  Listing of films.  Film Culture 37:7 Sum '65

BUCHOWETZKI, DIMITRI
  Sketch.  Photoplay 26:51 O '24

BUCKINGHAM, TOM
  Obit.  N.Y. Times p49 D 17 '39

BUCQUET, HAROLD SPENCER
  Exacting adventurer.  Lions Roar 1-4:no p# D '41
  They call him "Mr. K."  Lions Roar 3-1:no p# S '43
  Two Oscars?  Lions Roar 3-4:no p# Jl '44
  MGM's directors range from pioneers to newcomers.
    Lions Roar 3-4:no p# Jl '44
  Obit.  N.Y. Times p26 F 15 '46

BUCZKOWSKI, LEONARD
  The Polish cinema.  Film 31:26 Spg '62

BULAJIĆ, VELJKO (Velko)
  Biographical note.  International Film G 7:248 '70

BUÑUEL, LUIS
  Richardson, T.  The films of Luis Bunuel.  Sight &
    Sound 23-3:125 Ja/Mr '54
  Knight, A.  Films of Luis Bunuel.  Sat R 37:27 Jl 17 '54
  Bazin, A. & Donid-Valcroze, J.  Conversations with
    Bunuel.  Sight & Sound 24-4:181 Spg '55
  Bunuel, L.  Bunuel on Bunuel; letter.  Films In Review
    6-8:425 O '55
  Aubry, D. & Lacor, J. M.  Luis Bunuel.  Film Q 12-
    2:7 Win '58
  Prouse, D.  Interview.  Sight & Sound 29-3:118 Sum '60
  Bunuel, L.  A statement.  Film Culture 21:41 Sum '60
  Riera, E. G.  The eternal rebellion of Luis Bunuel;
    filmog.  Film Culture 21:42 Sum '60
  Aranda, F.  Bunuel in Spain.  Sight & Sound 30-2:70
    Spg '61
  Aranda, J. F.  Surrealist and Spanish giant.  Films &
    Filming 8-1:17 O '61
  Aranda, J. F.  Back from the wilderness.  Films &
    Filming 8-2:29 N '61

Talk with the director.   Newsweek 59:96 Mr 26 '62
Bunuel, L.   On Viridiana.   Film Culture 24:74 Spg '62
Kanesaka, K.   Interview.   Film Culture 24:75 Spg '62
Robinson, D.   Thank God I am still an atheist.   Sight &
    Sound 31-3:116 Sum '62
Cinema, an instrument of poetry.   Theatre Arts 46:18 Jl
    '62
Steel, R.   Anarchistic heart.   Christian Century 79:1259
    O 17 '62
Sarris, A.   Beyond the fringe.   Film Culture 28:29 Spg
    '63
Aranda, F.   Bunuel's Tristana.   Sight & Sound 32-3:123
    Sum '63
Cobos, J.   The face of '63--Spain.   Films & Filming
    10-1:39 O '63
Fuentes, C.   The macabre master of movie-making.
    Show 3-11:81 N '63
Beckley, P. V.   Two on the aisle.   Sat R 47:36 F 8 '64
Biography.   Current Biography 26:11 Mr '65
    Same.   Current Biography Yearbook 1965:62 '65
Carson, R.   An eye in the wilderness.   Holiday 37:127
    Ap '65
Interview at Cannes.   Cinema (BH) 2-6:38 Jl/Ag '65
Hammond, R. M.   Luis Alcoriza and the films of Luis
    Bunuel.   Film Heritage 1-1:25 Fall '65
Milne, T.   The Mexican Bunuel.   Sight & Sound 35-1:36
    Win '65/66
Director of the year; filmog.   International Film G 2:19
    '65
Kanesaka, K.   A visit to Luis Bunuel.   Film Culture
    41:60 Sum '66
Mussman, T.   Early surrealist expression in the film.
    Film Culture 41:8 Sum '66
Fieschi, J-A.   Bunuel's Mexican sketches.   Cahiers
    (Eng) 4:19 '66
Mardore, M.   Age of gold.   Cahiers (Eng) 3:47 '66
Harcourt, P.   Spaniard and surrealist.   Film Q 20-3:2
    Spg '67
Stein, E.   Bunuel's golden bowl.   Sight & Sound 36-4:172
    Aut '67
Capelle, A.   Exit Bunuel; interview.   Atlas 14:55 S '67
Gilliatt, P.   Current cinema.   New Yorker 44:163 Ap 20;
    66 Je 22 '68
Kael, P.   Current cinema.   New Yorker 44:109 F 15 '69
Verley, B.   Bunuel's Christ.   Film 56:23 Aut '69
Biography.   Time 94:NY16 N 28 '69
Michelson, A.   Bunuel on pilgrimage.   Commonweal 92:63
    Mr 27 '70

Carriere, J-C.   The Bunuel mystery.   Show 1-4:59
Ap 27 '70
Aranda, F.   Bunuel and Tristana.   Sight & Sound 39-2:73
Spg '70
Terrien, S.   Demons also believe.   Christian Century
87:1481 D 9 '70
MacLochlainn, A.   The films of Luis Bunuel and Georges
Franju.   Film Journal 1-2:16 Sum '71
Elsaesser, T.   Bunuel's Tristana.   Monogram 2:8 Sum
'71
Kerry, T. K. & Howard, J.   The super-ego Christian
asceticism and Bunuel's Simon.   Film 63:15 Aut '71

BURCKHARDT, RUDY
A report on the films of Rudy Burckhardt.   Vision 1-1:13
Spg '62
Sitney, P. A.   A view of Burckhardt.   Vision 1-1:13
Spg '62
Batten, M.   Notes on Rudy Burckhardt: motion seen.
Vision 1-1:15 Spg '62
Katz, A.   Rudolph Burckhardt: multiple fugitive.   Art N
62:38 D '63
Listing of films.   Film Culture 37:7 Sum '65

BURGE, STUART
Cox, F.   Stuart Burge; interview.   Plays & Players
16-9:64 Je '69
British cinema filmography.   Film 65:10 Spg '72

BURTON, MICHAEL and PHILIP
Mekas, J.   Notes on the new American cinema.   Film
Culture 24:6 Spg '62
Listing of films.   Film Culture 37:7 Sum '65

BUTE, MARY ELLEN
Starr, C.   Animation: abstract and concrete.   Sat R
35:46 D 13 '52
Bute, M. E.   Abstronics.   Films In Review 5-6:263
Je/Jl '54
Markopoulos, G.   Beyond audio visual space; filmog.
Vision 1-2:52 Sum '62
Batten, M.   Actuality and abstraction; interview.   Vision
1-2:55 Sum '62
Weinberg, G.   Interview.   Film Culture 35:25 Win '64/65
Pyres, J.   Notes on women directors.   Take One 3-2:7
N/D '70

BUTLER, DAVID
  Biographical note; filmog.   Movies & People 2:39 '40
  Parsons, L. O.   Cosmopolitan's citation for the best di-
    rection of the month.   Cosmop 123:12 D '47
  Butler, D.   Remembering Leo McCarey.   Action 4-5:11
    S/O '69

BUZZELL, EDDIE
  What happens to kid stars?   Lions Roar 1-2:no p# O '41
  He's been through the mill.   Lions Roar 1-9:no p# My
    '42
  Buzzell, E.   Movies for morale.   Lions Roar 2-4:no p#
    Ap '43
  He gets what he wants.   Lions Roar 3-1:no p# S '43
  MGM's directors range from pioneers to newcomers.
    Lions Roar 3-1:no p# S '43

BYARS, BILLY JR.
  Swisher, V. H.   Generating The genesis children.   After
    Dark 5-5:18 S '72

BYRNE, ERNEST G.
  Byrne, E. G.   How do you describe a mist?   Action
    1-2:22 N/D '66
  Byrne, E. G.   A real Irishman.   Action 2-3:14 Mr/Ap
    '68

CABANNE, WILLIAM CHRISTY
　　Biographical note.　Photoplay 9-4:42 Mr '16
　　Obit.　N. Y. Times p31 O 17 '50
　　　Screen World 2:233 '51

CACOYANNIS, MICHAEL
　　Cacoyannis, M.　The simple approach; filmmaking in
　　　Greece.　International Film A 1:49 '57
　　Michael Cacoyannis on a matter of size.　Films & Film-
　　　ing 6-4:13 Ja '60
　　Stanbrook, A.　Rebel with a cause.　Film 24:16 Mr/Ap
　　　'60
　　Personality of the month.　Films & Filming 6-10:5 Jl '60
　　Manus, W.　Michael Cacoyannis.　Films In Review
　　　13-10:638 D '62
　　Cacoyannis, M.　Greek to me.　Films & Filming 9-9:19
　　　Je '63
　　Dallas, A.　Michael Cacoyannis.　Film Comment 1-6:44
　　　Fall '63
　　Lyon, N.　Second fame; good food.　Vogue 145:230 My '65
　　Biography.　Current Biography 27:5 My '66
　　　Same.　Current Biography Yearbook 1966:34 '67
　　Lerman, L.　International movie report.　Mademoiselle
　　　64:117 F '67
　　Robbins, F.　Director Michael Cacoyannis and his Trojan
　　　women.　Show 2-8:29 O '71

CADE, SVEND
　　Obit.　N. Y. Times p29 Je 26 '52

CAHN, EDWARD
　　The man in the basement.　Lions Roar 4-1:no p# F '45

CAMMELL, DON
　　Liben, R. J.　Don Cammell performance pluperfect.
　　　Interview 23:10 Jl '72

CAMPANI, PAUL
　　Granja, V.　Paul Campani and Max Massimino-Garnier
　　　alive and well!　CTVD 6-3:9 Spg '69

CAMPBELL, COLIN
　　Carr, H. C.　Directors: the men who make the plays.
　　　Photoplay 8-1:80 Je '15

Aye, J.   Silent Jim Campbell.   Photoplay 9-6:41 My '16

CAMPBELL, MAURICE
Obit.   N. Y. Times p15 O 17 '42

CAMPBELL, WEBSTER
Sketch.   Motion Pic 10:117 N '15
His most difficult scene.   Motion Pic 15:47 Ap '18
Bruce, B.   Interview.   Motion Pic 20:68 O '20

CAMPION, TOBY
Campion, T.   7,000 feet of film.   Seventeen 27:86 Ja '68

CAMUS, MARCEL
Biographical note.   Unifrance 45:11 D '57
Sadoul, G.   Notes on a new generation.   Sight & Sound
28-3/4:111 Sum/Aut '59
Billard, G.   The men and their work.   Films & Filming
6-1:7 O '59
Meeting La nouvelle vague; conversation.   Films & Filming
6-1:7 O '59
Orpheus distending.   Time 76:62 S 19 '60

CANNON, WILLIAM D.
Listing of films.   Film Culture 37:7 Sum '65

CANUTT, YAKIMA
Zeitlin, D.   Great general slays 'em again.   Life 60:93
My 27 '66
Action man's action.   Action 1-1:14 S/O '66
Hagner, J. C.   Yak: super stuntman.   Classic Film
Collector 18:13 Sum '67
King of the stuntmen.   Those Enduring Matinee Idols
1-9:114 F/Mr '71
Canutt, Y.   The company remembers Stagecoach.   Action
6-5:26 S/O '71

CAPELLANI, ALBERT
Corliss, A.   "Cap," a sweet tempered director.   Photoplay 11-2:88 Ja '17

CAPOVILLA, MAURICE
Viany, A.   Who's who in the cinema novo.   CTVD 5-4:26
Sum '68

CAPRA, FRANK
Cohen, H.   Frank Capra.   Cinema Digest 3-4:12 Ap 10
'33

Baskette, K.   Success of his work.   Photoplay 47:31 D
    '34
Harrison, P.   Interview.   Motion Pic 49:55 Jl '35
Stuart, J.   Fine Italian hand.   Colliers 96:13 Ag 17 '35
Star director goes to town with Mr. Deeds.   Newsweek
    7:29 Ap 18 '36
Sketch.   Stage 13:62 Ap '36
Improviser.   American 121:77 Je '36
Work of.   Motion Pic 52:60 Ag '36
Johnston, A.   Capra shoots as he pleases.   Sat Evening
    Post 210:8 My 14 '38
Columbia's gem.   Time 32:35 Ag 8 '38
He makes a hit picture.   Life 5:46 S 19 '38
Daugherty, F.   He has the common touch.   Christian
    Science Mon Mag p5 N 9 '38
Sketch.   Time 34:43 Jl 24 '39
Spotlight on Hollywood.   Arts & Decoration 51:24 D '39
Hellman, G. T.   Thinker in Hollywood.   New Yorker
    16:23 F 24 '40
Biographical note; filmog.   Movies & People 2:39 '40
Jacobs, L.   Film directors at work.   Theatre Arts 25:43
    Ja '41
Hamman, M.   Meet Frank Capra making a picture.   Good
    Housekeeping 112:11 Mr '41
Harriman, M. C.   Mr. and Mrs. Frank Capra.   Ladies
    Home J 58:35 Ap '41
Benedict, P.   Frank Capra's secret!   Silver Screen
    12-3:34 Ja '42
Breaking Hollywood's pattern of sameness.   N. Y. Times
    Mag p18 My 5 '46
Capra, F.   We all should be actors.   Silver Screen
    16-11:54 S '46
New picture.   Time 48:54 D 23 '46
Work of.   Life 21:68 D 30 '46
Parsons, L. O.   Cosmopolitan's citation as one of the
    best directors of the month.   Cosmop 122:67 Ja '47
Rivkin, A.   Frank Capra sticks by the little man.   U. N.
    World 1:64 Mr '47
Wechsberg, J.   Meet Frank Capra.   Readers Digest
    51:80 O '47
Biography.   Current Biography 9:5 Ap '48
    Same.   Current Biography Yearbook 1948:90 '49
Parsons, L. O.   Cosmopolitan's citation for the best di-
    rection of the month.   Cosmop 124:13 Je '48
Minoff, P.   Frank talk with Capra.   Cue 25-47:16 N 24
    '56
Up with Frank Capra.   Newsweek 48:92 D 3 '56

Look applauds.   Look 21:14 Ap 2 '57
Stanbrook, A.   Ya gotta have heart.   Films & Filming
    6-12:6 S '60
Talk with the director.   Newsweek 58:97 D 18 '61
Zunser, J.   Frank Capra returns.   Cue 30-51:11 D 23 '61
Capra, F.   Do I make you laugh?   Films & Filming
    8-12:14 S '62
Fenin, G.   The face of '63--United States.   Films &
    Filming 9-6:55 Mr '63
Sarris, A.   Third line; filmog.   Film Culture 28:18
    Spg '63
Directors still dominate films.   Making Films 3-5:44 O '69
Richards, J.   Frank Capra and the cinema of populism;
    filmog.   Cinema (Lon) 5:22 F '70
Interview; filmog; biblio.   Discussion 3:entire issue '71
Capra, F.   The name above the title.   Action 6-3:5
    My/Je '71
Thompson, H.   Capra, 74, looks back at film career.
    N.Y. Times Bio Ed Je 24 '71
Bernds, E.   Dear Frank Capra.   Film Fan Mo 124:9 O '71
Bergman, M.   The telephone company, the nation, and
    perhaps the world.   Velvet Light Trap 3:24 Win '71/72
Richards, J.   Frank Capra and the cinema of populism.
    Film Society R 7-6:38 F; 7-7/8/9:61 Mr/Ap/My '72
Stein, E.   Capra counts his Oscars.   Sight & Sound
    41-3:162 Sum '72


CARBONNEAUX, NORBERT
    Biographical note.   Unifrance 45:11 D '57


CARDIFF, JACK
    British cinema filmography.   Film 65:10 Spg '72


CAREWE, EDWIN
    Service, F.   Interview.   Classic 19:60 Ap '24
    Tully, J.   Sketch.   Photoplay 28:17 S '25
    Obit.   N.Y. Times p21 Ja 23 '40
        Current Biography '40


CAREY, PATRICK
    Biographical note.   International Film G 7:98 '70


CARLSEN, HENNING
    Biographical note.   International Film G 5:66 '68


CARNÉ, MARCEL
    Spotlights five young Frenchmen who are giving French

cinema a new look. Films & Filming 5-3:18 D '58
Stanbrook, A. The Carne bubble. Film 22:12 N/D '59
The French film; discussion. Film 26:10 N/D '60
Hatch, R. Films. Nation 193:38 Jl 15 '61

## CARRERAS, MICHAEL
British cinema filmography. Film 65:10 Spg '72

## CARSON, L. M. KIT
Carson, L. M. K. More notes from the underground.
Cinema (BH) 5-1:20 Spg '69
Carson, L. M. K. A voice-over. Film Library Q
2-3:20 Sum '69
Carson, L. M. K. The loser here. Show 1-1:39 Ja '70
Zadan, C. An America dreamer. After Dark 3-11:18 Mr '71
Colaciello, R. Interview. Interview 2-3:22 n. d.
Carson, L. M. K. The mask falls ... and there's life:
American independents. AFI Report 3:12 N '72

## CARSTAIRS, JOHN PADDY
Filmography. Film 14:8 N/D '57
Carstairs, J. P. British laughter-makers. Films &
Filming 4-4:9 Ja '58
British feature directors; an index to their work. Sight &
Sound 27-6:291 Aut '58
Obit. Film R p17 '71/72

## CARTIER, RUDOLPH
The man to beat. Film 54:17 Win '71

## CASS, HENRY
British feature directors; an index to their work. Sight &
Sound 27-6:291 Aut '58

## CASSAVETES, JOHN
Broadway love story. Look 21:62 Je 11 '57
No torn shirts for him. TV Guide 5-40:18 O 5 '57
The chip's off his shoulder. TV Guide 7-48:28 N 28 '59
$40,000 method. Time 77:72 Mr 24 '61
People on the way up. Sat Evening Post 235:26 Ap 7 '62
Mekas, J. Cassavetes, the improvisation. Film Culture
24:8 Spg '62
Incoming tide; interview. Cinema (BH) 1-1:34 '62
Fenin, G. The face of '63--United States. Films &
Filming 9-6:55 Mr '63
Sarris, A. Oddities and one shots. Film Culture 28:45
Spg '63
Faces interview. Cinema (BH) 4-1:23 Spg '68

Austen, D.   Masks and faces; interview.   Films & Film-
    ing 14-12:4 S '68
Faces of the husbands.   New Yorker 45:32 Mr 15 '69
Guerin, A.   After Faces, a film to keep the man-child
    alive.   Life 66:53 My 9 '69
Biography.   Current Biography 30:10 Jl '69
    Same.   Current Biography Yearbook 1969:74 '70
Haskell, M. Three husbands hold court.  Show 1-2:67 F '70
On the scene.   Playboy 17-4:183 Ap '70
New Hollywood is old Hollywood.   Time 96:72 D 7 '70
Gillett, J.  Biographical note; filmog.  Focus On Film 6:11 Spg '71
Interview.   Playboy 18-7:55 Jl '71
Harmetz, A. Dear boss: I'm sorry I couldn't interview Gena
    ... but John Cassavetes could.  N. Y. Times sec2:11 F 13'72
Cassavetes, J.  What's wrong with Hollywood?  Film
    Culture 19:4 n. d.
Robert Aldrich comments on Cassavetes.  Dialogue On Film 2:7
    '72
Interview with Cassavetes and Peter Falk; Cassavetes filmog.
    as director; biblio.  Dialogue On Film 4:entire issue '72

CASTELLANI, RENATO
    Jorgenson, P. A.   Castellani's Romeo and Juliet; inten-
        tion and response.   Q Film Radio TV 10:1 Fall '55
    Castellani, R.   Putting gloss on prison.   Films & Film-
        ing 5-7:9 Ap '59

CASTLE, WILLIAM
    Sketch.   American 141:135 My '46
    Queer for fear.   Time 74:58 Ag 3 '59
    Kobler, J.   Master of movie horror.   Sat Evening Post
        232:30 Mr 19 '60

CATES, GILBERT
    Hartzband, M. & Wallach, G.   Problems of lighting in
        an airport terminal.   Making Films 4-1:37 F '70
    Cates, G.   Life with "Father."   Action 5-5:11 S/O '70

CATTANEO, TONY
    Wyatt Cattaneo productions.   Film 45:27 Spg '66

CAVALCANTI, ALBERTO
    Cavalcanti, A.   Sound in films.   Films 1-1:25 N '39
    de la Roche, C.   Cavalcanti in Brazil.   Sight & Sound
        24-3:119 Ja/Mr '55
    The big screens.   Sight & Sound 24-4:201 Spg '55
    Monegal, E. R.   Alberto Cavalcanti.   Q Film Radio TV
        9-4:342 Sum '55

Minish, G.   Cavalcanti in Paris.   Sight & Sound 39-3:135
    Sum '70
Taylor, J. R.   Surrealist admen.   Sight & Sound 40-4:187
    Aut '71
Interview.   Screen Sum '72

CAVALIER, ALAIN
    Graham, P.   The face of '63--France.   Films & Filming
    9-8:13 My '63

CAYATTE, ANDRÉ
    Interview.   Unifrance 33:7 D '54/Ja '55
    Cayatte, A.   My friend Bourvil.   Unifrance 48:17 O '58

CHABROL, CLAUDE
    Biographical note.   Unifrance 48:12 O '58
    Spotlights five young Frenchmen who are giving French
        cinema a new look.   Films & Filming 5-3:18 D '58
    Baxter, B.   Claude Chabrol.   Film 54:31 Spg '59
    6 films 6 faces.   Unifrance 50:25 Jl/S '59
    Sadoul, G.   Notes on a new generation.   Sight & Sound
        28-3/4:111 Sum/Aut '59
    Billard, G.   The men and their work.   Films & Filming
        6-1:7 O '59
    Meeting La nouvelle vague; conversation.   Films & Film-
        ing 6-1:7 O '59
    The French film; discussion.   Film 26:10 N/D '60
    Claude Chabrol.   Films & Filming 9-6:5 Mr '63
    Graham, P.   The face of '63--France.   Films & Filming
        9-8:13 My '63
    Cameron, I.   The Darwinian world of Claude Chabrol.
        Movie 10:4 Je '63
    Fieschi, J. & Shivas, M.   Interview.   Movie 10:16 Je '63
    Knight, A.   New life for the new wave.   Sat R 49:38
        Ag 20 '66
    Chabrol, C.   Hitchcock confronts evil.   Cahiers (Eng)
        2:67 '66
    Gow, G.   When the new wave becomes old hat.   Films &
        Filming 13-6:20 Mr; 13-7:26 Ap '67
    Dewey, L.   Cabrol rides the waves.   Film 55:32 Sum '69
    Wood, R.   Chabrol and Truffaut.   Movie 17:16 Win
        '69/70
    Allen, D.   Claude Chabrol.   Screen 11-1:55 F '70
    Milne, T.   Chabrol's schizophrenic spider.   Sight &
        Sound 39-2:58 Spg '70
    Interview.   Take One 3-1:22 S/O '70
    Nogueira, R. & Zalaffi, N.   Conversation with Chabrol.

Sight & Sound 40-1:2 Win '70/71
Milne, T. Songs of innocence. Sight & Sound 40-1:7
Win '70/71
Coment, M. ; Legrand, G. ; Torok, J. Interview. Movie
18:2 Win '70/71
Ebert, R. This man must commit murder. N. Y. Times
Bio Ed N 29 '70
Director of the year; filmog. International Film G p16 '70
Giard, R. Chabrol's Iliad. Film Heritage 6-3:26 Spg '71
Bucher, F. & Cowie, P. Welles and Chabrol. Sight &
Sound 40-4:188 Aut '71
Goldman, C. Claude Chabrol: Le Boucher. Applause
1-9:37 Ja 19 '72

CHAFFEE, JOAN
Kevles, B. L. Interview. Film Culture 38:15 Fall '65

CHAFFEY, DON
British feature directors; an index to their work. Sight
& Sound 27-6:292 Aut '58
British cinema filmography. Film 65:10 Spg '72

CHALMERS, THOMAS
Obit. Screen World 18:233 '67

CHANDET, LOUIS W.
Obit. Screen World 17:234 '66

CHAPLIN, CHARLES
Charlie Chaplin. Photoplay 7-3:35 F '15
Eubank, V. Interview. Motion Pic 9:75 Mr '15
Some expressions! McClure 45:27 Jl '15
Sketch. Motion Pic 9:93 Jl '15
McGuirk, C. J. Charles Chaplin. Motion Pic 9:121 Jl
'15 (and following issues)
Carr, H. C. Charlie Chaplin's story. Photoplay
8-2:27 Jl; 8-3:43 Ag; 8-4:107 S; 8-5:97 O '15
How I made my success. Theatre 22:120 S '15
Adams, F. P. Plutarch lights of history. Harper
62:300 Mr 25 '16
Gaddis, I. Sketch. Motion Pic 11:47 Ap '16
Fiske, M. M. Art of. Harper 62:494 My 6 '16
Grau, R. Salary of. Harper 62:496 My 6 '16
Smith, E. H. Charlie Chaplin's million-dollar walk.
McClure 47:26 Jl '16
Raymond, C. S. Sketch. Green Book 16:204 Ag '16
Todd, S. W. Personal side of. Motion Pic Classic 3:41
S '16

O'Higgins, H. Charlie Chaplin's art. New Republic
10:16 F 3 '17

Moore, R. F. Falling, on and off the screen. Motion
Pic 13:39 Mr '17

Briscoe, J. Sketch. Motion Pic 13:43 Ap '17

Cram, M. Taking Charlie seriously. Theatre 26:10
Jl '17

Ramsey, T. Chaplin--and how he does it. Photoplay
12-4:19 S '17

Hilbert, J. E. A day with Chaplin on location. Motion
Pic 14:59 N '17

Wagner, R. Mr. Charles Spencer Chaplin, the man you
don't know. Ladies Home J 35:82 Ag '18

Johnson, J. Charles, not Charlie. Photoplay 14-4:81 S
'18

What people laugh at. American 86:34 N '18

Peltret, E. Chaplin's new contract. Photoplay 15-3:72
F '19

Bilby, E. A. How pictures discovered Charlie Chaplin.
Photoplay 15-5:70 Ap '19

Carr, H. C. Sketch. Motion Pic Classic 8:18 Ap '19

Charlie Chaplin says laughs are produced by rules. Lit
Digest 61:80 My 3 '19

Charlie Chaplin is too tragic to play Hamlet. Current
Opinion 70:187 F '21

Ervine, S. J. Mr. Charles Chaplin. Living Age 309:107
Ap 9 '21

Jordan, J. Mother o' mine. Photoplay 20-2:45 Jl '21

Visit to London. Graphic 104:296 S 10 '21

Sketch. Sat R 132:400 O 1 '21

Charlie Chaplin's art dissected. Lit Digest 71:26 O 8 '21

Swaffer, H. Visit to London. Graphic 104:434 O 15 '21

Impressions of travels in Europe. Photoplay 21:64 D '21
(and following issues)

Burke, T. Tragic comedian. Outlook 130:100 Ja 18 '22
Same abridged. Lit Digest 72:48 Ja 28 '22

Science and Charlie Chaplin. Lit Digest 72:68 Ja 28 '22

Chaplin, C. Charlie's abroad. Photoplay 21-1:64 D '21;
21-2:20 Ja '22

Wright, W. H. Charlie's great secret. Photoplay
21-3:40 F '22

Charlie Chaplin as a comedian contemplates suicide.
Current Opinion 72:209 F '22

How Charlie Chaplin does it. World Work 43:425 F '22

Sheridan, C. The strange little man with the great big
heart. Metropolitan 55:27 F '22

Sketch. Canadian Bookman 4:130 Ap '22

Leight, E.  How Charlie Chaplin does it.  World Work
(Lon) 39:441 Ap '22
Carr, H.  Interview.  Motion Pic 23:22 My '22
Young, S.  Dear Mr. Chaplin.  New Republic 31:358
Ag 23 '22
We have come to stay.  Ladies Home J 39:12 O '22
In defense of myself.  Colliers 70:8 N 11 '22
Carr, H.  Compared with Harold Lloyd.  Motion Pic
24:55 N '22
St. Johns, A. R.  The loves of Charlie Chaplin.  Photo-
play 23-3:28 F '23
Birthplace in London.  Musical Courier 86:8 Je 7 '23
Charlie Chaplin.  Sunset 51:29 Jl '23
Higgins, B.  Appreciation.  Spectator 131:318 S 8 '23
Does the public know what it wants?  Ladies Home J
40:40 O '23
Carr, H.  His production of A woman in Paris.  Motion
Pic 25:28 D '23
Becomes a motion picture reformer.  Current Opinion
75:708 D '23
Wilson, B. F.  Interview.  Theatre 39:20 Ja '24
How much of Chaplin does Charlie own?  Lit Digest
80:44 F 2 '24
Hall, G. & Fletcher, A. W.  Interview.  Motion Pic
27:24 F '24
Grein, J. T.  Chaplin as film producer.  Illustrated
London N 164:462 Mr 15 '24
Tully, J.  The loneliest man in Hollywood.  Classic
19:40 Mr '24
Can art be popular?  Ladies Home J 41:34 O '24
York, C.  Charlie's unromantic wedding.  Photoplay
27-3:35 F '25
Bercovici, K.  Charlie Chaplin.  Colliers 76:5 Ag 15 '25
Wilson, E.  New Chaplin comedy.  New Republic 44:45
S 2 '25
Reniers, P.  Chaplin moves his stake to Alaska.  Inde-
pendent 115:368 S 26 '25
Ervine, St. J. & King, H.  Two English views of Chap-
lin.  Living Age 327:370 N 14 '25
Carr, H.  Interview 30:31 N '25
Woollcott, A.  Sandman's magic.  Colliers 77:13 Ja 30
'26
St. Johns, I.  Everything's rosy at Charlie's.  Photoplay
29-3:35 F '26
Underhill, H.  That Chaplin complex.  Motion Pic Classic
23:56 Ap '26
Hall, M.  The changeable Chaplin.  Motion Pic Classic
23:16 Ag '26

Ennis, B. How fame came to him with borrowed clothes. Motion Pic Classic 23:36 Jl '26

Green, I. E. Who made Charlie Chaplin? Motion Pic 32:49 S '26

Young, S. Charlot in Rome. New Republic 48:217 O 13 '26

St. Johns, A. R. Matrimonial troubles. Photoplay 31:30 Ja '27

Tully, J. Charlie Chaplin, his real life story. Pictorial R 28:8 Ja; 19 F; 22 Mr; 22 Ap '27

Manners, D. The riddle of the Chaplin marriage. Motion Pic 33:39 Mr '27

deBeauplan, R. From Charlot to Chaplin. Living Age 333:311 Ag 15 '27

Gilmore, F. The change in Chaplin. Motion Pic Classic 26:21 Ja '28

Young, S. Charlie Chaplin. New Republic 53:313 F 8 '28

Bakshy, A. Charlie Chaplin. Nation 126:247 F 29 '28

Bonnie Prince Charlie of the custard pies. Lit Digest 93:36 Mr 24 '28

Chaplin as Puck. Bookman 67:177 Ap '28

Hollriegel, A. Charles Chaplin at home. Living Age 334:1068 Jl '28

Smith, R. Has he lost his humor? Theatre 48:22 S '28

Bercovici, K. Day with Charlie Chaplin. Harper 158:42 D '28

Donnell, D. His mother. Motion Pic 36:31 D '28

Hall, G. Interview. Motion Pic 37:28 My '29

Whitaker, A. Home of. Photoplay 36:40 Je '29

Frank, W. Charles Chaplin. Scribner 86:237 S '29

Kisch, E. E. I work with Charlie Chaplin. Living Age 337:230 O 15 '29

To play Napoleon? Graphic 127:508 Mr 29 '30

Lang, H. No talkies for Charlie. Photoplay 37-6:47 My '30

Rose, D. Silence is requested. No. American 230:127 Jl '30

Fairbanks, D. Jr. Appreciation. Vanity Fair 34:47 Ag '30

Charlie Chaplin and talking pictures. Theatre Arts 14:908 N '30

Bercovici, K. My friend Charlie Chaplin. Delineator 117:12 D '30

Frink, C. Sketch. Motion Pic Classic 32:30 Ja '31

Peet, C. Chaplin's sanctification. Outlook 157:271 F 18 '31

Seldes, G.   Chaplin's masterpieces: City lights.   New
     Republic 66:46 F 25 '31
Charlie Chaplin defies the talkies.   Lit Digest 108:28 F
     28 '31
Ockham, D.   Tribute to genius.   Sat R 151:299 F 28 '31
Bakshy, A.   Charlie Chaplin falters.   Nation 132:250
     Mr 4 '31
Two Charlies.   Graphic 131:346 Mr 7 '31
Mr. Chaplin throws a party.   Graphic 131:322 Mr 7 '31
Betts, E.   Charlie Chaplin's pantomine.   Weekend R
     3:354 Mr 7 '31
Skinner, R. D.   City lights.   Commonweal 13:553 Mr 18
     '31
Sir Charlie?   Commonweal 13:537 Mr 18 '31
Good word for the talkies.   Lit Digest 108:17 Mr 21 '31
Woollcott, A.   Charlie, as ever was.   Colliers 87:18
     Mr 28 '31
Arnett, K.   Still kicking around.   Photoplay 39-4:39
     Mr '31
Wettach, A.   My colleague Charlie Chaplin.   Living Age
     340:43 Mr '31
Dumb shows and noise.   Review Of Reviews (Lon) 81:42
     Mr '31
Fergusson, F.   City lights.   Bookman 73:184 Ap '31
John Bull hit by a Chaplin pie.   Lit Digest 109:10 My 23
     '31
In the driftway.   Nation 132:583 My 27 '31
Chaplin abroad.   Living Age 340:410 Je '31
Vantine, W. C. K.   Sketch.   Motion Pic 41:34 Je '31
If Charlie plagiarized, what then?   Lit Digest 110:17
     S 12 '31
Spensley, D.   Hollywood wants him to return.   Motion
     Pic 42:49 S '31
Bartlett, A. C.   Charlie Chaplin's no-man; interview.
     American 112:78 O '31
Manners, D.   What love has cost him.   Movie Classic
     1:24 N '31
Shallert, E.   Sketch.   Movie Classic 2:42 Je '32
Charlie Chaplin and talkies.   Review Of Reviews 86:49
     Ag '32
Janeway, D.   His sons enter the movies.   Move Classic
     3:30 S '32
Derr, E.   His latest romance.   Movie Classic 3:29 O '32
Babcock, M.   His headline history.   Movie Classic 3:42
     N '32
Schallert, E.   Sketch.   Motion Pic 44:34 Ja '33
Taviner, R.   In search of happiness.   Photoplay 43:34
     My '33

Romance with Paulette Goddard.   Movie Classic 4:20
    Ag '33
Autobiographical.   Womans Home Companion 59:7 S '33
    (and following issues)
Lee, S.  Immortals of the screen.   Motion Pic 46:32 O
    '33
Bercovici, K.   Little stories of big men.   Good House-
    keeping 98:148 Ja '34
Schallert, E.   Expenditures for his sons.   Motion Pic
    46:41 Ja '34
Comedian sees the world; autobiography.   Womans Home
    Companion 60:7 S; 15 O; 15 N; 21 D '33; 61 Ja '34
Rozas, L. T.   Charlie Chaplin's decline.   Living Age
    346:319 Je '34
Nicholai, B.   Story of his marriage to Paulette Goddard.
    Movie Classic 6:40 Je '34
Darnton, C.   The woman who found Charlie Chaplin.
    Photoplay 46-3:27 Ag '34
Tully, J.   Can he come back?   Motion Pic 49:30 Jl '35
Churchill, W.   Everybody's language; can silent movies
    come back.   Colliers 96:24 O 26 '35
Taviner, R.   What love has done for Chaplin.   Photoplay
    48-5:28 O '35
Hogarth, D.   His quest for love.   Movie Classic 9:30 O
    '35
Chaplin: machine age Don Quixote.   Lit Digest 120:26 N 2
    '35
Eastman, M.   Appreciation.   Stage 13:26 N '35
Bewildered little fellow bucking modern times.   Newsweek
    7:18 F 8 '36
Mullen, S. M.   Chaplin, master of pantomime, laughter
    and tears.   Senior Scholastic 28:24 F 15 '36
Van Doren, M.   Charlie Chaplin.   Nation 142:232 F 19
    '36
Simpson, G.   Groucho Marx tells how he "discovered"
    the genius in Chaplin.   Motion Pic 51:39 My '36
Wilson, C.   Sketch.   Photoplay 50:25 S '36
No. 1 player.   Senior Scholastic 29:25 N 21 '36
Waley, H. D.   Is this Charlie.   Sight & Sound 7-25:10
    Spg '38
Charlie's lost again.   Christian Science Mon Mag p13
    Je 1 '38
Childhood recollections.   Readers Digest 33:69 D '38
Sketch.   Photoplay 53:46 Ap '39
Scripteaser; Great dictator's provisional script.   Time
    34:24 Ag 7 '39
Cooke, A.  Charlie Chaplin.  Atlantic 164:176 Ag '39

Same, abridged.    Readers Digest 35:34 S '39
Chaplin's new film.    Current History 51:52 S '39
Crichton, K.    Ride 'em Charlie!    Colliers 105:20 Mr 16
    '40
Comedy has its limits.    Christian Century 57:816 Je 26
    '40
Pringle, H. F.    Story of two mustaches.    Ladies Home J
    57:18 Jl '40
Charlie Chaplin's dictator.    Life 9:53 S 2 '40
Daughtery, F.    Two millions' worth of laughter.    Christian
    Science Mon Mag p7 S 7 '40
Van Gelder, R.    Chaplin draws a keen weapon.    N. Y.
    Times Mag p8 S 8 '40
Great dictator.    Senior Scholastic 37:32 S 16 '40
Wilson, D.    Chaplin talks.    Photoplay 54-12:20 D '40
Biography.    Current Biography '40
Wilson, R.    The new mystery of Mr. and Mrs. Chaplin.
    Photoplay 18-2:56 Ja '41
Frye, N.    Great Charlie.    Canadian Forum 21:148 Ag '41
Farber, M.    Little fellow.    New Republic 106:606 My 4
    '42
Hirschfeld, A.    Man with both feet in clouds.    N. Y.
    Times Mag p12 Jl 26 '42
Hitler and Chaplin at 54.    N. Y. Times Mag p17 Ap 18
    '43
Chaplin and Joan.    Newsweek 21:49 Je 21 '43
His marriage to Oona O'Neill.    Life 14:31 Je 28 '43
His marriage to Oona O'Neill.    Newsweek 21:46 Je 28 '43
His marriage to Oona O'Neill.    Time 41:70 Je 28 '43
Kilgallen, D.    Sketch.    Photoplay 23:21 Je '43
St. Johns, A. R.    Case against Chaplin.    Photoplay
    23-4:35 S '43
Reproduction of early Chaplin screen plays.    New States-
    man 26:232 O 9 '43
Chaplin as villain.    Newsweek 23:46 F 21 '44
Man and woman.    Time 43:24 Ap 3 '44
Charlie and Wayne.    Newsweek 23:29 Ap 10 '44
Fleming, J.    Modern times in Moscow.    Newsweek 23:42
    My 15 '44
Just a Peter Pan.    Time 45:15 Ja 1 '45
Case of Carol Ann.    Life 18:30 Ja 8 '45
The case of Carol Ann.    Newsweek 25:40 Ja 15 '45
Father for Carol Ann.    Newsweek 25:41 Ap 30 '45
Eisenstein, S. M.    Charlie the grown-up.    Sight & Sound
    15:53 Sum '46
Scheuer, P. K.    From rags to riches.    Colliers 119:15
    Ap 12 '47

His role in Monsieur Verdoux.    Newsweek 29:98 Ap 28 '47

Brown, J. M.    Charlie-into-Charles.    Sat R 30:24 My 3
   '47

His new film Monsieur Verdoux.    Time 49:98 My 5 '47

O'Hara, S.    Sketch.    New Republic 116:39 My 5 '47

Lewis, R.    Story of.    Theatre Arts 31:32 Je '47

Payne, R.    The man whose comic genius and pathos have
   given pleasure to millions.    World R 2:34 Ap '49

Agee, J.    Early work of.    Life 27:76 S 5 '49

Laugh's on us.    Nation 175:440 N 15 '52

Genet.    Letter from Paris.    New Yorker 28:175 N 15 '52

Unrehearsed Chaplin comedy.    Life 33:51 N 17 '52

Bentley, E.    Chaplin's mea culpa.    New Republic 127:30
   N 17 '52

Barrett, W.    Charlie as Charles.    American Mercury
   75:90 N '52

Huie, W. B.    Mr. Chaplin and the 5th freedom.    American Mercury 75:123 N '52

Miller, E.    Limelight; a great comedian sums up his life.
   Theatre Arts 36:76 N '52

Kerr, W.    Lineage of Limelight.    Theatre Arts 36:72 N
   '52

New light on Limelight.    Reporter 8:1 Ja 6 '53

Mr. Ferrer and Mr. Chaplin: threat by American Legion.
   Nation 176:90 Ja 31 '53

Process of dissolution.    Commonweal 57:441 F 6 '53

Tallenay, J. L.    Tragic vision of Charles Chaplin.    Commonweal 57:451 F 6 '53

Murray, W.    Limelight, Chaplin and his censors.    Nation
   176:247 Mr 21 '53

Glick, N.    Chaplin's film romance.    Commentary 15:295
   Mr '53

Cane and bowler.    Newsweek 41:37 Ap 27 '53

Stonier, G. W.    After Limelight?    New Statesman 45:581
   My 16 '53

Biography.    Colliers Yearbook 1953:128 '53

Micha, R.    Chaplin as Don Juan.    Sight & Sound 23-3:132
   Ja/Mr '54

People of the week.    U. S. News 36:14 F 19 '54

Little man and a plot.    Newsweek 43:48 Je 14 '54

Anderson, L.    In search of Charlie.    Sight & Sound 24-
   1:4 Je/S '54

Double play.    Sat Evening Post 227:10 S 4 '54

Ferguson, O.    Hallelujah, bum again.    New Republic
   131:44 N 22 '54

Gibbons, T.    Chaplin as Chaplin.    Film 3:16 F '55

Unfunny fellow.    Newsweek 46:31 N 21 '55

Film pioneers' roll of their living immortals.   Life
    40:123 Ja 23 '56
Callenbach, E.   Great Chaplin chase.   Nation 183:96
    Ag 4 '56
Halle, L. J.   Foreign relations and domestic behavior.
    Sat R 39:11 O 13 '56
Baker, P.   Clown with a frown.   Films & Filming 3-11:7
    Ag '57
Lane, J. F.   My life as Chaplin's leading lady; interview
    with Dawn Addams.   Films & Filming 3-11:12 Ag '57
Hinxman, M.   Interview.   Sight & Sound 27-2:76 Aut '57
Unfunny Charlie Chaplin.   Newsweek 50:108 S 9 '57
Chaplin and the little guy.   New Statesman 54:308 S 14 '57
Unfunny comic.   Time 70:48 S 23 '57
Kaufman, W.   Saturday Review goes to the movies.   Sat R
    40:26 S 28 '57
Lee, P.   Whither Chaplin?   America 98:12 O 5 '57
Fulford, R.   Chaplin; a king in decline.   New Republic
    137:22 O 7 '57
Felheim, M.   Monarch in exile.   Reporter 17:43 O 17 '57
O'Donnell, J. P.   Charlie Chaplin's stormy exile.   Sat
    Evening Post 230:19 Mr 8; 44 Mr 15; 36 Mr 22 '58
Why Chaplin paid up.   Newsweek 53:39 Ja 12 '59
Mayer, A. L.   The origins of United Artists.   Films In
    Review 10-7:390 Ag/S '59
Baggy little man now.   Newsweek 54:120 N 9 '59
Giesler, J.   Chaplin case; as told to P. Martin.   Sat
    Evening Post 232:38 N 21 '59
Beaumont, C.   Chaplin.   Playboy 7:81 Mr '60
Ross, W.   Charlie Chaplin; clown without a country.
    Coronet 48:121 Je '60
Crowther, B.   Modern, mellower times of Mr. Chaplin.
    N. Y. Times Mag p52 N 6 '60
Biography.   Current Biography 22:13 Mr '61
Rosen, C.   The saddest story of all.   Photoplay 59-5:50
    My '61
Spears, J.   Chaplin's collaborators.   Films In Review
    13-1:18 Ja '62
Charlie Chaplin.   Time 79:59 My 4 '62
Charlie Chaplin.   America 107:561 Ag 4 '62
Clurman, H.   Oona, Oxford, America and the book; in-
    terview.   Esquire 58:86 N '62
Biography.   Current Biography Yearbook 1961:100 '62
Sarris, A.   Pantheon directors; filmog.   Film Culture
    28:2 Spg '63
Brownlow, K.   The early days of Charlie Chaplin.   Film
    40:12 Sum '64

Charles the great.   Newsweek 64:78 Jl 27 '64

Lee, R.   The five Chaplins.   8mm Collector 9:4 S '64

Kearns, M.   The Chaplin story.   8mm Collector 9:4 S '64

Chaplin's film career.   8mm Collector 9:4 S '64

What they said about Chaplin.   8mm Collector 9:4 S '64

Chaplin's autobiography due soon.   8mm Collector 9:5
   S '64

Chaplin plans film with son.   8mm Collector 9:5 S '64

Kearns, M.   The films of Charlie Chaplin; filmog.   8mm
   Collector 9:5 S '64

Lemay, H.   Tantalizing look behind Chaplin's mask; his
   autobiography.   Life 57:24 O 2 '64

Little tramp as told to himself.   Time 84:132 O 2 '64

Kauffman, S.   Man named Chaplin.   New Republic 151:19
   O 3 '64

Tramp.   Newsweek 64:112 O 5 '64

Knight, A.   Travels with Charlie and friends.   Sat R
   47:45 O 10 '64

Houseman, J.   Charlie's Chaplin.   Nation 199:222 O 12
   '64

Junker, H.   Real life of the tramp.   Commonweal 81:104
   O 16 '64

Hatch, R.   Dapper wayfarer.   Harper 229:129 O '64

Wyndham, F.   Charles Chaplin at ease.   Vogue 144:112
   N 15 '64

McVay, D.   Chaplin revisited.   Films & Filming 11-2:10
   N '64

Russell, F.   Only the little tramp matters.   National R
   16:1066 D 1 '64

Gill, B.   Books.   New Yorker 40:236 D 12 '64

Cotes, P.   The little fellow's self portrait.   Films &
   Filming 11-3:11 D '64

Correction to Only the little tramp matters.   National R
   17:77 Ja 26 '65

Muggeridge, M.   Books.   Esquire 63:54 F '65

Macdonald, D.   On Chaplin, Verdoux and Agee.   Esquire
   63:18 Ap '65

Frank, G.   Charles Chaplin and his children.   Ladies
   Home J 82:70 My '65

Chaplin takes a walk.   Sight & Sound 35-1:20 Win '65

Robinson, D.   Chaplin meets the press.   Sight & Sound
   34:20 Win '65

Chaplin, G. edited by E. Miller.   Entrancing new actress.
   Seventeen 24:95 D '65

Hamblin, D. J.   Passionate clown comes back.   Life
   60:80A Ap 1 '66

Hamilton, J.   Charlie and his countess.   Look 30:96 Ap 19
   '66

Brownlow, K.    Watching Chaplin direct The countess from
   Hong Kong.    Film Culture 40:2 Spg '66
Brooks, L.    Charles Chaplin remembered.    Film Culture
   40:5 Spg '66
Ginsberg, A. & Orlovsky, P.    A letter to Chaplin.    Film
   Culture 40:7 Spg '66
The old maestro shows how it's done.    8mm Collector
   14:35 Spg '66
Custard pie of creation.    Newsweek 67:90 Je 6 '66
Bentley, E.    Charlie Chaplin and Peggy Hopkins Joyce.
   Moviegoer 3:10 Sum '66
Brownlow, K.    The Countess set.    Film 46:4 Sum '66
Gilliatt, P.    Genius of Chaplin.    Vogue 148:94 Jl '66
Hoover, M. L.    Chaplin on Chaplinism.    Tulane Drama
   R 11:188 Fall '66
Chaplin in the limelight.    Illustrated London N 249:20 D
   31 '66
Lee, R.    I was a Chaplin kid.    Classic Film Collector
   17:16 Win/Spg '67
Meryman, R.    Ageless master's anatomy of comedy.
   Life 62:80 Mr 10 '67
Kenner, H.    Anatomy of tepidity.    National R 15:59
   My 30 '67
The complete screenplay of The gold rush compiled by
   Timothy J. Lyons.    Cinema (BH) 4-2:17 Sum '68
Madeen, D.    Harlequin's stick.    Charlie's cane.    Film Q
   22-1:10 Fall '68
Rosen, P. G.    The Chaplin world-view.    Cinema J 9-1:2
   Fall '69
Charlie Chaplin's Monsieur Verdoux; press conference.
   Film Comment 5-4:34 Win '69
Hickey, T.    Accusations against Charles Chaplin for
   political and moral offenses.    Film Comment 5-4:44
   Win '69
Quixote with a bowler.    Time 95:54 Ja 5 '70
When silence was golden.    Screen Greats 1-2:74 Sum '71
Whitman, A.    Chaplin, 82, softens criticism of U. S.
   N. Y. Times Bio Ed O 22 '71
   Same.    Classic Film Collector 33:46 Win '71
Mills, I.    Chaplin's Mutual films.    Velvet Light Trap
   3:2 Win '71/72
Shivas, M.    Charles Chaplin.    N. Y. Times    Bio Ed
   D 12 '71
What directors are saying.    Action 7-1:36 Ja/F '72
Wolf, W.    Welcome back, Charlie; interview.    Cue 41-
   12:2 Mr 18 '72
Schickel, R.    Hail Chaplin--the early Chaplin.    N. Y. Times
   Bio Ed Ap 2 '72

Whitman, A.   The king of comedy.   N. Y. Times Bio Ed
    Ap 4 '72
The tramp for television.   Films & Filming 18-8:14
    My '72
Wolf, W.   Charlie Chaplin today--elder statesman of the
    arts.   Show 2-4:33 Je '72
Lyons, T. J.   Roland H. Totheroh interviewed: Chaplin
    films.   Film Culture 53/54/55:230 Spg '72
Sieger, E.   Chaplin.   Focus 7:33 Spg '72
Chaplin ovation.   Classic Film Collector 35:2X Sum '72
Twelve essays on Charlie Chaplin by various writers.
    Film Comment 8-3:8 S/O '72
Robinson, C. R.   The private life of Charlie Chaplin.
    Liberty 1-7:23 Win '72
Evans, C.   The sounds of silence.   Mise-En-Scene 1:23
    n. d.


CHATTERTON, BOB
    Listing of films.   Film Culture 37:7 Sum '65


CHAUVEL, CHARLES E.
    Obit.   N. Y. Times p35 N 12 '59
        Time 74:104 N 23 '59
    Bease, A.   Charles E. Chauvel; letter.   Films In Review
        11-2:118 F '60


CHOMETTE, HENRI
    Obit.   N. Y. Times p19 Ag 20 '41


CHOMSKY, MARVIN
    Whitney, D.   You've got 30 seconds to grab 'em by the
        throat.   TV Guide 20-41:18 O 7 '72


CHRISTENSEN, BENJAMIN
    Old master Christensen.   CTVD 3-1:5 Fall '64
    Gillett, J.   The mysterious X.   Sight & Sound 35-2:99
        Spg '66
    Higham, C.   Christensen continued.   Sight & Sound 35-4:
        207 Aut '66
    Routt, W. D.   Buried directors.   Focus 7:9 Spg '72


CHRISTIAN-JACQUE
    Christian-Jacque.   Making it international.   Films &
        Filming 7-1:10 O '60


CHUKHRAI, GRIGORI
    Herlinghaus, H.   A talk with Grigori Chukhrai.   Film
        Culture 26:34 Fall '62

Chukhrai, G.   Keeping the old on their toes.   Films &
     Filming 9-1:26 O '62
Vronskaya, J.   Recent Russian cinema.   Film 62:5 Sum
     '71

CHYTILOVÁ, VÉRA
     Sketch.   Film 51:33 Spg '68

CIMINO, MIKE
     Shaw, E.   A successful filmmaker appraises his craft.
          Making Films 3-1:21 F '69

CLAIR, RENÉ
     Art of Rene Clair.   Living Age 342:181 Ap '32
     Ogden, R.   Art of Rene Clair.   Bookman (Lon) 82:64
          Ap '32
     Marshall, M.   Art of Rene Clair.   Nation 134:659 Je 8
          '32
     Wellman, R.   Work of.   Town & Country 87:39 Ag 1 '32
     Rene Clair indicts entire film industry.   Cinema Digest
          1-9:30 S 5 '32
     Troy, W.   Rene Clair.   Nation 137:520 N 1 '33
     Causton, B.   A conversation with Rene Clair.   Sight &
          Sound 1-4:111 Win '33
     Ace director baffles Hollywood.   Lit Digest 121:28 Ja 25
          '36
     Van Doren, M.   Rene Clair goes west.   Nation 142:138
          Ja 29 '36
     M. Chomett's status.   New Yorker 16:13 S 14 '40
     Biography.   Current Biography 2:151 '41
     Farber, M.   Quick dissolve.   New Republic 110:788
          Je 12 '44
     Nichols, D. & Clair, R.   It happened tomorrow; excerpt.
          Theatre Arts 28:375 Je '44
     Grunberg, I.   Film directors in France.   Life & Letters
          56:155 F '48
     Koval, F.   Interview.   Sight & Sound 19-1:9 Mr '50
     Koval, F.   To the legend of Faust.   Films In Review
          2-1:19 Ja '51
     Clair, R. & Manvell, R.   Debate with a past self.   Sight
          & Sound 21-3:108 Ja/Mr '52
     The big screens.   Sight & Sound 24-4:209 Spg '55
     Rene Clair in Moscow.   Sight & Sound 25-3:130 Win
          '55/56
     Master challenged.   Newsweek 47:45 Ja 23 '56
     Clair, R.   Nothing is more artificial than neo-realism.
          Films & Filming 3-9:7 Je '57

Mushroom's edge.  New Yorker 34:44 N 29 '58
Editorial.  Film Culture 4-18:2 '58
Ford, C.  Cinema's first "immortal."  Films In Review
    11-9:513 N '60
Sarris, A.  Beyond the fringe.  Film Culture 28:29 Spg
    '63
Dale, R. C.  Rene Clair in Hollywood; interview.  Film
    Q 24-2:34 Win '70/71

CLAMPETT, BOB
    Barrier, M.  Interview with a master cartoon maker and
        puppeteer.  Funnyworld 12:12 Sum '70
    Gray, M. & Barrier, M.  Interview.  Classic Film
        Collector 31:extra one Sum '71

CLARK, BRUCE
    Three men and their movie.  Show 2-2:23 Ap '71

CLARK, JAMES
    The crisis we deserve.  Sight & Sound 39-4:172 Aut '70

CLARKE, SHIRLEY
    Breitrese, H.  Films of Shirley Clarke.  Film Q 13-4:57
        Sum '60
    Young, C. & Bachmann, G.  New Wave--or gesture?
        Film Q 14-3:6 Spg '61
    Frost bit.  Newsweek 59:81 Ja 29 '62
    Mekas, J.  Notes on the new American cinema.  Film
        Culture 24:6 Spg '62
    Archer, E.  Woman director makes the scene.  N. Y.
        Times Mag p46 Ag 26 '62
    Fenin, G.  The face of '63--United States.  Films &
        Filming 9-6:55 Mr '63
    Clarke, S.  The cool world.  Films & Filming 10-3:7
        D '63
    Berg, G.  Interview.  Film Culture 44:52 Spg '67
    A conversation.  Film Culture 46:44 O '68
    Weiner, P.  New American cinema; filmog.  Film 58:22
        Spg '70
    Pyres, J.  Notes on women directors.  Take One 3-2:7
        N/D '70
    Rice, S.  Image and images; interview.  Take One 3-2:20
        N/D '70
    Cooper, K.  Shirley Clarke.  Filmmakers Newsletter
        5-8:34 Je '72
    Pelt, H.  Shirley Clarke at Venice; interview.  Film
        Comment 2-2:31 n. d.

CLAVELL, JAMES
British cinema filmography.    Film 65:10 Spg '72

CLAXTON, WILLIAM F.
Stoop, N. M.   Through a lens, clearly.    After Dark
12-3:16 Jl '70

CLAYTON, JACK
A free hand.   Sight & Sound 28-2:60 Spg '59
Personality of the month.    Films & Filming 8-3:7 D '61
Cowie, P.   The face of '63--Great Britain.    Films &
Filming 9-5:19 F '63
Desert island films.    Films & Filming 9-11:11 Ag '63
McVay, D.   The house that Jack built.    Films & Filming
14-1:4 O '67
British cinema filmography.    Film 65:10 Spg '72

CLAYTON, JOHN
Who's who in filmmaking; selected filmog.    Sightlines
3-2:4 N/D '69

CLEMENT, DICK
The crisis we deserve.    Sight & Sound 39-4:172 Aut '70
British cinema filmography.    Film 65:10 Spg '72

CLÉMENT, RENÉ
Koval, F.   Interview.   Sight & Sound 19-4:149 Je '50
Eisner, L. H.   Style of Rene Clement.    Film Culture
3-2(12):21 S '57; 3-3(13):11 O '57
Clement, R.   On being a creator.    Films & Filming
7-1:39 O '60
Merralls, J.   The films of Rene Clement.    Film Journal
(Aus) 18:3 O '61
Graham, P.   The face of '63--France.    Films & Filming
9-8:13 My '63
Sarris, A.   Beyond the fringe.    Film Culture 28:29 Spg
'63
Genet.   Letter from Paris.   New Yorker 41:142 S 18 '65
Guy, R.   Is Paris burning?   Cinema (BH) 3-3:4 Jl '66
McVay, D.   The darker side of life.    Films & Filming
13-3:19 D '66

CLIFT, DENISON
Obit.   N.Y. Times p27 D 21 '61

CLIFTON, ELMER
Service, F.   Interview. Motion Pic Classic 12:58 Ag '21

Underhill, H.   Interview.   Motion Pic 22:60 O '21
Hall, G.   Interview.   Motion Pic 23:75 Je '22
Great whaling days commemorated on the screen.   Current
    Opinion 75:75 Jl '23
Rittenhouse, M.   What is an epic picture?   Motion Pic
    31:54 Je '26
Obit.   N. Y. Times p23 O 17 '49
    Screen World 1:234 '49

CLINE, EDDIE
    Obit.   N. Y. Times p41 My 24 '61

CLOUZOT, HENRI-GEORGES
    Genet.   Letter from Paris.   New Yorker 30:111 F 12 '55
    Frenchman's horror.   Newsweek 46:116 N 28 '55
    Tennant, S.   Henri-Georges Clouzot.   Film 8:20 Mr/Ap
        '56
    Mignani, R. & Bianchi, P.   Henri-Georges Clouzot. Yale
        French Studies 17:21 '56
    Berger, J.   Clouzot as Delilah.   Sight & Sound 27-4:196
        Spg '58
    Sety, G.   Clouzot: he plans everything from script to
        screen.   Films & Filming 5-3:7 D '58
    Interview.   Cinema (BH) 5-4:14 Win '69
    What directors are saying.   Action 5-2:16 Mr/Ap '70

CLURMAN, HAROLD
    Biography.   Current Biography 20:6 F '59
        Same.   Current Biography Yearbook 1959:72 '60
    Sarris, A.   Oddities and one shots.   Film Culture 28:45
        Spg '63
    O'Neill in Japanese.   Time 92:47 Ag 30 '68
    Clurman, H.   Memories of Awake and sing.   TV Guide
        20-10:31 Mr 4 '72

COCTEAU, JEAN
    Russell, P.   The cleverest epigrammatist since Oscar
        Wilde.   Shadowland 6-6:27 Ag '22
    Bower-Shore, C.   Appreciation.   Bookman (Lon) 84:195
        Jl '33
    Old faces and feet in Paris.   Time 48;76 D 9 '46
    Cocteau with eagle.   Newsweek 29:84 Mr 31 '47
    Pilcher, V.   His career as dramatist, artist, poet and
        filmmaker.   Theatre Arts 31:12 Ap '47
    Jean Cocteau.   Theatre Arts 31:60 Ap '47
    Millstein, G.   Jean Cocteau.   Cue 18-2:15 Ja 8 '49
    Artists and statesmen.   Life 29:76 Ag 7 '50

Koval, F. Interview. Sight & Sound 19-6:229 Ag '50
Genet. Letter from Paris. New Yorker 27:40 Ja 12 '52
Fowlie, W. French literary scene. Commonweal
  56:202 My 30 '52
Cocteau, J. Conversations. Sight & Sound 22-1:6 Jl/S
  '52
Fowlie, W. Note on Jean Cocteau. Poetry 84:85 My '54
Lions in their lairs. Vogue 123:88 Je '54
Cocteau on filming of Orphee and Les enfants terribles.
  Film 4:8 Mr '55
Poet with a brush. Newsweek 45:98 My 16 '55
Index to Picasso's palate. Life 39:210 S 19 '55
Green fever. Time 66:20 O 31 '55
Ceremony makes a rebel immortal. Life 39:158 N 7 '55
Chapsal, M. Jean Cocteau joins the immortals. Re-
  porter 13:39 D 15 '55
Prince of Parisians. Newsweek 48:91 S 3 '56
Cocteau a la mode. Nation 183:504 D 8 '56
Turnell, M. Legend of Jean Cocteau. Commonweal
  65:285 D 14 '56
Turnell, M. Achievement of Cocteau. Commonweal
  65:309 D 21 '56
Oxenhandler, N. Poetry in three films of Jean Cocteau;
  filmog. Yale French Studies 17:14 '56
Peyre, M. Man who subdued a gift. Sat R 40:19 Ja 26
  '57
Ballet Russe brings La dame a la licerne to the Met.
  Dance 31:24 Ap '57
Cocteau in the chapel. Newsweek 50:69 Jl 15 '57
Cocteau turns muralist for fisherman's chapel. Life 43:8
  Jl 29 '57
Ehrensperger, M. Cocteau, Garbo and Giedion. Sat R
  41:39 Je 21 '58
France. Atlantic 201:27 Je '58
Memory of Diaghilev and Nijinsky. Vogue 133:156 F 15
  '59
Phelps, R. Apollo's son is seventy. Sat R 42:14 Jl 4
  '59
Interview. Unifrance 51:24 O/D '59
Counting on a miracle. Newsweek 54:102 N 2 '59
Fowlie, W. Paris letter. Poetry 96:373 S '60
Bendix, H. Encounter with Cocteau; interview. Harper
  221:24 D '60
Cocteau vin. Newsweek 59:80 Ja 15 '62
Alpert, H. Self-portrait. Sat R 45:35 Ja 20 '62
Self-portrait. Esquire 58:108 S '62
Obit. Americana Annual 1964:736 '64

British Book Year 1964:622 '64
Illustrated London N 243:645 O 19 '63
Musical America 83:61 N '63
Nation 197:282 N 2 '63
N. Y. Times p1 O 12 '63
New Yorker 39:200 N 2 '63
Newsweek 62:81 O 21 '63
Publisher W 184:32 O 21 '63
Screen World 15:219 '64
Time 82:38 O 18 '63
Funeral. N. Y. Times p32 O 17 '63
Kenner, H. Hommage a Monsieur Jean. National R
    15:441 N 19 '63
Foulke, A. To the young of 2000 A. D. Vogue 143:72
    Ja 1 '64
Death and the poet. Show 4-1:74 Ja '64
Sorell, W. Appreciation of Jean Cocteau. Dance 38:38
    F '64
Cantwell, R. Poet and the boxer. Sports Illustrated
    20:62 Mr 2 '64
Peeters, G. How Cocteau managed a champion. Sports
    Illustrated 20:66 Mr 2 '62
Oxenhandler, N. On Cocteau. Film Q 18-1:12 Fall '64
Artist was the medium. Time 89:96 Je 16 '67
Fowlie, W. Notes on a spiritual odyssey. Sat R 50:28
    Je 17 '67
Maloff, S. Camera eye. Newsweek 70:73 Jl 24 '67
Brown, F. Impersonation of angels; excerpt. Harper
    Bazaar 101:210 O '68
Axtholm, P. I neglected to live. Newsweek 72:56 D 30
    '68
Roudiez, L. S. Portrait of a Parisian personality. Sat
    R 52:95 Ja 4 '69
Clurman, H. French characters. Nation 208:88 Ja 20 '69
Phillips, H. E. All Cocteau program at Julliard opera
    theatre. Opera News 33:23 Je 14 '69
Roud, R. Memories of Resnais. Sight & Sound 38-3:124
    Sum '69
Steegmuller, F. Onward and upward with the arts. New
    Yorker 45:130 S 27 '69
Phelps, R. Colette, Cocteau and Proust. Mademoiselle
    72:124 D '70
Raynes, T. Unreal realism: cyphers of the poet. Cinema
    (Lon) 8:3 '71
Amberg, G. The testament of Jean Cocteau. Film
    Comment 7-4:23 Win '71/72
The testament of Jean Cocteau. Castle Of Frankenstein
    5:36 n. d.

COHEN, HERMAN
On being a teenage werewolf; interview. Films & Filming 6-12:15 S '60

COHEN, NORMAN
British cinema filmography. Film 65:10 Spg '72

COHEN, ROBERT
Survey among unsuccessful applicants for the Ford
Foundation film grants. Film Comment 2-3:10 Sum '64

COHEN, SAUL B.
Cohen, S. B. Three American filmmakers. Film Comment 3-2:2 Spg '65

COLLA, RICHARD A.
Colla, R. A. First time out. Action 5-5:28 S/O '70

COLLINS, LEWIS D.
Everson, W. K. Lewis D. Collins; letter. Films In Review 5-9:492 N '54

COLLINSON, PETER
British cinema filmography. Film 65:10 Spg '72

COLPI, HENRI
Graham, P. The face of '63--France. Films & Filming
9-8:13 My '63
Colpi, H. Debasement of the art of montage. Cahiers
(Eng) 3:44 '66

COMFORT, LANCE
British feature directors; an index to their work. Sight
& Sound 27-6:292 Aut '58
Obit. Film R p29 '66/68

CONNER, BRUCE
Brown, R. K. Interview. Film Culture 33:15 Sum '64
Listing of films. Film Culture 37:7 Sum '65
Alexander, T. K. San Francisco's hipster cinema. Film
Culture 44:70 Spg '67
Savonarola in nylon skeins. Time 91:50 Ja 5 '68
"I was obsessed..."; discussion. Film Library Q 2-3:23
Sum '69
Discussion; filmog. Film Comment 5-4:16 Win '69

CONRAD, TONY
    Tony Conrad on The flicker.    Film Culture 41:1 Sum '66
    Mussman, T.    Interview.    Film Culture 41:3 Sum '66
    Conrad, T.    Inside the dream syndicate.    Film Culture
        41:5 Sum '66

CONWAY, JACK
    Biographical note.    Photoplay 9-4:42 Mr '16
    Jack Conway--actor-director.    Cue 4-9:3 D 28 '35
    Biographical note; filmog.    Movies & People 2:40 '40
    They love to act.    Lions Roar 1-11/12:no p# Jl/Ag '42
    Conway--Hollywood's first star!    Lions Roar 2-4:no p#
        Ap '43
    MGM's directors range from pioneers to newcomers.
        Lions Roar 3-4:no p# Jl '44
    Conway, J.    The uses of color.    Sight & Sound 13-50:27
        Jl '44
    Two Oscars?    Lions Roar 3-4:no p# Jl '44
    Obit.    N. Y. Times p21 O 13 '52
        Screen World 4:176 '53

COOK, FIELDER
    Cook, F.    A big hand for the little agents.    Action 1-1:8
        S/O '66

COOKE, ALAN
    British cinema filmography.    Film 65:10 Spg '72

COOPER, MERIAN C.
    Behlmer, R.    Merian C. Cooper.    Films In Review
        17-1:17 Ja '66

COPPOLA, FRANCIS FORD
    Biography.    Newsweek 69:96 F 20 '67
    Koszarski, R.    The youth of Francis Ford Coppola; inter-
        view.    Films In Review 19-9:529 N '68
    Cutts, J.    The dangerous age; interview.    Films & Film-
        ing 15-8:4 My '69
    Taylor, J. R.    Francis Ford Coppola.    Sight & Sound
        38-1:21 Win '68/69
    Sweeney, L.    The movie business is alive and well and
        living in San Francisco.    Show 1-4:34 Ap '70
    Fensch, T.    Amateurs on the campus make professional
        films.    Making Films 5-2:12 Ap '71
    McGillivray, D.    Biographical note; filmog.    Focus On
        Film 11:6 Aut '72

CORMAN, ROGER
   Knight, A.   New Roger Corman.   Sat R 45:34 F 10 '62
   Titillater.   Newsweek 63:87 Je 29 '64
   Joyce, P.   Roger Corman starts the long ride home.
      Film 43:28 Aut '65
   Alpert, H.   Psychedelia.   Sat R 50:36 S 2 '67
   Godard in Hollywood.   Take One 1-10:13 Je '68
   A letter from Roger Corman.   Take One 1-12:13 Jl/Ag
      '68
   Wallace, E.   Roger Corman's gothic world.   Screen Edu-
      cation 45:72 Jl/Ag '68
   Should directors produce?   Action 3-4:10 Jl/Ag '68
   Diehl, D.   Corman: a double life.   Action 4-4:10 Jl/Ag '69
   Herman, G.   Corman and the art of film.   Brighton
      Film R 16:18 Ja '70
   Diehl, D.   The Simenon of cinema.   Show 1-5:27 My '70
   Interview.   Take One 2-12:6 Jl/Ag '70
   Strick, P.   Ma Barker to von Richthofen; interview.
      Sight & Sound 39-4:179 Aut '70
   Koszarski, R.   The films of Roger Corman; filmog.
      Film Comment 7-3:43 Fall '71
   Goldman, C.   Interview. Film Comment 7-3:49 Fall '71
   Sayer, J.   Interview.   Take One 1-9:8 n. d.
   Jack Nicholson comments on Roger Corman.   Dialogue On
      Film 1:16 '72

CORNELIUS, HENRY
   Filmography.   Film 14:8 N/D '57
   British feature directors; an index to their work.
      Sight & Sound 27-6:292 Aut '58

CORNELL, JONAS
   Sketch.   Film 51:33 Spg '68
   Filmmaking in Sweden.   Interview 1-7:25 n. d.

CORNFIELD, HUBERT
   Alpert, H.   Hubert Cornfield makes a ripple.   Sat R
      43:26 F 27 '60
   Johnson, A.   Interview.   Film Q 15-3:39 Spg '62
   Hubert Cornfield.   Films & Filming 8-10:5 Jl '62
   The directors select the best films.   Cinema (BH) 1-5:14
      Ag/S '63

CORSO, GREGORY
   Bye, bye Beatnik.   Newsweek 62:65 Jl 1 '63
   Scully, J.   Audience swam for their lives.   Nation 198:244
      Mr 9 '64
   Notes from the other sides of April.   Esquire 62:86 Jl '64

Corso, G.   Life, death and dancing.   Esquire 64:34 Jl '65
Listing of films.   Film Culture 37:7 Sum '65
Moraes, D.   Somewhere else with Allen and Gregory.
   Horizon 11:66 Win '69

COSMATOS, GEORGE
   On location with The beloved.   Films & Filming 17-5:59
      F '71

COSTA-GAVRAS (GAVRAS, KOSTANTINOS)
   Georgakas, D.   Costa-Gavras talks.   Take One 2-6:12
      Jl/Ag '69
   Kael, P.   Current cinema.   New Yorker 45:168 D 13 '69
   Costa-Gavras talks about Z.   Cineaste 3-3:12 Win '69/70
   Austen, D.   Pointing out the problems; interview.   Films
      & Filming 16-9:32 Je '70
   What directors are saying.   Action 5-4:30 Jl/Ag '70
   On the scene.   Playboy 17-11:205 N '70
   Kael, P.   Current cinema.   New Yorker 46:172 D 12 '70
   Mellen, J.   Arthur London and Costa-Gavras: the politics
      of The confession.   Cineaste 4-3:25 Win '70/71
   Semprun, J.   Interview.   Film Society R 6-5:43 Ja '71
   Davis, M. S.   Agent provocateur of films.   N. Y. Times
      Bio Ed Mr 21 '71
   O'Brien, G.   Interview.   Interview 1-12:18 n. d.

COSTELLANI, RENATO
   Lane, J. F.   The face of '63--Italy.   Films & Filming
      9-7:11 Ap '63

COTÉ, GUY L.
   Cote, G. L.   Cinema sans sense.   Q Film Radio TV
      7-4:335 Sum '53

COTES, PETER
   Cotes, P.   Cinema has the edge on TV.   Films & Filming
      4-6:9 Mr '58

COURNOT, MICHEL
   Maeghts' museum.   Vogue 144:190 O 15 '64

COUSTEAU, JACQUES-YVES
   Underwater wonders.   Life 29:119 N 27 '50
   Fish men explore a new world undersea.   National Geo-
      graphic 102:431 O '52
   Sea monsters and sharks at eye level.   Harper 206:31
      F '53

Fish men discover a 2, 200 year old Greek ship.   National
    Geographic 105:1 Ja '54
To the depths of the sea by bathyscaphe.   National Geo-
    graphic 106:67 Jl '54
Diving through an undersea avalanche.   National Geographic
    107:538 Ap '55
Calypso explores for underwater oil.   National Geographic
    108:155 Ag '55
Dugan, J.   Pioneer undersea explorer.   Holiday 18:94
    S '55
World underwater.   Newsweek 47:96 F 13 '56
Exploring Davy Jone's locker with Calypso.   National
    Geographic 109:149 F '56
Personality of the month.   Films & Filming 2-10:3 Jl '56
Wildlife in the water.   Life 41:70 O 22 '56
People are talking about.   Vogue 128:102 N 15 '56
Biography.   Nature 179:73 Ja 12 '57
Biography.   Colliers Yearbook 1957:692 '57
Calypso explores an undersea canyon.   National Geographic
    113:373 Mr '58
Tornabene, L.   Fascination of the unknown.   Cosmop
    148:28 Ja '60
Explorer's dream.   Newsweek 55:62 Mr 14 '60
Poet of the depths.   Time 75:66 Mr 28 '60
Diving saucer takes to the deep.   National Geographic
    117:570 Ap '60
Inflatable ship opens era of airborne undersea expeditions.
    National Geographic 120:142 Jl '61
Jacques-Yves Cousteau receives National Geographic
    Society medal at White House.   National Geographic
    120:146 Jl '61
Dugan, J.   Portrait of homo aquatious.   N. Y. Times Mag
    p38 Ap 21 '63
Fish men.   Newsweek 62:64 Jl 29 '63
Ocean-bottom homes of skin divers.   Popular Mechanic
    120:98 Jl '63
Fish named Ulysses.   Readers Digest 83:188 S '63
To sea in a saucer.   Business Week p88 F 15 '64
Tufty, B.   Seanauts launched.   Science News Letter
    85:118 F 22 '64
At home in the sea.   National Geographic 125:465 Ap '64
Johnson, W.   Man's future beneath the sea.   Senior
    Scholastic 85:6 Ja 7 '65
Underwater pioneer.   Senior Scholastic 85:20 Ja 7 '65
Miller, E.   Talk with Cousteau.   Seventeen 24:56 F '65
Up from success.   Time 86:72 O 22 '65
Working for weeks on the sea floor.   National Geographic
    129:498 Ap '66

Tretta, G.   Not to be missed.   Harper Bazaar 101:160
    My '68
How we film under the sea.   Popular Science 194:65 F '69
Dying oceans.   Time 96:64 S 28 '70
Davidson, S.   Cousteau searches for his whale.   N. Y.
    Times Mag p32 S 10 '72

COUTARD, RAOUL
    Lennen, P.   Sergeant of the cinema.   Show 1-13:16 S 17
        '70
    Kent, L.   Coutard: War can be beautiful.   N. Y. Times
        Bio Ed S 12 '71

COUTINHO, EDUARDO
    Viany, A.   Who's who in the cinema novo.   CTVD 5-4:26
        Sum '68

COWAN, BOB
    Listing of films.   Film Culture 37:7 Sum '65

CRABTREE, ARTHUR
    British feature directors; an index to their work.   Sight &
        Sound 27-6:292 Aut '58

CRAIGIE, JILL
    Filmography.   Film 14:8 N/D '57

CRAMA, NICO
    Biographical note.   International Film G 7:163 '70

CRANE, FRANK HALL
    Obit.   N. Y. Times p15 S 4 '48

CRICHTON, CHARLES
    Filmography.   Film 14:8 N/D '57
    British feature directors; an index to their work.   Sight &
        Sound 27-6:292 Aut '58

CROMWELL, JOHN
    Reed, E.   Some actors.   Theatre Arts 20:446 Je '36
    Biographical note; filmog.   Movies & People 2:40 '40
    Sarris, A.   Likable but elusive; filmog.   Film Culture
        28:35 Spg '63
    Lyons, D.   Interview.   Interview 19:18 F '72

CRONE, GEORGE J.
    Obit.   N. Y. Times p19 D 21 '57

CROSLAND, ALAN
   Calhoun, D.  Sketch.  Motion Pic Classic 27:33 Je '28
   Flicker veteran.  Cue 3-38:3 Jl 20 '35

CRUZE, JAMES
   Condon, M.  "Jimmie" Cruze; interview.  Photoplay
      6-4:117 S '14
   The cruise of Cruze and Bracy.  Movie Pictorial 2-1:13
      Jl; 2-2:13 Ag; 2-3:13 S '15
   Rement, F.  Interview.  Motion Pic Classic 7:41 N '18
   Cohn, A. A.  Stronger than onions.  Photoplay 16-4:64
      S '19
   St. Johns, I.  Sketch.  Photoplay 26:32 S '24
   Sketch.  Classic 20:40 O '24
   Donnell, D.  Cruze, trail-breaker.  Motion Pic Classic
      22:26 S '25
   Tully, J.  Sketch.  Vanity Fair 29:82 D '27
   Cruikshank, H.  Sketch.  Motion Pic Classic 27:33 My '28
   Walker, H. L.  Hospitality of Mr. and Mrs. Cruze.
      Motion Pic Classic 29:32 Ap '29
   Condon, F.  Cruze, director.  Colliers 96:17 Mr 28 '36
   Obit.  Current Biography '42
      N. Y. Times p19 Ag 5 '42
      Newsweek 20:6 Ag 17 '42
      Time 40:76 Ag 17 '42
   Will.  N. Y. Times p22 S 3 '42
   Geltzer, G.  James Cruze.  Films In Review 5-6:283
      Je/Jl '54
   Cohen, J.  Cruze's last efforts; letter.  Films In Review
      5-7:382 Ag/S '54

CUKOR, GEORGE
   Penfield, C.  Work of.  Stage 13:60 Je '36
   Work of.  Motion Pic 52:76 S '36
   Small, F.  Interview on the filming of Romeo and Juliet.
      Photoplay 50:46 S '36
   Spotlight on Hollywood.  Arts & Decoration 51:24 D '39
   Biographical note; filmog.  Movies & People 2:40 '40
   Haines, W.  Home of.  Vogue 98:88 N 1 '41
   How Cukor directs Garbo.  Lions Roar 1-3:no p# N '41
   Men do all right, too.  Lions Roar 1-10:no p# Je '42
   For the duration.  Lions Roar 2-3:no p# D '42
   Biography.  Current Biography '43
   New villains for old.  Lions Roar 3-3 (sup):no p# Ap '44
   MGM's directors range from pioneers to newcomers.
      Lions Roar 3-4:no p# Jl '44
   Houston, P.  Cukor and the Kanins.  Sight & Sound 24-4:
      186 Spg '55

Gow, G. The quest for realism; discussion. Films & Filming 4-3:13 D '57

Tozzi, R. V. George Cukor; filmog. Films In Review 9-2:53 F '58

Reid, J. H. So he became a ladies' man. Films & Filming 6-11:9 Ag '60

Reid, J. H. Women, and still more women. Films & Filming 6-12:10 S '60

Tynan, K. Genius and the girls. Holiday 29:99 F '61

Cutts, J. Biographical note. Films & Filming 8-10:25 Jl '62

Sarris, A. Second line; filmog. Film Culture 28:11 Spg '63

Gillett, J. & Robinson, D. Conversation with George Cukor. Sight & Sound 33:188 Aut '64

Overstreet, R. Interview; filmog. Film Culture 34:1 Fall '64

Seidenbaum, A. Why they let George do it. McCalls 92:189 O '64

Should directors produce? Action 6-4:20 Jl/Ag '71

Clarens, C. Cukor and Justine. Sight & Sound 38-2:75 Spg '69

What directors are saying. Action 6-4:20 Jl/Ag '71

The professional director speaks. Making Films 5-4:40 Ag '71

Phillips, G. George Cukor; interview; filmog. Film Comment 8-1:53 Spg '72

What directors are saying. Action 7-3:29 My/Je '72

Wolf, W. A Hollywood giant keeps the torch burning. Cue 41-39:2 S 23 '72

McClelland, D. Candid Cukor, by George! After Dark 5-7:50 N '72


CUMMINGS, IRVING
Sketch. Motion Pic Supplement 1:53 S '15
Wright, E. Interview. Motion Pic 12:76 S '16
Roberts, S. Sketch. Motion Pic 16:42 O '18
Naylor, H. S. Interview. Motion Pic 23:42 Mr '22
Biographical note; filmog. Movies & People 2:40 '40
Obit. British Book Year 1960:506 '60
    N. Y. Times p86 Ap 19 '59
    Screen World 11:216 '60


CURTIZ, MICHAEL
Cohen, H. W. Pittsburgh cinema critic extra in Hollywood. Cinema Digest 2-1:30 N 14 '32
Biographical sketch. Time 36:78 Ag 19 '40
Biographical note. filmog. Movies & People 2:40 '40

Martin, P.   Hollywood's champion language assassin.
Sat Evening Post 220:22 Ag 2 '47
Samuels, G.   Director Hollywood's leading man.   N. Y.
Times Mag p23 O 26 '52
Curtiz, M.   Talent shortage is causing two-year produc-
tion delay.   Films & Filming 2-9:9 Je '56
Obit.   British Book Year 1963:867 '63
    N. Y. Times p35 Ap 12 '62
    Newsweek 59:69 Ap 23 '62
    Screen World 14:222 '63
    Time 79:48 Ap 20 '62
Sarris, A.   Likable but elusive; filmog.   Film Culture
28:35 Spg '63
Nolan, J. E.   Michael Curtiz; filmog.   Films In Review
21-9:525 N '70
Behlmer, R. & Pinto, A.   Letters.   Films In Review
22-2:114 F '71
Mundy, R.   Death plays and wax works.   Cinema (Lon)
9:8 n. d.


CZINNER, PAUL
    Knight, A.   Bolshoi ballet: how the film was made.
    Dance 32:38 Ja '58
    Bourne, D.   Tenth row center at the Bolshoi ballet.
    Reporter 18:37 F 20 '58
    Documenting the stage.   Opera News 27:28 D '62

DAALDER, RENÉE
Biographical note.　International Film G 6:133 '69

DA COSTA, MORTON
There's money in a strawhat.　Theatre Arts 31:6 Jl '47
Da Costa, M.　Auntie and I.　Films & Filming 5-4:11
Ja '59
Keating, J.　Dossier on Da Costa.　Theatre Arts 43:22
Jl '59

DAHL, GUSTAVO
Viany, A.　Who's who in the cinema novo.　CTVD 5-4:26
Sum '68

D'ALMEIDA, JULIO
Round take on the cinema novo.　Cinema (Lon) 5:15 F '70

DAMIAMI, DAMIANO
Lane, J. F.　The face of '63--Italy.　Films & Filming
9-7:11 Ap '63

DANELIA, GEORGI (Also:　DANELIYA)
Vronskaya, J.　Recent Russian cinema.　Film 62:5 Sum
'71

DANSKA, HERBERT
Survey among unsuccessful applicants for the Ford Found-
ation film grants.　Film Comment 2-3:10 Sum '64
Listing of films.　Film Culture 37:7 Sum '65

d'ARRAST, H. d'ABBADIE
Weinberg, H. G.　Immemoriam--1897-1968.　Film Comment 5-3:36 Fall '69

DAS GUPTA, CHIDANANDA
Indian cinema today.　Film Q 22:27 Sum '69

DASSIN, JULES
Jules Dassin, young director.　Lions Roar 1-7:no p#
Mr '42
A director and his pals.　Lions Roar 1-11/12:no p#　Jl/
Ag '42
New faces among MGM directors too.　Lions Roar 1-11/
12:no p#　Jl/Ag '42

101

Early feet.   Lions Roar 3-1:no p# S '43
MGM's directors range from pioneers to newcomers.
   Lions Roar 3-4:no p# Jl '44
Dassin, J.   The truth of fantasy.   Lions Roar 3-4(sup):
   no p# Jl '44
Parsons, L. O.   Cosmopolitan's citation as the best di-
   rector of the month.   Cosmop 123:59 Jl '47
Personality of the month.   Films & Filming 4-1:5 O '57
Grenier, C.   Jules Dassin; interview.   Sight & Sound
   27-3:141 Win '57/58
Alpert, H.   Greek passion.   Sat R 41:14 D 20 '58
Bluestone, G.   Interview.   Film Culture 4-17:3 '58
Talk with a movie maker.   Newsweek 56:130 O 24 '60
Hammel, F.   A director's return.   Cue 31-10:11 Mr 10
   '62
Nolan, J.   Jules Dassin; filmog.   Films In Review 13-9:
   572 N '62
Sarris, A.   Minor disappointments; filmog.   Film Culture
   28:41 Spg '63
Hamilton, J.   Melina Mercouri rehearses Never on Sun-
   day for Broadway.   Look 31:66 Ja 24 '67
Madsen, A.   The race race.   Take One 1-11:16 My/Je
   '68
Madsen, A.   Too late blues.   Sight & Sound 37-4:184
   Aut '68
Skow, J.   Uptight!   Sat Evening Post 24-2:36 Ja 25 '69
Wolf, W.   Durably demonstrating the art of entwining
   careers.   Cue 39-9:9 F 28 '70
Gow, G.   Style and instinct; interview.   Films & Filming
   16-5:22 F '70; 16-6:66 Mr '70
What directors are saying.   Action 5-3:30 My/Je '70
Biography.   Current Biography 32:18 Mr '71


DAVES, DELMER
   Fenin, G.   The face of '63--United States.   Films &
      Filming 9-6:55 Mr '63
   Whitehall, R.   On the 3:10 to Yuma.   Films & Filming
      9-7:51 Ap '63
   Knight, A.   Auteur theory.   Sat R 46:22 My 4 '63
   Whitehall, R.   A summer place.   Films & Filming 9-8:48
      My '63
   Should directors produce?   Action 3-4:10 Jl/Ag '68
   Wicking, C.   Interview.   Screen 10-4/5:55 Jl/O '69
   Wallington, M.   Auteur and genre: the westerns of Del-
      mer Daves.   Cinema (Lon) 4:6 O '69
   Daves, D.   Closing the gap.   Action 5-2:25 Mr/Ap '70
   Screenwriters symposium; filmog.   Film Comment 6-4:86
      Win '70/71

Whitman, M. Second sight. Films Illustrated 2-13:34
Jl '72

Daves, D. You've come a long way, baby. Action
7-5:29 S/O '72

DAVIDSON, CARSON
Who's who in filmmaking; filmog. Sightlines 2-2:4 N/D
'68

D'AVINO, CARMEN
D'Avino, C. A statement; filmog. Film Culture 29:74
Sum '63

Mancia, A. & Van Dyke, W. Four artists as filmmakers.
Art In America 55:67 Ja '67

Stack, D. Animation, pixilation and Mr. D'Avino. Cinema
(BH) 4-4:24 D '68

DAVIS, DESMOND
Hutchinson, D. Take two nice guys like them: Desmond
Davis and Roy Millichip. Films & Filming 16-3:51 D
'69

Davis, D. The sullen art. Films & Filming 17-8:36
My '71

British cinema filmography. Film 65:10 Spg '72

DAVIS, PETER
The selling of the pentagon; interview. Film Library Q
4-4:10 Fall '71

DAWLEY, J. SEARLE
Obit. N.Y. Times p25 Mr 30 '49

DAWN, NORMAN
Fielding, R. Norman Dawn: pioneer worker in special
effects cinematography. Journal Soc Motion Pic Television Engineers 72:15 Ja '63

DAY, ROBERT
Nolan, J. E. Films on TV; filmog. Films In Review
21-6:368 Je/Jl '70

DEAN, BASIL
His opinion of the American theatre. Theatre 42:9 O '25
Talking pictures. 19th Century 106:823 D '29

De ALMEIDA, FARIA
Granja, V. Faria De Almeida's first feature. CTVD
6-4:13 Fall '69

de ANDRADE, JOAQUIM PEDRO
    Viany, A.   Who's who in the cinema novo.   CTVD 5-4:26
      Sum '68

de ANTONIO, EMILE
    de Antonio, E.   The point of view in Point of order.
      Film Comment 2-1:35 Win '64
    Rush to judgment; a conversation with Mark Lane and
      Emile de Antonio.   Film Comment 4-2/3:2 Fall/Win
      '67
    Westerbeck, C. J. Jr.   Some out-takes from radical
      filmmaking.   Sight & Sound 39-3:140 Sum '70
    Weiner, B.   Radical scavenging; interview.   Film Q
      25-1:3 Fall '71
    Kent, L.   Eat, drink & make 'Millhouse.'   N.Y. Times
      Bio Ed O 17 '71
    O'Brien, G.   Interview.   Interview 19:28 F '72

DEARDEN, BASIL
    Filmography.   Film 14:8 N/D '57
    Personalities of the month.   Films & Filming 4-4:5 Ja '58
    British feature directors; an index to their work.   Sight &
      Sound 27-6:293 Aut '58
    Two on a tandem.   Films & Filming 12-10:26 Jl '66
    British cinema filmography.   Film 65:10 Spg '72
    Obit.   Film R p17 '71/72

DEGELIN, EMILE
    Biographical note.   International Film G 8:86 '71

DE GRASSE, JOSEPH
    Obit.   N.Y. Times p35 My 26 '40

DE HIRSCH, STORM
    De Hirsch, S.   Roman notebook.   Film Culture 25:75
      Sum '62
    Markopoulos, G.   Three filmmakers.   Film Culture
      35:23 Win '64/65
    Listing of films.   Film Culture 37:7 Sum '65
    A conversation.   Film Culture 46:44 O '68
    Pyros, J.   Notes on women directors.   Take One 3-2:7
      N/D '70

DEITCH, GENE
    Deitch, G.   An American in Prague.   Film Library Q
      2-4:20 Fall '69

DE LA CERDA, CLEMENTE
Focus on a director.   International Film G 8:276 '71

DELLUC, LOUIS
Blumer, R. H.   The camera as snowball:  France 1918-
1927.   Cinema J 9-2:31 Spg '70

DEL RUTH, ROY
Cavanaugh, I.   Roy Del Ruth.   Cinema Digest 1-10:10 S
19 '52
Cheatham, M.   Stars in the ascendant.   Silver Screen
6-5:53 Mr '36
Biographical note; filmog.   Movies & People 2:41 '40
Roy Del Ruth: musical marked man.   Lions Roar 1-3:no
p# N '41
Anything for a laugh.   Lions Roar 1-10:no p# Je '42
Musical magic.   Lions Roar 2-4:no p# Ap '43
Screen's Vanity fair.   Lions Roar 3-3:no p# Ap '44
Anything could have happened!  Lions Roar 3-4(sup):no
p# Jl '44
MGM's directors range from pioneers to newcomers.
Lions Roar 3-4:no p# Jl '44
Parsons, L. O.   Cosmopolitan's citation for the best di-
rection of the month.   Cosmop 125:13 S '48
Obit.   N. Y. Times p31 Ap 28 '61
Screen World 13:221 '62

DELVAUX, PAUL
Milne, T.   Countries of the mind.   Sight & Sound 41-2:75
Spg '72

DeMILLE, CECIL B.
Carr, H. C.   Directors: the men who make the plays.
Photoplay 8-1:80 Je '15
Own, K.   The kick-in prophets.   Photoplay 8-5:82 O '15
Wise man of the movies.   Theatre 27:58 Ja '18
Mistley, M.   Interview.   Motion Pic Classic 6:54 Jl '18
Haskins, H.   Work of.   Motion Pic Classic 7:16 S '18
Naylor, H. S.   Interview.   Motion Pic 18:36 N '19
Peltret, E.   An interview in the air.   Photoplay 17-1:36
D '19
St. Johns, A. R.   His views of marriage.   Photoplay
19:28 D '20
Opinions on marriage.   Photoplay 19:24 My '21
Naylor, H. S.   Interview.   Motion Pic 21:28 Je '21
They hunt the grizzly.   Outing 79:200 F '22
Hall, G. & Fletcher, A. W.   Interview.   Motion Pic
23:24 Ap '22

The chances of color photoplay in moving pictures.
   American Photo 17:14 Ja '23
St. Johns, A. R.  Sketch.  Photoplay 24:50 O '23
Work of.  Classic 18:24 N '23
Home of.  Classic 18:34 D '23
Schallert, E.  How the Red Sea was made to open.
   American Projectionist 2-9:5 S '24
Mullett, M. B.  How Cecil DeMille works and what he
   knows about us; interview.  American 100:34 Jl '25
Kiesling, B. C.  Sketch.  Motion Pic Classic 22:28 N '25
Tully, J.  An estimate.  Vanity Fair 26:56 Ap '26
Smith, A.  The utmost in directors.  Motion Pic 31:65
   Je '26
Macpherson, J.  Sketch.  Motion Pic 33:30 Mr '27
Smith, F. J.  Interview regarding The king of kings.
   Photoplay 32:38 Jl '27
The public is always right.  Ladies Home J 44:13 S '27
Belfrage, C.  Interview.  Motion Pic Classic 26:21 F '28
Thorp, D.  Interview.  Motion Pic Classic 29:23 Je '29
Calhoun, D.  Charges of hokum and his defense.  Motion
   Pic Classic 31:36 My '30
Shaffer, R.  Interview.  Photoplay 38:30 S '30
Interview.  Movie Classic 1:60 F '32
Calhoun, D.  Predicts Hollywood doomed.  Movie Classic
   3:42 S '32
Keen, J. C.  Cecil B. DeMille.  Cinema Digest 2-5:13
   Ja 9 '33
Moffitt, J. C.  Moffitt discusses DeMille and Sign of the
   cross.  Cinema Digest 2-10:4 F 20 '33
Whipple, S.  Yes--Mr. DeMille.  Cinema Digest 3-5:10
   Ap 17 '33
What's wrong with the movies.  Motion Pic 46:42 S '33
Hamilton, S.  The last of the veteran showmen.  Photo-
   play 44:32 O '33
Grant, J.  The "yes-man" legend.  Movie Classic 5:34
   D '33
Biographical sketch.  Time 24:36 Ag 27 '34
How I make a spectacle.  Photoplay 46:43 O '34
Reynolds, Q.  Shooting stars.  Colliers 95:12 F 9 '35
Grant, J.  His sense of humor.  Movie Classic 8:82
   My '35
Brenan, A. S.  Sketch.  Stage 12:53 Ag '35
Cecil Blount DeMille, deus ex machina.  Cue 3-45:3 S 7
   '35
Harrison, M.  Interview.  Movie Classic 10:12 Mr '36
Orme, M.  Twenty-fifth anniversary as a film producer.
   Illustrated London N 192:300 F 19 '38

Benon, A.  When C. B. picks 'em they stay picked.
   Silver Screen 8-4:51 F '38
Spotlight on Hollywood.  Arts & Decoration 51:24 D '39
Planning a cinema on the Virgin Mary.  Time 35:44 Ap 22
   '40
Biographical note; filmog.  Movies & People 2:41 '40
Nugent, F. S.  Sixty reels of DeMille.  N. Y. Times Mag
   p10 Ag 10 '41
Van Ryn, F.  When you see Paramount, remember
   DeMille.  Readers Digest 41:35 S '42
Biography.  Current Biography 3:189 '42
Durant, J.  DeMille: colossus of celluloid.  Sat Evening
   Post 215:24 F 6 '43
Hopper, H.  His married life.  Photoplay 22:26 My '43
Sammis, F. R.  Sketch.  Photoplay 25:29 N '44
The dollar assessment: his controversy with the American
   federation of radio artists.  Time 45:53 F 5 '45
AFRA and Mr. DeMille.  New Republic 112:164 F 5 '45
DeMille's dollar.  Newsweek 25:41 F 5 '45
Yes, Cecil DeMille can still vote.  Sat Evening Post 217:
   104 F 24 '45
My favorite tree.  American Forests 51:99 Mr '45
Must union members give up their American rights?
   Readers Digest 47:93 Jl '45
Stand up and be counted.  Vital Speeches 12:48 N 1 '45
House united.  Vital Speeches 13:151 D 15 '46
Biography.  National Cylopaedia G:150 '46
Reid, L.  Don't say glamour to C. B. DeMille.  Silver
   Screen 17-10:49 Ag '47
The cinematic talent of a movie pioneer.  Time 50:99
   O 27 '47
Well, J. A. & Glenn, J. A.  DeMille loses again.
   American Federationist 55:10 Ja '48
While Rome burns.  Vital Speeches 14:495 Je 1 '48
Brainbridge, J.  Story of his filming of Samson and
   Delilah.  Life 27:138 D 5 '49
Small, C.  Rock of Hollywood.  Colliers 125:13 F 25;
   125:30 Mr 4 '50
Feldman, J. & M.  C. B. DeMille's virtues.  Films In
   Review 1-9:1 D '50
Lardner, J.  While Tolstoy sleeps.  Newsweek 45:66
   F 21 '55
The director and the public; symposium.  Film Culture
   1-2:15 Mr/Ap '55
Going like 70.  Time 65:106 My 9 '55
The big screens.  Sight & Sound 24-4:209 Spg '55
DeMille directs his biggest spectacle.  Life 39:142 O 24
   '55

DeMille, C. B.   After 70 pictures.   Films In Review
    7-3:97 Mr '56
Zunser, J.   DeMille the great is 75.   Cue 25-31:12
    Ag 4 '56
Hill, G.   Most colossal of all.   N. Y. Times Mag p16
    Ag 12 '56
Cole, C.   Forget spectacle--it's the story that counts;
    interview.   Films & Filming 3-1:7 O '56
Gray, M.   New treatment for the old testament.   Films &
    Filming 3-1:8 O '56
Baker, P.   Showman for the millions; filmog.   Films &
    Filming 3-1:9 O '56
In the grand tradition.   Newsweek 48:112 N 5 '56
Close call for Mr. DeMille.   Life 41:120 N 12 '56
New pictures.   Time 68:120 N 12 '56
Mount Sinai to Main Street.   Time 68:82 N 19 '56
Mr. DeMille and Moses.   Look 20:77 N 27 '56
Hamilton, M.   Man of imagination.   Flying 59:40 D '56
DeMille on DeMille.   Newsweek 51:92 Ja 27 '58
DeMille, C. B.   How to be a critic.   Films & Filming
    4-6:11 Mr '58
Obit.   Americana Annual 1960:212 '60
    British Book Year 1960:507 '60
    Current Biography 20:6 Mr '59
    Current Biography Yearbook 1959:92 '60
    Illustrated London N 234:186 Ja 31 '59
    Life 46:26 F 2 '59
    N. Y. Times p1 Ja 22 '59
    Newsweek 53:84 F 2 '59
    Screen World 11:216 '60
    Time 73:54 F 2 '59
Funeral.   N. Y. Times p19 Ja 24 '59
Will.   N. Y. Times p31 Ja 28 '59
Boyd, M.   God and DeMille in Hollywood.   Christian
    Century 76:230 F 25 '59
DeMille's epic story of films' first epic; excerpt from his
    autobiography.   Life 47:154 O 19 '59
Weales, G.   Gospel according to DeMille.   Reporter 21:38
    D 24 '59
Sarris, A.   Third line; filmog.   Film Culture 28:18
    Spg '63
DeMille, A.   Goodnight, C. B.   Esquire 61:119 Ja '64
Miller, D.   Films on TV.   Films In Review 15-2:110
    F '64
Biography.   National Cylopaedia 47:614 '65
Arthur, A.   C. B. DeMille's human side.   Films In Re-
    view 18-4:221 Ap '67

Dreis, D. D. Ready when you are, C. B. After Dark
12-1:22 My '70

deMILLE, WILLIAM C.
One of the Merriwold dramatists. Bookman 29:627 Ag '09
Owen, K. The kick-in prophets. Photoplay 8-5:82 O '15
Smith, F. J. Interview. Motion Pic Classic 12:36 Ap
'21
A message of hope. Photoplay 19:54 My '21
The audience and motion pictures. Drama 11:344 Jl '21
St. Johns, A. R. Sketch. Photoplay 24:50 O '23
Doyle, T. Interview. Classic 20:66 S '24
Bigoted and bettered pictures. Scribner 76:231 S '24
Film drama has infantile paralysis. Current Opinion
77:608 N '24
Prudes and pictures. Scribner 81:311 Mr '27
Screen speaks. Scribner 85:367 Ap '29
Cruikshank, H. Sketch. Motion Pic Classic 29:35 Ap '29
Mickey vs. Popeye. Forum 94:295 N '35
Saga of the deMilles. Newsweek 14:42 O 9 '39
Goodbye Messrs. Chips. Time 61:68 Je 29 '53
Obit. N. Y. Times p89 Mr 6 '55
Newsweek 45:71 Mr 14 '55
Screen World 7:233 '56
Time 65:92 Mr 14 '55
Wilson Library B 29:678 My '55
Funeral. N. Y. Times p27 Mr 9 '55
Geltzer, G. William C. deMille. Films In Review
7-6:264 Je/Jl '56
Dyer, E. William C. deMille. Films In Review 7-10:
538 D '56
Geltzer, G. William C. deMille; letter. Films In Re-
view 8-1:45 Ja '57
Biography. National Cyclopaedia 45:382 '62

DEMY, JACQUES
Graham, P. The face of '63--France. Films & Filming
9-8:13 My '63
Billard, G. Jacques Demy and his other world. Film Q
18-1:23 Fall '64
Bastide, F. R. Phenomenon of Les parapluies de
Cherbourg. Vogue 144:184 N 1 '64
Demy, J. I prefer the sun to the rain. Film Comment
3-2:61 Spg '65
Director of the year; filmog. International Film G 3:21
'66
Interview. Film Heritage 2-3:17 Spg '67

Scheuer, P. K.   Frenchman in Hollywood.   Action 3-6:10
   N/D '68
Kael, P.   Current cinema.   New Yorker 45:122 F 22 '69
Gow, G.   Lola in Los Angeles; interview.   Films & Film-
   ing 16-7:13 Ap '70
Strick, P.   Demy calls the tune.   Sight & Sound 40-4:187
   Aut '71
Petrie, G.   Interview; filmog.   Film Comment 7-4:46
   Win '71/72

DENHAM, REGINALD
   Fruit of a bad seed.   Theatre Arts 39:33 D '55
   140 years before the footlights.   Sat R 52:43 My 24 '69

de OLIVEIRA, MANOEL
   de Oliveira's struggle to create.   CTVD 1-2:12 Sum '62

de PALMA, BRIAN
   Is Hollywood's new freedom for real?   Show 2-1:27 Mr
   '71
   What directors are saying.   Action 6-3:28 My/Je '71
   The professional director speaks.   Making Films 5-4:40
   Ag '71

DEREN, MAYA
   Farber, M.   Maya Deren's films.   New Republic 115:555
   O 28 '46
   Deren, M.   Maya Deren's films; reply.   New Republic
   115:630 N 11 '46
   Bower, A.   Five avant-garde films.   Nation 168:25
   Ja 1 '49
   Mephisto's musings.   Musical America 73:9 My '53
   Obit.   N. Y. Times p23 O 14 '61
   Deren, M.   On a film in progress.   Film Culture 22/23:
   160 '61
   Deren, M.   A statement of principles.   Film Culture
   22/23:161 '61
   Reynolds, C.   Maya Deren.   Popular Photo 50:83 F '62
   Arnheim, R.   To Maya Deren.   Film Culture 24:1 Spg
   '62
   Poetry and the film; a symposium.   Film Culture 29:55
   Sum '63
   Deren, M.   The Cleveland lecture.   Film Culture 29:64
   Sum '63
   Deren, M.   The very eye of night; filmog.   Film Culture
   29:70 Sum '63
   Writing of Maya Deren.   Film Culture 39:1 Win '65

Pyros, J.   Notes on women directors.   Take One 3-2:7
   N/D '70
Cornwell, R.   Activists of the avant-garde.   Film Library
   Q 5-1:29 Win '71/72

de RENZY, ALEX
   Sex trip.   Time 96:44 Jl 20 '70

de ROCHEMONT, LOUIS
   Superior documentary.   Newsweek 34:72 Jl 4 '49
   Lyons, E.   Louis de Rochemont; maverick of the movies.
      Readers Digest 55:23 Jl '49
   Biography.   Current Biography 10:13 N '49
      Same.   Current Biography Yearbook 49:144 '50
   MacCann, R. D.   Louis de Rochemont turns facts into fiction
      --with care.   Christian Science Mon Mag p14 D 30 '50
   Biographical note.   Time 58:102 Ag 13 '51
   Gehman, R. B.   de Rochemont--a pictorial journalist who re-
      cords the American scene on film.   Theatre Arts 35:58 O '51
   Zolotow, M.   Want to be a movie star?   Sat Evening
      Post 224:24 Mr 29 '52
   Out of the studios and into the streets; Louis de Rochemont
      and The march of time; interview.   AFI Report 3:17 N '73

de SANTIS, GIUSEPPE
   Lane, J. F.   de Santis and Italian neo-realism.   Sight &
      Sound 19-6:245 Ag '50
   New names.   Sight & Sound 25-3:120 Win '55/56

DESCHNER, DONALD
   Survey among unsuccessful applicants for the Ford Found-
      ation film grants.   Film Comment 2-3:10 Sum '64

DE SETA, VITTORIO
   New names.   Sight & Sound 25-3:119 Win '55/56
   Pistol-toting director.   Newsweek 56:108 N 21 '60
   Lane, J. F.   The triumph of Italy's realism.   Films &
      Filming 8-3:38 D '61
   De Seta, V.   Notes on Banditi a Orgosolo.   Film Culture
      24:36 Spg '62

DE SICA, VITTORIO
   Fong, M.   His direction of Shoeshine: a student's
      analysis.   Hollywood Q 4:14 Fall '49
   Jacobson, H. L.   De Sica's Bicycle thieves and Italian
      humanism.   Hollywood Q 4-1:28 Fall '49
   Koval, F.   Interview.   Sight & Sound 19-2:61 Ap '50

Hawkins, R. F.  De Sica dissected.  Films In Review
    2-5:26 My '51
Lambert, G.  The case of De Sica.  Sight & Sound
    20-2:41 Je '51
Miracle man.  New Yorker 28:29 Ap 5 '52
Keating, J.  Shoe shine boy heads for Hollywood.  Cue
    21-15:14 Ap 12 '52
Picker, M.  De Sica in Chicago; letter.  Films In Re-
    view 3-5:251 My '52
Biography.  Current Biography 13:16 Jl '52
    Same.  Current Biography Yearbook 1952:142 '53
De Sica, V.  Illiberal censorship?  Film 7:15 Ja/F '56
Young, V.  Umberto D: Vittorio De Sica's super-natural-
    ism.  Hudson R  8:592 Win '56
Sargeant, W.  Bread, love and neo-realism.  New Yorker
    33:35 Je 29; 35 Jl 6 '57
De Sica, V.  British humour?  It's the same in Italy;
    filmog.  Films & Filming 5-7:10 Ap '59
Bester, A.  Vittorio De Sica.  Holiday 31:143 Mr '62
De Sica on Sophia Loren.  Vogue 140:102 N 1 '62
Lane, J. F.  The face of '63--Italy.  Films & Filming
    9-7:11 Ap '63
How they live and die in Naples.  Horizon 5:49 S '63
De Sica, V.  What's right with Hollywood.  Films &
    Filming 10-2:47 N '63
McVay, D.  Poet of poverty.  Films & Filming 11-1:12
    O; 11-2:51 N '64
Dragadze, P.  Vittorio De Sica's Roma; interview.
    Travel & Camera 33:26 Ap '70
Salute of the week.  Cue 40-52:1 D 25 '71
Flatley, G.  The victory of De Sica.  N. Y Times Bio
    Ed Ja 16 '72
Lyons, D.  Interview.  Interview 19:12 F '72
Johnson, D.  A director who makes serious pictures.
    Show 2-1:45 Mr '72
What directors are saying.  Action 7-3:29 My/Je '72

de TOTH, ANDRE
    Bangs, B.  Problem child with good intentions.  Silver
        Screen 15-5:32 Mr '45
    Howard, M.  The amazing de Toths.  Silver Screen
        17-9:43 Jl '47
    Marriage is such fun.  Photoplay 33:58 Ag '48

DEVILLE, MICHEL
    Graham, P.  The face of '63--France.  Films & Filming
        9-8:13 My '63

Interview.    Film 55:28 Sum '69

DEXTER, JOHN
British cinema filmography.    Film 65:10 Spg '72

DICKINSON, THOROLD
The big screens.   Sight & Sound 24-4:209 Spg '55
Dickinson, T.   Heaven preserve us from the passive
audience!  Film 5:7 S/O '55
Dickinson, T.   The sponsoring of films.    Film 8:14 Mr/
Ap '56
Dickinson, T.   Conference in Paris.   Sight & Sound
26-1:38 Sum '56
Dickinson, T.   The personal style.   Films 12:20 Mr/Ap
'57
Dickinson, T.   This documentary business.   Film
Culture 3-3(13):5 O '57
Filmography.   Film 14:8 N/D '57
British feature directors; an index to their work.   Sight
& Sound 27-6:293 Aut '58
Tidal wave.   New Yorker 35:33 Mr 14 '59
Dickinson, T.   Power among men.   Film 22:32 N/D '59
Dickinson, T. & Orrem, M.   The start at the Slade.
Film 28:22 Mr/Ap '61
Dickinson, T.   Working with Pearson.   Silent Pic 2:5
Spg '69

DICKSON, PAUL
British feature directors; an index to their work. Sight &
Sound 27-6:293 Aut '58

DI DONATO, WILLIAM
Listing of films.    Film Culture 37:7 Sum '65

DIETERLE, WILLIAM (Wilhelm)
William Dieterle, carpenter in celluloid.   Cue 4-1:3
N 2 '35
Lawson, R.   The director Hollywood forget to remember.
Screen Book 19-1:51 Ag '37
Work of.   Motion Pic 54:58 D '37
Dieterle, W.   The great god box office.   Cinema
Progress 3-1:12 F/Mr '38
Biographical note; filmog.   Movies & People 2:41 '40
Director William Dieterle.   Lions Roar 2-3:no p# D '42
Biography.   Current Biography '43
William D. Dieterle--synonym for dynamic.   Lions Roar
3-5:no p# D '44

Koval, F.   Interview.   Sight & Sound 19-3:107 My '50
Dieterle, W.     Europeans in Hollywood.   Sight & Sound
    22-1:39 Jl/S '52
Luft, H. G.   William Dieterle.   Films In Review 8-4:148
    Ap '57
Luft, H. G.   Dieterle; letter.   Films In Review 8-6:301
    Je/Jl '57
Pinto, A. & Rialp, F.   The films of William Dieterle;
    filmog.   Films In Review 19-8:499 O '68

DILLON, EDWARD
    Biographical Note.   Photoplay 9-4:42 Mr '16

DISNEY, WALT
    Carr, H.   Only unpaid movie star.   American 111:55
        Mr '31
    Hurwitz, L. T.   P. Roy and W. Disney, comparison of
        their methods.   Creative Art 8:359 My '31
    His work points the way to a new art of the cinema.   Lit
        Digest 110:19 Ag 8 '31
    Mickey Mouse's musical career.   Golden Book 14:343 N
        '31
    Seldes, G.   Disney and others.   New Republic 71:101
        Je 8 '32
    Syring, R. H.   One of the great geniuses!   Silver Screen
        3-1:46 N '32
    Merry Christmas from Mickey and Minnie Mouse.
        Delineator 121:15 D '32
    Noah's ark, a Silly symphony by Walt Disney.   Newsweek
        1:27 Ap 29 '33
    Moffitt, J.   Walt Disney to blame?   Cinema Digest 4-4:7
        Je 5 '33
    On the screen; Three little pigs.   Lit Digest 116:29 O 14
        '33
    Fuller, M.   Three little pigs.   Publisher W 124:1431
        O 21 '33
    Mickey Mouse, financier.   Lit Digest 116:41 O 21 '33
    Mechanical mouse.   Sat R 10:252 N 11 '33
    Grant, J.   How his cartoons are made.   Movie Classic
        5:30 N '33
    Ferguson, O. C.   Ozep and Walt Disney.   New Republic
        77:253 Ja 10 '34
    Parents' magazine medal to Walt Disney.   Parents 9:17
        Ja '34
    Skolsky, S.   His real story.   Cosmop 96:52 F '34
    Lejeune, C. A.   Disney-time; not-so-silly symphonies.
        Theatre Arts 18:84 F '34

Macaroni Mickey mousse, a favorite recipe.  Better
  Home & Garden 12:42  F '34
Thurber, J.  Odyssey of Disney.  Nation 138:363 Mr 28
  '34
Grasshopper and the ants; from a Walt Disney Silly
  symphony.  Good Housekeeping 98:37 Ap '34
McCord, D. F.  Are his animated cartoons a menace to
  children?  Photoplay 45:30 Ap '34
Mann, A.  Mickey Mouse's financial career.  Harper
  168:714 My '34
Jamison, J.  Around the world with Mickey Mouse.  Ro-
  tarian 44:22 My '34
Big bad wolf; from a Walt Disney Silly symphony.  Good
  Housekeeping 98:37 My '34
Greene, G.  Three little pigs in England.  Living Age
  346:273 My '34
His profits from films exaggerated.  Harper 168:714
  My '34
Wise little hen; from a Walt Disney Silly symphony.
  Good Housekeeping 98:37 Je '34
Johnston, A.  Biographical.  Womans Home Companion
  61:12 Jl '34
Bragdon, C.  Mickey Mouse and what he means.  Scribner
  96:40 Jl '34
Johnston, A.  Mickey Mouse.  Womans Home Companion
  61:12 Jl '34
Flying mouse; from a Walt Disney Silly symphony.  Good
  Housekeeping 99:37 Jl '34
Peculiar penguins; from a Walt Disney Silly symphony.
  Good Housekeeping 99:37 Ag '34
Mickey Mouse's friends find him in Portland museum.
  Newsweek 4:29 S 15 '34
Goddess of spring; from a Walt Disney Silly symphony.
  Good Housekeeping 99:37 S '34
Tortoise and the hare; from the Walt Disney Silly sym-
  phony.  Good Housekeeping 99:27 O '34
Golden touch; from a Walt Disney Silly symphony.  Good
  Housekeeping 99:37 N '34
Work of.  Fortune 10:88 N '34
Water babies; from the Walt Disney Silly symphony.  Good
  Housekeeping 99:34 D '34
Mickey Mouse in The band concert.  Good Housekeeping
  100:37 Ja '35
Cookie Carnival; from a Walt Disney Silly symphony.
  Good Housekeeping 100:27 F '35
Mickey's garden; from the Walt Disney Mickey Mouse.
  Good Housekeeping 100:37 Mr '35

Robber kitten; from the Walt Disney Silly symphony.
    Good Housekeeping 100:37 Ap '35
Mullen, S. M.   Master of cartoons.   Scholastic 26:10
    My 18 '35
Walt Disney's Mickey Mouse in Mickey's fire brigade.
    Good Housekeeping 100:37 My '35
His creations.   Theatre World 23:233 My '35
Who killed Cock Robin?   from a Walt Disney Silly sym-
    phony.   Good Housekeeping 100:37 Je '35
Mickey's magic hat; from a Walt Disney Mickey Mouse.
    Good Housekeeping 101:37 Jl '35
Ferguson, O.   Extra added attractions: Band concert and
    Who killed Cock Robin?   New Republic 83:363 Ag 7 '35
Music land; from the Walt Disney Silly symphony.   Good
    Housekeeping 101:37 Ag '35
Cock of the walk; from the Walt Disney Silly symphony.
    Good Housekeeping 101:37 S '35
Burnett, D.   Rise of Donald Duck, Mickey Mouse's
    enemy.   Pictorial R 37:19 O '35
Three little wolves; from a Walt Disney Silly symphony.
    Good Housekeeping 101:37 O '35
Mickey Mouse in On ice.   Good Housekeeping 101:37 N '35
Broken toys; from a Walt Disney Silly symphony.   Good
    Housekeeping 101:37 D '35
That awful word art.   Christian Century 53:137 Ja 22 '36
Mickey Mouse in Through the mirror.   Good Housekeep-
    ing 102:37 Ja '36
Disney receives ribbon of the French Legion of honor.
    Publisher W 129:605 F 1 '36
Elmer Elephant, from the Walt Disney Silly symphony.
    Good Housekeeping 102:39 F '36
Mickey's rival, from a Walt Disney Mickey Mouse.  Good
    Housekeeping 102:37 Mr '36
Mickey Mouse; Alpine Mickey.   Good Housekeeping 102:39
    Ap '36
Mickey Mouse in Moving day.   Good Housekeeping 102:39
    My '36
Mickey Mouse; Mickey's circus.   Good Housekeeping
    102:37 Je '36
Three mouseketeers, from a Walt Disney silly symphony.
    Good Housekeeping 103:37 Jl '36
Trell, M.   Disney's staff.   Pictorial R 37:30 Ag '36
Toby Tortoise returns from a Walt Disney Silly symphony.
    Good Housekeeping 103:45 Ag '36
Walt Disney's Mickey Mouse presents Donald and Pluto.
    Good Housekeeping 103:37 S '36
Mickey Mouse is eight years old.   Lit Digest 122:18 O 3
    '36

Country cousin; from a Walt Disney Silly symphony. Good
Housekeeping 103:37 O '36
Walt Disney's Mickey Mouse presents Mickey's elephant.
Good Housekeeping 103:37 N '36
Greene, G.  Christmas Disney season at Tatler theatre,
London.  Spectator 157:1122 D 25 '36
More kittens; from a Walt Disney Silly symphony.  Good
Housekeeping 103:38 D '36
Walt Disney's Mickey Mouse presents Don Donald.  Good
Housekeeping 104:37 Ja '37
Walt Disney's Mickey Mouse presents Mickey's amateurs.
Good Housekeeping 104:37 F '37
Walt Disney's Silly symphony: Hiawatha.  Good House-
keeping 104:37 Mr '37
Walt Disney's Mickey Mouse presents Pluto's quinpuplets.
Good Housekeeping 104:37 Ap '37
Walt Disney's Mickey Mouse: Donald's ostrich.  Good
Housekeeping 104:37 My '37
Mickey Mouse, and Silly symphony featuring Donald Duck.
Canadian 87:50 My '37
Walt Disney's Academy awards revue.  Commonweal
26:160 Je 4 '37
Walt Disney's Mickey Mouse presents Clock cleaners.
Good Housekeeping 104:37 Je '37
Pearson, R. M.  Artist's point of view.  Forum 98:271
N '37
Mouse and man.  Time 30:19 D 27 '37
McGinnis, E. W.  Christmas fare in the movies: Snow
White.  St. Nicholas 65:47 D '37
Snow White and the seven dwarfs.  Good Housekeeping
105:35 N; 35 D '37
Snow White and the seven dwarfs.  Scholastic 31:8 Ja 22
'38
Ferguson, O.  Walt Disney's Grimm reality.  New Re-
public 93:339 Ja 26 '38
Boone, A. R.  First full-length cartoon movie.  Popular
Science 132:50 Ja '38
Daugherty, F.  Mickey Mouse comes of age.  Christian
Science Mon Mag p8 F 2 '38
Walt Disney.  Silver Screen 8-6:51 Ap '38
Morkovin, B. V.  Cooperative imagination.  Cinema
Progress 3-2:14 My/Je '38
Awarded honorary degrees.  Time 31:28 Je 20 '38
Best, K.  Appreciation.  Stage 15:16 Je '38
Calverton, V. F.  Snow White fiasco.  Current History
48:46 Je '38
Stillwell, M.  Walt Disney's $10,000,000 surprise.  Reader
Digest 32:25 Je '36

Walt Disney, M. A. , M. S. Newsweek 12:18 Jl 4 '38

Brashares, C. W. Walt Disney as theologian. Christian Century 55:963 Ag 10 '38

Grauer, G. W. Snow White debate continues. Christian Century 55:993 Ag 17 '38

Cartoons. Theatre Arts 22:674 S '38

Ferdinand in the movies. Publisher W 134:1524 O 22 '38

Ferdinand the bull. Scholastic 33:10 N 12 '38

Baskette, K. His great new plans. Photoplay 52:48 N '38

Goofy and Wilbur. Good Housekeeping 108:84 My '39

Charlot, J. But is it art? American Scholar 8-3:260 Jl '39

Sound and laughter; why Donald Duck is irresistible even on the radio. Living Age 356:475 Jl '39

Story of Pinocchio. Good Housekeeping 109:39 O; N '39

Pinocchio; a puppet comes to life in a new color cartoon. Scholastic 35:20E D 18 '36

Martin, J. Librarian to Walt Disney. Wilson Library B 14:292 D '39

Color-shooting in fairland; building the story of Pinocchio. Popular Mechanic 73:17 Ja '40

Peterson, E. T. At home with Walt Disney. Better Home & Garden 18:13 Ja '40

Walt Disney's Pinocchio. Theatre Arts 24:6 Ja '40

Burton, T. Walt Disney's Pinocchio. Sat R 21:17 F 17 '40

Ferguson, O. It's a Disney; Pinocchio. New Republic 102:346 Mr 11 '40

Disney, Jiminy, etc. Scholastic 36:10 Ap 8 '40

Mickey preferred. Current History 51:7 Ap '40

Smith, P. J. Music of the Walt Disney cartoons. Etude 58:438 Jl '40

Cobb, J. Cartoons; Disney originals on view at Kennedy's. N. Y. Times Mag p17 Ag 18 '40

Robins, S. Disney again tries trailblazing; Fantasia. N. Y. Times Mag p6 N 3 '40

Disney's cinesymphony: Fantasia. Time 36:52 N 18 '40

Hoollering, F. Fantasia; Walt Disney plus Bach or Beethoven. Nation 151:513 N 23 '40

Ferguson, O. Both fantasy and fancy: Disney's Fantasia. New Republic 103:724 N 25 '40

Hartung, P. T. Once in a lifetime; Fantasia is a rare treat. Commonweal 23:152 N 29 '40

Gessner, R. Class in Fantasia. Nation 151:543 N 30 '40

Fantasia is a new art form in which cartoons and music combine. Scholastic 37:34 D 9 '40

Daugherty, F. How Donald comes out of the paint pots. Christian Science Mon Mag p6 D 14 '40

Hollister, P.  Walt Disney, genius at work.  Atlantic
    166:689 D '40
Biography.  Current Biography '40
Biographical note; filmog.  Movies & People 2:41 '40
Low, D.  Appreciation of his work.  New Republic 106:16
    Ja 5 '41
Mickey Mouse on parade.  Time 37:32 Ja 6 '41
Haggin, B. H.  Fantasia.  Nation 152:53 Ja 11 '41
Peck, A. P.  What makes Fantasia click?  Scientific
    American 164:28 Ja '41
MacDonald, A. S.  Midwinter Drama; Fantasia.  Inde-
    pendent Woman 20:15 Ja '41
Boone, A. R.  Mickey Mouse goes classical.  Popular
    Science 138:65 Ja '41
Isaacs, H. R.  New horizons; Fantasia and fantasound.
    Theatre Arts 25:55 Ja '41
Story of.  Ladies Home J 58:20 Mr '41
Mulvey, K.  Sketch.  Womans Home Companion 68:21
    Mr '41
Mr. and Mrs. Disney.  Ladies Home J 58:20 Mr '41
Cartoon characters lend new romance to the stars.
    Science Newsletter 39:229 Ap 12 '41
Goofy.  Good Housekeeping 112:78 Ap '41
Bower, A.  Snow White and the 1, 200 dwarfs; attempts to
    organizing the Disney employees.  Nation 152:565
    My 10 '41
Labor fantasia; NLRB forces issue of second employee
    election in Walt Disney plant.  Business Week p48
    My 17 '41
Disney designs army, navy insignia.  Life 10:10 My 26
    '41
Mulvey, K.  Keeping up with Hollywood.  Womans Home
    Companion 68:21 My '41
Disney developments.  Business Week p46 Je 14 '41
Benchley in Disneyland.  Newsweek 17:55 Je 30 '41
Hartung, P. T.  Stars, strikes and dragons.  Common-
    weal 34:377 Ag 8 '41
La Farge, C.  Walt Disney and the art form.  Theatre
    Arts 25:673 S '41
Ferguson, O.  Two for the show: Dumbo.  New Republic
    105:537 O 27 '41
Disney rides a baby elephant back into hearts of his fans.
    Newsweek 18:61 O 27 '41
Pluto lends a paw.  Good Housekeeping 113:113 O '41
Pollen man.  New Yorker 17:14 N 1 '41
Kracauer, S.  Dumbo.  Nation 153:463 N 8 '41
Low, D.  Leonardo da Disney.  New Republic 106:16 Ja 5
    '42

Disney family of carrot cartoons. N. Y. Times Mag p25 Ja 11 '42

Iwerks, U. Movie cartoons come to life. Popular Mechanic 77:34 Ja '42

Donald Duck joins up. N. Y. Times Mag p20 F 22 '42

New spirit, Disney's tax film. Life 12:48 Mr 16 '42

Rough sketches. Good Housekeeping 114:4 Mr '42

Walt and the professors. Time 39:58 Je 8 '42

Farber, M. Saccharine symphony; Bambi. New Republic 106:893 Je 29 '42

Pluto at the zoo. Good Housekeeping 115:174 Jl '42

Teacher Disney. Time 40:49 Ag 17 '42

Walt Disney goes to war. Life 13:61 Ag 31 '42

Walt Disney; great teacher; his films for war are revolutionizing the technique of education. Fortune 26:90 Ag '42

Martin, J. Bringing Bambi to the screen. Nature 35:350 Ag '42

Mickey Mouse and Donald Duck for victory. Popular Science 141:98 S '42

Hallet, Trail of Bambi; origin deep in Maine's Katahdin forests. Colliers 110:58 O 3 '42

McEvoy, J. P. Of mouse and man; from newsboy to screen magician. Reader Digest 41:85 O '42

Movie cartoons show how an antitank gun works. Popular Science 141:62 O '42

Disney's troupe goes to war. N. Y. Times Mag p20 N 15 '42

Bambi. Good Housekeeping 115:4 S; 8 O; 4 N '42

Crichton, K. Riot from Rio; Disney's South American film. Colliers 110:90 D 19 '42

Delehanty, T. Disney studio at war. Theatre Arts 27:31 Ja '43

Wanger, W. Film phenomena. Sat R 26:19 F 6 '43

Jacobson, E. People you know. Sat Evening Post 215: 35 My 15 '43

Pluto. Good Housekeeping 117:14 Jl '43

Donald Duck. Good Housekeeping 117:11 Ag '43

Wanger, W. Mickey Icarus, 1943. Sat R 26:18 S 4 '43

Goofy. Good Housekeeping 117:8 S '43

Mickey Mouse and Donald Duck join the colors. School Arts 43:7 S '43

How Disney combines living actors with his cartoon characters. Popular Science 145:106 S '44

Ahl, F. N. Techniques in educational films. Social Studies 35:344 D '44

Saga of Pluto. N. Y. Times Mag p28 F 4 '45

But is it art?   Business Week p72 F 10 '45
Reid, A.   Mr. Disney's dream world.   Colliers 115:33
    F 24 '45
Brown, J. M.   Seeing things.   Sat R 28:22 F 24 '45
Churchill, E.   Walt Disney's animated war.   Flying 36:50
    Mr '45
Studio artists pose Donald Duck for the old masters of
    art.   Life 18:10 Ap 16 '45
Daugherty, F.   Donald's back again!   Christian Science
    Mon Mag p14 N 10 '45
Stuffed duck?   Time 46:98 D 3 '45
Farber, M.   Make mine Muzak.   New Republic 114:769
    My 27 '46
Rivkin, A.   Hollywood letter.   Free World 11:62 My '46
MacGowan, K.   Work of.   Hollywood Q 1:376 Jl '46
Stanford, B.   Disney's health films.   Discovery 7:255
    Ag '46
Mosdell, D.   His full-length picture technique.   Canadian
    Forum 26:180 N '46
Mad cocktail party.   Time 48:31 D 2 '46
Nugent, F.   That million-dollar mouse.   N. Y. Times
    Mag p22 S 21 '47
Mr. Harper.   After hours.   Harper 196:573 Je '48
Mighty Mouse.   Time 52:96 O 25 '48
What I know about girls.   Parents 24:22 Ja '49
Wallace, I.   Mickey Mouse and how he grew.   Colliers
    123:20 Ap 9 '49
Mosdell, D.   Work of.   Canadian Forum 29:206 D '49
Money from mice.   Newsweek 35:84 F 13 '50
Brown, J. M.   Recessional.   Sat R 33:28 Je 3 '50
Disney, W.   How I cartooned "Alice."   Films In Review
    2-5:7 My '51
Battle of wonderland.   Time 58:90 Jl 16 '51
Biography.   Current Biography Ap '52
    Same.   Current Biography Yearbook 1952:148 '53
Starr, C.   Animation: abstracts and concrete.   Sat R
    35:46 D 13 '52
Peter Pan; real Disney magic.   Newsweek 41:96 F 16 '53
Walt Disney builds half-pint history.   Popular Science
    162:118 F '53
Disney, Mrs. W.   I live with a genius.   McCalls 80:39
    F '53
What I've learned about animals.   American 155:22 F '53
He'll double as a top-notch salesman.   Business Week
    p43 Mr 21 '53
Silver anniversary for Walt and Mickey.   Life 35:82 N '53
Alexander, J.   Amazing story of Walt Disney.   Sat

Evening Post 226:24 O 31; 225:27 N 7 '53

Lubin, E. R. Disney is still creative. Films In Review 5-3:115 Mr '54

Disney comes to TV. Newsweek 43:85 Ap 12 '54

Whitcomb, J. Girls behind Disney's characters. Cosmop 136:50 My '54

Why I like making nature films. Womans Home Companion 81:38 My '54

Wirsig, W. Disneyland; going onto television. Womans Home Companion 81:12 Je '54

Fishwick, M. Aesop in Hollywood. Sat R 37:38 Jl 10 '55

Lurking camera. Atlantic 194:23 Ag '54

Disney on the dial. Newsweek 44:62 N 8 '54

Row, D. Leonardo da Disney. New Republic 131:42 N 22 '54

Minoff, P. He sets a Disney pace. Cue 23-52:14 D 25 '54

Disney does it again. Newsweek 44:60 D 27 '54

Father goose. Time 64:42 D 27 '54

Wood, C. TV personalities biographical sketch book. TV Personalities p96 '54

Starr, C. Professional movies for home showing. House Beautiful 97:147 F '55

McEvoy, J. P. McEvoy in Disneyland. Reader Digest 66:19 F '55

Wonderful world. Newsweek 45:60 Ap 18 '55

Mouse that turned to gold. Business Week p72 Jl 9 '55

Spectacular plus. Newsweek 46:32 Jl 25 '55

Gordon, A. Walt Disney. Look 19:29 Jl 26 '55

Greatest triple play in show business. Reader Digest 67:69 Jl '55

Newest travel lure, Disneyland. Travel 104:16 Jl '55

Disneyland. Life 39:39 Ag 15 '55

Eddy, D. Amazing secret of Walt Disney. American 160:29 Ag '55

Kids' dream world come true. Popular Science 167:92 Ag '55

Lipton, N. C. Disneyland's circarama. Popular Photo 39:96 D '55

Disney, M. S., M. A. CTA 51:6 D '55

McKenney, J. D. Walt Disney, showman and educator, remembers Daisy. CTA 51:4 D '55

Woodson, W. D. Through the jungles of Disneyland. American Forests 62:20 Ja '56

Walt Disney receives Audubon medal. Audubon 58:25 Ja '56

Liston, J. M.  Land that does away with time.  Better
Home & Garden 34:62 F '56
Rare antiques in Disneyland.  American Home 56:14 S '56
Sound effects and realism at Disneyland.  Radio & TV
News 56:52 Ag '56
Stoltz, J. H.  Steamboat 'round the bend.  Scholastic
69:75 N 8 '56
How they evolved, story of Walt Disney.  Sat Evening
Post 229:160 N 17 '56
Miller, D.  My dad, Walt Disney.  Sat Evening Post
229:25 N 17; 26 N 24; 29 D 1; 38 D 8; 36 D 15;
24 D 22; 24 D 29 '56; 24 Ja 5 '57
Biography.  Colliers Yearbook 1956:518 '56
Clean sweep for Disneyland.  American City 72:15 F '57
Gay '90s favorites from Main Street, Disneyland.  Better
Home & Garden 35:96 My '57
How to make a buck.  Time 70:76 Jl 29 '57
If you plan to visit Disneyland.  Sunset 119:16 Ag '57
McHugh, T.  Walt Disney's mechanical wonderland.
Popular Mechanic 108:138 N '57
Halevy, J.  Disneyland and Las Vegas.  Nation 186:510
Je 7 '58
Disneyland discussion.  Nation 186:1 Je 28 '58
Cahn, R.  Intrepid kids of Disneyland.  Sat Evening Post
230:22 Je 28 '58
Electronics at Disneyland.  Radio & TV News 59:39 Je '58
Disneyland and son.  Time 73:54 Je 29 '59
Disneyland adds submarine and monorail.  Popular
Mechanic 112:77 Jl '59
Stranvinsky replies to Walt Disney.  Sat R 43:81 Mr 12
'60
Wolfert, I.  Walt Disney's magic kingdom.  Reader Digest
76:144 Ap '60
Martin, P.  Walt Disney shoots the works.  Sat Evening
Post 233:38 D 10 '60
Christmas in Disneyland.  Sunset 125:42 D '60
Smith, E. M.  Keeping Disneyland in proportion.  Hor-
ticulture 39:27 Ja '61
Gardener's visit to Disneyland.  Sunset 126:100 Mr '61
Miller, W. L.  Marginal utility in the Magic kingdom.
New Republic 145:21 Ag 21 '61
Wolters, L.  Wonderful world of Walt Disney.  Todays
Health 40:26 Ap '62
Wide world of Walt Disney.  Newsweek 60:48 D 31 '62
Menen, A.  Dizzled in Disneyland.  Holiday 34:68 Jl '63
DeRoos, R.  Magic worlds of Walt Disney.  National
Geographic 14:1570 Ag '63

Wallace, K.   Onward and upward with the arts.   New
    Yorker 39:104 S 7 '63
Cohen, D.   Preview of Disney's world's fair shows.
    Science Digest 54:8 D '63
Zimmermann, G.   Giant at the fair.   Look 28:28 F 11
    '64
Birmingham, S.   Greatest one-man show on earth.
    McCalls 91:98 Jl '64
Davidson, B.   Fantastic Walt Disney.   Sat Evening Post
    237:66 N 7 '64
Birmingham, S.   Imagination unlimited.   Reader Digest
    85:272 N '64
Ciardi, J.   Foamrubbersville.   Sat R 42:20 Je 19 '65
Litwak, L. E.   Fantasy that paid off.   N. Y. Times Mag
    p22 Je 27 '65
Tinker Bell, Mary Poppins, cold cash.   Newsweek 66:74
    Jl 12 '65
Disney's live-action profits.   Business Week p78 Jl 24 '65
Whitaker, F.   Day with Disney.   American Artist 29:44
    S '65
Sayers, F. C.   Too long at the sugar bowls.   Library J
    90:4538 O 15 '65
Bradbury, R.   Machine-tooled happyland.   Holiday 38:100
    O '65
Disneyland East.   Newsweek 66:82 N 29 '65
Sayers, F. C.   Walt Disney accused; interview.   Horn
    Book 41:602 D '65
Scholastic and Disney sign book agreement.   Publisher W
    , 189:30 Ap 4 '66
Magic kingdom.   Time 87:84 Ap 15 '66
McDonald, J.   Now the bankers come to Disney.   Fortune
    73:139 My '66
AFA honors Walt Disney.   American Forests 72:10 D '66
Obit.   British Book Year 1967:591 '67
    Broadcasting 71:72 D 19 '66
    Current Biography 28:45 F '67
    Current Biography Yearbook 1967:473 '68
    Economist 221:1327 D 24 '66
    Film R p21 '66/68
    Illustrated London N 249:16 D 24 '66
    National R 19:17 Ja 10 '67
    N. Y. Times p1 D 16 '66
    Newsweek 68:57 D 26 '66
    Screen World 18:234 '67
    Senior Scholastic 89:17 Ja 6 '67
    Time 88:71 D 23 '66
Funeral.   N. Y. Times p33 D 17 '66

Morgenstern, J. Walt Disney, imagineer of fun. Newsweek 68:68 D 26 '66

Nathan, P. Footnote to Walt. Publisher W 191:48 Ja 2 '67

Mineral king proposal. American Forests 73:21 F '67

Walt Disney films; filmog. Film Fan Mo 68:entire issue F '67

Bright, J. Disney's fantasy empire. Nation 204:299 Mr 6 '67

Bigart, H. Men who made the world move. Sat R 50:63 Ap 22 '67

Rider, D. Walt Disney. Film 48:21 Spg '67

Reddy, J. Living legacy of Walt Disney. Reader Digest 90:165 Je '67

Disney with Walt. Forbes 100:39 Jl 1 '67

Izard, R. S. Walt Disney: master of laughter and learning. Peabody J Education 45:36 Jl '67

Maltin, L. Walt Disney's films; filmog. Films In Review 18-8:457 O '67

Sheed, W. Films. Esquire 68:26 N '67

Kreuger, M. In the limelight. American Record G 34:346 D '67

Rialp, F. Walt Disney; additional filmog. Films In Review 19-3:191 Mr '68

Schickel, R. Bringing forth the mouse; excerpt from The Disney version. American Heritage 19:24 Ap '68

Schickel, R. Myth and reality; excerpt from The Disney version. American Heritage 19:94 Ap '68

Uncle Walt. Time 91:82 My 3 '58

First complaint; Walt Disney commemorative stamp. Christian Century 85:739 My 29 '68

Smith, D. R. Additional filmog. Films In Review 19-5:313 My '68

What, no Donald Duck? Newsweek 72:35 S 23 '68

Kilgore, A. The Disney assault. Film Fan Mo 87:3 S '68

Bayer, A. Happy 40th, Mickey. Life 65:57 O 25 '68

Disney, R. Unforgettable Walt Disney. Reader Digest 94:212 F '69

Marx, W. Disney imperative. Nation 209:76 Jl 28 '69

Disney without Walt. Newsweek 74:90 O 20 '69

Murray, T. Men who followed Mickey Mouse. Duns R 94:34 D '69

Beckerman, H. From Steamboat Willie to The yellow submarine. Making Films 3-6:14 D '69

Tripping on Disney. Newsweek 75:88 Ja 19 '70

Maltin, L. The Disney studio today. Film Fan Mo 104:19 F '70

Zinsser, W.  Walt Disney's psychedelic Fantasia.  Life
    68:15 Ap 3 '70
Rider, D.  Disney world.  Films & Filming 16-9:95 Je '70
Disney on parade.  Newsweek 67:69 O 5 '70
Ten greatest men of American business as you picked
    them.  Nations Business 59:46 Mr '71
Goldberger, P.  Mickey Mouse teaches the architects.
    N. Y.  Times Mag p40 O 22 '70

DITVOORST, ADRIAAN
    Biographical note.  International Film G 5:118 '68
    Biographical note.  International Film G 8:209 '71

DJURKOVIC, DEJAN
    Biographical note.  International Film G 8:283 '71

DMYTRYK, EDWARD
    English, R.  What makes a Hollywood communist?  Sat
        Evening Post 223:30 My 19 '51
    Reply to R. English.  Nation 172:482 My 26 '51
    Dyer, E. V.  Letter.  Films In Review 10-7:438 Ag/S
        '59
    Tozzi, R.  Edward Dmytryk; filmog.  Films In Review
        13-2:86  F '62
    Nolan, J. E.  Edward Dmytryk.  Films In Review 13-2:
        86  F '62
    Dmytryk, E.  The director and the editor.  Action 4-2:23
        Mr/Ap '69
    Dmytryk, E.  Whose is the right of the first cut?
        Making Films 3-3:11 Je '69
    The cinema of Edward Dmytryk.  Films Illustrated 1-4:14
        O '71

DOLLER, MIKHAIL
    Obit.  N. Y.  Times p92 Mr 23 '52

DONEHUE, VINCENT J.
    Obit.  Screen World 18:234 '67

DONEN, STANLEY
    Knight, A.  From dance to film director.  Dance 28:21
        Ag '54
    Knight, A.  Dance in the movies.  Dance 32:13 O '58
    What to do with star quality.  Films & Filming 6-11:11
        Ag '60
    Moanin' for Donen; filmog.  Film 27:21 Ja/F '61
    Luft, H. G.  Donen at work.  Films In Review 12-2:127
        F '61

Sarris, A.    Esoterica; filmog.    Film Culture 28:22 Spg
    '63
Quotemanship.    Action 3-3:20 Jl/Ag '68
Lloyd, P.    Stanley Donen.    Brighton Film R 18:17 Mr '70

DONIOL-VALCRAZE, JACQUES
    Three directors.    Films & Filming 7-1:12 O '60

DONNER, CLIVE
    Donner, C.    These are the most selfish actors of all.
        Films & Filming 4-7:7 Ap '58
    British feature directors; an index to their work.    Sight &
        Sound 27-6:293 Aut '58
    A free hand.    Sight & Sound 28-2:60 Spg '59
    Perkins, V. F.    Clive Donner and some people.    Movie
        3:22 O '62
    Cameron, I. & Shivas, M.    What's new pussycat; inter-
        view.    Movie 14:12 Aut '65
    Joyce, P.    Nothing but the best?    Film 45:16 Spg '66
    Gow, G.    The urge of some people.    Films & Filming
        15-10:4 Jl '69
    British cinema filmography.    Film 65:10 Spg '72

DONNER, JÖRN
    Donner, J.    After three films.    Sight & Sound 35-4:190
        Aut '66
    Jorn Donner: an outsider at home.    Films & Filming
        15-3:70 D '68
    Reyner, L.    Jorn Donner.    Film 54:33 Spg '69
    Biographical note.    International Film G 6:67 '69
    Donner, J.    After six films.    Sight & Sound 39-2:75
        Spg '70
    Director of the year; filmog.    International Film G p17
        '72

DONNER, VYVYAN
    Obit.    Screen World 17:236 '66

DONSKOY, MARK (Also  DONSKOI)
    Gillett, J.    Mark Donskoy; filmog.    Focus On Film 1:10
        Mr/Ap '70
    Hibbin, N.    Director of the year; filmog.    International
        Film G 8:15 '71

DORSKY, NATHANIEL
    Listing of films.    Film Culture 37:7 Sum '62

dos SANTOS, NELSON PEREIRA
Viany, A.   Who's who in the cinema novo.   CTVD 6-1:27
Fall '68

DOUGLAS, GORDAN
Maltin, L.   Making of a pro.   Action 5-6:19 N/D '70

DOVZHENKO, ALEXANDER
Peet, C.   Poet who works with a motion picture camera.
Outlook 156:353 O 29 '30
Leyda, J.   An index to the creative work of Alexander
Dovzhenko.   Sight & Sound (special sup) Index Series
# 12 N '47
Obit.   N. Y. Times p38 N 27 '56
Shibeck, C.   Dovzhenko and Dupont; letter.   Films In
Review 8-2:93 F '57
Montagu, I.   Dovzhenko--poet of life eternal.   Sight &
Sound 27-1:44 Sum '57
Robinson, D.   Dovzhenko.   Silent Pic 8:11 Aut '70
Carynnyk, M.   The Dovzhenko papers; filmog.   Film
Comment 7-3:34 Fall '71

DOWNEY, ROBERT (A Prince)
Listing of films.   Film Culture 37:7 Sum '65
Brenner, R.   Truth and soul the Robert Downey way.
After Dark 11-2:40 Je '69
Mahoney, S.   Robert Downey makes vile movies.   Life
67:63 N 28 '69
Downey's Pound.   New Yorker 46:30 F 28 '70
Downey, R.   Past master (Preston Sturges).   New York
3-33:46 Ag 17 '70
Sarlin, B.   Robert Downey goes to the dogs.   Show
1-6:59 O '70

DOWNS, ALLEN
Survey among unsuccessful applicants for the Ford
Foundation film grants.   Film Comment 2-3:10
Sum '64
Film Comment announces the recipients of the 1964
anniversary awards.   Film Comment 2-3:3 Sum '64

DRAGIĆ, NEDELJKO
Biographical note.   International Film G 7:248 '70

DRASIN, DAN
Mekas, J.   Notes on the new American cinema.   Film
Culture 24:6 Spg '62

DRASKOVIC,  BORO
  Biographical note.   International Film G 8:282 '71

DREYER,  CARL
  Winge, J. H.   Interview.   Sight & Sound 18-72:16 Ja '50
  Rowland, R.   Carl Dreyer's world.   Hollywood Q 5-1:53
    Fall '50
  Moor, P.   Tyrannical Dane.   Theatre Arts 35:35 Ap '51
  Dreyer, C. T.   Film style.   Films In Review 3-1:15
    Ja '52
  Fenns, M.   Carl Dreyer's new film.   Films In Review
    6-1:19 Ja '55
  The big screens.   Sight & Sound 24-4:209 Spg '55
  Neergaard, E.   The word.   Sight & Sound 24-4:172 Spg
    '55
  Luft, H. G.   Dreyer's next picture; letter.   Films In
    Review 6-9:478 N '55
  Dreyer, C.   Thoughts on my craft.   Sight & Sound 25-3:
    128 Win '55/56
  Trolle, B.   The world of Carl Dreyer.   Sight & Sound
    25-3:122 Win '55/56
  Everson, W. K.   Rudy Mate: his work with Carl Dreyer.
    Films & Filming 2-2:7 N '55
  Marcussen, E. B.   Danish film production.   American
    Scandanavian R 43:338 D '55
  Luft, H. G.   Carl Dreyer--a master of his craft.   Q
    Film Radio TV 11-2:181 Win '56
  Gunsten, D.   Filmmaker of genius.   American Scanda-
    navian R 46:229 S '58
  Talmey, A.   Men of the North.   Vogue 137:89 Ap 15 '61
  Luft, H.   Dreyer, an interview.   Films & Filming
    7-9:11 Je '61
  Cowie, P.   Dreyer at 75.   Films & Filming 10-6:45 Mr
    '64
  Kelman, K.   Dreyer; filmog.   Film Culture 35:1 Win
    '64/65
  Milne, T.   Darkness and light.   Sight & Sound 34-4:167
    Aut '65
  Bond, K.   The world of Carl Dreyer.   Film Q 19-1:26
    Fall '65
  An interview with Carl Th. Dreyer.   Film Culture 41:58
    Sum '66
  Lerner, C.   My way of working is in relation to the
    future; interview.   Film Comment 4-1:62 Fall '66
  Delahaye, M.   Interview.   Cahiers (Eng) 4:7 '66
  Duperley, D.   Carl Dreyer, utter bore?  or total genius?
    Films & Filming 14-5:45 F '68

Obit.   N. Y.  Times p47 Mr 21 '68
   Newsweek 71:100 Ap 1 '68
   Screen World 21:233 '70
Hart, H.   Carl Theodore Dreyer: 1889-1968.   Films In
   Review 19-4:193 Ap '68
Monty, I.   Great Dane.   Sight & Sound 37-2:75 Spg '68
Luft, H. G.   A tribute to Carl Th. Dreyer.   Cinema (BH)
   4-2:48 Sum '68
Drum, D. D.   Carl Dreyer's shorts; filmog. of shorts.
   Films In Review 20-1:34 Ja '69
Drum, D. D.   Another Dreyer vignette.   Films In Re-
   view 20-4:26 Ap '69
Dreyer in double reflection; an annotated translation of
   Carl Dreyer's 1946 essay A little on film style.
   Cinema (BH) 6-2:8 Fall '70
Patterson, G. G.   Eloquent though silent.   Filmograph
   1-4:31 '70
Bordwell, D.   Carl Dreyer's Jesus film.   Film Comment
   8-2:59 Sum '72


DUARTE, ANSELMO
   Viany, A.   Who's who in the cinema novo.   CTVD 5-4:26
   Sum '68


DUDOW, SLATAN
   Bean, R.   The face of '63--Germany.   Films & Filming
   9-9:41 Je '63


DULAC, GERMAINE
   Obit.   N. Y  Times p19 Jl 23 '42
   Blumer, R. H.   The camera as snowball: France 1918-
   1927.   Cinema J 9-2:31 Spg '70
   Feldman, J. & H.   Women directors.   Films In Review
   1-8:9 N '50
   Pyros, J.   Notes on women directors.   Take One 3-2:7
   N/D '70
   Cornwell, R.   Activists of the avant-garde.   Film Library
   Q 5-1:29 Win '71/72


DUNNE, PHILIP
   Screenwriters symposium; filmog.   Film Comment 6-4:86
   Win '70/71


DUNNING, GEORGE
   Interview.   International Film G 1:163 '64

DUPONT, EWALD ANDRÉ
    Fraenkel, H.   Sketch.   Motion Pic Classic 23:52 Ap '26
    Devensky, D.   Ewald Andre Dupont, a one-time genius?
        Classic Film Collector 36:18 Fall '72

DUPONT, JACQUES
    Three directors.   Films & Filming 7-1:12 O '60

DURSTON, DAVID E.
    How do you make a color film on a tiny budget and make
        it good?   Making Films 3-4:43 Ag '69

DUVIVIER, JULIEN
    Biographical note; filmog.   Movies & People 2:41 '40
    Biography.   Current Biography '43
    Biographical note.   Unifrance 10:5 Je '51
    The directors choose the best films.   Cinema (BH) 1-5:14
        Ag/S '63
    Obit.   British Book Year 1968:589 '68
        Current Biography 29:45 Ja '68
        Current Biography Yearbook 1968:454 '69
        N. Y. Times p45 O 30 '67
        Newsweek 70:67 N 13 '67
        Screen World 19:231 '68
        Time 90:90 N 10 '67

DWAN, ALLAN
    Biographical note.   Photoplay 9-4:42 Mr '16
    Johnson, J.   A brief memorandum on Allan Dwan.
        Photoplay 11-6:70 My '17
    Cheatham, M. S.   Interview.   Motion Pic 18:52 D '19
    Haskins, H.   Interview.   Motion Pic Classic 10:21 Je '20
    St. Johns, A. R.   Interview.   Photoplay 18:56 Ag '20
    Bruce, B.   Interview.   Motion Pic 20:38 S '20
    Fletcher, A. W.   Interview.   Motion Pic 25:24 F '23
    Pope, F. T.   Interview.   Photoplay 24:63 S '23
    Wilson, B.   Interview.   Classic 20:38 D '24
    Sketch.   National 53:356 Mr '25
    Must actors have temperament?   Motion Pic 31:53 F '26
    Biographical note; filmog.   Movies & People 2:41 '40
    Sarris, A.   Esoterica; filmog.   Film Culture 28:22 Spg
        '63
    Smith, J. M.   Allan Dwan.   Brighton Film R 17:17 F '70
    Schikel, R.   Good days, good years.   Harper 241:46 O '70
    Dwan, A.   As it was.   Making Films 5-3:35 Je '71
    What directors are saying.   Action 6-4:20 Jl/Ag '71

DWOSKIN, STEPHEN
  Dawson, J. & Johnston, C.   More British sounds.   Sight
    & Sound 39-3:144 Sum '70
  British cinema filmography.   Film 65:10 Spg '72

EADY, DAVID
  Filmography.   Film 14:8 N/D '57

EAGLE, ARNOLD
  Kevles, B. L.   Interview.   Film Culture 38:35 Fall '65
  Weinberg, G.   The backroom boys.   Film Culture 41:87
    Sum '66

EAMES, CHARLES
  Twirling toy run by sun.   Life 44:22 Mr 24 '58
  Solar powered display.   Radio & TV News 60:39 D '38
  Talmey, A.   Eames.   Vogue 134:124 Ag 15 '59
  Personalities.   Progressive Architecture 41:59 Ag '60
  Huxtable, A. L.   Designers with a dash.   N. Y. Times
    Mag p77 N 6 '60
  Peter, J.   Visit with Charles Eames.   Look 25:58b
    Je 20 '61
  Biography.   Current Biography 26:9 Ja '65
    Same.   Current Biography Yearbook 1965:139 '65
  Anti-casting couch.   Time 95:37 Ja 5 '70
  Schrader, P.   The films of Charles Eames; filmog.
    Film Q 23-3:2 Spg '70

EASON, REEVES (BREEZY)
  Marshall, J.   Catastrophe maker.   Colliers 118:28
    Ag 10 '46
  Obit.   N. Y. Times p37 Je 13 '56

EDMONDS, ROBERT
  Edmonds, R.   Chicago style.   Action 4-4:29 Jl/Ag '69

EDWARDS, BLAKE
  Franklyn, I. R.   Blake Edwards.   Films In Review
    10-4:249 Ap '59
  Sarris, A.   Esoterica; filmog.   Film Culture 28:22 Spg
    '63
  Zeitlin, D.   Greatest pie fight ever creates a horrendous
    splaat!   Life 59:84 Jl 9 '65
  Hauduroy, J. F.   Interview.   Cahiers (Eng) 3:21 '66
  Haller, R.   Peter Gunn: the private eye of Blake Edwards.
    Film Heritage 3-4:21 Sum '68
  Filmography.   Film Comment 6-4:101 Win '70/71
  Lightman, H. A.   Wild rovers; case history of a film.
    American Cinematographer 52-7:654 Jl '71

EDWARDS, WALTER
   Biographical note.   Photoplay 9-4:42 Mr '16

EICHBERG, RICHARD
   Obit.   N. Y. Times p23 My 9 '52

EISENSTEIN, SERGEI M.
   Mass movies.   Nation 125:507 N 9 '27
   Krutch, J. W.   Season in Moscow.   Nation 126:716
      Je 27 '28
   Richman, A.   S. M. Eisenstein.   Dial 86:311 Ap '29
   Eisenstein and Pudovkin.   Theatre Arts 13:664 S '29
   Heiman, B.   Sketch.   Theatre 52:16 Jl '30
   Calhoun, D.   Interview.   Motion Pic Classic 32:58 O '30
   Mirsky, D. S.   The art of Eisenstein.   Virginia Q R
      7:522 O '31
   Wilson, E.   Eisenstein in Hollywood.   New Republic
      68:320 N 4 '31
   Mexican film and Marxian theory.   New Republic 69:99
      D 9 '31
   Eisenstein on Hollywood.   Cinema Digest 1-1:8 My 16 '32
   Eisenstein's plans.   Living Age 342:462 Jl '32
   Maugard, A. B.   Mexico into cinema.   Theatre Arts
      16:926 N '32
   Sinclair, U.   Thunder over Eisenstein.   New Republic
      75:210 Jl 5 '33
   Troy, W.   Eisenstein muddle.   Nation 137:83 Jl 19 '33
   Discussion.   New Republic 75:344 Ag 9; 76:49 S 6 '33
   Woodward, H.   Eisenstein and Upton Sinclair; reply to
      W. Troy.   Nation 137:410 O 11 '33
   Kunitz, J.   Eisenstein's resurgence.   New Republic
      98:222 Mr 29 '39
   Hoellering, F.   Eisenstein has been subordinated to the
      orders of the monolithic state.   Nation 148:413 Ap 8 '39
   Maddow, B.   Eisenstein and the historical films.   Holly-
      wood Q 1-1:26 O '45
   Boos and bravos.   Time 47:93 Ap 1 '46
   Biography.   Current Biography 7:20 My '46
      Same.   Current Biography Yearbook 1946:175 '47
   Soviet movies.   Life 21:91 O 14 '46
   Agee, J.   Films.   Nation 164:495 Ap 26 '47
   Eisenstein, S. M.   Purveyors of spiritual poison.   Sight &
      Sound 16-63:103 Aut '47
   Obit.   Current Biography 9:9 Mr '48
      Current Biography Yearbook 1948:184 '49
      N. Y. Times p24 F 12 '48
      Newsweek 31:58 F 23 '48

Time 51:96 F 23 '48

Down with marazm. Time 51:36 F 23 '48

Lania, L. The man who died twice. U. S. World 2:20 Ap '48

Wollenberg, H. H. Two masters. Sight & Sound 17-65: 46 Spg '48

Solski, W. His career: case history of an artist under dictatorship. Commentary 7:252 Mr '49

Eisenstein, S. M. Dickens, Griffith and the film today. Sight & Sound 19-4:169 Je; 19-5:216 Jl; 19-6:256 Ag; 19-7:294 N '50

Seton, M. Vignettes of Eisenstein. Films In Review 2-4:29 Ap '51

Seton, M.; Reisz, K.; McLeod, L. Unfair to Eisenstein? Sight & Sound 20-2:54 Je '51

Ingster, B. Sergei Eisenstein. Hollywood Q 5-4:380 Sum '51

Burford, R. Eisenstein's religiosity. Films In Review 4-2:110 F '53

Seton, M. Eisenstein's images and Mexican art. Sight & Sound 23-1:8 Jl/S '53

Seton, M. Taking Eisenstein to France. Film 2:19 D '54

Leyda, J. Eisenstein's Mexican tragedy. Sight & Sound 27-6:305 Aut '58

Sylvester, D. Strike. New Statesman 56:490 O 11 '58

Leyda, J. Eisenstein's Bezhin Meadow. Sight & Sound 28-2:74 Spg '59

Eisenstein, S. One path to colour. Sight & Sound 30-2:84 Spg '61

Leyda, J. Care of the past. Sight & Sound 31:47 Win '61

Sarris, A. Beyond the fringe. Film Culture 28:29 Spg '63

Berson, A. & Keller, J. Shame and glory in the movies. National R 16:17 Ja 14 '64; Correction 16:124 F 11 '64

Eisenstein--the facts; filmog. International Film G 1:49 '64

Gettesman, R. Sergei Eisenstein and Upton Sinclair. Sight & Sound 34-3:142 Sum '65

Eisenstein, S. M. Organic unity and pathos in the composition of Potemkin. Cahiers (Eng) 3:26 '66

Robinson, D. The two Bezhin Meadows. Sight & Sound 37-1:33 Win '67/68

Levine, N. Influence of the Kabuki theater on the films of Eisenstein. Modern Drama 12:18 My '69

Sklar, R. Griffith's Russian fans. Nation 211:249 S 2 '70

Morse, D.   Style in Ivan the terrible.   Monogram 1:28
   Ap '71
Hill, S. P.   Le Kuleshov; reminiscences of Eisenstein.
   Film Journal 1-3/4:28 Fall/Win '72
Kuleshov, L.   A critique of Eisenstein's films.   Film
   Journal 1-3/4:31 Fall/Win '72

EKMAN, HASSE
   Gohrn-Ohm, M.   Hasse Ekman.   American Scandanavian
   R 36:47 Mr '48
   Note.   International Film G 2:41 '65

ELDRIDGE, JOHN
   Filmography.   Film 14:8 N/D '57

ELEK, JUDIT
   Biographical note.   International Film G 7:136 '70

EL-MAZZAOUI, FARID
   El-Mazzaoui, F.   Film in Egypt.   Hollywood Q 4-3:245
   Spg '50

ELVEY, MAURICE
   Interview.   N.Y. Dramatic Mirror 68:8 N 6 '12
   British feature directors; an index to their work.   Sight &
   Sound 27-6:293 Aut '58
   Obit.   N.Y. Times p37 Ag 29 '67
   Screen World 19:232 '68

EMMER, LUCIANO
   Margolis, H. F.   Luciano Emmer and the art film.
   Theatre Arts 30:461 Ag '46
   Margolis, H. F.   Luciano Emmer and the art film.
   Sight & Sound 16-61:1 Spg '47
   The film renaissance in Italy.   Hollywood Q 2-4:353 Jl
   '47
   Koval, F.   Interview with Emmer.   Sight & Sound 19-9:
   354 Ja '51

EMSHWILLER, ED
   Emshwiller, E.   A statement; filmog.   Film Culture
   29:71 Sum '63
   Listing of films.   Film Culture 37:7 Sum '65
   Mullins, J.   Interview; filmog.   Film Culture 42:107
   Fall '66
   Mancia, A. & Van Dyke, W.   Four artists as filmmakers.
   Art In America 55:69 Ja '67

Whitehall, R.   The films of Ed Emshwiller.   Film Q
   20-3:46 Spg '67
Whitehall, R.   Relativity re-affirms Emshwiller's stature.
   Filmmakers Newsletter 1-1:6 N '67
Weiner, P.   New American cinema; filmog.   Film 58:22
   Spg '70

ENDFIELD, CYRIL (Cy)
   Endfield, C.   The inhibitions of filmmakers.   Film 15:10
   Ja/F '58

ENGEL, MORRIS
   Long way from Hollywood.   Womans Home Companion
   83:22 N '56
   Mekas, J.   Morris Engel: the low-budget feature.   Film
   Culture 24:7 Spg '62
   Bellow, S.   Art of going it alone.   Horizon 5:108 S '62

ENGLE, HARRISON
   (Frequent contributor to Film Comment)

ENGLISH, EDWARD
   Survey among unsuccessful applicants for the Ford
   Foundation film grants.   Film Comment 2-3:10 Sum '64

ENGLISH, JOHN
   Fernett, G.   Jack English looks back.   Classic Film
   Collector 21:52 Sum '68
   Malcomson, R. M.   The sound serial.   Views & Reviews
   3-1:13 Sum '71

ENRICO, ROBERT
   Graham, P.   The face of '63--France.   Films & Filming
   9-8:13 My '63

ENRIGHT, RAY
   Parsons, L. O.   Cosmopolitan's citation for the best
   direction of the month.   Cosmop 124:13 F '48
   Obit.   Screen World 17:236 '66

ERENDS, RONNY
   Biographical note.   International Film G 6:132 '69

ERIKSEN, DAN
   We need studios, yes! but we need producers more.
   Making Films 1-4:12 O '67

ERSKINE, CHESTER
  Barnes, H.   His plans for the season.   Theatre 52:14
    Ag/S '30

ESCOREL, EDUARDO
  Viany, A.   Who's who in the cinema novo.   CTVD
    5-4:26 Sum '68

ESPINOSA, JULIO GARCIA
  Douglas, M. E.   The Cuban cinema; filmog.   Take One
    1-12:6 Jl/Ag '68
  Espinosa, J. G.   Peru, for an imperfect cinema.   CTVD
    8-1(29):20 Spg '71
  Espinosa, J. G.   For an imperfect cinema.   Afterimage
    3:55 Sum '71

ÉTAIX, PIERRE
  Graham, P.   The face of '63--France.   Films & Filming
    9-8:13 My '63

EVANS, DARYL
  The lure of the feature film.   Making Films 3-1:12 F '69

EVANS, MAX
  Evans, M.   Directing The wheel.   American Cinema-
    tographer 53-5:527 My '72

FÁBRI, ZOLTÁN
Biographical note. International Film G 2:94 '65

FAIRCHILD, WILLIAM
Filmography. Film 14:8 N/D '57
British feature directors; an index to their work. Sight &
Sound 27-6:294 Aut '58

FANCK, ARNOLD
Trace, M. Upon that mountain. Silent Pic 14:31 Spg '72

FANT, KENNE
Note. International Film G 2:41 '65

FARIAS, ROBERTO
Viany, A. Who's who in the cinema novo. CTVD 5-4:26
Sum '68

FARROW, JOHN
Farrow wins Catholic literary award. Publisher W
144:2030 N 27 '43
Parsons, L. O. Cosmopolitan's citation for the best
direction of the month. Cosmop 125:13 N '48
Obit. British Book Year 1964:623 '64
N. Y. Times p7 Ja 29 '63
Newsweek 61:63 F 11 '63
Screen World 15:220 '64
Time 81:70 F 8 '63

FASSBINDER, RAINER WERNER
Wilson, D. Anti-cinema. Sight & Sound 41-2:99 Spg '72

FEIGELSON, JULIUS D.
Feigelson, J. D. The windsplitter. American Cinematographer 52-8:768 Ag '71

FEIST, FELIX
Obit. N. Y. Times p21 S 4 '65

FEJER, TAMAS
Biographical note. International Film G 1:103 '64

FEJOS, PAUL
Wunscher, C. Paul Fejos. Films In Review 5-3:124 Mr '54

Kraft, R.  Fejos' Broadway; letter.  Films In Review
   5-4:204 Ap '54

## FELDMAN, HARRY
Survey among unsuccessful applicants for the Ford
   Foundation film grants.  Film Comment 2-3:10 Sum '64

## FELDMAN, ROBERT
Film Comment announces the recipients of the 1964 anniversary awards.  Film Comment 2-3:3 Sum '64

## FELLINI, FEDERICO
New names.  Sight & Sound 25-3:120 Win '55/56
Young, V.  La Strada; cinematic intersections.  Hudson R
   9:437 Fall '56
Fellini: a personal statement.  Film 11:8 Ja/F '57
Biography.  Current Biography 18:33 Je '57
   Same.  Current Biography Yearbook 1957:184 '58
Bluestone, G.  Interview.  Film Culture 3-3(13):3 O '57
Knight, A.  Noblest Roman of them all.  Sat R 40:28 N 9
   '57
Gow, G.  The quest for realism; discussion.  Films &
   Filming 4-3:13 D '57
People are talking about.  Vogue 131:56 Ja 15 '58
Stanbrook, A.  The hope of Fellini.  Film 19:17 Ja/F '59
Fellini, F.  My sweet life.  Films & Filming 5-7:7 Ap '59
Fellini, F.  My experience as a director.  International
   Film A 3:29 '59
Weaver, W.  Letter from Italy.  Nation 190:260 Mr 19
   '60
Lane, J. F.  Fellini tells why.  Films & Filming 6-9:30
   Je '60
Rosmer, M.  Three hours in hell.  Reporter 24:40 Mr 30
   '61
Steel, R.  Moviemaker as moralist.  Christian Century
   78:488 Ap 19 '61
Neville, R.  Poet-director of The sweet life.  N. Y.
   Times Mag p17 My 14 '61
Pepper, R. G.  Rebirth in Italy; three great movie di-
   rectors.  Newsweek 58:66 Jl 10 '61
Peri, E.  Interview.  Film Q 51-1:30 Fall '61
Bergtal, E.  Lonely crowd in La dolce vita.  America
   106:13 O 7 '61
Duprey, R. A.  Bergman and Fellini, explorers of the
   modern spirit.  Catholic World 194:13 O '61
Federico Fellini.  Esquire 57:92 F '62
The screen answers back.  Films & Filming 8-8:12 My
   '62

End of the sweet parade. Esquire 59:98 Ja '63

La dolce far miente. Time 81:46 Mr 1 '63

Navonne, J. J. Fellini's La dolce Italia. Commonweal
77:639 Mr 15 '63

Bachmann, G. Fellini eight and a half. Film Journal
(Aus) 21:116 Ap '63

Lane, J. F. The face of '63--Italy. Films & Filming
9-7:11 Ap '63

Free. New Yorker 39:19 Jl 6 '63

Dizzy doings on a set; making of 8-1/2. Life 55:95 Jl 19
'63

Alpert, H. From 1/2 through 8-1/2. N. Y. Times Mag
p20 Jl 21 '63

What Fellini thinks Mastroianni thinks about women. Vogue
142:50 Ag 15 '63

8-1/2 interview. Cinema (BH) 1-5:19 Ag/S '63

Fellini, F. 9-1/2: the movie director as an artist.
Show 4-5:86 My '64

Bachmann, G. Interview. Sight & Sound 33:82 Spg '64

Bachmann, G. Disturber of the peace; interview. Mademoiselle 60:152 N '64

Mazzocchi, G. How I create; interview. Atlas 9:182
Mr '62

Liber, N. New fantasy by the 8-1/2 man. Life 59:50
Ag 27 '65

Walter, E. Private jokes of Federico Fellini. Vogue
146:274 S 1 '65

Ross, L. Profiles. New Yorker 41:63 O 30 '65

Ross, L. 10-1/2. Newsweek 41:63 O 30 '65

Wolf, W. Italy's movie greats. Cue 34-45:14 N 6 '65

Walter, E. Federico Fellini; wizard of film. Atlantic
216:62 D '65

Director of the year; filmog. International Film G 2:11
'65

Meehan, T. Fantasy, flesh and Fellini. Sat Evening
Post 239:24 Ja 1 '66

Lyon, N. Second fame; good food. Vogue 147:152 Ja 1
'66

Davis, M. S. First the pasta, then the play. N. Y.
Times Mag p10 Ja 2 '66

Interview. Playboy 13:55 F '66

Harcourt, P. The secret life of Federico Fellini. Film
Q 19-3:4 Spg '66

Walter, E. The wizardry of Fellini. Films & Filming
12-9:18 Je '66

Paolucci, A. Italian film. Massachusetts R 7:556 Sum
'66

Levine, I. R.   I was born for the cinema; a conversation with Federico Fellini.   Film Comment 4-1:77 Fall '66

Kast, P.   Giulietta and Federico.   Cahiers (Eng) 5:24 '66

Fellini talks about the face of Anouk Aimee.   Vogue 150:160 O 1 '67

Williams, F.   Fellini's voices.   Film Q 21-3:21 Spg '68

Morini, S.   Mastroianni at home.   Vogue 152:134 N 15 '68

Eason, P.   Notes on double structure and the films of Fellini.   Cinema (Lon) 2:22 Mr '69

Alpert, H.   Fellini at work.   Sat R 52:14 Jl 12 '69

Hughes, E.   Old Rome alla Fellini.   Life 67:56 Ag 15 '69

What directors are saying.   Action 4-5:32 S/O '69

Herman, D.   Federico Fellini.   American Imago 26:251 Fall '69

Fellini on Fellini on Satyricon.   Cinema (BH) 5-3:2 Fall '69

Interview.   Cinema (BH) 5-3:12 Fall '69

Langman, B.   Working with Fellini.   Mademoiselle 70:74 Ja '70

Morini, S.   Federico Fellini on Satyricon.   Vogue 155:168 Mr 1 '70

Rollin, B.   He shoots dreams on film.   Look 34:48 Mr 10 '70

Kael, P.   Current cinema.   New Yorker 46:134 Mr 14 '70

Rome B.C., A. F.   Time 95:76 Mr 16 '70

Both sides new.   Show 1-4:20 Ap '70

What directors are saying.   Action 5-3:30 My/Je '70

Fellini's formula.   Esquire 74:62 Ag '70

Myhers, J.   Fellini's continuing autobiography.   Cinema (BH) 6-2:40 Fall '70

Highet, G.   Whose Satyricon, Petronius's or Fellini's?   Horizon 12:42 Aut '70

Interview; filmog; biblio.   Discussion 1:Entire Issue '70

Dillard, R. H. W.   If we were all devils; Fellini's Satyricon as horror film.   Contempora 1-5:26 Ja/Ap '71

Garrett, G. P.   Fellini: a selected checklist of available secondary materials published in English (books, screenplays, interviews, critical pieces).   Contempora 1-5:33 Ja/Ap '71

McBride, J.   The director as superstar.   Sight & Sound 41-2:78 Spg '72

Hale, W.   Fellini's Rome & Losey's Trotsky.   N. Y. Sun News sec 3:7 O 8 '72

Ingrid Thulin comments on Fellini.   Dialogue On Film 3:16 '72


FENTON, LESLIE

Howe, H.   Sketch.   Photoplay 36:41 N '29

Alpert, K.   Interview.   Photoplay 39:45 F '31

FERGUSON, GRAEME
  Ferguson, G.   North of Superior: the world's largest
    motion picture.   American Cinematographer 52-9:898
    S '71

FERNÁNDEZ, EMILIO
  El Indio.   Time 48:101 N 11 '46
  Crichton, K.   Uprising of El Indio.   Colliers 119:28 Ja 4
    '47
  Fernandez, E.   After the revolution.   Films & Filming
    9-9:20 Je '63

FERNO, JOHN
  Biographical note.   International Film G 8:209 '71

FERRER, JOSE
  Underwood, M.   Joe and Uta.   Colliers 113:20 My 20 '44
  Biography.   Current Biography My '44
  Old play in Manhattan.   Time 48:78 O 21 '46
  Frank, S.   Broadway's new matinee idol.   Sat Evening
    Post 219:28 Mr 8 '47
  Funke, L.   Broadway stars--ten years ago and today.
    N. Y. Times Mag p25 Ap 20 '47
  Ferrer, J.   Is the Bergman legend true?   Silver Screen
    18-11:24 S '48
  His portrayal of the tramp in The silver whistle.   News-
    week 32:86 D 6 '48
  Best actor.   Life 25:51 D 20 '48
  Television no terror.   Theatre Arts 33:46 Ap '49
  Sketch.   Photoplay 36:120 O '49
  Advice to the players.   Christian Science Mon Mag p15
    Ag 19 '50
  Jose Ferrer as Cyrano.   Cue 19-38:17 S 23 '50
  Holliday, K.   No one in the world like him.   Silver
    Screen 21-3:42 Ja '51
  Hine, A.   People and prospects.   Holiday 9:22 F '51
  Mr. Harper.   After hours.   Harper 202:102 F '51
  Bardolatry.   Time 57:82 Mr 19 '51
  Millstein, G.   All the stage is his world.   N. Y. Times
    Mag p20 Mr 25 '51
  Oscars for Jose and Judy.   Life 30:38 Ap 9 '51
  Alig, W. B.   Starring Jose Ferrer.   Americas 3:9 S '51
  Brown, J. M.   Amazing Mr. Ferrer.   Sat R 35:22 F 9
    '52
  Phenomenon called Ferrer.   Life 39:99 F 11 '52
  Keating, J.   Man of parts.   Cue 21-17:11 Ap 26 '52
  Forecasts and side glances.   Theatre Arts 36:13 Ap '52

Theatre Arts spotlights.   Theatre Arts 36:52 My '52

Shrinking of Jose Ferrer.   Life 33:51 S 29 '52

Mr. Ferrer and Mr. Chaplin; threat by American Legion.
     Nation 176:90 Ja 31 '53

One-man reperatory.   Cue 22-45:16 N 7 '53

Gibbs, W.   Theatre.   New Yorker 29:76 D 19 '53

Millstein, G.   Fabulous Jose Ferrer.   Colliers 132:34
     D 25 '53

Haves, H.   Happy hunchback.   Sat R 36:27 D 26 '53

Biography.   Americana Annual 1953:241 '53

Hayes, R.   Portrait of the artist as Mr. Ferrer.   Com-
     monweal 59:378 Ja 15 '54

Four parts in eight weeks.   Theatre Arts 38:32 Ja '54

Carlson, T.   Come closer darling.   Silver Screen 24-4:31
     F '54

Peet, C.   All around star.   Senior Scholastic 64:6 Mr 3
     '54

Frazier, G.   Jose Ferrer; stage-master.   Coronet 36:83
     Je '54

Clooney, R.   On being Mrs. Jose Ferrer; as told to
     M. L. Runbeck.   Good Housekeeping 142:66 My '56

McCall visits.   McCalls 84:6 Jl '57

Jose sings out.   Newsweek 56:98 Jl 25 '60

Kolodin, I.   Name is Ferrer, not Farrar; acting in
     Gianni Schicchi.   Sat R 43:33 O 8 '60

Gelman, M.   Jose Ferrer.   Theatre 3-1:21 Ja '61

Condon, R.   Ole Jose.   Holiday 29:123 Mr '61

Meltsir, A.   Highly improbable, uproariously happy
     marriage of Rosemary Clooney and Jose Ferrer.
     Coronet 50:145 Ag '61

Funke, L.   & Booth, J. E.   Actor's method:  his life.
     N. Y. Times Mag p35 O 1 '61

Corbin, J.   Break-up.   Photoplay 61-1:6 Ja '62

Ferrer, J.   In who's who of the critics.   Films & Film-
     ing 8-8:14 My '62

The screen answers back.   Films & Filming 8-8:12 My
     '62

Ferrer, J.   Cyrano and others; interview.   Films &
     Filming 8-10:13 Jl '62

FERRER, MEL
     Holliday, K.   Fabulous Ferrer.   Silver Screen 20-9:41
          Jl '50
     Making of a movie matador.   Life 29:55 Jl 10 '50
     Hill, G.   Jet propulsion, Hollywood type.   Colliers
          126:28 Jl 29 '50
     Hine, A.   People and prospects.   Holiday 9:22 F '51

Life in the afternoon.   Newsweek 37:54 Ap 23 '51
La Jolla players.   Theatre Arts 35:4 Ag '51
Hall, G.   Ever meet a quinto phreniac?   Silver Screen
    23-5:24 Mr '53
Idyl for Audrey.   Life 39:44 Jl 18 '55
Jones, M. W.   My husband doesn't ruin me.   Photoplay
    49-4:52 Ap '56
Tolstoy, Ferrer, Hepburn, $6 million.   Newsweek 48:53
    Jl 30 '56
Scandal in rehearsal.   Life 42:56 F 4 '57
Celebrities on a stylish spree.   Life 47:103 S 7 '59


FERRERI, MARCO
    Lane, J. F.   The face of '63--Italy.   Films & Filming
        9-7:11 Ap '63


FERRY, ISIDORO M.
    Cobos, J.   The face of '63--Spain.   Films & Filming
        10-1:39 O '63


FEUILLADE, LOUIS
    Lacassin, F.   Louis Feuillade. Sight & Sound 34-1:42
        Win '64/65
    Roud, R.   Memories of Resnais.   Sight & Sound 38-3:124
        Sum '69


FEYDER, JACQUES
    Obit.   N. Y. Times p25 My 26 '48


FIELD, MARY
    Who's who in audio-visual education.   Audio Visual G
        16:22 Ja '50


FISHER, TERENCE
    British feature directors; an index to their work.  Sight &
        Sound 27-6:294 Aut '58
    Fisher, T.   Horror is my business.   Films & Filming
        10-10:7 Jl '64
    British cinema filmography.   Film 65:10 Spg '71


FITZMAURICE, GEORGE
    The art of directing.   N. Y. Dramatic Mirror 75:23 Mr 11
        '16
    Smith, F. J.   Interview.   Motion Pic 10:47 Ap/My '20
    Evans, D.   Sketch.   Photoplay 18:43 Jl '20
    Obit.   Current Biography '40
        N. Y. Times p21 Je 14 '40
        Newsweek 15:8 Je 24 '40

FITZPATRICK, JAMES A.
Voice unglobed.  Time 37:67 Je 30 '41
We reluctantly say farewell to ...  Lions Roar 1-2:no p#
    O '41
Rosie and the weather.  New Yorker 24:13 Jl 10 '48
Where are they now?  Newsweek 61:12 Je 3 '63

FLAHERTY, ROBERT
Indomitable children of the north.  Travel 39:16 Ag '22
How I filmed Nanook of the north.  World Work (Lon)
    44:553 S; 44:632 O '22
Wetalltook's islands.  World Work (Lon) 45:324 Ja;
    45:422 F; 45:538 Mr '23
Freelick, L.  New movie prophet.  Asia 23:396 Je '23
Sketch.  World Work (Lon) 41:426 Ap '23
Weller, S. M.  Interview.  Motion Pic Classic 26:25 O
    '27
Ramsaye, T.  Sketch.  Photoplay 33:58 My '28
Man of Aran.  Newsweek 4:39 O 20 '34
Hobsen, H.  Man of films.  Christian Science Mon Mag
    p8 N 6 '35
Ferguson, O.  Flaherty and the films.  New Republic
    90:323 Ap 21 '37
Flaherty, R.  North Sea.  Sight & Sound 7-26:62 Sum '38
Documentary daddy.  Time 37:69 F 3 '41
Most unforgettable character I've met.  Readers Digest
    40:41 Mr '42
Brinnin, J M.  Pioneer documentary filmmakers.  Harper
    Bazaar 81:146 D '47
Old master.  Time 52:94 S 20 '48
How he began to make documentary films.  Life 25:151
    O 4 '48
Foster, I. W.  Partners and pioneers.  Christian Science
    Mon Mag p5 Ja 15 '49
Over the magazine editor's desk.  Christian Science Mon
    Mag p15 Ja 15 '49
Biography.  Current Biography 10:15 Mr '49
    Same.  Current Biography Yearbook 1949:199 '50
How he made the Louisiana story in the bayous of Louisi-
    ana.  Travel 92:12 My '49
Taylor, R. L.  Moviemaker.  New Yorker 25:30 Je 11;
    28 Je 18; 28 Je 25 '49
Houston, P.  Interview.  Sight & Sound 18-71:16 Aut '49
Grim, gallant story of Comeck the Eskimo.  Reader
    Digest 57:169 Jl '50
Gray, H.  Robert Flaherty and the naturalistic docu-
    mentary.  Hollywood Q 5-1:41 Fall '50

Knight, A.   Flaherty festival.   Sat R 34:27 Ja 6 '51
Film: language of the eye.   Theatre Arts 35:30 My '51
Obit.   Americana Annual 1952:249 '52
   Current Biography 12:26 S '51
   Current Biography Yearbook 1951:205 '52
   France Illustrated 7:144a Ag 11 '51
   Illustrated London N 219:187 Ag 4 '51
   N. Y. Times p25 Jl 24 '51
   Newsweek 38:57 Ag 6 '51
   Screen World 3:177 '52
   Time 58:81 Jl 30 '51
Weinberg, H. G.   A farewell to Flaherty.   Films In Review 2-8:14 O '51
Houston, J.   A tribute.   Sight & Sound 21-2:64 O/D '51
Grierson, J.   Flaherty as innovator.   Sight & Sound 21-2:64 O/D '51
Sammis, E.   Flaherty at Abbeville.   Sight & Sound 21-2:68 O/D '51
Flaherty, F.   Flaherty way.   Sat R 35:50 S 13 '52
Wynkip, M. H.   The Flaherty memorial.   Films In Review 4-2:105 F '53
Starr, C.   Film seminar in Vermont.   Sat R 39:32 O 13 '56
Flaherty, R.   Flaherty's quest for life.   Films & Filming 5-4:8 Ja '59
Bob; a conversation.   Film 21:23 S/O '59
Sarris, A.   Pantheon directors; filmog.   Film Culture 28:2 Spg '63
Van Dongen, H.   Robert J. Flaherty 1884-1951.   Film Q 18-4:3 Sum '65
Visions in an ice-blue eye.   Time 87:90 Ja 28 '66
Trevelyan, C. F.   Art of movie making.   U. S. Camera 29:68 Ag '66
Sadoul, G.   A Flaherty mystery.   Cahiers (Eng) 11:46 S '67
Who's who in filmmaking.   Sightlines 1-1:4 S/O '67
Fondiller, H. V.   Bob Flaherty remembered.   Popular Photo 66:98 Mr '70
Robert Flaherty (Barneuw's file); correspondence.   Film Culture 53/54/55:161 Spg '71
Werner, P.   Frances Flaherty: hidden and seeking.   Filmmakers Newsletter 5-9/10:28 Sum '72

FLEISCHER, RICHARD
   Fleischer, R.   Underwater filming.   Films In Review 5-7:333 Ag/S '54
   Sarris, A.   Minor disappointments; filmog.   Film Culture 28:41 Spg '63

Listing of films.   Film Culture 37:7 Sum '65

Symposium: adding to the director's tools.   Action 3-6:26
   N/D '68

Gow, G.   Don't throw them away; filmog.   Films & Filming 17-3:20 D '70

What directors are saying.   Action 6-3:28 My/Je '71

The professional director speaks.   Making Films 5-4:40
   Ag '71

Lawrence, J.   Richard Fleischer: establishment director
   in the shifting scene.   Todays Filmmaker 1-2:24 N '71


FLEISCHMANN, PETER
   Baby, Y.   Interview.   Atlas 19:56 Je '70


FLEMING, VICTOR
   Work of.   Motion Pic 54:70 S '37
   Biographical note; filmog.   Movies & People 2:41 '40
   Directed by Victor Fleming.   Lions Roar 1-1:no p# S '41
   Action Fleming.   Lions Roar 1-9:no p# My '42
   A director named Fleming.   Lions Roar 3-2:no p# Ja '44
   MGM's directors range from pioneers to newcomers.
      Lions Roar 3-4:no p# Jl '44
   Fleming, V.   Directing--then and now.   Lions Roar
      3-4:no p# Jl '44
   Obit.   N.Y. Times p21 Ja 7 '49
      Newsweek 33:54 Ja 17 '49
      Screen World 1:234 '49
      Time 53:85 Ja 17 '49
   Sarris, A.   Likable but elusive; filmog.   Film Culture
      28:35 Spg '63
   Reid, J. H.   Fleming: the apprentice years.   Films &
      Filming 14-4:39 Ja '68


FLEMYNG, GORDON
   British cinema filmography.   Film 65:10 Spg '72


FLICKER, THEODORE
   Hentoff, N.   Instant theater.   Reporter 24:46 Mr 30 '61


FLOOD, JAMES
   Obit.   N.Y. Times p20 F 6 '53


FLOREY, ROBERT
   Tarrent, E.   Sketch.   Motion Pic Classic 27:40 Ag '28
   Herring, R.   His method of making movies.   Creative
      Art 4:360 My '29
   Spears, J.   Robert Florey; filmog.   Films In Review 11-4:
      210 Ap '60

Maltin, L.   Directors on TV; partial TV filmog.   Film
   Fan Mo 126:22 D '71
Mundy, R.   Death plays and wax works.   Cinema (Lon)
   9:8 n. d.


FONT, JOSE LUIS
   Katz, J.   Interview.   Vision 1-2:25 Sum '62


FONTOURA, ANTONIO CARLOS
   Viany, A.   Who's who in the cinema novo.   CTVD 5-4:26
   Sum '68


FORBES, BRYAN
   Forbes, B.   Breaking the silence.   Films & Filming
      6-10:7 Jl '60
   The cost of independence.   Sight & Sound 30-3:111 Sum '61
   Personality of the month.   Films & Filming 7-12:5 S '61
   Cowie, P.   The face of '63--Great Britain.   Films &
      Filming 9-5:19 F '63
   How to get into films, by the people who got in them-
      selves.   Films & Filming 9-10:11 Jl '63
   Fixx, J. F.   From Hollywood with love.   Sat R 48:12
      D 25 '65
   King Rat; interview.   Cinema (BH) 3-1:32 D '65
   Lerman, L.   International movie report.   Mademoiselle
      64:118 F '67
   On the scene.   Playboy 14-4:155 Ap '67
   Forbes, B.   Eric Portman; a tribute.   Plays & Players
      17-5:23 F '69
   Houston, P.   Forbes' first fifteen.   Sight & Sound 38-4:
      182 Aut '69
   Biography.   British Book Year 1970:146 '70
   Forbes, B.   Elstree, a leaving report.   Films Illustrated
      1-1:6 Jl '71
   Forbes, B.   Kate: a memoir of Katharine Hepburn.
      Films Illustrated 1-3:17 S '71
   Gruen, J.   He says 'Yes, yes, Nanette!'   N. Y. Times
      Bio Ed O 24 '71
   Goldman, C.   Long ago tomorrow and before; filmog.
      Applause 1-9:36 Ja 19 '72
   British cinema filmography.   Film 65:10 Spg '72


FORD, ALEKSANDER
   Moskowitz, G.   Aleksander Ford and the Polish cinema.
      Sight & Sound 27-3:136 Win '57/58
   The Polish cinema.   Film 31:26 Spg '62

FORD, CHARLES HENRI
    Colaciello, R.   Interview.   Interview 2-2:26 n. d.

FORD, DEREK
    British cinema filmography.   Film 65:10 Spg '72

FORD, FRANCIS
    How he became a photoplayer.   Motion Pic 9:112 F '15
    Willis, R.   Interview.   Motion Pic 9:101 Je '15
    Obit.   N. Y.  Times p19 S 7 '53

FORD, JOHN
    Cruikshank, H.   Sketch.   Motion Pic Classic 30:45 Ja '30
    Men behind megaphones.   Cue 4-13:3 Ja 25 '36
    Sketch.   Motion Pic 52:62 O '36
    Sharpe, H.   Work of.   Photoplay 50:14 O '36
    Jacobs, L.   Work of.   One Act Play 3:88 Ja '40
    Biographical note; filmog.   Movies & People 2:41 '40
    Daugherty, F.   John Ford wants it real.   Christian
        Science Mon Mag p5 Je 21 '41
    Biography.   Current Biography '41
    Wootten, W. P.   An index to the films of John Ford.
        Sight & Sound (special sup) Index Series # 13 F '48
    Nugent, F. S.   Hollywood's favorite rebel.   Sat Evening
        Post 222:25 Jl 23 '49
        Same abridged.   Reader Digest 55:53 O '49
    Anderson, L.   John Ford.   Films In Review 2-2:5 F '51
    Knight, A.   Watch the Fords go by.   Sat R 35:28 Ag 23
        '52
    Samuels, G.   Director Hollywood's leading man.   N. Y.
        Times Mag p22 O 26 '52
    Johnson, G.   John Ford: maker of Hollywood stars.
        Coronet 35:133 D '53
    Cockshott, G.   The curious cult of John Ford.   Film 2:8
        D '54
    In praise of John Ford; letters.   Film 3:25 F '55
    The director and the public; a symposium.   Film Culture
        1-2:15 Mr/Ap '55
    Mitry, J.   John Ford.   Films In Review 2-7:305 Ag/S
        '55
    Days of a pioneer.   Films & Filming 2-2:19 N '55
    Reed, A. C.   John Ford.   Arizona Highways 32:4 Ap '56
    Failure makes good.   TV Guide 4-38:25 S 22 '56
    Killanin, M.   Poet in an iron mask.   Films & Filming
        4-5:9 F '58
    Down with Rebecca.   Newsweek 52:104 S 22 '58
    Young, C.   The old dependables.   Film Q 13-1:2 Fall '59

Gillett, J.   Working with Ford.   Sight & Sound 29-1:21
    Win '59/60
Taylor, J. R.   Ford omnibus.   Sight & Sound 30-3:122
    Sum '61
McVay, D.   The five worlds of John Ford.   Films &
    Filming 8-9:14 Je '62
Tupper, L.   Letter.   Films In Review 13-6:382 Je/Jl '62
Barkun, M.   Notes on the art of John Ford.   Film
    Culture 25:9 Sum '62
Sarris, A.   Cactus Rosebud or the Man who shot Liberty
    Valance.   Film Culture 25:13 Sum '62
Mitchell, G. J.   Filmography.   Films In Review 14-3:129
    Mr '63
Fenin, G.   The face of '63--United States.   Films &
    Filming 9-6:55 Mr '63
Letters.   Films In Review 14-4:246 Ap '63
Letters.   Films In Review 14-5:314 My '63
Sarris, A.   Pantheon director; filmog.   Film Culture
    28:2 Spg '63
The directors choose the best films.   Cinema (BH) 1-5:14
    Ag/S '63
Wootten, W. P. Jr.   Letter.   Films In Review 14-10:631
    D '63
Hill, S. P.   Letter.   Films In Review 15-1:60 Ja '64
Bogdanovich, P.   Autumn of John Ford.   Esquire 61:102
    Ap '64
Mitchell, G. J.   Ford on Ford.   Films In Review 15-6:
    321 Je/Jl '64
Peck, S.   Autumn of John Ford.   N. Y. Times Mag p124
    N 29 '64
Houston, P.   Producing for Ford.   Sight & Sound 34-1:18
    Win '64/65
Ford on Ford; discussion.   Cinema (BH) 2-2:42 '64
Bates, D.   A John Ford footnote.   Sight & Sound 35-1:51
    Win '65/66
Taylor, J. R.   A Ford footnote.   Sight & Sound 35-2:103
    Spg '66
Kennedy, B.   A talk with John Ford.   Action 3-5:6 S/O
    '68
Ford and Kennedy on the western; discussion.   Films In
    Review 20-1:29 Ja '69
Our way west: Burt Kennedy talks to John Ford.   Film &
    Filming 16-1:30 O '69
Beresford, B.   Decline of a master.   Film 56:4 Aut '69
Interview.   Focus 5:3 O '69
Schickel, R.   Good days, good years.   Harper 241:44
    O '70

McBride, J.   County Mayo Gu Bragh; interview.  Sight &
Sound 40-1:43  Win '70/71
Everson, W. K   John Ford goes to war--against VD.
Film Fan Mo 119:14 My '71
Anderson, L.  John Ford.   Cinema (BH) 6-3:21 Spg '71
Everson, W. K.   Forgotten Ford.   Focus On Film 6:13
Spg '71
Richards, J.   Ford's lost world.   Focus On Film 6:20
Spg '71
Haggard, M.   Ford in person.   Focus On Film 6:33 Spg
'71
Eyles, A.   Ford in print.   Focus On Film 6:38 Spg '71
Ford on 16mm.   Focus On Film 6:40 Spg '71
Campbell, R.   John Ford; filmog.   Velvet Light Trap
2:entire issue Ag '71
Wood, R.   Shall we gather at the river?  the late films
of John Ford.   Film Comment 7-3:8 Fall '71
John Ford on Stagecoach.   Action 6-5:10 S/O '71
Ford, D.   The west of John Ford and how it was made.
Action 6-5:35 S/O '71
Zolotow, M.   The American west of John Ford.  TV Guide
19-49:19 D 4 '71
McBride, J.   Straight shooting.   Silent Pic 13:18 Win/Spg
'72
Ketkin, A.   John Ford and the western.   Mise-En-Scene
1:34 n. d.

FOREMAN, CARL
Darkness at High noon.   Nation 176:21 Ja 10 '53
Cogley, J.   Matter of ritual.   Commonweal 66:149 My 10
'57
Personality of the month.   Films & Filming 3-9:3 Je '57
Alpert, H.   Return of Carl Foreman.   Sat R 40:26 S 21
'57
Houston, P. & Cavander, K.   Interview. Sight & Sound
27-5:220 Sum '58
Foreman, C.   What film shall we make next?   Inter-
national Film A 2:118 '58
Foreman, C.   Introduction.   International Film A 3:9 '59
Lane, J. F.   Big guns.   Films & Filming 6-11:28 Ag '60
Of peregrinating producers.   Sat R 43:52 D 24 '60
Lerman, L.   Catch up with Guns of Navarone.   Made-
moiselle 53:78 My '61
Zunser, J.   Prodigal's return.   Cue 30-22:10 Je 3 '61
The cost of independence.   Sight & Sound 30:3:112 Sum '61
Debate: movies vs. theatre.   N. Y. Times Mag p10 Ap 29
'62

The screen answers back.    Films & Filming 8-8:12 My
   '62
Cowie, P.    The face of '63--Great Britain.    Films &
   Filming 9-5:19 F '63
Desert island films.    Films & Filming 9-11:11 Ag '63
James, H.    To the spoils go The victors.    Cinema (BH)
   1-5:9 Ag/S '63
Foreman, C.    The road to The victors.    Films & Film-
   ing 9-12:11 S '63
Alpert, H.    Something worth fighting for; interview.
   Sat R 46:16 D 28 '63
Oren, U.    Carl Foreman in Israel.    Film Comment
   2-3:40 Sum '64
Foreman, C.    A pat on the back for film actors.    Inter-
   national Film G 1:40 '64
Goodfriend, A.    Carl Foreman's London.    Sat R 52:32
   Ag 16 '69
The sense of adventure; interview.    Films & Filming
   16-2:14 N '69
Foreman, C.    Confessions of a frustrated screenwriter;
   filmog.    Film Comment 6-4:22 Win '70/71
Gow, G.    Interrogation; interview; filmog.    as writer,
   producer, director.    Films & Filming 18-11:14 Ag '72
Rose, T.    Interview.    Movie Maker 6-9:616 S '72

FORMAN, MILOŠ
   Dyer, P. J.    Star-crossed in Prague.    Sight & Sound
      35-1:34 Win '65/66
   Arkadin.    Film clips.    Sight & Sound 35-1:46 Win '65/66
   Hooper, M.    Forman.    Film 45:34 Spg '66
   Adula's dream.    Newsweek 68:110 S 19 '66
   Levy, A.    Watch out for the hook, my friend.    Life
      62:77 Ja 20 '67
   Blue, J. & de Bosio, G.    Interview.    Cahiers (Eng) 8:53
      F '67
   Chill wind on the new wave.    Sat R 50:10 D 23 '67
   Sarris, A.    Movers.    Sat R 50:10 D 23 '67
   Biography.    British Book Year 1969:150 '69
   Director of the year; filmog.    International Film G 6:12
      '69
   Forman, M.    How I came to America to make a film and
      wound up owing Paramount $140, 000.    Show 1-2:38
      F '70
   Czechs in exile.    Newsweek 76:70 Jl 27 '70
   Pelt, H.    Getting the great ten percent; interview.    Film
      Comment 6-3:58 Fall '70
   Conaway, J.    Milos Forman's America is like Kafka's--

basically comic. N. Y. Times Bio Ed Jl 11 '71
Gow, G.   A Czech in New York; interview; filmog. Films
    & Filming 17-12:20 S '71
What directors are saying.   Action 6-6:22 N/D '71
Interview; filmog; biblio.  Dialogue On Film 3:1 '72

FORMAN, TOM
    Sketch.   Motion Pic 10:113 D '15
    McGaffey, K. Return to motion pictures. Motion Pic 17:36 Je '19
    Shelley, H.   Rise of.   Motion Pic Classic 11:32 N '20
    Boone, A.   Interview.   Photoplay 19:55 Ja '21
    Underhill, H.   Interview.   Motion Pic 21:72 F '21

FORZANO, GIOVACCHINO
    Fischer-Williams, B.  Don't call me maestro; interview.
        Opera News 20:6 Ja 1 '66
    Obit.   N. Y. Times p46 O 29 '70
        Opera News 35:33 D 5 '70
        Time 96:67 N 9 '70

FOSTER, NORMAN
    Service, F.   His separation marriage.   Motion Pic 44:47
        Ag '32

FOSSE, BOB
    Coleman, E.   Dance man leaps to the top.   N. Y. Times
        Mag p26 Ap 19 '59
    Joel, L.   Gwen Verdon and Bob Fosse.   Dance 35:18 Jl
        '61
    Bob Fosse.   Dance 37:32 Ap '63
    Swisher, V. H.   Bob Fosse translates Sweet Charity from
        stage to screen.   Dance 43:22 F '69
    Hemming, R.   Robert Fosse; interview.   Senior Scholastic
        96:14 F 2 '70
    Picard, L.   Interview.   Interview 20:8 Mr '72
    Loney, G.   The many facets of Bob Fosse.   After Dark
        5-2:22 Je '72
    Vallance, T.   Biographical note; credits.   Focus On Film
        10:6 Sum '72

FRAKER, WILLIAM A.   (Bill)
    What directors are saying.   Action 4-6:28 N/D '69
    Eyles, A.   William A. Fraker; filmog.   Focus On Film
        5:5 Win '70
    Cinematographer turned director.   Todays Filmmaker
        1-2:35 N '71

FRAMPTON, HOLLIS
  Snow, M.   Interview; filmog.    Film  Culture  48/49:6
    Win/Spg '70

FRANCIS, FREDDIE
  British cinema filmography.   Film 65:10 Spg '72
  Jensen, P.   Interview.   Photon 22:32 '72

FRANJU, GEORGES
  Grenier, C.   Franju.   Sight & Sound 26-4:186 Spg '57
  Biographical note.   Unifrance 48:13 O '58
  Spotlights five young Frenchmen who are giving French
    cinema a new look.   Films & Filming 5-3:18 D '58
  Sadoul, G.   Notes on a new generation.   Sight & Sound
    28-3/4:111 Sum/Aut '59
  Cameron, I.   Eyes without a face.   Film 26:22 N/D '60
  Directors of the year; filmog.   International Film G 4:9 '67
  Milne, T.   Songs of innocence.   Sight & Sound 40-1:7
    Win '70/71
  Gow, G.   Franju.   Films & Filming 17-11:80 Ag '71
  MacLochlainn, A.   The films of Luis Bunuel and Georges
    Franju; selected filmog.   Film Journal 1-2:16 Sum '71

FRANK, ROBERT
  Mekas, J.   Notes on the new American cinema.   Film
    Culture 24:6 Spg '62
  Survey among unsuccessful applicants for the Ford Found-
    ation film grants.   Film Comment 2-3:10 Sum '64
  Listing of films.   Film Culture 37:7 Sum '65
  Weiner, P.   New American cinema; filmog.   Film 58:22
    Spg '70

FRANKEL, CYRIL
  Filmography.   Film 14:8 N/D '57
  British feature directors; an index to their work.   Sight &
    Sound 27-6:294 Aut '58
  Frankel, C.   What establishes a style?   Films & Filming
    7-12:10 S '61

FRANKENHEIMER, JOHN
  Backstage at Playhouse 90.   Time 70:43 D 2 '57
  Personality of the month.   Films & Filming 7-11:5 Ag '61
  TV's problems and prospects; discussion.   Playboy 13:35
    N '61
  Meyersberg, P.   John Frankenheimer.   Movie 5:35 D '62
  Jennings, C. R.   John Frankenheimer.   Horizon 5:35
    Mr '63

Fenin, G.   The face of '63--United States.   Films &
Filming 9-6:55 Mr '63
Sarris, A.   Minor disappointments; filmog.   Film Culture
28:41 Spg '63
Big-bang bagatelle.   Newsweek 63:112 Ap 20 '64
Frankenheimer, J.   Seven ways with Seven days in May.
Films & Filming 10-9:9 Je '64
Biography.   Current Biography 25:3 O '64
Same.   Current Biography Yearbook 1964:134 '64
Criticism as creation.   Sat R 47:12 D 26 '64
Schlesinger, A. Jr.   The director vs. the film.   Show
5-2:16 Mr '65
Thomas, J.   The smile on the face of the tiger.   Film Q
19-2:2 Win '65/66
Casty, A.   Realism and beyond; the films of John
Frankenheimer.   Film Heritage 2-2:21 Win '66/67
Alpert, H.   Hollywood in Budapest.   Sat R 50:20 D 23 '67
Directors of the year; filmog.   International Film G 4:26
'67
Wolf, W.   Moviemakers with conviction.   Cue 37-17:16
Ap 27 '68
Higham, C.   Frankenheimer.   Sight & Sound 37:91 Spg '68
Two-thirds of greatness.   Time 92:107 D 13 '68
Filmer, P.   Three Frankenheimer films: a sociological
approach.   Screen 10-4/5:160 Jl/O '69
Pratley, G.   Interview.   International Film G 6:29 '69
AuWerter, R.   Interview.   Action 5-3:6 My/Je '70
Wolff, A.   A man and his movie: John Frankenheimer's
The horsemen.   Show 2-5:34 Jl '71
O'Brien, J.   Interview.   Interview 2-5:27 Ag '71

FRANKLIN, CHESTER
Biographical note.   Photoplay 9-4:42 Mr '16
Brownlow, K.   The Franklin kid pictures.   Films In Re-
view 23-7:396 Ag/S '72

FRANKLIN, SIDNEY A.
Cohn, A. A.   Sketch.   Photoplay 17:51 Ja '20
Sketch.   Motion Pic 33:94 Mr '27
Work of.   Motion Pic 53:20 My '37
Zerbe, B.   Franklin the thorough.   Cinema Progress
2-3:12 Ag '37
Biographical note; filmog.   Movies & People 2:42 '40
It's their baby.   Lions Roar 2-3:no p# D '42
Just what the doctor ordered.   Lions Roar 3-2:no p#
Ja '44
He collects trophies. Lions Roar 3-2:no p#  Ja '44

Envoy to everywhere.  Lions Roar 3-4:no p# Jl '44
Obit.  N. Y. Times Bio Ed My 20 '72
Brownlow, K.  The modest pioneer; filmog.  Focus On
    Film 10:30 Sum '72
Brownlow, K.  The Franklin kid pictures.  Films In Re-
    view 23-7:396 Ag/S '72

FRANKLIN, WENDELL
    Keats, C.  I was shooting the militants from a white
        viewpoint.  Action 7-1:13 Ja/F '72

FRAZEE, ED
    Biographical Note.  Photoplay 9-4:42 Mr '16

FREARS, STEPHEN
    British cinema filmography.  Film 65:10 Spg '72

FRENCH, HAROLD
    Filmography.  Film 14:8 N/D '57
    British feature directors; an index to their work.  Sight
        & Sound 27-6:294 Aut '58

FREND, CHARLES
    Filmography.  Film 14:8 N/D '57
    British feature directors; an index to their work.  Sight &
        Sound 27-6:294 Aut '58

FRENKE, EUGENE (Eŭgen)
    Hunter, L.  Sketch.  Motion Pic 48:14 Ja '35
    Dillon, F.  Work of.  Motion Pic 49:40 F '35

FRENO, JOHN
    Biographical sketch.  International Film G 3:117 '66

FREUND, KARL
    Luft, H. G.  Karl Freund.  Films In Review 14-2:93
        F '63
    Freund, K.  Letter reply to Luft.  Films In Review
        14-4:249 Ap '63
    Hanson, C. L.  The mummy.  Cinema (BH) 2-5:30
        Mr/Ap '65
    Brockway, D.  One of the screen's greatest cameramen.
        8mm Collector 13:2 Fall/Win '65
    Deschner, D.  Karl Freund.  Cinema (BH) 5-4:24 Win '69
    Obit.  Classic Film Collector 24:14 Sum '69 (reprint
        from Variety)
    Journal Optical Society 59:1686 D '69

Luft, H. G.   Cinematographer Karl Freund.   Film Journal
   1-1:52 Spg '71
Filmography (as cinematographer and director).   Film
   Comment 8-2:35 Sum '72
Mundy, R.   Death plays and wax works.   Cinema (Lon)
   9:8 n. d.

FRIČ, MARTIN
   Dewey, L.   Czechoslovakia; silence into sound.   Film
      60:5 n. d.

FRIEDKIN, WILLIAM
   The director says.   Making Films 2-1:43 F '68
   What directors are saying.   Action 4-5:32 S/O '69
   Friedkin, W.   Anatomy of a chase.   Take One 3-6:25
      Jl/Ag '71
   Friedkin, W.   Anatomy of a chase.   Action 7-2:8 Mr/Ap
      '72
   What directors are saying.   Action 7-3:28 My/Je '72
   Shedlin, M.   Interview.   Film Q 25-4:2 Sum '72
   Chase, C.   Everyone's reading it.   Billy's filming it.
      N. Y. Times sec2:1 Ag 27 '72
   Spinelli, A. L.   Location New York for The French con-
      nection.   Todays Filmmaker 2-1:32 Ag '72
   The director says.   Making Films 6-4:25 Ag '72
   Eyles, A.   Biographical sketch; filmog.   Focus On Film
      8:4 n. d.

FRISCH, LARRY
   Frisch, L.   A filmmaker's report on the Arab-Israeli
      war.   Action 2-6:20 N/D '67
   Frisch, L.   Biafra.   Action 4-2:17 Mr/Ap '69

FRIZELL, VARICK
   Weinberg, G.   The backroom boys.   Film Culture 41:90
      Sum '66

FUEST, ROBERT
   British cinema filmography.   Film 65:10 Spg '72
   Knight, K. & Nicholson, P.   On the set of Phibes II.
      Cinefantastique 2-2:38 Sum '72

FULLER, SAMUEL
   Mealand, R.   Books into films; Dark page.   Publisher W
      146:1662 O 21 '44
   He keeps them happy.   Look 17:110 Mr 24 '53
   Sarris, A.   Second line; filmog.   Film Culture 28:11 Spg
      '63

Fuller, S.   What is film?   Cinema (BH) 2-2:22 '64

Goodman, E.   Low-budget movies with pow!   N. Y. Times Mag p42 F 28 '65

Hanson, C. L.   Caine--a new film by Samuel Fuller. Cinema (BH) 3-6:30 Win '67

Godard in Hollywood.   Take One 1-10:13 Je '68

Baker, B.   Samuel Fuller--minor but interesting; filmog. Kinema 2:no p# Je '69

Canhan, K.   The world of Samuel Fuller; filmog.   Film 55:4 Sum '69

Canhan, K.   Samuel Fuller's action films.   Screen 10-6:80 N '69

McArthur, C.   Samuel Fuller's gangster films.   Screen 10-6:93 N '69

What directors are saying.   Action 4-6:28 N/D '69

Bjorkman, S.   Interview, Paris 1965.   Movie 17:25 Win '69/70

Shivas, M.   Interview, California 1969.   Movie 17:29 Win '69/70

Morse, D.   Reflections on Samuel Fuller.   Brighton Film R 16:15 Ja '70

Interview.   Cinema (Lon) 5:6 F '70

What directors are saying.   Action 5-4:30 Jl/Ag '70`

What directors are saying.   Action 6-1:30 Ja/F '71

Belton, J.   Are you waving that flag at me?   Velvet Light Trap 4:10 Spg '72

FUNT, ALLEN

Talking out of turn.   Newsweek 30:52 N 10 '47

Beatty, J.   Watch out for candid mike!   American 146:32 Jl '48

McEvoy, J. P.   Eavesdropper without inhibitions.   Reader Digest 53:115 Ag '48

Funt's fun.   Newsweek 32:62 S 20 '48

Hamburger, P.   Peeping Funt.   New Yorker 25:72 Ja 7 '50

Allen Funt's candid camera shows druggists how to sell. Business Week p78 Ja 5 '52

There's nothing funny about money; excerpt from Eavesdropper at large.   Colliers 130:74 S 27 '52

Shaman, H.   How to make a comedy film.   Popular Photo 36:105 Ap '55

Lardner, J.   Air.   New Yorker 35:54 Jl 4 '59

Allen Funt.   Newsweek 54:52 N 2 '59

Flagler, J. M.   Profiles.   New Yorker 36:59 D 10 '60

Godfrey on campus.   Newsweek 56:49 D 19 '60

Martin, P.   I call on the candid camera man.   Sat Evening

Post 234:26 My 27 '61
Engle, H.   Hidden cameras and human behavior; interview.
Film Comment 3-4:42 Fall '65
Biography.   Current Biography 27:5 D '66
Same.   Current Biography Yearbook 1966:109 '67
Smile!   Time 89:63 Mr 3 '67
Smile, you're off.   Newsweek 69:86 Mr 6 '67
Five happy moments.   Esquire 74:140 D '70

FURIE, SIDNEY
Sidney Furie.   Film 34:20 Win '62
Cowie, P.   The face of '63--Great Britain.   Films &
Filming 9-5:19 F '63
Interview at Cannes.   Cinema (BH) 2-6:39 Jl/Ag '65
British cinema filmography.   Film 65:10 Spg '72

GAÁL, ISTVÁN
    Biographical note.    International Film G 6:93 '69
    Biographical note.    International Film G 8:175 '71

GADE, SVEND
    Smith, A.    Sketch.    Classic 19:38 Mr '24

GADNEY, ALAN
    Winogura, D.    Interview.    Cinefantastique 2-1:6 Spg '72

GANCE, ABEL
    Koval, F.    France's greatest director.    Films In Review
        3-9:436 N '52
    Biographical note.    Unifrance 32:3 O/N '54
    The big screens.    Sight & Sound 24-4:209 Spg '55
    Personality of the month.    Films & Filming 6-8:3 My '60
    Granja, V.    Abel Gance and the new picture writing.
        CTVD 6-1:6 Fall '68
    Brownlow, K.    The charm of dynamite.    Film 54:8 Spg
        '69
    Brownlow, K.    Abel Gance: the spirit of genius.    Films
        & Filming 16-2:32 N; 16-3:26 D '69
    Blumer, A. H.    The camera as snowball: France 1918-
        1927.    Cinema J 9-2:31 Spg '70
    Brownlow, K.    Bonaparte et la revolution.    Sight &
        Sound 41-1:18 Win '71 /72

GARDNER, CYRIL
    Obit.    N. Y. Times 11:3 Ja 2 '43

GARDNER, ROBERT
    Statement by Robert Gardner at the opening ceremony of
        the Festival Popoli.    Film Comment 2-1:13 Win '64
    Gardner, R.    Can the will triumph?    Film Comment
        3-1:28 Win '65
    Gardner, R.    Chronicles of the human experience: Dead
        birds.    Film Library Q 2-4:25 Fall '69

GARFEIN, JACK
    Bachmann, G.    Interview.    Film 27:26 Ja/F '61
    Sarris, A.    Minor disappointments; filmog.    Film Culture
        28:41 Spg '63
    Johnson, A.    Jack Garfein; interview. Film Q 17-1:36 Fall
        '63
                                161

GARNETT, TAY
  Acrobat to film director.   Cue 3-43:3 Ag 24 '35
  Sketch.   Motion Pic 54:21 O '37
  The director's problems.   Photoplay 53:30 S '39
  Biographical note; filmog.   Movies & People 2:41 '40
  Living action.   Lions Roar 2-5:no p# Jl '43
  Ace action artisan.   Lions Roar 3-2:no p# Ja '44
  MGM's directors range from pioneers to newcomers.
      Lions Roar 3-4:no p# Jl '44
  Ladies' man.   Lions Roar 3-5:no p# D '44
  Sarris, A.   Likable but elusive; filmog.   Film Culture
      28:35 Spg '63
  What directors are saying.   Action 5-1:28 Ja/F '70
  Thomas, B.   Tay Garnett: a man for all films.   Action
      7-5:12 S/O '72

GARNETT, TONY
  Interview.   Afterimage 1:no p# Ap '70

GARREL, PHILIPPE
  Interview.   Afterimage 3:59 Aut '70

GARRETT, OTIS
  Obit.   N. Y. Times 27:1 Mr 20 '40

GASSAN, ARNOLD
  Listing of films.   Film Culture 37:7 Sum '65

GATTI, ARMAND
  Graham, P.   The face of '63--France.   Films & Filming
      9-8:13 My '63

GAVIGAN, GERRY
  Gavigan, G.   The call of the wild.   Movie Maker 6-8:532
      Ag '72

GAVRAS, KOSTANTINOS
  (See:  COSTA-GAVRAS)

GEESINK, JOOP
  Biographical note.   International Film G 4:125 '67

GEHR, ERNIE
  Mekas, J.   Interview.   Film Culture 53/54/55:25 Spg '72
  Program notes by Ernie Gehr; filmog.   Film Culture
      53/54/55:36 Spg '72

GENINA, AUGUSTO
   Obit. N. Y. Times p86 S 29 '57

GEORGIADIS, VASSILIS
   Georgiadis, V. Focus on a director. International Film
      G 8:168 '71

GERASIMOV, SERGEI
   Gerasimov, S. Socialist realism and the Soviet cinema.
      Films & Filming 5-3:11 D '58
   Gerasimov, S. All is not Welles. Films & Filming
      5-12:8 S '59
   Gerasimov, S. A clash of conscience. Films & Filming
      7-6:7 Mr '61
   Reflections on Soviet culture. UNESCO Courier 20:21 N
      '67
   Hudson, R. Interview. Film 54:12 Spg '69
   Vronskaya, J. Recent Russian cinema. Film 62:5 Sum
      '71

GERMI, PIETRO
   Lane, J. F. The face of '63--Italy. Films & Filming
      9-7:11 Ap '63
   Bachmann, G. Man is no longer enough for man. Films
      & Filming 12-12:25 S '66

GERRARD, DOUGLAS
   Obit. Screen World 2:234 '51

GERSON, BARRY
   Listing of films. Film Culture 37:7 Sum '65

GHATAK, RITWIK
   Ray, S. K. New Indian directors. Film Q 14-1:63
      Fall '60

GIBLYN, CHARLES
   Bartless, R. A pioneer without whiskers. Photoplay
      12-4:131 S '17

GIBSON, ALAN
   British cinema filmography. Film 65:10 Spg '72

GIDAL, PETER
   Gidal, P. Some notes on underground film. Film 62:13
      Sum '71

GIESBERS, WIM
   Biographical note.   International Film G 7:335 '70

GILBERT, LEWIS
   Gilbert, L.   Drama from lives of men around us.
      Films & Filming 2-12:9 S '56
   Filmog.   Film 14:8 N/D '57
   British feature directors; an index to their work.  Sight
      & Sound 27-6:295 Aut '58
   Gilbert, L.   Ferry to Hong Kong ... and why we went
      round the world to make all of it.   Films & Filming
      5-10:19 Jl '59
   Robinson, W. R.   The movies as a revolutionary moral
      force (Alfie)  Contempora My/Ag '71
   British cinema filmography.   Film 65:10 Spg '72

GILLETTE, BURTON
   Obit.   Classic Film Collector 34:X-2 Spg '72

GILLIAT, SIDNEY
   Filmography.   Film 14:8 N/D '57
   British feature directors; an index to their work.  Sight
      & Sound 27-6:295 Aut '58

GILLING, JOHN
   Filmography.   Film 14:8 N/D '57
   British feature directors; an index to their work.  Sight
      & Sound 27-6:295 Aut '58

GILROY, FRANK
   Gilroy is here.   Time 83:43 Je 19 '64
   Prideaux, T.   Gilroy's small world confounds the big
      time.   Life 57:72 S 4 '64
   Biography.   Current Biography 26:16 O '65
      Same.   Current Biography Yearbook 1965:163 '65
   Leaf, P.   Two desperate characters.   Making Films
      5-5:8 O '71
   Gilroy, F.   First feature: Desperate characters.  Action
      6-6:3 N/D '71
   Simon, J.   A nice man.   New York 5-32:66 Ag 7 '72

GIMBEL, PETER
   Gimbel, P.   The hunt for the great white shark.  Ameri-
      can Cinematographer 52-9:872 S '71

GLENNON, BERT
   Obit.   N.Y. Times 23:6 Jl 1 '67

GLENVILLE, PETER

Feydeau, father of pure farce. Theatre Arts 41:66 Ap
'46

Filmography. Film 14:8 N/D '57

British feature directors; an index to their work. Sight
& Sound 27-6:295 Aut '58

Roll call for Rashomon. Theatre Arts 43:12 F '59

Magic moments of musicals. Theatre Arts 43:21 O '59

Larger slice of life. Theatre Arts 44:22 O '60

Peter Glenville. Films & Filming 8-8:5 My '62

Glenville, P. Reflections of Becket. Films & Filming
10-7:7 Ap '64

Fixx, J. F. Great Gallic welcome. Sat R 48:17 D 25
'65

Peter Glenville talks about the Burtons. Vogue 150:282
S 1 '67

British cinema filmography. Film 65:10 Spg '72

GODARD, JEAN-LUC

Larcenous talent. Time 77:58 Mr 17 '61

Godard, J-L. But "wave" adds brightness. Films &
Filming 7-12:7 S '61

Godard, J-L. Montage, Mon beau souci. Film Culture
22/23:37 '61

Milne, T. Jean-Luc Godard and Vivre sa vie. Sight &
Sound 32-1:1 Win '61/62

Fieschi, J. Godard: cut sequence. Movie 6:21 Ja '63

Graham, P. The face of '63--France. Films & Filming 9-8:13 My '63

Marcorelles, L. Jean-Luc Godard's half-truths. Film Q
17-3:4 Spg '64

Feinstein, H. Interview. Film Q 17-3:8 Spg '64

Sarris, A. Waiting for Godard. Film Culture 33:2 Sum
'64

Interview. N. Y. Film B #46 '64

Zand, N. Interview. Atlas 9:56 Ja '65

Godard on pure film. Cinema (BH) 2-5:38 Mr/Ap '65

Jean-Luc Godard interviews Michelangelo Antonioni.
Movie 12:31 Spg '65

Milne, T. Jean-Luc Godard, ou La Raison Ardente.
Sight & Sound 34-3:106 Sum '65

Gill, B. Current cinema. New Yorker 41:99 Ag 21 '65

Godard est Godard. New Yorker 41:43 O 9 '65

Godard, J-L. An interview with Antonioni. Cahiers
(Eng) 1:19 Ja '66

Godard, J-L. Bergmanorama. Cahiers (Eng) 1:56 Ja
'66

Goldman, J. Godard: cult or culture? Films & Filming 12-9:36 Je '66

My anger has to strike. Atlas 11:375 Je '66

Wittig, M. Lacunary films. New Statesman 72:102 Jl 15 '66

Sharits, P. J. Red, blue, Godard. Film Q 19-4:24 Sum '66

Kael, P. Movie brutalists. New Republic 155:24 S 24 '66

Lu Clezio talks to Godard. Atlas 12:54 S '66

Godard, J-L. Montage, mon beau souci. Cahiers (Eng) 3:45 '66

Godard, J-L. One or two things. Sight & Sound 36-1:2 Win '66/67

Two arts in one; conversation. Cahiers (Eng) 6:25 D '66

Godard, J-L. Modern life. Take One 1-3:7 F '67

Godard, J-L. & Delahaye, M. Interview with Robert Bresson. Cahiers (Eng) 8:5 F '67

Godard, J-L. Three thousands hours of cinema. Cahiers (Eng) 10:10 My '67

Bertolucci, B. Versus Godard. Cahiers (Eng) 10:16 My '67

Delahaye, M. Jean-Luc Godard and the children of art. Cahiers (Eng) 10:18 My '67

Delahaye, M. Jean-Luc Godard on the urgency of art. Cahiers (Eng) 10:33 My '67

Roud, R. Godard. Making Films 1-4:17 O '67

Armitage, P. Honest to Godard. Film 50:13 Win '67

Moullet, L. Jean-Luc Godard. Cahiers (Eng) 12:22 D '67

Fieschi, J-A. The difficulty of being Jean-Luc Godard. Cahiers (Eng) 12:38 D '67

Biography. British Book Year 1967:151 '67

The truth 24 times a second. Newsweek 71:90 F 12 '68

Infuriating magician. Time 91:90 F 16 '68

Larcenous talent. Time 77:58 Mr 17 '68

Alpert, H. Film ferment. Sat R 51:39 Mr 30 '68

Kael, P. Current cinema. New Yorker 44:156 Ap 6 '68

Gilliatt, P. Current cinema. New Yorker 44:157 My 11 '68

Christgau, R. Godard: master of the clean home movie. Ramparts 6:59 Je 15 '68

Sheed, W. Films. Esquire 69:56 Je '68

Godard in Hollywood. Take One 1-10:13 Je '68

MacBean, J. R. Politics, painting and the language of signs in Godard's Made in USA. Film Q 22:18 Spg '68

Federman, R. Jean-Luc Godard and Americanism.
Film Heritage 3-3:1 Spg '68
Goldwasser, N. Made in U. S. A. : the paper tiger in
your tank. Cineaste 1-4: Spg '68
Siegel, J. E. Between art and life: the films of Jean-
Luc Godard. Film Heritage 3-3:11 Spg '68
Sarris, A. Jean-Luc versus Saint Jean. Film Heritage
3-3:27 Spg '68
Sontag, S. Godard. Partisan R 35:290 Spg '68
MacBean, J. R. Politics and poetry. Film Q 21-4:14
Sum '68
Clouzot, C. Godard and the U. S. Sight & Sound 37-3:
110 Sum '68
Quotemanship. Action 3-3:20 Jl/Ag '68
Roud, R. One plus one. Sight & Sound 37-4:182 Aut '68
Fabrizio, T. Godard and the U. S. Sight & Sound 37-4:
215 Aut '68
Kael, P. Current cinema. New Yorker 44:141 O 5 '68
Struggle on two fronts. Film Q 22:20 Win '68
MacBean, J. R. Weekend, or the self critical cinema
of cruelty. Film Q 22:35 Win '68
Struggle on two fronts; conversation with Jean-Luc Godard.
Film Q 22-2:20 Win '68/69
Pechter, W. S. For and against Godard. Commentary
47:59 Ap '69
Biography. Current Biography 30:12 My '69
Same. Current Biography Yearbook 1969:167 '70
Crofts, S. The films of Jean-Luc Godard. Cinema
(Lon) 3:27 Je '69
Ross, W. S. Splicing together Jean-Luc Godard; inter-
view. Esquire 72:72 Jl '69
Roud, R. Memories of Resnais. Sight & Sound 38-3:124
Sum '69
Weightman, J. Whatever happened to Godard? Encounter
33:56 S '69
What directors are saying. Action 4-5:32 S/O '69
Goodwin, M. Interview. Take One 2-10:8 Mr/Ap '70
Jean-Luc Godard, including notes on two films: British
sounds, Pravada. Afterimage 1:no p# Ap '70
Flatley, G. Godard says bye-bye to Bardot and all that.
N. Y Times Bio Ed My 17 '70
Gilliatt, P. Current cinema. New Yorker 46:102 My 2;
46:88 My 30 '70
Godard: a select bibliography. Take One 2-11:11 My/Je
'70
Silverstein, N. Godard and revolution. Films & Film-
ing 16-9:96 Je '70

Isaac, D.   The social gospel of St. Jean-Luc Godard.
Film Culture 48/49:49 Win/Spg '70
Dawson, J.   Raising the red flag.   Sight & Sound 39-2:90
Spg '70
What directors are saying.   Action 5-4:30 Jl/Ag '70
Interview.   Evergreen R p47 S '70
MacBean, J. R.   See you at Mao.   Film Q 24-2:15 Win
'70/71
Westerbeck, C. L. Jr.   A terrible day is born.   Sight &
Sound 40-2:80 Spg '71
MacBean, J. R.   At the crossroads.   Sight & Sound
40-3:144 Sum '71
Cast, D.   Godard's truths.   Film Heritage 6-4:19 Sum
'71
Elsaesser, T.   Godard's sounds.   Monogram 2:7 Sum '71
Roud, R.   Long live Godard and Gorin.   Sight & Sound
41-3:123 Sum '72
Rosenbaum, J.   Theory and practice; the criticism of
Jean-Luc Godard.   Sight & Sound 41-3:124 Sum '72
Lesage, J.   Radical French cinema in context.   Cineaste
5-3:42 Sum '72
MacBean, J. R.   Godard and the Dziga Vertov group:
film and dialectics.   Film Q 26-1:30 Fall '72
Godard in Hollywood.   Take One 1-10:13 n. d.
Goodwin, M.   Interview.   Interview 1-11:6 n. d.

GODFREY, BOB
Godfrey, B.   The animated cartoon 1963.   International
Film G 1:171 '64
Bob Godfrey films.   Film 45:29 Spg '66
Animation quartet.   International Film G 3:175 '66

GODREY, PETER
Morris, G.   From Gate to Gate.   Theatre Arts 29:58
Ja '45
Obit.   Screen World 22:237 '71

GOLAN, MENAHEM
Biographical note.   International Film G 6:103 '69

GOLD, JACK
Robinson, D.   Case histories of the next renascence.
Sight & Sound 38:37 Win '68
Spiers, D.   Interview.   Screen 10-4/5:115 Jl/O '69
British cinema filmography.   Film 65:10 Spg '72

GOLDBECK, WILLIS
    The power of "suggestions." Lions Roar 2-5:no p# Jl
        '43
    One man's meat. Lions Roar 3-3:no p# Ap '44
    MGM's directors range from pioneers to newcomers.
        Lions Roar 3-4:no p# Jl '44
    He sees 'em coming up. Lions Roar 4-1:no p# F '45

GOLDMAN, PETER
    Listing of films. Film Culture 37:7 Sum '65
    Andrew Sarris on Peter Goldman. Film Culture 42:111
        Fall '66
    Peter Goldman discusses Echoes of silence. Film
        Culture 42:112 Fall '66

GOLDSTONE, JAMES
    Butts, J. Facing up to reality; interview. Films &
        Filming 18-4:28 Ja '72
    Brown, V. A talk with James Goldstone. Action 7-3:22
        My/Je '72

GORDON, BERT I.
    Shooting movies with a Nikon. U. S. Camera 30:68 Ja
        '67

GORDON, ROBERT
    Wawa moves east. Time 85:40 F 5 '65

GORDON, STUART
    Listing of films. Film Culture 37:7 Sum '65

GORIN, JEAN-PIERRE
    Flatley, G. Godard says bye-bye to Bardot and all that.
        N. Y. Times Bio Ed My 17 '70
    Goodwin, M. & Wise, N. Raymond Chandler, Mao Tse-
        Tung and Tout va bien; interview. Take One 3-6:22
        Jl/Ag '71
    Roud, R. Long live Godard and Gorin. Sight & Sound
        41-3:123 Sum '72
    Lesage, J. Radical French cinema in context. Cineaste
        5-3:42 Sum '72
    MacBean, J. R. Godard and the Dziga Vertov group:
        film and dialectics. Film Q 26-1:30 Fall '72
    Goodwin, M. Interview with Godard. Interview 1-11:6
        n. d.

GOSHO, HEINOSUKE
  Anderson, J. L. & Richie, D.   The films of Heinosuke
    Gosho.   Sight & Sound 26-2:76 Aut '56
  Note.   International Film G 2:33 '65

GOULDING, EDMUND
  Biographical note; filmog.   Movies & People 2:42 '40
  With cameras on Claudia.   Cue 12-35:8 Ag 28 '43
  Whistles a tune to an arranger for background music to
    a film.   Time 49:48 My 19 '47
  Obit.   N. Y. Times 24:2 D 25 '59
    Screen World 11:219 '60
  Sarris, A.   Likable but elusive; filmog.   Film Culture
    28:35 Spg '63

GRADUS, BEN
  What they say.   Making Films 4-3:46 Je '70

GRAF, LOUIS C.
  Obit.   Screen World 19:233 '68

GRANIER-DEFERRE, PIERRE
  Ehrlich, H.   It's smashing to be stinky.   Look 35-4:28
    F 23 '71

GRAS, ENRICO
  Emmer, L. & Gras, E.   The film renaissance in Italy.
    Hollywood Q 2-4:353 Jl '47

GREAVES, WILLIAM
  Who's who in filmmaking; selected filmog.   Sightlines
    3-1:6 S/O '69
  Greaves, W.   Log: in the company of men.   Film Library
    Q 3-1:29 Win '69/70

GREBELSKY, GARY
  Grebelsky, G.   A super-16 production experience.   Film-
    makers Newsletter 5-11:30 S '72

GREEN, ALFRED E.
  Obit.   N. Y. Times p33 S 6 '60
    Screen World 12:221 '61

GREEN, GUY
  British feature directors; an index to their work.   Sight
    & Sound 27-6:295 Aut '58
  Guy Green.   Films & Filming 9-5:5 F '63

Guy Green talks about The magus.  Films & Filming
  15-4:59 Ja '69

GREENE, DAVID
  British cinema filmography.  Film 65:10 Spg '72

GREENFIELD, AMY
  Greenfield, A.  Dance as film.  Filmmakers Newsletter
  4-1:26 N '70

GREFÉ, WILLIAM
  Grefe, W.  Filming in Florida.  Action 6-6:6 N/D '71

GREGORETTI, UGO
  Lane, J. F.  The face of '63--Italy.  Films & Filming
  9-7:11 Ap '63

GRÉMILLON, JEAN
  Hackett, H.  Jean Gemillon.  Sight & Sound 16-62:60
  Sum '47

GRIERSON, JOHN
  Grierson, J.  Future for British film.  Spectator 148:691
    My 14 '32
  Grierson, J.  One hundred percent cinema.  Spectator
    155:285 Ag 23 '35
  Grierson, J.  Dramatizing housing needs and city planning
    in the city.  Films 1-1:85 N '39
  Grierson, J.  Postwar patterns.  Hollywood Q 1-2:159
    Ja '46
  Story of.  Time 48:101 D 16 '46
  Grierson, J.  Notes on the tasks of an international film
    institute.  Hollywood Q 2-2:192 Ja '47
  Grierson, J.  Prospect for documentary.  Sight & Sound
    17-66:55 Sum '48
  Grierson, J.  Flaherty as innovator.  Sight & Sound
    21-2:64 O/D '51
  Grierson, J.  The front page.  Sight & Sound 21-4:143
    Ap/Je '52
  Grierson, J.  The BBC and all that.  Q Film Radio TV
    9-1:46 Fall '54
  Grierson, J.  The prospect for cultural cinema.  Film
    7:20 Ja/F '56
  A tough man with an unbroken heart.  Vision 1-2:75 Sum
    '62
  Who's who in filmmaking.  Sightlines 1-2:4 N/D '67
  Interview.  Take One 2-9:17 Ja/F '70

Ellis, J. C.　John Grierson's first years at the National
　　film board.　Cinema J 10-1:2 Fall '70
Obit.　N. Y. Times Bio Ed F 21 '72
Jacoby, I.　A small packet of Scottish dynamite.　Sight-
　　lines 5-5:10 My/Je '72
Sussex, E.　John Grierson.　Sight & Sound 41-2 Spg '72
Sussex, E.　The golden years of Grierson.　Sight &
　　Sound 41-3:149 Sum '72
Grierson's hammer.　Films & Filming 18-10:14 Jl '72
Sussex, E.　Grierson on documentary; the last interview.
　　Film Q 26-1:24 Fall '72

GRIES, TOM
　　Cyrano de Bergerac; Stanley Kramer production.　Theatre
　　　　Arts 34:32 N '50
　　Gries, T.　Why directors criticize critics.　Action 4-1:13
　　　　Ja/F '69
　　Tom Gries on critics.　Making Films 3-6:37 D '69

GRIFFIN, FRANK
　　Biographical note.　Photoplay 9-4:42 Mr '16

GRIFFITH, DAVID WARK
　　Man who "made" the movies.　Theatre 19:311 Je '14
　　Man who "made" the movies.　Leslie W 119:104 Jl 30 '14
　　Worley, E. M.　Man who "made" the movies.　McClure
　　　　43:109 S '14
　　Stanhope, S. A.　The world's master picture producer.
　　　　Photoplay 7-2:57 Ja '15
　　Barry, R.　Interview.　Editor 41:407 Ap 24 '15
　　The Griffith way.　Photoplay 7-5:75 Ap '15
　　Katterjohn, M. W.　Work of.　Green Book 13:897 My '15
　　Guiterman, A.　Sketch.　Womans Home Companion 42:9
　　　　Je '15
　　Carr, H. C.　Directors: the men who make the plays.
　　　　Photoplay 8-1:80 Je '15
　　Courtlandt, R.　Interview.　Motion Pic 10:90 Ag '15
　　Sketch.　N. Y. Dramatic Mirror 75:26 Ap 22; 76:26 Jl 15
　　　　'16
　　Gordon, H. S.　The story of David Wark Griffith.　Photo-
　　　　play 10-1:28 Je; 10-2:122 Jl; 10-3:78 Ag; 10-4:79 S;
　　　　10-5:86 O; 10-6:27 N '16
　　Moving pictures vs. one-night stands.　Independent 88:447
　　　　D 11 '16
　　Destiny of motion pictures.　N. Y. Dramatic Mirror
　　　　77:45 Ja 27 '17
　　Darnell, J.　Personal side.　Motion Pic 12:95 Ja '17

What I demand of movie stars.   Motion Pic Classic 3:40
    F '17
Denig, L.   Proposed production of war pictures.   Dramatic Mirror 77:8 O 27 '17
Wise man of the movies.   Theatre 27:58 Ja '18
Carr, H. C.   Griffith, maker of battle scenes, sees real
    war.   Photoplay 13-4:23 Mr '18
Visit to the trenches.   Current Opinion 64:258 Ap '18
Haskins, H.   Work of.   Motion Pic Classic 7:16 S '18
Carr, H.   Interview.   Motion Pic Classic 7:16 D '18
Carr, H. C.   How Griffith picks his leading women.
    Current Opinion 66:30 Ja '19
Naylor, H. S.   Interview.   Motion Pic 18:28 S '19
Smith, F. J.   Sketch.   Motion Pic Classic 10:27 Mr '20
Work of.   Theatre 31:389 My '20
How I get along with people.   Hearst 38:36 S '20
Mullett, M. P.   Greatest moving picture producer in the
    world.   American 91:32 Ap '21
Motion pictures.   Mentor 9:2 Jl '21
Youth, the spirit of the movies.   Illustrated World
    36:194 O '21
The miracle man of the movies.   National 50:421 Ja '22
Savage, R.   Interview.   Theatre 35:108 F '22
Another dreamer who wants to stop all war.   Graphic
    105:518 Ap 29 '22
Dickens and Griffith of the movies.   Lit Digest 73:31
    Ja 10 '22
Carr, H.   Interview.   Motion Pic 24:23 Ag '22
Leeds, S.   Sketch.   Classic 16:23 Mr '23
Are motion pictures destructive of good taste?   Arts &
    Decoration 19:12 S '23
Carr, H.   Work of.   Classic 18:24 N '23
Real truth about breaking into the movies.   Womans Home
    Companion 51:16 F '24
Movies 100 years from now.   Colliers 73:7 My 3 '24
Redway, S.   Sketch.   Motion Pic Classic 22:30 O '25
Stearns, M. M.   How do you like the show?   Colliers
    77:8 Ap 24 '26
Tully, J.   Interview.   Vanity Fair 27:80 N '26
Smith, F. J.   Interview.   Photoplay 31:30 D '26
The motion picture--today and tomorrow.   Theatre 46:21
    O '27
Wilson, B. F.   Work of.   Motion Pic Classic 26:21 N
    '27
London, M.   D. W. Griffith.   Overland 86:137 My '28
Cruikshank, H.   Appreciation.   Motion Pic Classic 30:35
    N '29

Braverman, B. G.   Pioneer motion picture producer.
    Theatre Guild 8:28 F '31

Personalities prominent in the press.   Cinema Digest
    1-3:7 Je 13 '32

Hall, H.   Griffith gets garrulous.   Cinema Digest 3-7:3
    My 1 '33

Lee, S.   Immortals of the screen.   Motion Pic 46:32 O
    '33

Mastin, M.   Star-maker whose dreams turned to dust.
    Photoplay 45:50 My '34

Hall, L.   Interview.   Stage 13:112 Ag '36

Mackaye, M.   Birth of a nation.   Scribner 102:40 N '37
    Same, abridged.   Reader Digest 32:103 Ja '38

His movies now ancient history.   Life 4:2 Ap 25 '38

Stern, S.   Pioneer of the film art.   N. Y. Times Mag
    p16 N 10 '40

Bravermann, B.   D. W. Griffith, creator of film form.
    Theatre Arts 29:240 Ap '45

Stern, S.   An index to the creative work of D. W.
    Griffith; The Triangle productions.   Sight & Sound
    (special sup) Index Series # 7 Ag '46

Noble, P.   A note on an idol.   Sight & Sound 15-59:81
    Aut '46

Stern, S.   An index to the creative work of D. W.
    Griffith: Hearts of the world.   Sight & Sound (special
    sup) Index Series # 10 My '47

Griffith, D. W. & Stern, S.   The Birth of a nation;
    reply to Peter Noble.   Sight & Sound 16-61:32 Spg '47

Stern, S.   The Griffith controversy.   Sight & Sound
    17-65:49 Spg '48

Obit.   Illustrated London N 213:134 Jl 31 '48
    Life 25:31 Ag 2 '48
    N. Y. Times p15 Jl 24 '48
    Newsweek 32:55 Ag 2 '48
    Time 52:72 Ag 2 '48

Agre, J.   D. W. Griffith.   Nation 167:264 S 4 '48

Stern, S.   D. W. Griffith--an appreciation.   Sight &
    Sound 17-67:109 Aut '48

Stern, S.   D. W. Griffith and the movies.   American
    Mercury 68:308 Mr '49

Leyda, J.   Art and death of D. W. Griffith.   Sewanee
    R 57:350 Ap '49

Feldman, J. & H.   The D. W. Griffith influence.   Films
    In Review 1-5:11 Jl/Ag '50

Eisenstein, S. M.   Dicks, Griffith and the film today.
    Sight & Sound 19-4:169; 19-5:216 Jl; 19-6:256 Ag;
    19-7:294 N '50

Dickinson, T.   Griffith and the silent film.   Sight &
  Sound 21-2:84 O/D '51

Stern, S.   Griffith and Poe.   Films In Review 2-9:23 N
  '51

Stern, S.   The cold war against D. W. Griffith.   Films
  In Review 7-2:49 F '56

Drum, D. D.   Porter and Griffith; letter.   Films In Review 7-3:138 Mr '56

Stern, S.   The Soviet directors' debt to D. W. Griffith.
  Films In Review 7-5:202 My '56

Everson, W. K.   Griffith and Ince; letter.   Films In
  Review 8-2:94 F '57

Salerno, A. J.   Griffith in Louisville; letter.   Films In
  Review 8-4:187 Ap '57

Vaughan, D.   Victor Sjostrom and D. W. Griffith.   Film
  15:13 Ja/F '58

Carr, C. C.   D. W. Griffith; letter.   Films In Review
  10-3:188 Mr '59

Stern, S.   Biographical hogwash.   Films In Review 10-5:
  284 My '59

Mayer, A. L.   The origins of United Artists.   Films In
  Review 10-7:390 Ag/S '59

Letters; reply to Stern.   Films In Review 10-7:441 Ag/S
  '59

Gessner, R.   Moving image.   American Heritage 11:30
  Ap '60

Sarris, A.   Pantheon directors; filmog.   Film Culture
  28:2 Spg '63

Crowthers, B.   Birth of the Birth of a nation.   N. Y.
  Times Mag p24 F 7 '65

Stern, S.   Griffith.   Film Culture 36:entire issue.   Spg/
  Sum '65

Niemeyer, G. C.   D. W. Griffith, in retrospect, 1965.
  Film Heritage 1-1:13 Fall '65

Ridlon, S. D.   The master revisited.   8mm Collector
  13:5 Fall/Win '65

Johnson, W.   Birth of an art.   Senior Scholastic 88:4
  Mr 4 '66

Meyer, R. J.   The films of David Wark Griffith.   Film
  Comment 4-2/3:92 Fall/Win '67

Nathan, P.   Rights and permissions.   Publisher W 192:
  71 N 13 '67

Roseman, H. C.   How good was Griffith?   Classic Film
  Collector 17:17 Win/Spg '67

Night watch.   Classic Film Collector 18:39 Sum '67 (reprint from The Villager, N '53)

Kael, P.   Current cinema.   New Yorker 44:102 F 24 '68

Biograph, Griffith and fate.　Silent Pic 1:no p# Win '68/69

The simplicity of true greatness.　Silent Pic 4:18 Aut '69

Mae Marsh, Robert Harron and D. W. Griffith.　Silent
　　Pic 4:10 Aut '69

Griffith, a big step forward to Judith.　Silent Pic 5:9
　　Win '69/70

Farnett, G.　D. W. Griffith: 1931.　Film Fan Mo 105:8
　　Mr '70

Sklar, R.　Griffith's Russian fans.　Nation 211:249 S 21
　　'70

Zimmerman, P. D.　Griffith--films' old master.　News-
　　week 77:87 Mr 8 '71

Griffith, D. W.　The movies 100 years from now.　Views
　　& Reviews 3-2:10 Fall '71

Dorr, J.　The movies, Mr. Griffith and Carol Dempster.
　　Cinema (BH) 7-1:23 Fall '71

Plaut, J.　Roots of film realism in a Griffith one-reeler.
　　Filmograph 2-1:41 '71

Casty, A.　The films of D. W. Griffith.　Journal Popu-
　　lar Film 1-2:67 Spg '72

Lenning, A.　D. W. Griffith and the making of an un-
　　conventional masterpiece.　Film Journal 1-3/4:2
　　Fall/Win '72

Larson, R.　A retrospective look at the films of D. W.
　　Griffith and Andy Warhol.　Film Journal 1-3/4:80
　　Fall/Win '72

GRIGSBY, MICHAEL
　　Crick, P.　Michael Grigsby and Unit five seven.　Film
　　38:8 Win '63

GRINDE, NICK
　　Where's vaudeville at?　Sat Evening Post 202:44 Ja 11
　　'30

　　Whimsy by the mile.　Reader Digest 28:61 Ja '36

　　Pictures for peanuts.　Sat Evening Post 218:14 D 25 '45

　　Handmade language.　Sat Evening Post 221:34 Jl 10 '48

GROENING, HOMER
　　Who's who in filmmaking; filmog.　Sightlines 1-6:4 Jl/Ag
　　'68

GRØNLYKKE, SVEN
　　Adams, S.　Four Dane directors; interview.　CTVD
　　7-2:26 Spg '70

　　Biographical note.　International Film G 8:117 '71

GROOMS, CHARLES (Red)
Grand Pop Moses.  Time 85:76 Ap 9 '65
Listing of films.  Film Culture 37:7 Sum '65
Berrigan, T.  Red power.  Art N 65:44 D '66
Kroll, J.  People painter.  Newsweek 69:98 Ja 30 '67
Rosenberg, H.  Art world; exhibition.  New Yorker
    43:100 F 25 '67
News of art.  Horizon 9:78 Win '67
Goodrich, D. L.  Anybody want to buy Chicago.  Sat
    Evening Post 242:36 F 8 '69

GROSBARD, ULU
Ulu Grosbard discusses The subject was roses with
    Ernest Shaw.  Making Films 2-2:22 Ap '68

GROULX, GILLES
Biographical note; filmog.  Cahiers (Eng) 4:43 '66

GRUMMAN, FRANCIS
Again: the director/cameraman.  Making Films 4-3:42
    Je '70

GRUNDGENS, GUSTAV
Donaldson, G.  Gustav Grundgens' films; filmog.  Films
    In Review 16-1:63 Ja '65
Luft, H. G.  Letter.  Films In Review 16-3:185 Mr '65

GUERRA, RUI
Viany, A.  Who's who in the cinema novo.  CTVD 5-4:26
    Sum '68

GUEST, VAL
British feature directors; an index to their work.  Sight
    & Sound 27-6:295 Aut '58
Guest, V.  British films were never bad.  Films &
    Filming 7-1:34 O '69
Cowie, P.  The face of '63--Great Britain.  Films &
    Filming 9-5:19 F '63
British cinema filmography.  Film 65:10 Spg '72

GUILLERMIN, JOHN
Filmography.  Film 14:8 N/D '57
British feature directors; an index to their work.  Sight
    & Sound 27-6:296 Aut '58
British cinema filmography.  Film 65:10 Spg '72

GUITRY, SACHA
Sketch.    Sat R 114:452 O 12 '12
Steell, W.    Work of.    Theatre 17:23 Ja '13
Kitchen, K.    Sketch.    Theatre 20:118 S '14
Sketch.    Current Opinion 59:102 Ag '15
Classical color of Sacha Guitry's triviality.    Current
 Opinion 67:99 Ag '19
Last thoughts on the Guitry season.    Athenaeum 1920
 1:809 Je 8 '20
Guitrys in London.    Living Age 306:32 Jl 3 '20
French polish on British and American stages.    Lit
 Digest 66:31 Jl 10 '20
Interviewing Bernard Shaw and Sacha Guitry.    Living Age
 311:555 N 26 '21
Guitrys in London.    Living Age 314:243 Jl 22 '22
Lewisohn, L.    Guitry.    Nation 116:373 Mr 28 '23
Clark, B. H.    Famous theatrical family.    Theatre 37:24
 Mr '23
The Guitrys.    Sat R 135:768 Je 9 '23
Interviewing Sacha Guitry    Living Age 320:188 Ja 26 '24
Guitrys.    Lit Digest 90:29 S 4 '26
Yvonne and Sacha.    Lit Digest 92:28 Ja 15 '27
Macdougall, A. R.    Famous Guitrys now playing in New
 York Arts & Decoration 26:56 Ja '27
Mason, E.    Interview.    Theatre 45:32  Mr '27
deCroisset, F.    Persons and personages.    Living Age
 345:231 N '33
Off stage and on; autobiographical.    Atlantic 155:643 Je;
 156:34 Jl; 173 Ag; 324 S '35
Guitry's growing up.    Time 26:77 O 14 '35
Preshelden, S.    Memory serves very well.    Christian
 Science Mon Mag p9 D 4 '35
Blum, L.    Sacha Guitry.    Theatre Arts 21:740 S '37
Questioned by the F. B. I.    Vogue 104:97 O 15 '44
Paris' No. 1 jack-of-all theatrics.    Time 47:46 Mr 18
 '46
Descaves, P.    J'Accuse.    Hollywood Q 1-4:435 Jl '46
Joseph, R.    Je confirme.    Hollywood Q 2:206 Ja '47
Ordeal of Sacha Guitry.    Time 51:32 Je 7 '48
Nathan, G. J.    Formula of the Guitry comedy.    American
 Mercury 68:468 Ap '49
Love marches on.    Life 27:53 D 12 '49
Men who fascinate women.    Look 19:74 O 4 '55
Obit.    Americana Annual 1958:537 '58
 British Book Year 1958:512 '58
 Illustrated London N 231:201 Ag 3 '57
 N. Y. Times p26 Jl 24 '57

Newsweek 50:65 Ag 5 '57
Time 70:75 Ag 5 '57
Wilson Library B 32:19 S '57
Marcorelles, L.   Sacha Guitry.   Sight & Sound 27-2:101
   Aut '57
Hatch, R.   Films.   Nation 185:332 N 5 '57
Ford, C.   Sacha Guitry; letter.   Films In Review 8-9:474
   N '57
Clurman, H.   French characters.   Nation 208:88 Ja 20
   '69
Roud, R.   Memories of Resnais.   Sight & Sound 38-3:124
   Sum '69

GUNN, GILBERT
   British feature directors; an index to their work.   Sight
   & Sound 27-6:296 Aut '58

GURROLA, JUAN JOSE
   Riera, E.   A new Mexican cinema.   CTVD 6-3:21 Spg '69

GUY, ALICE
   (See: BLACHE, ALICE GUY)

GUY-BLACHÉ, ALICE
   (See: BLACHE, ALICE GUY)

GYARMATHY, LIVIA
   TV technician shortage; excerpts from address.   Elec-
   trical World 83:32 Mr '70
   Biographical note.   International Film G 7:138 '70

HAANSTRA, BERT
  Biographical note. International Film G 2:117 '65
  Director of the year; filmog. International Film G 3:28
    '66
  Biographical note. International Film G 8:208 '71
  Cowie, P. Biographical note; filmog. Focus On Film
    9:10 Spg '72

HAAS, HUGO
  Biographical note. Time 58:102 Ag 27 '51
  Obit. Screen World 19:233 '68
    Screen World 20:235 '69

HÄDRICH, ROLF
  Bean, R. The face of '63--Germany. Films & Filming
    9-9:41 Je '63

HAFER, RICK
  David and Goliath. Making Films 5-4:18 Ag '71

HAGMANN, STUART
  Hagmann, S. Reflections on The strawberry statement.
    Action 5-5:26 S/O '70

HALAS, JOHN
  Halas and Batchelor; profile of a partnership. Film
    4:15 Mr '55
  Animated cartoon. Design 64:33 S '62
  Filmography. International Film G 1:65 '64
  Halas and Batchelor. International Film G 2:175 '65
  Halas and Batchelor. Film 45:28 Spg '66
  Animated cartoon. Design 70:25 Win '68

HALE, SONNIE
  Obit. N.Y. Times p37 Je 10 '59

HALEY, JACK JR.
  Gelman, M. Haley's young lions. Television 24:22 Jl
    '67
  Haley, J. Jr. Years from now, when you talk about
    this.... Action 5-5:14 S/O '70

HALL, ALEXANDER
  The man with the baton. Lions Roar 3-2:no p# Ja '44

Cosmopolitan's citation for the best direction of the
month. Cosmop 119:61 D '45
Obit. Classic Film Collector 22:56 Fall/Win '68 (re-
print from Variety)
N.Y. Times p31 Ag 1 '68
Screen World 20:235 '69

## HALL, PETER

Hewes, H. Bloodless revolution. Sat R 43:43 S 17 '60
Fay, G. London panorama. Theatre Arts 46:68 Ja '62
Biography. Current Biography 23:17 F '62
Same. Current Biography Yearbook 1962:179 '63
Hewes, H. Forward with anger. Sat R 45:21 Ap 7 '62
British cinema filmography. Film 65:10 Spg '62
Marowitz, C. Three theatres of Peter Hall. Theatre
Arts 46:62 S '62
Brien, A. Openings; London. Theatre Arts 46:57 D '62
Play that never was. Time 82:37 Ag 2 '63
Avoiding a method. Theatre Arts 47:24 Ag '63
Living figures. Opera News 29:6 N 14 '64
Heinitz, T. Thwarted attempt to present Schonberg's
Moses and Aaron at Royal Opera House. Sat R 48:43
Jl 31 '65
Gow, G. In search of a revolution; interview. Films &
Filming 15-12:40 S '69
Imm, V. What's in a name; interview. Opera News
34:19 N 1 '69
The crisis we deserve. Sight & Sound 39-4:172 Aut '70
Biography. British Book Year 1972:143 '71

## HALLER, DANIEL

Interview. Castle of Frankenstein 7:16 n.d.

## HAMER, FRED BOOTH

Obit. N.Y. Times p19 D 31 '53

## HAMER, ROBERT

Lockhart, F.B. Interview with Hamer. Sight & Sound
21-2:74 O/D '51
Filmography. Film 14:8 N/D '57
British feature directors; an index to their work. Sight
& Sound 27-6:296 Aut '58
A free hand. Sight & Sound 28-2:60 Spg '59
Vincent, J. Hamer's potted lifemanship. Films & Film-
ing 5-10:27 Jl '59
Obit. Film R p45 '64/65

HAMILTON, GUY
  Filmography.   Film 14:8 N/D '57
  Hamilton, G.   Films must give the public what it wants.
    Film 15:6 Ja/F '58
  British film directors; an index to their work.   Sight &
    Sound 27-6:296 Aut '58
  Cowie, P.   The face of '63--Great Britain.   Films &
    Filming 9-5:19 F '63
  British cinema filmography.   Film 65:10 Spg '72

HANCOCK, TONY
  Houston, P.   The Punch and Judy man.   Sight & Sound
    31-3:120 Sum '62

HANI, SUSUMU
  Iwabutchi, M.   Japanese cinema 1961.   Film Culture
    24:85 Spg '62
  Richie, D.   The face of '63--Japan.   Films & Filming
    9-10:15 Jl '63
  Toshiyama, T.   Susumu Hani; report and interview.
    CTVD 4-2:7 Spg '66
  Richie, D.   In Japan, the nude scene--tortured first
    love.   Atlas 16:64 N '68
  Blue, J.   Susumu Hani; interview; filmog.   Film Com-
    ment 5-2:24 Spg '69

HANOUN, MARCEL
  Talking about people.   Film 31:5 Spg '62
  Schultz, V.   Hanoun: the cinema of ambiguity.   Film
    Culture 53/54/55:115 Spg '72

HARLAN, VEIT
  Patalas, E.   The Kolberg case.   Sight & Sound 35-1:22
    Win '65/66

HARRINGTON, CURTIS
  Harrington, C.   The dangerous compromise.   Hollywood
    Q 3-4:405 Sum '48
  Harrington, C.   Distribution center for experimental
    films.   Hollywood Q 3-4:450 Sum '48
  Harrington, C.   Personal chronicle: the making of an
    experimental film.   Hollywood Q 4-1:42 Fall '49
  Arrogant gesture.   Theatre Arts 34:42 N '50
  Made in Japan.   Theatre Arts 35:26 D '51
  Two pennies' worth of films.   Theatre Arts 36:66 Ag '52
  Harrington, C.   Ghoulies and ghosties.   Q Film Radio TV
    7-2:191 Win '52

Tyler, P. Two down and one to go? Film Culture 21:33
Sum '60

Young, C. & Bachmann, G. New wave--or gesture?
Film Q 14-3:6 Spg '61

Young, C. West coast report. Sight & Sound 30-3:137
Sum '61

Curtis Harrington on Night tide. Cinema (BH) 1-2:22 '62

Harrington, C. A statement; filmog. Film Culture
29:69 Sum '63

Survey among unsuccessful applicants for the Ford Foundation film grants. Film Comment 2-3:10 Sum '64

Palmer, J. Interview. Film Culture 34:38 Fall '64

Gow, G. Up from the underground; filmog. Films &
Filming 17-11:16 Ag '71

McAsh, I. The gingerbread man; filmog. Films Illustrated 1-3:10 S '71

What directors are saying. Action 6-6:22 N/D '71


HARRIS, HILARY
Listing of films. Film Culture 37:7 Sum '65
Steele, R. Hilary Harris returns. Film Heritage 2-3:25
Spg '67
Gardner, R. The making of The Nuer. Film Library Q
4-3:8 Sum '71


HARRIS, JAMES B.
The Bedford incident; interview. Cinema (BH) 3-1:28
D '65


HART, NEAL
Obit. N.Y. Times p23 Ap 4 '49


HARTFORD-DAVIS, ROBERT
British cinema filmography. Film 65:10 Spg '72


HARTMAN, DON
Biographical note. Theatre Arts 35:45 Ag '51
Newman, I. Secretary in wonderland. Good Housekeep-
ing 141:42 O '55
Obit. N.Y. Times p27 Mr 24 '58
Screen World 10:222 '59
Time 71:82 Mr 31 '58


HARVEY, ANTHONY
Robinson, D. Case histories of the next renascence.
Sight & Sound 38:36 Win '68
Scheuer, P. K. Directors Guild award winner. Action
4-2:11 My/Je '69

British cinema filmography.   Film 65:10 Spg '72

## HAS, WOJCIECH
Toepplitz, K.   The films of Wojciech Has.   Film Q
18-2:2 Win '64

## HATHAWAY, HENRY
Men behind megaphones.   Cue 4-17:3 F 22 '36
Crichton, K.   Lives of a Hollywood director.   Colliers
98:20 S 5 '36
Biographical note; filmog.   Movies & People 2:42 '40
Reid, J. H.   The best second fiddle.   Films & Filming
9-2:14 N '62
Sarris, A.   Likable but elusive; filmog.   Film Culture
28:37 Spg '63
The directors choose the best films.   Cinema (BH)
1-5:14 Ag/S '63
Knight, A.   No pro like an old pro.   Sat R 52:31 Je 21
'69
Eyles, A.   Henry Hathaway; filmog.   Focus On Film 1:7
Ja/F '70
Scheuer, P. K.   Henry Hathaway.   Action 5-3:28 My/Je
'70
Nogueira, R.   Interview.   Focus On Film 7:11 n. d.
Canham, K.   Hathaway's films; filmog.   Focus On Film
7:22 n. d.
Hathaway on 16 mm.   Focus On Film 7:62 n. d.
Letters.   Focus On Film 8:55 n. d.

## HATTON, MAURICE
British cinema filmography.   Film 65:10 Spg '72

## HAUPE, WLODZIMIERZ
The Polish cinema.   Film 31:26 Spg '62

## HAWKINS, RICHARD C.
Hawkins, R. C.   Perspective on 3-D.   Q Film Radio TV
7-4:325 Sum '53

## HAWKS, HOWARD
Men behind megaphones.   Cue 4-15:3 F 8 '36
Work of.   Lit Digest 121:24 F 15 '36
Biographical note; filmog.   Movies & People 2:42 '40
Crichton, K.   Flying Hawks; director Howard Hawks
makes his greatest movie, Air Force.   Colliers 111:
36 Ja 16 '43
Alpert, H.   In the land of the blue Teal Eye.   Sat R 35:
28 Ag 16 '52

Rivette, J. & Truffaut, F.   Howard Hawks; filmog.
    Films In Review 7-9:443 N '56
Movie discoverer's latest find.   Life 45:163 N 17 '58
Sarris, A.   The world of Howard Hawks.   Films & Film-
    ing 8-10:20 Jl '62
Bogdanovich, P.   Howard Hawks; interview.   Movie 5:7
    D '62
Rivette on Hughes.   Movie 5:19 D '62
Discussion of his films by various writers; filmog.   Movie
    5:21 D '62
Man's favorite director; interview.   Cinema (BH) 1-6:10
    N/D '63
Wood, R.   Who the hell is Howard Hawks?   Focus 1:3
    '67; 2:8 '67
Austin, D.   Gunplay and horses; interview.   Films &
    Filming 15-1:25 O '68
Wellman, W. Jr.   Howard Hawks: the distance runner.
    Action 5-6:8 N/D '70
Wise, N.   The Hawksian woman.   Take One 3-3:17 Ja/F
    '71
Kasindorf, M.   The Hawk.   Newsweek 77:95 F 8 '71
Peary, G. & Groark, S.   Hawks at Warner Brothers:1932
    Velvet Light Trap 1:12 Je '71
Do I get to play the drunk this time?   an encounter with
    Howard Hawks.   Sight & Sound 40-2:97 Spg '71
Davis, P.   Bogart, Hawks and The big sleep revisited--
    frequently.   Film Journal 1-2:3 Sum '71
Brackett, L.   A comment on the Hawksian woman.   Take
    One 3-6:19 Jl/Ag '71
Ford, G.   Mostly on Rio Lobo.   Film Heritage 7-1:1
    Fall '71
Belton, J.   Hawks and company.   Cinema (Lon) 9:19 n.d.

HAY, WILL
    Smith, C.   Will Hay.   Film 16:13 Mr/Ap '58

HAYERS, SIDNEY
    British cinema filmography.   Film 65:10 Spg '72

HAYWARD, STAN
    Crick, P.   The freelance vision of Stan Hayward.   Film
        42:10 Win '64

HEIN, BIRGIT
    Thomas, A.   German underground.   Afterimage 2:45
        Aut '70

HEIN, WILHELM
    Thomas, A.  German underground.  Afterimage 2:45
        Aut '70

HELICZER, PIERO
    Listing of films.  Film Culture 37:7 Sum '65

HELLER, FRANKLIN
    Heller, F.  Turning on The electric company.  Action
        7-2:22 Mr/Ap '72

HELLMAN, MONTE
    Johnston, C.  Interview.  Cinema (Lon) 6/7:39 Ag '70
    Walker, B.  Two-lane blacktop.  Sight & Sound 40-1:34
        Win '70/71
    On the road with a new Hellman.  Show 2-1:16 Mr '71
    Harmetz, A.  M's turn for the big time?  N.Y. Times
        Bio Ed My 16 '71
    What directors are saying.  Action 6-4:20 Jl/Ag '71
    The professional director speaks.  Making Films 5-4:40
        Ag '71
    Goodwin, M.  Interview.  Interview 2-5:8 Ag '71

HENABERY, JOSEPH E.
    Cohn, A. A.  Sketch.  Photoplay 17:88 Ja '20

HENDERSON, DEL
    Biographical note.  Photoplay 9-4:42 Mr '16
    Obit.  N.Y. Times p39 D 5 '56

HENDERSON, LUCIUS J.
    Obit.  N.Y. Times p25 F 19 '47

HENLEY, HOBART
    Ames, H.  Sketch.  Motion Pic 11:72 My '16
    Van Loan, H. H.  Sketch.  Motion Pic Classic 4:35
        Ap '17
    Shaw, O.  Interview.  Motion Pic Classic 10:28 Mr '20
    Fredericks, J.  Interview.  Motion Pic 20:68 S '20
    Obit.  N.Y. Times p23 My 23 '64
        Screen World 16:220 '64

HENNING-JENSEN, ASTRID
    Biographical note.  International Film G 6:61 '69

HENREID, PAUL
    Rhea, M.  Strangers in arms.  Photoplay 20-4:44 Mr '42

Sharpe, H.   Enter Paul Henreid.   Photoplay 22-2:37 Ja
'42
Sketch.   Theatre Arts 26:188 Mr '42
Sharpe, H.   Story of.   Photoplay 22:36 Ja '43
Wilson, E.   The man with the smoldering eyes.   Silver
Screen 13-3:24 Ja '43
Biography.   Current Biography '43
Henreid, P.   How to have a happy marriage.   Photoplay
24-3:38 F '44
Hall, G.   Women who have been kind to me.   Silver
Screen 14-4:32 F '44
A romance I can't forget.   Photoplay 24:55 Mr '44
Deere, D.   Hearthside pirate.   Photoplay 29-1:50 Je '46
O'Leary, D.   End of fantasy.   Silver Screen 17-1:37
N '46
Henreid, P.   The actor as director.   Films In Review
3-6:270 Je/Jl '52
Nolan, J. E.   Films on TV.   Films In Review 20-5:305
My '69
The director-actor: a conversation.   Action 5-1:21 Ja/F
'70

HENRIKSEN, R. LASSE
Biographical note.   International Film G 7:176 '70

HENRIKSON, ANDERS
Note.   International Film G 2:41 '65

HERBERT, JAMES
Greenspun, R.   Quick--who are David Rimmer and
James Herbert?   N. Y. Times sec 2:17 O 8 '72

HERSKÓ, JÁNOS
Biographical note.   International Film G 8:176 '71

HERZOG, WERNER
Baxter, B.   Werner Herzog.   Film 64:35 Spg '69

HESSLER, GORDON
British cinema filmography.   Film 64:10 Spg '72

HEYES, DOUGLAS
Nolan, J. E.   Films on TV.   Films In Review 22-10:
628 D '71

HIGGINS, DICK
Listing of films.   Film Culture 37:7 Sum '65

Intermedia.    Library  J  93:2213  Je  1  '68
Gruen,  J.    Underground.    Vogue  154:160  O  1  '69

HILL,  GEORGE  ROY
Stage  to  film.    Action  3-5:12  S/O  '68
Flynn,  C.    Interview;  filmog.    Focus  6:9  Spg  '70
What  directors  are  saying.    Action  6-1:30  Ja/F  '71

HILL,  JAMES
Cowie,  P.    The  face  of  '63--Great  Britain.    Films  &
Filming  9-5:19  F  '63

HILL,  JEROME
Hill,  J.    Making  a  documentary--Albert  Schweitzer.
Film  Culture  3-2(12):10  '57
Zunser,  J.    Millionaire  makes  movies.    Cue  30-7:17
F  18  '61
How  to  build  a  sound  castle.    Horizon  3:108  Jl  '61
Same.    Design  63:22  S  '61
Listing  of  films.    Film  Culture  37:7  Sum  '65
Jurors  named  anniversary  awards.    Film  Comment
2-2:50  n. d.

HILL,  ROBERT  F.
Obit.    Screen  World  18:236  '67

HILLER,  ARTHUR
Alpert,  H.    New  faces.    Sat  R  49:24  D  24  '66
What  directors  are  saying.    Action  6-3:28  My/Je  '71
The  professional  director  speaks.    Making  Films  5-4:40
Ag  '71
Brown,  R.    Hiller  directs  Hospital.    Todays  Filmmaker
1-2:38  N  '71

HINDLE,  WILL
Hindle,  W.    Chinese  firedrill.    Cineaste  1-4  Spg  '68

HIRSCH,  TIBOR
Make  your  wedding  pictures  tell  a  story.    Popular  Photo
46:62  Je  '60
Valentina  Pereyaslavec.    Dance  34:36  N  '60
How  a  rave-notice  travelog  was  made.    Popular  Photo
52:94  F  '63
Survey  among  unsuccessful  applicants  for  the  Ford
Foundation  film  grants.    Film  Comment  2-3:10  Sum  '64

HIRSZMAN, LEON
  Viany, A.  Who's who in the cinema novo.  CTVD
    5-4:26 Sum '68

HITCHCOCK, ALFRED
  VanDoren, A.  Alfred Hitchcock.  Nation 144:305 Mr 13
    '37
  Hitchcock, A.  My own methods.  Sight & Sound 6-22:61
    Sum '37
  VanDoren, M.  Work of.  Nation 146:193 F 12 '38
  Director's problems.  Living Age 354:172 Ap '38
  Goodman, E.  Mysterious Mr. Hitchcock.  Cinema Prog-
    ress 3-2:9 My/Je '38
  Lady vanishes; and a British trencherman is again spot-
    lighted.  Newsweek 12:28 O 17 '38
  Sketch.  Life 6:66 Je 19 '39
  Roberts, K.  Mystery man.  Colliers 104:22 Ag 5 '39
  Story of.  Life 7:33 N 20 '39
  Spotlight on Hollywood.  Arts & Decoration 51:24 D '39
  Wanger, W.  Hitchcock, Hollywood genius.  Current
    History 52:13 D 24 '40
  Biographical note; filmog.  Movies & People 2:42 '40
  Jacobs, L.  Film directors at work.  Theatre Arts 35:40
    Ja '41
  Biography.  Current Biography '41
  Hitchcock brews thriller.  House & Garden 82:34 Ag '42
  Farber, M.  Hitchcock in stride.  New Republic 108:182
    F 8 '43
  Johnston, A.  300-pound prophet comes to Hollywood.
    Sat Evening Post 215:12 My 22 '43
  The man who weighed to much.  Cue 12-51:10 D 18 '43
  Alfred Hitchcock reduces as plant expands.  Life 15:12
    D 27 '43
  Farber, M.  Among the missing.  New Republic 110:116
    Ja 24 '44
  Ascetic sadist.  Time 43:94 Ja 31 '44
  Vallee, W. L.  Mr. Hitchcock.  Silver Screen 15-8:50
    Je '45
  The famed Hitchcock movie technique goes into action on
    Spellbound.  Cue 14-43:12 O 27 '45
  Alfred Hitchcock, director and extra.  N.Y. Times Mag
    p20 O 28 '45
  Nugent, F. S.  Assignment in Hollywood.  Good House-
    keeping 121:12 N '45
  Nugent, F. S.  Hitchcock discovers love.  N.Y. Times
    Mag p12 N 3 '46
  Alfred Hitchcock builds a movie.  Cue 16-44:11 N 1 '47

Note.   Vogue 211:109 F 15 '48
Rope:   new thriller makes first dramatic use of color.
   Life 25:57 Jl 26 '48
Bright star meets top director.   Cue 17-41:17 O 9 '48
Parsons, L. O.   Cosmopolitan's citation for the best
   direction of the month.   Cosmop 125:12 O '48
Enjoyment of fear.   Good Housekeeping 128:39 F '49
Kane, L.   The shadow world of Alfred Hitchcock.   Theatre
   Arts 33:32 My '49
Hart, H.   On suspense and other film matters; interview.
   Films In Review 1-3:21 Ap '50
Core of the movie chase; interview.   N.Y. Times Mag
   p22 O 29 '50
Death in the crystal ball.   Coronet 29:38 D '50
Film crasher Hitchcock.   Cue 20-20:19 My 19 '51
Wise man of Kumin.   Coronet 30:38 Je '51
Benchley, N.   Off stage.   Theatre Arts 35:28 Ag '51
Knight, A.   Star behind the camera.   Sat R 36:33 F 21
   '53
Rosengren, J.   After-effects of a crime.   American
   Photo 47:16 Jl '53
Alfred Hitchcock, actor.   N.Y. Times Mag p78 Ap 25 '54
Dial ham for murder.   Life 36:126 My 24 '54
Harvey, E.   Dial M for murder.   Colliers 133:90 Je 11
   '54
Monroe, K.   My five greatest mysteries.   Coronet 38:74
   S '55
Minoff, P.   A master of suspense tackles a fresh
   medium.   Cue 24-41:17 O 15 '55
Sarris, A.   The trouble with Hitchcock.   Film Culture
   1-5/6:31 Win '55
de la Roche, C.   Conversation with Hitchcock.   Sight &
   Sound 25-3:157 Win '55/56
Fat silhouette.   Time 66:46 D 26 '55
Woman who knows too much.   McCalls 83:12 Mr '56
Kass, R.   Films and TV.   Catholic World 182:465 Mr '56
Alfred Hitchcock, director.   Newsweek 47:105 Je 11 '56
Failure makes good.   TV Guide 4-38:25 S 22 '56
Havemann, E.   We present Alfred Hitchcock.   Theatre
   Arts 40:27 S '56
Havemann, E.   His pleasure is scaring people.   Reader
   Digest 69:165 S '56
Hitchcock speaking; interview.   Cosmop 141:66 O '56
Nash, O.   How to harass a Hitchcock; poem.   House &
   Garden 110:42 '56
Wood, C.   TV personalities biographical sketch book.
   TV Personalities p25 '56

Murder with English on it. N.Y. Times Mag p17 Mr 3
'57

Millstein, G. Harrison horror story. N.Y. Times Mag
p44 Jl 21 '57

Martin, P. I call on Alfred Hitchcock. Sat Evening
Post 230:36 Jl 27 '57

Hush mush. Theatre Arts 41:14 S '57

Hitchcock's world. Look 21:51 N 26 '57

Gow, G. The quest for realism; discussion. Films &
Filming 4-3:13 D '57

Robinson, S. Alfred Hitchcock in the hundred-pound
murder. McCalls 85:58 Ap '58

British film directors; an index to their work. Sight &
Sound 27-6:296 Aut '58

Master of suspense explains his art. Life 47:72 Jl 13
'59

Alfred Hitchcock talking. Films & Filming 5-10:7 Jl '59

Kauffmann, S. Movies. New Republic 141:23 Ag 10 '59

Clark, B. P. Reply to Kauffmann. New Republic 141:3
S 14 '59

Whitcomb, J. Master of mayhem. Cosmop 147:22 O '59

Pitt, J. A master of suspense. Films & Filming 6-2:9
N '59

Pitt, J. Improving on the formula. Films & Filming
6-3:9 D '59

Phantom face in the foliage. Life 49:54 Jl 11 '60

Biography. Current Biography 21:18 Jl '60

Same. Current Biography Yearbook 1960:189 '61

My recipe for murder. Coronet 48:49 S '60

Violence. Esquire 56:107 Jl '61

Alfred, squeeze me a grape. Time 79:54 My 18 '62

Cameron, I. Mechanics of suspense. Movie 3:5 O '62

Lineberry, W. P. & Floyd, E. R. Violence bores me.
Senior Scholastic 81:23 N 14 '62

Davidson, B. Alfred Hitchcock presents. Sat Evening
Post 235:62 D 15 '62

Higham, C. Hitchcock's world. Film Q 16-2:3 Win
'62/63

Cameron, I. & Perkins, V. F. Hitchcock; interview.
Movie 6:4 Ja '63

Cameron, I. Hitchcock II--suspense and meaning. Movie
6:8 Ja '63

In charge. New Yorker 39:36 Mr 30 '63

Fenin, G. The face of '63--United States. Films &
Filming 9-6:55 Mr '63

Shayon, R. L. Screens and screams. Sat R 46:44
Ap 20 '63

Redbook dialogue.   Redbook 120:70 Ap '63

Sarris, A.   Pantheon directors; filmog.   Film Culture
    28:2 Spg '63

Kaytor, M.   Hitchcock dinner hour; with recipes.   Look
    27:42 Ag 27 '63

Hitchcock on style; interview.   Cinema (BH) 1-5:4 Ag/S
    '63

Houston, P.   The figure in the carpet.   Sight & Sound
    32-4:159 Aut '63

Richards, J-J.   Letter.   Films In Review 15-1:59 Ja '64

Weaver, J. D.   Man behind the body.   Holiday 36:85
    S '64

Truffaut: author of book about Hitchcock.   New Yorker
    40:45 O 31 '64

Director of the year; filmog.   International Film G p25
    '64

Cameron, I. & Jeffery, R.   The Universal Hitchcock.
    Movie 12:21 Spg '65

Hitchcock's three nightmares.   Newsweek 67:89 Ja 24 '66

Jacobs, L. Jr.   Master of cinema!   U.S. Camera 29:72
    Ja '66

Vermilye, J.   An Alfred Hitchcock index; filmog.   Films
    In Review 17-4:231 Ap '66

Hitchcock and the dying art.   Film 46:9 Sum '66

Bond, K.   The other Alfred Hitchcock.   Film Culture
    41:30 Sum '66

Sonbert, W.   Alfred Hitchcock: master of morality.
    Film Culture 41:35 Sum '66

Interview.   Take One 1-1:14 S/O '66

Arkadin.   Film Clips.   Sight & Sound 35-4:202 Aut '66

Bazin, A.   Hitchcock vs. Hitchcock.   Cahiers (Eng)
    2:51 '66

Truffaut, F.   Skeleton keys.   Cahiers (Eng) 2:61 '66

Chabrol, C.   Hitchcock confronts evil.   Cahiers (Eng)
    2:67 '66

Alston, E.   Alfred Hitchcock probes the American man's
    aversion to carving.   Look 31:50 Ja 10 '67

Avallone, M.   Whatever happened to Alfred Hitchcock?
    Films In Review 18-7:454   Ag/S '67

Madson, O.   Fear and laughter.   Atlantic 221:116 Ja '68

A talk with Alfred Hitchcock.   Action 3-3:8 My/Je '68

Hitchcock on TV.   Film Fan Mo # 84 Je '68

Hitchcock, A.   The birds.   Take One 1-10:6 Je '68

Braudy, L.   Hitchcock, Truffaut and the irresponsible
    audience.   Film Q 21-4:21 Sum '68

Hitchcock tells young film directors how easy it all is.
    Making Films 2-4:38 Ag '68

Houston, P. Hitchcockery. Sight & Sound 37-4:188 Aut '68
Millar, G.   Hitchcock versus Truffaut.   Sight & Sound
    38-2:82 Spg '69
Wollen, P.   Hitchcock's vision.   Cinema (Lon) 3:2 Je '69
Houston, P.   Hitch on Topaz.   Sight & Sound 39-1:16
What directors are saying.   Action 5-1:28 Ja/F '70
Amory, C.   Trade winds.   Sat R 53:14 F 7 '70
Durgnat, R.   The strange case of Alfred Hitchcock.
    Films & Filming 16-5:58 F; 16-6:58 Mr; 16-7:59 Ap;
    16-8:58 My; 16-9:114 Je; 16-10:52 Jl; 16-11:57 Ag;
    16-12:84 S; 17-1:60 O; 17-2:35 N '70
Samuels, C. T. Hitchcock. American Scholar 39:295 Spg '70
Mundy, P.   Another look at Hitchcock.   Cinema (Lon)
    6/7:10 Ag '70
Hitchcock, A.   Spellbound.   Sight & Sound 39-4:186 Aut
    '70
Belton, J.   Reply to Samuels.   American Scholar 39:728
    Aut '70
Patterson, G. G.   Eloquent though silent.   Filmograph
    1-4:31 '70
Walker, M.   The age of Alfred Hitchcock.   Movie 18:10
    Win '70/71
What directors are saying.   Action 6-4:20 Jl/Ag '71
The professional director speaks.   Making Films 5-4:40
    Ag '71
Mamber, S.   The television films of Alfred Hitchcock.
    Cinema (BH) 7-1:2 Fall '72
McAsh, I.   Technical Hitchcock.   Films Illustrated
    1-3:22 S '71
Flatley, G.   I tried to be discreet with that nude corpse.
    N.Y. Times Bio Ed Je 18 '72
Castell, D.   Alfred Hitchcock; filmog.   Films Illustrated
    2-13:22 Jl '72
Cleave, A.   Other people's pictures; Frenzy.   Movie
    Maker 6-8:546 S '72
Schickel, R.   We're living in a Hitchcock world, all
    right.   N.Y. Times Mag p22 O 29 '72
Rudkin, D.   Celluloid apocalypse; notes on The birds.
    Cinema (Lon) 9:14 n.d.
Hitchcock, A.   It's a bird; it's a plane; it's The birds.
    Take One 1-10:6 n.d.
Tumlin, J. S.   Audience as protagonist in three Hitch-
    cock films.   Mise-En-Scene 1:2 n.d.
American Film Institute University advisory committee
    seminar. Dialogue On Film 2-1:entire issue '72
Interview; filmog; biblio. Dialogue On Film 5:entire issue
    '72

HITCHENS, GORDON
  Chicago's midwest film festival grows up.   Popular Photo
    53:97 O '63
  Sunday on the river.   Popular Photo 54:134 My '64
  Survey among unsuccessful applicants for the Ford Found-
    ation film grants.   Film Comment 2-3:10 Sum '64

HOBL, PAVEL
  Gray, P.   One kind of filmmaking.   Tulane Drama R
    11:150 Fall '66

HOFFMAN, JERZY
  Biographical note; filmog.   Focus On Film 3:17 My/Ag
    '70

HOFFMANN, KURT
  Bean, R.   The face of '63--Germany.   Films & Filming
    9-9:41 Je '63

HOGAN, JAMES P.
  Obit.   N.Y. Times p13 N 6 '43

HOLLAND, PAT
  Dawson, J. & Johnston, C.   More British sounds.   Sight
    & Sound 39-3:144 Sum '70

HOLMES, BEN
  Obit.   N.Y. Times p23 D 3 '43

HOLMES, BURTON
  They stand out from the crowd.   Lit Digest 117:13 F 17
    '34
  Scenic wonders of the world.   Popular Mechanics 63:337
    S '34
  Hardy perennial.   New Yorker 18:13 F 6 '43
  Biography.   Current Biography My '44
  Seven wonders of the modern world.   Science Digest 20:69
    Ag '46
  Bronson, A.   Burton Holmes, American traveler.   Ameri-
    can Mercury 63:735 D '46
  Wallace, I.   Great globe-trotter.   Sat Evening Post 219:23
    My 10 '47
  If I were taking my first trip.   American 149:32 My '50
  Obit.   Americana Annual 1959:324 '59
    British Book Year 1959:511 '59
    Current Biography 19:24 O '58
    Current Biography Yearbook 1958:200 '58

Life 45:8 Ag 11 '58
N. Y. Times p27 Jl 23 '58
Newsweek 52:50 Ag 4 '58
Screen World 10:222 '59
Time 72:64 Ag 4 '58
Wilson Library B 33:175 '58
Biography. National Cylopaedia 44:510 '62

HOLT, SETH
A free hand. Sight & Sound 28-2:60 Spg '59
The British cinema. Movie 1:7 Je '62
Sarris, A. Oddities and one shots. Film Culture 28:45
Spg '63
Gough-Yates, K. Interview. Screen 10-6:4 N '69
Obit. Film R p18 '71/72
N. Y. Times p37 F 16 '71

HOM, JESPER
Biographical note. International Film G 8:117 '71

HOPKINSON, PETER
Hopkinson, P. Facts out of focus. Films & Filming
4-4:13 Ja '58

HOPPER, DENNIS
Southern, T. Loved house of the Dennis Hoppers. Vogue
146:138 Ag 1 '65
Space odyssey. Time 94:73 Jl 25 '69
Not-so-easy riders: Dennis Hopper and Peter Fonda.
Vogue 154:129 Ag 1 '69
Macklin, A. Easy rider: the initiation of Dennis Hopper.
Film Heritage 5-1:1 Fall '69
What directors are saying. Action 4-5:32 S/O '69
Dennis Hopper, riding high. Playboy 16-12:250 D '69
Darrack, B. Easy rider runs wild in the Andes. Life
68:48 Je 19 '70
Nolan, T. You can bring Dennis Hopper to Hollywood but
you can't take Dodge City out of Kansas. Show 1-9:20
Jl 23 '70
Burke, T. Dennis Hopper saves the movies. Esquire
74:139 S '70
Flatley, G. Dennis Hopper. N. Y. Times Bio Ed O 18
'70
Movies: and everybody's doing it. Look 34-22:42 N 3 '70
Knight, A. & Alpert, H. Sex stars of 1970. Playboy
17-12:220 D '70
Hopkins, H. Dennis Hopper's America. Art In America
59:87 My '71

Goodwin, M.  Home is the Hopper.  Interview 2-4:25
    Jl '71
O'Brien, G. & Netter, M.  Interview.  Interview 19:24
    F '72

HORN, LEONARD
    What directors are saying.  Action 5-4:30 Jl/Ag '70

HORNE, JAMES W.
    James Horne's own story.  Photoplay 9-3:109 F '16
    James W. Horne.  Those Enduring Matinee Idols 1-9:117
        F/Mr '71

HORNER, HARRY
    Designing a Magic flute.  Theatre Arts 40:58 Ja '56
    Lingg, A. M.  Sounding the depths; interview.  Opera
        News 28:33 Ja 25 '64

HOUGH, JOHN
    British cinema filmography.  Film 65:10 Spg '72

HOUSSEIN, ROBERT
    Biographical note.  Unifrance 45:8 D '57
    Graham, P.  The face of '63--France.  Films & Filming
        9-8:13 My '63

HOUWER, ROB
    Bean, R.  The face of '63--Germany.  Films & Filming
        9-9:41 Je '63

HOVING, HATTUM
    Biographical note.  International Film G 4:125 '67

HOWARD, CY
    Howard, C.  A monastic, lonely business.  Action 5-5:22
        S/O '70
    Eyles, A.  Cy Howard; filmog.  Focus On Film 4:12 S/O
        '70

HOWARD, DAVID
    Obit.  N.Y. Times p17 D 22 '41

HOWARD, WILLIAM KERRIGAN
    Cruikshank, H. J.  Sketch.  Motion Pic Classic 27:21
        Jl '28
    Manners, D.  Sketch.  Motion Pic 36:55 O '28
    Obit.  N.Y. Times p 19 F 22 '54

Screen World 6:224 '55
Time 63:78 Mr 1 '54
Everson, W. K. William Kerrigan Howard; filmog.
Films In Review 5-5:224 My '54

HUAN, LE
Hitchens, G. Filmmaking under the bomb. Film Comment 5-2:86 Spg '69

HUBBARD, LUCIEN
Obit. N.Y. Times Bio Ed Ja 1 '72

HUBLEY, JOHN
Hubley, J. & Schwartz, Z. Animation learns a new language. Hollywood Q 1-4:360 Jl '46
Up from Bugs. New Yorker 37:18 Ag 5 '61
Robinson, D. Evolution of a cartoonist. Sight & Sound 31:17 Win '61
Rieder, H. Memories of Mr. Magoo. Cinema J 8-2:17 Spg '69
Archibald, L. John Hubley. Film Library Q 3-2:5 Spg '70

HUDSON, BILL
A young black filmmaker's view. Film Library Q 4-1:10 Win '70/71

HUGGINS, ROY
Vogel, N. Television and film writing. Writers Digest 48:12 Ap '68
Huggins, R. What's wrong with the television series? Action 4-5:28 S/O '69

HUGHES, KEN
Filmography. Film 14:8 N/D '57
British feature directors; an index to their work. Sight & Sound 27-6:297 Aut '58
Hughes, K. Those nutty intellectuals. Films & Filming 8-4:9 Ja '63
Eyles, A. Ken Hughes and Cromwell. Focus On Film 4:18 S/O '70
British cinema filmography. Film 65:10 Spg '72
Eyles, A. A passion for cinema; filmog. Focus On Film 6:42 n.d.
Richards, P. D. & Nolan, J. E. Letters. Focus On Film 8:14 n.d.

HUGHES, RUPERT
  Interview. N.Y. Dramatic Mirror 65:11 Mr 8 '11
  Bacon, G. V. Biographical sketch. Green Book 10:743
    N '13
  His early work. Strand (NY) 50:531 N '15
  Mannering, M. Character sketch. National 46:227 My
    '17
  Home of. Theatre 26:91 Ag '17
  Black, A. W. Interview. National 48:356 S '19
  St. Johns, A. R. Interview. Photoplay 20:21 Jl '21
  New talent from the films. Photoplay 21:55 Ja '22
  Goldbeck, W. Interview. Motion Pic 24:43 S '22
  Art of moving picture composition. Arts & Decoration
    19:9 My '23
  Tully, J. His defense of the movies. Classic 20:34 S
    '24
  Rupert Hughes indicts religion. Current Opinion 77:754
    D '24
  Getting paid for having a good time. American 110:42
    Ag '30
  Calamity with sound effects. New Outlook 162:21 S '33
  Brief for Hughes. Sat Evening Post 206:23 Mr 3 '34
  Early days in the movies. Sat Evening Post 207:18 Ap 6;
    30 Ap 13 '35
  McOmie, M. We create beauty ourselves; interview.
    Better Home & Garden 13:54 Ap '35
  Broun, H. Rupert Hughes and the Screen Writers' Guild.
    Nation 142:678 My 27 '36
  Discussion. Nation 142:662 My 27: 755 Je 10 '36
  Biographical sketch. Current History 51:38 Ja '40
  Hughes, R. TV won't ruin everything. Films In Review
    2-3:24 Mr '51
  Comediens have courage. Coronet 30:53 Je '51
  Obit. British Book Year 1957:575 '57
    Musical America 76:35 O '56
    N.Y. Times p27 S 10 '57
    Newsweek 48:78 S 17 '56
    Publisher W 170:1606 S 24 '56
    Time 68:98 S 17 '56
    Wilson Library B 31:219 N '56


HUGO, IAN
  Nin, A. Poetics of the film; filmog. Film Culture
    31:12 Win '63/64
  Survey among unsuccessful applicants for the Ford Found-
    ation film grants. Film Comment 2-3:10 Sum '64

HUMBERSTONE, H. BRUCE
  Parsons, L. O.  Cosmopolitan's citation for the best
    direction of the month.  Cosmop 122:66 My '47

HUNT, PETER
  Hunt, P.  A sense of personality is what every director
    is seeking.  Action 7-1:3 Ja/F '72
  British cinema filmography.  Film 65:10 Spg '72

HUNTER, T. HAYES
  Obit.  N. Y. Times p21 Ap 18 '44

HUNTINGTON, LAWRENCE
  Filmography.  Film 14:8 N/D '57
  British feature directors; an index to their work.  Sight
    & Sound 27-6:297 Aut '58

HURST, BRIAN DESMOND
  Hurst, B. D.  The director.  Films & Filming 3-5:27 F
    '57
  Filmography.  Film 14:8 N/D '57
  British feature directors; an index to their work.  Sight
    & Sound 27-6:397 Aut '58

HURTADO, ANGEL
  Listing of films.  Film Culture 37:7 Sum '65

HUSSEIN, WARRIS
  British cinema filmography.  Film 65:10 Spg '72
  Goldgram, S. & Hackett, P.  Warris Hussein and The
    possession of Joel Delaney.  Interview 24:42 Ag '72

HUSTON, JOHN
  Designed his own home.  Harper Bazaar 81:72 Jl '47
  Allen, L.  On the set with John Huston.  Cinema (Holly-
    wood) 1-2:7 Jl '47
  Biography.  Current Biography 10:30 F '49
    Same.  Current Biography 1949:287 '50
  Farber, M.  Hollywood's fair-haired boy.  Nation 168:642
    Je 4 '49
  Questions.  New Yorker 25:21 Je 4 '49
  Griffith, R.  Wyler, Wellman and Huston.  Films In Re-
    view 1-1:1 F '50
  Biographical note.  Newsweek 35:88 Je 12 '50
  Agee, J.  Undirectable director.  Life 29:129 S 18 '50
  Huston, J.  A tribute to Robert Flaherty.  Sight & Sound
    21-2:64 O/D '51

Reisz, K. Interview. Sight & Sound 21-3:130 Ja/Mr '52

African queen. Theatre Arts 36:48 F '52

Ross, L. Onward and upward with the arts. New Yorker 28:32 My 24; 29 My 31; 32 Je 7; 39 Je 14 '52

Mage, D. A. The way John Huston works. Films In Review 3-8:393 O '52

Hine, A. Paris in the 90's; Moulin Rouge on location. Holiday 13:26 Ap '53

Huston's hectic 72 hours in New York. Life 38:163 F 14 '55

Godley, J. In the wake of the whale. Vogue 126:118 N 15 '55

Director John Huston; a remarkable man and the movies in 1956. Newsweek 47:67 Ja 9 '56

Barnes, P. The director on horseback. Q Film Radio TV 10-3:281 Spg '56

Knight, A. Director of Moby Dick. Sat R 39:29 Je 9 '56

Alpert, H. Quest of Captain Ahab. Sat R 39:29 Je 9 '56

John Huston on Moby Dick; a conversation with Edward Lauret. Film 10:11 N/D '56

An encounter with John Huston; excerpts from a conversation with Edward Lauret. Film Culture 2-2(8):1 '56

John Huston's big stage. Newsweek 52:87 Jl 21 '58

Grenier, C. Huston at Fontainebleau. Sight & Sound 27-6:280 Aut '58

Bester, A. John Huston's unsentimental journey. Holiday 25:111 My '59

Archer, E. Taking life seriously. Films & Filming 5-12:13 S '59

Archer, E. Small people in a big world. Films & Filming 6-1:9 O '59

McIntyre, A. T. Making The misfits; or waiting for Monroe. Esquire 55:74 Mr '61

The screen answers back. Films & Filming 8-8:12 My '62

John Huston, actor. Newsweek 61:102 Mr 18 '63

Fenin, G. The face of '63--United States. Films & Filming 9-6:55 Mr '63

Sarris, A. Fallen idols; filmog. Film Culture 28:30 Spg '63

The directors choose the best films. Cinema (BH) 1-5:14 Ag/S '63

John Cardinal Huston. Life 55:61 N 22 '63

Lawrenson, H. The nightmare of the iguana. Show 4-1:46 Ja '64

Problems in paradise. Newsweek 64:90 S 14 '64

Barry, N. John Huston's best of all worlds. House & Garden 126:140 D '64

Sage, T.   Giraffe in Piazza del Popolo.   National R 17:
105 F 9 '65

Noah.   Look 29:21 Jl 27 '65

Ark that John built.   Life 59:43 Ag 13 '65

Ross, L.   Our far flung correspondents.   New Yorker
41:185 S 25 '65

Bachmann, G.   How I make films; interview.   Film Q
19-1:3 Fall '65

Maestro Huston.   Newsweek 67:89 Mr 7 '66

John Huston, the Bible and James Bond.   Cahiers (Eng)
5:7 '68

Wright, I.   Ireland for the Irish.   Sight & Sound 36-4:177
Aut '67

Miller, E.   Extraordinary debut.   Seventeen 27:138 O '68

Ehrlich, H.   Anjelica.   Look 32:66 N 12 '68

Taylor, J. R.   John Huston and the Figure in the carpet.
Sight & Sound 28-2:70 Spg '69

Koningsberger, H.   From book to film via John Huston.
Film Q 22:2 Spg '69

Takes; interview.   New Yorker 45:31 Je 14 '69

Wolf, W.   John Huston makes a today spy film.   Cue
38-26:10 Je 28 '69

Sarris, A.   Director of the month.   Show 1-1:28 Ja '70

Huston, J.   Eugene O'Neill, playwright.   Action 5-3:32
My/Je '70

Nogueira, R.   A walk with love and death.   Films Illustrated 1-3:6 S '71

Filmog; including screen plays.   Film Comment 6-4:101
Win '70/71

Taylor, C. & O'Brien, G.   Huston! interview.   Interview
25:42 S '72

Ford, D.   A talk with John Huston.   Action 7-5:21 S/O
'72

Buckner, G.   A director's progress: Huston in perspective; filmog.   Film Journal (Aus) 4:entire issue n. d.

Bressi, J. F.   Huston and Bogart.   Mise-En-Scene 1:66
n. d.

Archer, E.   John Huston--the Hemingway tradition in
American film.   Film Culture 19:66 n. d.

HUSZÁRIK, ZOLTÁN
Kuttna, M.   Hungarian Sindbad.   Sight & Sound 41-2:69
Spg '72

HUTCHINSON, CHARLES
Mullett, M. B.   Stunt king of the movies.   American
95:18 F '23

IBANEZ, JUAN
    Riera, E.    A new Mexican cinema.    CTVD 6-3:21
        Spg '69

ICHIKAWA, KON
    Richie, D.    Japan: the younger talents.    Sight & Sound
        29-2:78 Spg '68
    Richie, D.    The face of '63--Japan.    Films & Filming
        9-10:15 Jl '63
    Outdoing Olympia.    Newsweek 64:106 S 21 '64
    Triumph in Cannes.    Sports Illustrated 22:17 My 31 '65
    Note.    International Film G 2:33 '65
    Richie, D.    The several sides of Kon Ichikawa.    Sight &
        Sound 35-2:84 Spg '66
    Dewey, L.    The range of Ichikawa.    Film 46:28 Sum '66
    Coleman, J.    Ichikawa.    New Statesman 72:236 Ag 12 '66
    Milne, T.    The skull beneath the skin.    Sight & Sound
        35-4:185 Aut '66
    The uniqueness of Kon Ichikawa; a symposium.    Cinema
        (BH) 6-2:30 Fall '70
    Director of the year; filmog.    International Film G p23
        '70

IIMURA, TAKAHIKO
    Listing of films.    Film Culture 37:7 Sum '65
    Linder, C.    Interview; filmog.    Filmmakers Newsletter
        1-2:4 D '67

IMAI, TADASHI
    Note.    International Film G 2:33 '65

IMAMURA, SHOHEI
    Iwabutchi, M.    Japanese cinema 1961.    Film Culture
        24:85 Spg '62
    Biographical note.    International Film G 8:193 '71

INCE, JOHN EDWARD JR.
    Doyle, B. H.    Letter.    Films In Review 11-9:566 N '60

INCE, RALPH
    Johnson, J.    Ince of Atlantic; interview.    Photoplay
        8-3:103 Ag '15
    How to get into moving pictures.    Motion Pic 12:101 S
        '16

Lane, T.   Interview.   Motion Pic 18:32 Ja '20

INCE, THOMAS HARPER
Wing, W. E.   Tom Ince of Inceville.   N. Y. Dramatic
   Mirror D 24 '13
Sketch.   Green Book 12:647 O '14
Inceville.   N. Y. Dramatic Mirror 72:30 D 23 '14
Present needs of photoplays.   N. Y. Dramatic Mirror
   72:23 D 23 '14
Troubles of a motion picture producer.   Motion Pic
   9:113 My '15
Carr, H. C.   Directors: the men who make the plays.
   Photoplay 8-1:80 Je '15
Carr, H. C.   Ince: Rodin of shadows.   Photoplay 7-2:81
   Jl '15
Duncan, R. C.   The Ince studio.   Picture Play Mr '16
Ince completes a world drama.   Photoplay 9-6:32 My '16
Interview.   N. Y. Dramatic Mirror 75:20 Je 17 '16
Sketch.   N. Y. Dramatic Mirror 76:26 Jl 15 '16
Grau, R.   Sketch.   American 82:52 Ag '16
Ince, T. H.   What does the public want.   Photoplay
   Ja '17
Ince, T. H.   The art of motion picture directing.
   Pictures & Picturegoer Ag 10 '18
The star is here to stay.   Munsey 65:338 N '18
A few more inches about Ince.   Photoplay J Ja '19
Ince, T. H.   The early days at Kay Bee.   Photoplay
   15-4:42 Mr '19
Carr, H.   Work of.   Classic 18:24 N '23
Edgerton, G.   Dias Dorados, a beautiful California
   estate.   Arts & Decoration 21:16 Je '24
Home of.   Classic 19:38 Je '24
Home of.   Photoplay 26:62 Je '24
Memoirs of T. H. Ince.   Exhibiters Herald D 13 '24
Ellis, F. J.   The passing of a great showman.   Story
   World Ja '25
Produced by Thomas H. Ince.   Exceptional Photoplays
   Ja '25
Everson, W. K.   Griffith and Ince; letter.   Films In
   Review 8-2:94 F '57
Mitchell, G.   Thomas H. Ince.   Films In Review 11-8:
   464 O '60
Eastes, O. Jr.   The Aesop of Inceville.   8mm Collector
   12:14 '65
Ince, E.   Thomas Ince; letter.   Silent Pic 6:14 Spg '70
The life of Thomas H. Ince: 1882-1924.   Silent Pic 14:4
   Spg '72

INGRAHAM, LLOYD
  Biographical note.   Photoplay 9-4:42 Mr '16
  Obit.   N. Y. Times p29 Ap 5 '56

INGRAM, REX
  Montanye, L.   Interview.   Motion Pic Classic 12:58 Jl
      '21
  Robinson, J.   Interview.   Photoplay 20:42 Ag '21
  Beach, B.   Interview.   Motion Pic 22:22 Ja '22
  Stem, C. H.   Sketch.   Classic 16:22 My '23
  How I discover stars.   Photoplay 24:36 Je '23
  Carr, H.   Work of.   Classic 18:24 N '23
  Howe, H.   How he makes them act.   Photoplay 25:52
      D '23
  Morz, C.   Six men with names.   New Republic 38:152
      Ap 2 '24
  Robinson, S.   Word-portrait of his wife.   Motion Pic
      28:24 N '24
  Hall, G.   A day at the Cine studio at Nice.   Motion Pic
      33:52 Jl '27
  Art advantages of the European scene.   Theatre Arts
      47:24 Ja '28
  They stand out from the crowd.   Lit Digest 116:9 Jl 2
      '33
  Sketch.   Time 31:36 Mr 14 '38
  Obit.   N. Y. Times p57 Jl 23 '50
      Newsweek 36:59 Jl 31 '50
      Screen World 2:234 '51
      Time 56:55 Jl 31 '50
  Geltzer, G.   Hollywood handsomest director; filmog.
      Films In Review 3-5:213 My '52

INGSTER, BORIS
  Ingster, B.   Serge Eisenstein.   Hollywood Q 5-4:380
      Sum '51

IOCELIANI, OTAR
  A Russian six.   Films & Filming 13-12:27 S '67

IVANDA, BRANKO
  Biographical note.   International Film G 8:282 '71

IVANOV, S.
  Integral experience.   Films & Filming 18-11:11 Ag '72

IVENS, JORIS
  Ferguson, O. Guest artist. New Republic 86:278 Ap 15;

87:18 My 13 '36

Stebbins, R. & Leyda, J.   Artist in documentary.   Mag
    Art 31:392 Jl '38

Pacific flight.   Asia 39:508 S '39

Ivens, J.   Collaboration in documentary.   Film 1-2:30
    Spg '40

Apprentice to films; autobiographical.   Theatre Arts
    30:179 Mr; 244 Ap '46

Grenier, C.   Joris Ivens; social realist versus lyric
    poet.   Sight & Sound 27-4:204 Spg '58

Director of the year; filmog.   International Film G 5:14
    '68

Hitchens, G.   Interview.   Film Culture 53/54/55:190
    Spg '72


IVORY, JAMES
    Music of Satyajit Ray.   American Record G 32:1109
        Ag '66
    Savages.   Sight & Sound 40-4:208 Aut '71
    Varble, S.   Interview.   Interview 2-2:15 n.d.


IWERKS, UB
    Smith, D. R.   Ub Iwerks, 1901-1971.   Funnyworld
        14:32 Spg '72

JABOR, ARNALDO
 Codignola, L. Enter two newcomers. Atlas 14:57
  S '67
 Viany, A. Who's who in the cinema novo. CTVD
  5-4:26 Sum '68

JACKMAN, FRED
 Obit. N.Y. Times p17 Ag 29 '59

JACKSON, PATRICK
 Filmography. Film 14:8 N/D '57
 British feature directors; an index to their work. Sight
  & Sound 27-6:297 Aut '58
 A free hand. Sight & Sound 28-2:60 Spg '59

JACOBS, KEN
 Listing of films. Film Culture 37:7 Sum '65
 Sitney, P. A. Avant garde film. Afterimage 2:19
  Aut '70

JACOBS, LEWIS
 Jacobs, L. Experimental cinema in America. Holly-
  wood Q 3-2:111 Win '47/48; 3-3:278 Spg '48
 Listing of films. Film Culture 37:7 Sum '65
 Deschin, J. Filmmaker, director, author, teacher;
  interview. Popular Photo 58:12 F '66

JANCSÓ, MIKLÓS
 Biographical note. International Film G 2:94 '65
 Arkadin. Film clips. Sight & Sound 36-3:156 Sum '67
 Biographical note. International Film G 4:101 '67
 Gilliatt, P. Current cinema. New Yorker 45:106
  Mr 29 '69
 Gilliatt, P. Current cinema. New Yorker 45:124
  My 17 '69
 Hatch, R. Films. Nation 208:740 Je 9 '69
 Director of the year; filmog. International Film G 6:16
  '69
 Crick, P. Three East European directors. Screen
  11-2:64 Mr/Ap '70
 Robinson, D. Quite apart from Miklos Jancso. Sight
  & Sound 39-2:84 Spg '70
 Czigany, L. Jancso country. Film Q 26-1:44 Fall '72

206

JARROTT, CHARLES
    Emerson, W.    Beneath that bland exterior lay a spark of
        terror.    Action 7-1:18 Ja/F '72
    British cinema filmography.    Film 65:10 Spg '72

JARVA, RISTO
    Biographical note.    International Film G 8:143 '71

JASON, LEIGH
    Jason, L.    Art and the box office.    Cinema Progress
        4-1/2:9 Je/Jl '39

JEFFRIES, LIONEL
    Star to director.    Film 60:2 n.d.

JEKEL, GUS
    Jekel, G.    Overcome, conquer that animation phobia.
        Action 2-4:20 Jl/Ag '67

JENNINGS, HUMPHREY
    Wright, B.    Humphrey Jennings.    Sight & Sound 19-8:311
        D '50
    Vedres, N.    A memoir.    Sight & Sound 20-1:24 My '51
    Lambert, G.    Jennings' Britain.    Sight & Sound 20-1:24
        My '51
    Anderson, L.    Only connect: some aspects of the work of
        Humphrey Jennings.    Sight & Sound 23-4:181 Ap/Je '54
    Dand, C. H.    Britain's screen poet.    Films In Review
        6-2:73 F '55
    Bronowski, J.    Recollections of Humphrey Jennings.    20th
        Century 165:44 Ja/F '59
    Anderson, L.    Only connect: some aspects of the work
        of Humphrey Jennings.    Film Q 15-2:5 Win '61/62
    Jennings, H.    Work sketches of an orchestra.    Film Q
        15-2:12 Win '61/62
    Noxen, G.    How Humphrey Jennings came to film.    Film
        Q 15-2:19    Win '61/62
    Sanson, W.    The making of Fires were started.    Film Q
        15-2:27 Win '61/62
    Merralls, J.    Humphrey Jennings; a biographical sketch.
        Film Q 15-2:29 Win '61/62
    Merralls, J.    Some thoughts on Jennings.    Film Journal
        (Aus) 5:8 n.d.

JERSEY, WILLIAM C. JR.
    Jersey, W. C. Jr.    Some thoughts on film technique.
        Film Comment 2-1:15 Win '64

Jurors named anniversary awards.    Film Comment
2-2:49 n. d.

## JESSUA, ALAIN
Delahaye, M.    Meeting with Alain Jessua.    Cahiers (Eng)
11:37 S '67
Petrie, G.    Interview.    Cinema (Lon) 9:32 n. d.

## JEWISON, NORMAN
Norman Jewison discusses thematic action in the Cin-
cinnati kid; interview.    Cinema (BH) 2-6:4 Jl/Ag '65
The Russians ... Nyet yet.    Action 1-1:16 S/O '66
Knight, A.    New faces.    Sat R 49:25 D 24 '66
Lipscomb, J.    Improvise.    Films are made of whimsy.
Life 63:86 N 10 '67
Should directors produce?    Action 3-4:10 Jl/Ag '68
Symposium: adding to the director's tools.    Action 3-6:26
N/D '68
Canham, C.    A day in the life of Gaily Gaily.    Cineaste
2-3:13 Win '68/69
Jewison, N.    Turning on in Salzburg.    Action 4-4:14
Jl/Ag '69
Eyles, A.    Norman Jewison; filmog.    Focus On Film
1:13 Mr/Ap '70
Gow, G.    Confrontations; interview; filmog.    Films &
Filming 17-4:20 Ja '71
What directors are saying.    Action 6-3:28 My/Je '71
The professional director speaks.    Making Films 5-4:40
Ag '71
Robbins, F.    Norman Jewison, by George he's done it.
Show 2-10:44 D '71
Williams, J.    The man behind Fiddler on the roof; inter-
view.    Films Illustrated 1-6:13 D '71

## JIREŠ, JAROMIL
Sarris, A.    Movers.    Sat R 50:38 D 23 '67

## JISSOJI, AKIO
Biographical note.    International Film G 9:184 '72

## JODOROWSKY, ALEXANDRO
O'Brien, G.    Interview.    Interview 2-3:3 n. d.

## JOHNSON, EMORY
Obit.    Screen World 12:222 '61

JOHNSON, LAMONT
    Award winner: Lamont Johnson.   Action 6-3:21 My/Je '71

JOHNSON, NUNNALLY
    Biography.   Current Biography 2:442 '41
    Biography.   National Cylopaedia G:513 '46
    Entertains Hollywood celebrities with a mermaid party.
       Life 22:102 Ja 13 '47
    Johnson, N.   The long and the short of it.   Films &
       Filming 3-9:10 Je '57
    Filmography.   Film Comment 6-4:101 Win '70/71

JONES, CHUCK
    Benayoun, R.   The Roadrunner and other characters;
       interview.   Cinema J 8-2:10 Spg '69
    Barrier, M.   Interview.   Funnyworld 13:4 Spg '71

JONES, DICK
    Biographical note.   Photoplay 9-4:42 Mr '16

JONES, F. RICHARD
    Smith, F. J.   Interview.   Motion Bic Classic 12:97
       Mr '21
    Cheatham, M.   Interview.   Motion Pic 21:67 Je '21

JONES, GROVER
    Movie magician.   Colliers 96:26 S 21 '23
    Magic lantern.   Sat Evening Post 209:10 O 3; 38 N 14
       '36; 16 Ja 23; 17 Mr 6; 34 Ap 10 '37
    On location.   Colliers 98:24 D 5 '36
    Knights of the keyhold.   Colliers 101:25 Ap 16 '38
    Star shadows.   Colliers 101:18 Ap 30 '38
    Obit.   Current Biography '40
       N. Y. Times p27 S 25 '40
    Gag man.   Time 36:63 O 7 '40

JORDON, LARRY
    Survey among unsuccessful applicants for the Ford
       Foundation film grants.   Film Comment 2-3:10 Sum '64
    Weiner, P.   New American cinema; filmog.   Film 58:22
       Spg '70

JOSE, EDWARD
    Keene, M.   Interview.   Motion Pic Classic 9:36 Ja '20

JOST, JON
    Letter and editor's note.   Women & Film 2:75 '72

JULIAN, RUPERT
     How to get into motion pictures.   Motion Pic Classic
        3:39 D '16
     Obit.   N. Y.  Times p16 D 31 '43

JUTRA, CLAUDE
     Biographical note; filmog.   Cahiers (Eng) 4:45 '66

KADAR, JAN
 Director.  New Yorker 41:23 F 12 '66
 Lerman, L.  International movie report.  Mademoiselle
   64:117 F '67
 Choen, J.  Discussion.  Film Comment 4-2/3:68 Fall/
   Win '68
 Czechs in exile.  Newsweek 76:70 Jl 27 '70
 The Czech who bounced back.  Films Illustrated 1-10:34
   Ap '72

KALATOZOV, MIKHAIL (Michael)
 Ambassador; Soviet union's official ambassador to the
   movie industry.  Time 43:54 Je 12 '44

KAMERLING, NORMAN
 Listing of films.  Film Culture 37:7 Sum '65

KANAI, KATSU
 Biographical note.  International Film G 9:184 '72

KANIN, GARSON
 Biographical note; filmog.  Movies & People 2:42 '40
 Jacobs, L.  Film directors at work.  Theatre Arts
   25:225 Mr '41
 I direct.  Theatre Arts 25:640 S '41
 Biography.  Current Biography '41
 Houghton, N.  Kanins on Broadway.  Theatre Arts
   30:731 D '46
 Bomb and the Parker 51.  Theatre Arts 32:43 O '48
 Note.  Harper Bazaar 83:94 D '49
 Biography.  Current Biography 13:31 O '52
 Same.  Current Biography Yearbook 1952:294 '53
 Biographical sketch.  Good Housekeeping 140:14 F '55
 Houston, P.  Cinema and the Kanins.  Sight & Sound
   24-4:186 Spg '55
 Ingenue or leading lady?  Vogue 138:114 O 15 '61
 Sarris, A.  Likable but elusive; filmog.  Film Culture
   28:35 Spg '63
 Miller, D.  Films on TV.  Films In Review 15-10:626
   D '64
 Lydon, S.  Faa-bu-lous long run of Gordon and Kanin.
   N.Y. Times Mag '64 O 5 '69
 Private Kate.  McCalls 97:58 F '70

Mr. and Mrs.  Films Illustrated 1-11:36 My '72
Houston, P. & Gillet, J.  Kanin talking; interview.
   Sight & Sound 41-3:134 Sum '72

KAPLAN, NELLY
   Harris, K.  Interview.  Women & Film 2:33 '72

KARDOS, FERENC
   Biographical note.  International Film G 5:101 '68

KARGER, MAXWELL
   Jameson, C.  Interview.  Motion Pic Classic 7:24 F '19

KARLSON, PHIL
   Sarris, A.  Esoterica; filmog.  Film Culture 28:22
      Spg '63

KARLSSON, FINN
   Adams, S.  Four Dane directors; interview.  CTVD
      7-2:26 Spg '70
   Biographical note.  International Film G 7:90 '70

KARMEN, ROMAN
   Vernichtungslager.  Time 44:36 Ag 21 '44

KARMITZ, MARIN
   Interview.  Cineaste 4-2:21 Fall '70
   Lesage, J.  Radical French cinema in context.  Cineaste
      5-3:42 Sum '72

KAST, PIERRE
   Biographical note.  Unifrance 45:10 D '57
   Billard, G.  The men and their work.  Films & Filming
      6-1:7 O '59

KATZ, MAX
   Listing of films.  Film Culture 27:7 Sum '65

KAUTNER, HELMUT
   Bean, R.  The face of '63--Germany.  Films & Filming
      9-9:41 Je '63

KAWALEROWICZ, JERZY
   Kawalerowicz, J.  Angles on the angels.  Films &
      Filming 8-2:14 N '61

KAYE, STANTON
Listing of films.   Film Culture 37:7 Sum '65

KAZAN, ELIA
Isaacs, H. R.   First rehearsals; Elia Kazan directs a
modern legend; Jacobowsky and the colonel.   Theatre
Arts 28:143 Mr '44
Audience tomorrow.   Theatre Arts 29:568 O '45
Sketch.   Vogue 107:104 Ja 1 '46
Double-barreled director Kazan.   Cue 16-6:9 F 8 '47
Entr'acte.   Theatre Arts 31:10 Je '47
Schumach, M.   Director named Gadge.   N. Y. Times Mag
p18 N 9 '47
Stevens, V.   Actor and director of stage and screen.
Theatre Arts 31:18 D '47
Biography.   Current Biography Ja '48
Elia Kazan, prizewinner of the year.   Cue 17-16:14 Ap 17
'48
Sketch.   World R 6:39 Ag '49
Long, long ago.   Theatre Arts 34:39 S '50
Elia Kazan on Zapata.   Sat R 35:22 Ap 5 '52
Kazan talks.   Time 59:106 Ap 21 '52
Shapes of things; testimony in newspaper advertisement.
Nation 174:394 Ap 26 '52
Poling, J.   Handy Gadget.   Colliers 129:56 My 31 '52
Where I stand.   Reader Digest 61:45 Jl '52
Anderson, R.   Walk a ways with me.   Theatre Arts
38:30 Ja '54
The director and the public; a symposium.   Film Culture
1-2:15 Mr/Ap '55
Durniak, J.   Amateurs can be great; interview.   Popular
Photo 36:134 My '55
Knight, A. & Hewes, H.   Saturday Review goes to the
movies.   Sat R 39:22 D 29 '56
Archer, E.   Genesis of a genius; filmog.   Films & Film-
ing 3-3:7 D '56
Hume, R.   New baby.   Films & Filming 3-3:9 D '57
Archer, E.   Elia Kazan--the genesis of a style.   Film
Culture 2-2(8):5 '56
Archer, E.   The theatre goes to Hollywood.   Films &
Filming 3-4:13 Ja '57
Writers and motion pictures; introduction to Face in the
crowd.   Atlantic 199:67 Ap '57
Morehouse, W.   Keeping up with Kazan.   Theatre Arts
41:20 Je '57
Kazan, E.   The writer and motion pictures.   Sight &
Sound 27-1:20 Sum '57

Ten best for a repertory theatre. N.Y. Times Mag p74
    N 9 '58
Personality of the month. Films & Filming 7-7:5 Ap '61
Director. Newsweek 58:112 O 16 '61
What makes a woman interesting? Vogue 139:26 Ja 15 '62
Bean, R. Elia Kazan on The young agony; interview.
    Films & Filming 8-6:26 Mr '62
The screen answers back. Films & Filming 8-8:12 My
    '62
Winter, J. Phoney Kazan; letter. Films & Filming
    8-10:11 Jl '62
Theatre: new stages, new plays, new actors. N.Y. Times
    Mag p18 S 23 '62
Morgan, T. Elia Kazan's great expectations. Harper
    225:66 S '62
America, America; excerpt. Vogue 140:172 O 1 '62
Director's heritage. N.Y. Times Mag p106 O 7 '62
Fenin, G. The face of '63--United States. Films &
    Filming 9-6:55 Mr '63
Sarris, A. Fallen idols; filmog. Film Culture 28:30
    Spg '63
On location with Elia Kazan. Show 3-7:62 Jl '63
Famous feuds: Strasberg vs. Kazan. Show 3-7:88 Jl '63
Silke, J. R. Kazan the violent. Cinema (BH) 1-6:4
    N/D '63
Fixx, J. F. Who cares what the boss thinks? Sat R
    46:14 D 28 '63
Arthur Miller ad libs on Elia Kazan. Show 4-1:54 Ja '64
The life and times of Elia Kazan. Films & Filming
    10-8:35 My '64
Elia Kazan ad libs on The changeling and its critics.
    Show 5-1:38 Ja '65
Dundy, E. How to succeed in the theatre without really
    being successful. Esquire 63:88 My '65
Frankel, H. Son of the oven maker; excerpt from inter-
    view. Sat R 50:26 Mr 4 '67
Delahaye, M. Preface to an interview; filmog. Cahiers
    (Eng) 9:9 Mr '67
Member of the tribe. Newsweek 69:96D My 29 '67
Trailleur, R. Elia Kazan and the House Un-American
    Activities Committee. Film Comment 4-1:43 Sum '68
Kael, P. Current cinema. New Yorker 45:211 N 22 '69
What directors are saying. Action 5-1:28 Ja/F '70
Sarris, A. Director of the month; filmog. Show 1-2:29
    F '70
Cowie, P. Director of the year; filmog. International
    Film G 8:23 '71

Gussow, M.   Elia Kazan, novelist and moviemaker,
  prefers the pen.   N.Y. Times Bio Ed F 18 '72
O'Brien, G.   Interview.   Interview 20:10 Mr '72
Changas, E.   Elia Kazan's America.   Film Comment
  8-2:8 Sum '72
Silver, C. & Zucker, J.   Visiting Kazan; interview.
  Film Comment 8-2:15 Sum '72
The inspired adolescent.   Films & Filming 18-10:14 Jl
  '72
Elia Kazan.   Movie 19:entire issue.   n. d.

## KEARNEY, PHILIP
Survey among unsuccessful applicants for the Ford Foundation film grants.   Film Comment 2-3:10 Sum '64

## KEATON, BUSTER
Peltret, E.   Interview.   Motion Pic Classic 12:64 Mr '21
Keaton, B.   Before and after taking.   Photoplay 20-4:31
  S '21
Goldbeck, W.   Interview.   Motion Pic 22:28 O '21
St. Johns, A. R.   Interviewing Joseph Talmadge Keaton.
  Photoplay 22-5:51 O '22
Home of.   Classic 16:38 Ag '23
Brand, H.   Sketch.   Motion Pic Classic 23:32 Je '26
Why I never smile.   Ladies Home J 43:20 Je '26
Keaton, J.   Sketch.   Photoplay 31:98 My '27
Dickey, J.   Interview.   Motion Pic 35:42 Ap '28
Appearance in Steamboat Bill Jr.   Nation (Lon) 43:561
  Jl 28 '28
Van Dyke, S.   Oh Buster!   You wouldn't kid us, would
  you?   Silver Screen 2-6:22 Ap '32
Burden, J.   Sketch.   Movie Classic 2:32 Je '32
Moffit, J. C.   Page on publicity with premieres.   Cinema
  Digest 1-7:9 Ag 8 '32
Bannon, J.   His divorce.   Movie Classic 3:31 O '32
Janeway, D.   His "land yacht."   Movie Classic 3:32 N
  '32
Reid, A.   Strictly for laughs.   Colliers 113:66 Je 10 '44
Turned circus performer in Paris.   Newsweek 30:50
  O 20 '47
Agee, J.   Great stone face.   Life 27:82 S 5 '49
Gloomy Buster is back again; Keaton is up to his old
  tricks on TV.   Life 28:145 Mr 13 '50
Minoff, P.   Even the veteran comics are putting it on
  film.   Cue 22-1:7 Ja 3 '53
Shulman, M.   Then and now.   N.Y. Times Mag p19
  My 9 '54

Buster at bay.   Life 39:132 D 12 '55
Film pioneers' roll of their living immortals.   Life
   40:119 Ja 23 '56
Old comic and pupil.   Life 42:91 My 6 '57
Bishop, C.   Great stone face.   Film Q 12:10 Fall '58
Bishop, C.   Interview.   Film Q 12:15 Fall '58
Baxter, B.   Buster Keaton.   Film 18:8 N/D '58
DeRoos, R.   Biggest laugh in movie history.   Coronet
   46:98 Ag '59
Celebrities on a stylish spree.   Life 47:103 S 7 '59
Robinson, D.   Buster.   Sight & Sound 29:41 Win '59
Great stone face talks.   Newsweek 55:90 Ja 25 '60
Still playing it deadpan.   Life 49:132 O 10 '60
Happy pro.   New Yorker 39:36 Ap 27 '63
Sarris, A.   Second line; filmog.   Film Culture 28:11
   Spg '63
Maltin, L.   My favorite Buster Keaton.   8mm Collector
   8:15 My '64
Mosby, A.   Buster Keaton sneers at today's big bosoms.
   8mm Collector 8:12 My '64 (reprint from El Paso
   Herald Post)
Estes, O. Jr.   Keaton--genius of ingenius comedy!  8mm
   Collector 8:12 My '64
Keaton, B.   How I broke into the movies.   8mm Collector
   8:13 My '64
Bergen, E.   Keaton; interview.   8mm Collector 8:13 My
   '64
Beckett; production of his first screenplay for Evergreen
   theatre.   New Yorker 40:22 Ag 8 '64
Watch out, Buster, you're being watched.   Life 57:85
   Ag 14 '64
Brownlow, K.   Interview.   Film 42:6 Win '64
Gillett, J. & Blue, J.   Keaton at Venice.   Sight & Sound
   34:26 Win '65
Lorca, F. G.   Buster Keaton takes a walk.   Sight &
   Sound 35-1:24 Win '65
Scold and the Sphinx.   Time 87:52 F 11 '66
Agee, J.   Buster Keaton; excerpt from Agee on film.
   Life 60:63 F 11 '66
Obit:   British Book Year 1967:595 '67
   8mm Collector 14:29 Spg '66 (reprints from N. Y.
   Times; N. Y. Daily News; Philadelphia Evening Bulletin)
   Film R p22 '66/68
   National R 18:167 F 22 '66
   Screen World 18:237 '67
   Time 87:82 F 11 '66
Morgenstern, J.   What a Buster!  Newsweek 67:30 F 14 '66

Houston, P.   Buster.   Sight & Sound 35-2:72 Spg '66
Friedman, A. B.   Interview.   Film Q 19-4:2 Sum '66
Foley, E.   Mrs. Keaton looks back on her life with
    Buster.   Classic Film Collector 16:22 Fall '66 (re-
    print from Philadelphia Evening Bulletin)
Adieu Buster.   Cahiers (Eng) 2:5 '66
McCaffrey, D.   The mutual approval of Keaton and Lloyd.
    Cinema J 6 '66/67
Morley, S.   Tribute to Keaton.   Films & Filming 13-10:
    42 Jl '67
Rhode, E.   Buster Keaton.   Encounter 29:35 D '67
Coleman, J.   Damfino.   New Statesman 75:149 F 2 '68
Houston, P.   The great blank page.   Sight & Sound
    37-2:63 Spg '68
Gilliatt, P.   Current cinema.   New Yorker 46:118 S 26
    '70
Zimmerman, P. D.   Buster Keaton's comic world.
    Newsweek 76:96 O 5 '70
Kauffmann, S.   Buster Keaton festival.   New Republic
    163:24 O 24 '70
Kanfer, S.   Great stone face.   Time 96:94 N 2 '70
A bibliography of interest to film collectors.   Classic
    Film Collector 33:4 Win '71
Evans, C.   The sound of silence.   Mise-En-Scene 1:23
    n. d.


KEIGHLEY, WILLIAM
    Biographical note; filmog.   Movies & People 2:42 '40
    Voice of lux.   Newsweek 26:100 N 19 '45
    Keighley, W.   Why blame Hollywood?   Silver Screen
        18-3:22 Ja '48
    Biography.   Current Biography 9:24 N '48
        Same.   Current Biography Yearbook 1948:338 '49


KELLY, ANTHONY
    Obit.   N. Y. Times p17 S 26 '53


KELLY, GENE
    Stars of tomorrow.   Lions Roar 1-11/12:no p# Jl/Ag '42
    Meet Pal Joey.   Lions Roar 2-2:no p# N '42
    Kelly, G.   A letter to my daughter Kerry.   Silver
        Screen 13-5:30 Mr '43
    Tintype ... Gene Kelly.   Lions Roar 2-4:no p# Ap '43
    Proctor, K.   Hey, Irish!   Photoplay 22-6:36 My '43
    Mrs. Kelly's boy.   Lions Roar 2-5:no p# Jl '43
    The man on the flying trapeze.   Lions Roar 3-2:no p#
        Ja '44

Kelly ain't kickin'.   Lions Roar 3-2:no p# Ja '44
Harris, E.   If you were Gene Kelly's house guest.
    Photoplay 24-3:54 F '44
Kelly, B.   It's like this to be Mrs. Gene Kelly.   Photo-
    play 25-1:36 Je '44
Arnold, M.   Keeping up with Gene Kelly.   Photoplay
    26-2:38 Ja '45
Crichton, K.   Dancing master.   Colliers 115:20 My 19
    '45
Enton, H.   Where's Gene Kelly?   Photoplay 27-6:56 N '45
Biography.   Current Biography D '45
Frazier, G.   Starboard bound.   Photoplay 28-2:47 Ja '46
Isaacs, H. R.   Portrait of a dancing actor.   Theatre
    Arts 30:149 Mr '46
O'Leary, D.   Always on his toes!   Silver Screen 17-6:40
    Ap '47
Boger, F.   My kids, the Kellys.   Photoplay 33-3:54 Ag
    '48
Biographical note.   Newsweek 35:84 Mr 27 '50
Martin, P.   Fastest moving star in pictures.   Sat Even-
    ing Post 223:24 Jl 8 '50
Chandler, D.   Strictly from hunger.   Photoplay 41-2:56
    F '52
Sakol, J.   Traveling man.   Photoplay 42-2:50 Ag '52
Gene Kelly's invitation to the dance.   Look 17:88 Mr 24
    '53
Hyanes, J.   Gene Kelly: all the world loves to dance.
    Cue 22-18:12 My 2 '53
Gene Kelly: man in motion.   Coronet 35:105 N '53
Harvey, E.   Legs and a legend.   Colliers 133:24 Mr 5
    '54
Bruce, J.   He changes their lives.   Silver Screen 24-8:
    40 Je '54
Knight, A.   Invitation to the dance.   Dance 30:14 Je '56
Wood, C.   TV personalities biographical sketchbook.   TV
    Personalities p13 '57
Musical comedy is serious business.   Theatre Arts 42:18
    D '58
Alpert, H.   Old friends in new jobs: producing Flower
    drum song.   Dance 32:52 D '58
Brazel, A.   Dancing is a man's game.   Dance 33:30 F
    '59
Dance Magazine's 1958 award winner.   Dance 33:31 Mr
    '59
Dance Magazine's annual awards.   Dance 33:31 Ap '59
Shayon, R. L.   Shall we dance?   Sat R 42:61 My 16 '59
Kelly's Pontiac show.   Dance 33:36 Je '59

An evening with Fred Astaire and Gene Kelly.   TV Guide
    7-44:8 O 31 '59
Making ballet jump.   Newsweek 56:83 Jl 18 '60
Gene Kelly's French frolic.   Life 49:55 Ag 29 '60
September calendar; Museum of modern art presents a
    Gene Kelly dance film festival.   Dance 36:36 S '62
Sarris, A.   Oddities and one shots.   Film Culture 28:45
    Spg '63
Behlmer, R.   Gene Kelly; filmog.   Films In Review
    15-1:6 Ja '64
Amory, C.   Celebrity register.   McCalls 91:66 Mr '64
Gotta sing! gotta dance!   Film 40:9 Sum '64
Cutts, J.   Kelly.   Films & Filming 10-11:38 Ag '64;
    10-12:34 S '64
Some notes for young dancers.   Dance 39:49 S '65
Dancing in the dark.   Dance 39:103 D '65
Interview.   Cinema (BH) 3-4:24 D '66
Swisher, V. M.   Gene and Jack and the beanstalk. Dance
    41:52 F '67
Sextuple threat.   Time 90:56 Ag 4 '67
Kelly, G.   Directing Dolly.   Action 4-2:8 Mr/Ap '69
What directors are saying.   Action 5-3:30 My/Je '70
Song and dance man.   Screen Greats 1-2:42 Sum '71

KENNEDY, BURT
    Interview.   Cinema (BH) 4-1:14 S '68
    Kennedy, B.   A talk with John Ford.   Action 3-5:6 S/O
        '68
    Ford and Kennedy on the western; discussion.   Films In
        Review 20-1:29 Ja '69
    Our way west: Burt Kennedy talks to John Ford.   Films
        & Filming 16-1:30 O '69
    Filmography.   Film Comment 6-4:101 Win '70/71

KERN, JAMES V.
    Obit.   Screen World 18:237 '67

KERR, JAMES
    Survey among unsuccessful applicants for the Ford
        Foundation film grants.   Film Comment 2-3:10 Sum '64

KERSHNER, IRVIN
    Young, C. & Bachmann, G.   New wave--or gesture?
        Film Q 14-3:6 Spg '61
    Young, C.   West Coast report.   Sight & Sound 30-3:137
        Sum '61

A discussion: personal creation in Hollywood: can it be
  done?   Film Q 15-3:16 Spg '62
Sarris, A.   Director of the month.   Show 1-5:16 My '70

KESSLER, BRUCE
  Guy, R.   Interview.   Cinema (BH) 4-1:45 S '68

KHAN, MEHBOOB
  Ray, S. K.   New Indian directors.   Film Q 14-1:63 Fall
    '60

KIMMELMAN, KEN
  Ken Kimmelman finds new esthetic in film art.   Making
    Films 2-6:24 D '68

KIMMINS, ANTHONY
  Sketch.   World R p23 O '48
  Filmography.   Film 14:8 N/D '57
  Obit.   Film R p45 '64/65
    Illustrated London N 244:869 My 30 '64
    N. Y. Times p43 My 20 '64

KIMMINS, PAT
  British feature directors; an index to their work.   Sight
    & Sound 27-6:297 Aut '58

KING, ALLAN
  Rosenthal, A.   The fiction documentary; interview.
    Film Q 23-4:9 Sum '70

KING, HENRY
  West, V.   Sketch.   Motion Pic 9:101 Ap '15
  Cheatham, M.   Interview.   Motion Pic Classic 12:56
    Mr '21
  Evans, D.   Sketch.   Photoplay 23:34 D '22
  Cruikshank, H.   Sketch.   Motion Pic Classic 29:33 My
    '29
  King, H.   Art and the box office.   Cinema Progress
    4-1/2:9 Je/Jl '39
  Biographical note; filmog.   Movies & People 2:43 '40
  Eagle eye.   American 131:88 Je '41
  Martin, P.   Give me a volcano.   Sat Evening Post
    219:22 My 31 '47
  The big screens.   Sight & Sound 24-4:209 Spg '55
  King, H. Filmmakers as goodwill ambassadors.   Films
    In Review 9-8:425 O '58

Shibuk, C. & North, C. The life and films of Henry
King. Films In Review 9-8:427 O '58
Braff, R. E. Partial filmog. Films In Review 14-3:188
Mr '63
Mitchell, G. J. Henry King. Films In Review 15-6:375
Je/Jl '64
Cherry, R. Henry King, the flying director. Action
4-4:6 Jl/Ag '69
Pickard, R. The tough race. Films & Filming 17-12:38
S '71

KING, LOUIS
Parsons, L. O. Cosmopolitan's citation for the best
direction of the month. Cosmop 127:126 Ag '49

KINOSHITA, KEISUKE
Iwabutchi, M. Japanese cinema 1961. Film Culture
24:85 Spg '62
Note. International Film G 2:34 '65

KINUGASA, TEINOSUKE
Note. International Film G 2:34 '65

KIRSANOV, DIMITRI
Michel, W. S. In memoriam of Dimitri Kirsanov, a
neglected master. Film Culture 3-5(15):3 D '57

KIRSCHHEIMER, MANNY
Survey among unsuccessful applicants for the Ford Foundation film grants. Film Comment 2-3:10 Sum '64

KIRSH, JOHN
A free hand. Sight & Sound 28-2:60 Spg '59

KIRSTEN, RALF
Bean, R. The face of '63--Germany. Films & Filming
9-9:41 Je '63

KIRTMAN, LEONARD
MacDonough, S. The Zanuck of sexploitation. Show
2-6:36 Ag '71

KIVIKOSKI, ERKKO
Biographical note. International Film G 8:142 '71

KJAERULFF-SCHMIDT, PALLE
Biographical note. International Film G 5:66 '68

KLEIN, LARRY
  Can you make a feature for $37,500?   Making Films
      2-5:36 O '68

KLEIN, WILLIAM
  Cameron, I.   Interview.   Movie 8:20 Ap '63
  Caulfield, P.   William Klein.   Modern Photo 29:84 Ja '65

KLINE, HERBERT
  Hollywood fights back.   Nation 142:612 My 13 '36
  Forgotten village.   Theatre Arts 25:336 My '41
  Film without make believe.   Mag Art 35:58 F '42
  New faces among MGM directors too.   Lions Roar 1-11/
      12:no p# Jl/Ag '42
  Filmmaking in Mexico City.   Theatre Arts 27:679 N '43
  About the shape of films to come.   Theatre Arts 30:58
      Ja '46

KLOPČIČ, MATJAŽ
  Biographical note.   International Film G 8:282 '71

KLOS, ELMAR
  Cohen, J.   Discussion.   Film Comment 4-2/3:68 Fall/
      Win '68

KLUGE, ALEXANDER
  Dictionary of young German filmmakers.   CTVD 4-2:11
      Spg '66
  Nettlebeck, G. U.   Bewilderment of Anita.   Atlas 12:50
      D '66

KNEIFEL, ED
  Survey among unsuccessful applicants for the Ford Found-
      ation film grants.   Film Comment 2-3:10 Sum '64

KNIGHT, DERRICK
  Knight, D.   Time for a change.   Film 42:33 Win '64
  Short film profile.   International Film G 3:173 '66

KNOWLES, BERNARD
  British feature directors; an index to their work.   Sight
      & Sound 27-6:297 Aut '58

KOBAKHIDZE, MICHAEL
  A Russian six.   Films & Filming 13-12:27 S '67

KOBAYASHI, MASAKI
  Richie, D.   Japan: the youngest talents.   Sight & Sound
    29-2:78 Spg '60
  Iwabutchi, M.   Japanese cinema 1961.   Film Culture
    24:85 Spg '62
  Silke, J. R.   Harakiri, Kobayashi, humanism; interview.
    Cinema (BH) 1-4:32 Je/Jl '63
  Yoshiyama, T.   Chrysanthemums and corn.   CTVD 2-3:3
    Win '63/64
  Note.   International Film G 2:34 '65

KOCHENRATH, HANS PETER
  Thomas, A.   German underground.   Afterimage 2:45
    Aut '70

KOHON, DAVID
  Cobos, J.   The face of '63--Spain.   Films & Filming
    10-1:39 O '63

KONCHALOVSKY, ANDREI
  A Russian six.   Films & Filming 13-12:27 S '67

KORDA, ALEXANDER
  Helorin, M. A.   Alexander Korda ... screen pioneer.
    Naborhood Theatre G 2-33:3 Je 16 '34
  Lejeune, C. A.   British film and others.   Fortnightly R
    143:291 Mr '35
  Lejeune, C. A.   Alexander Korda, a sketch.   Sight &
    Sound 4-13:5 Spg '35
  Britain's best.   Time 26:44 S 9 '35
  Countney, W. B.   New worlds for Alexander.   Colliers
    97:25 F 15 '36
  Biographical sketch.   Time 27:43 Ap 6 '36
  Underdog now lion.   Lit Digest 122:19 Jl 18 '36
  Sherwood, L. E.   Work of.   Vogue 88:90 S 1 '36
  Biographical note; filmog.   Movies & People 2:43 '40
  Biography.   Current Biography 7:34 S '46
    Same.   Current Biography Yearbook 1946:306 '47
  Artist at work.   Time 50:98 N 17 '47
  Obit.   Americana Annual 1957:433 '57
    British Book Year 1957:576 '57
    Current Biography 17:34 Mr '56
    Current Biography Yearbook 1956:346 '57
    Illustrated London N 228:166 F 4 '56
    N.Y. Times p31 Ja 24 '56
    Screen World 8:223 '57
    Time 67:90 F 6 '56

Gilliat, S. ; Greene, G. ; Richardson, R.   Sir Alexander
  Korda.   Sight & Sound 25-4:214 Spg '56
Dalrymple, I.   Alexander Korda.   Q Film Radio TV
  11-3:294 Spg '57

KORDA, ZOLTAN
  Obit.   Illustrated London N 239:683 O 21 '61
  N. Y. Times p88 O 15 '61

KORTNER, FRITZ
  Obit.   N. Y. Times p31 Jl 24 '70
  Screen World 22:238 '71

KORTY, JOHN
  Survey among unsuccessful applicants for the Ford Found-
    ation film grants.   Film Comment 2-3:10 Sum '64
  Callenback, E. & Johnson, A.   Feature production in
    San Francisco: interview.   Film Q 19-3:20 Spg '66
  Interview.   New Yorker 46:27 Je 6 '70
  Geist, K.   Interview.   Interview 1-9:23 n. d.

KÓSA, FERENC
  Biographical note.   International Film G 6:93 '69

KOSTER, HENRY (Hermann Kosterlitz)
  Koster, H.   Director's notebook--why teach cinema?
    Cinema Progress 4-1/2:3 Je/Jl '39
  Biographical note; filmog.   Movies & People 2:43 '40
  MGM's directors range from pioneers to newcomers.
    Lions Roar 3-4:no p# Jl '44
  Great team.   Lions Roar 4-1:no p# F '45
  Samuels, G.   Director, Hollywood's leading man.   N. Y.
    Times Mag p23 O 26 '52

KOSTERLITZ, HERMANN
  (See: KOSTER, HENRY)

KOTCHEFF, TED
  British cinema filmography.   Film 65:10 Spg '70

KOVÁCS, ANDRÁS
  Biographical note.   International Film G 4:102 '67

KOZINTSEV, GRIGORI
  Kozintsev, G.   Deep screen.   Sight & Sound 28-3/4:156
    Sum/Aut '59
  Personality of the month.   Films & Filming 7-6:3 Mr '61

Kozintsev, G.   The Hamlet in me.   Films & Filming
    8-12:20 S '62
Kozintsev, G.   Over the Parisiana.   Sight & Sound 32-1:
    46 Win '62/63
A meeting with Grigori Kozintsev.   Film 49:27 Aut '67
New filmmakers.   Sat R 50:15 D 23 '67
Director of the year; filmog.   International Film G p24
    p72

KOZOMARA, LJUBISA
    Biographical note.   International Film G 8:281 '71

KRAMER, ROBERT
    Kael, P.   Current cinema.   New Yorker 46:136 O 24 '70

KRAMER, STANLEY
    Biographical note.   Newsweek 36:81 Jl 17 '50
    Small, C.   Genius on a low budget.   Colliers 126:26
        S 16 '50
    Crowther, B.   A movies on B budgets.   N.Y. Times
        Mag p24 N 12 '50
    New horizon.   Time 56:100 N 13 '50
    Mr. Kramer has come up fast.   Life 29:76 N 20 '50
    Kramer, S.   The independent producer.   Films In Review
        2-3:1 Mr '51
    Biography.   Current Biography 12:28 My '51
        Same.   Current Biography Yearbook 1951:356 '52
    Houston, P.   Kramer and company.   Sight & Sound 22-1:
        20 Jl/S '52
    Alpert, H.   Postwar generation in arts and letters. Sat R
        36:16 Mr 14 '53
    Kramer, S.   Kramer on the future.   Films In Review
        4-5:250 My '53
    Half a step behind.   Time 62:108 D 14 '53
    Into surgery for Not as a stranger.   Colliers 135:78 F 4
        '55
    Play the picture.   Theatre Arts 39:20 Ag '55
    Talk with Stanley Kramer: creative side of motion picture
        making.   Popular Photo 37:106 S '55
    Hollywood in Spanish.   Sat R 39:32 S 22 '56
    Bachmann, G.   The impact of television on motion pic-
        tures; interview.   Film Culture 3-2(12):3 '57
    Personality of the month.   Films & Filming 6-4:5 Ja '60
    Kramer, S.   Politics, social comment and my emotions.
        Films & Filming 6-9:7 Je '60
    Talk with the director.   Newsweek 56:114 O 17 '60
    Peterson, R.   Stanley Kramer; letter.   Films In Review

12-5:318 My '61
Hill, S. P. Producer Kramer; letter. Films In Review
12-7:447 Ag/S '61
Alpert, H.; Knight, A. Haunting question; producer-di-
rector at work. Sat R 44:43 D 2 '61
Crowther, B. Hollywood's producer of controversy. N.Y.
Times Mag p76 D 10 '61
Steel, P. Kramer's Nuremberg. Christian Century
79:332 Mr 14 '62
Cowie, P. The defiant one. Films & Filming 9-6:15
Mr '63
Fenin, G. The face of '63--United States. Films &
Filming 9-6:55 Mr '63
Kramer, S. Sending myself the message. Films &
Filming 10-5:7 F '64
McGivern, W. P. Ship of fools; has Stanley Kramer got
a tiger by the tail? Show 4-8:57 S '64
Decter, M. Movies and messages. Commentary 40:77
N '65
He could wither you with a glance. Life 62:69 Je 30 '67
Ronan, M. Interview. Senior Scholastic 92:16 F 1 '68
A recipe for greatness. Films & Filming 14-6:5 Mr '68
Kramer, S. Nine times across the generation gap.
Action 3-2:11 Mr/Ap '68
What directors are saying. Action 4-6:28 N/D '69
Omatsu, M. Guess who came to lunch? Take One 1-9:20
n. d.

KRISTL, VLADO
Stanislavsky: revolutionary of the modern theatre.
UNESCO Courier 16:12 N '63
K is for Kuri and Kristl. Film 42:36 Win '64

KUBELIKA, PETER
Mekas, J. Interview; filmog. Film Culture 44:42 Spg '67
Working for the next 1000 years; filmog. Cinema (Lon)
9:28 n. d.

KUBRICK, STANLEY
Biography. Time 67:106 Je 4 '56
Personality of the month. Films & Filming 2-12:5 S '56
Twenty-nine and running: the director with Hollywood by
the horns. Newsweek 50:96 D 2 '57
Stang, J. Film fan to filmmaker. N. Y. Times Mag p34
O 12 '58
Kubrick, S. Words and movies. Sight & Sound 30-1:14
Win '60/61

Biography.   Current Biography 24:23 F '63
    Same.   Current Biography Yearbook 1963:224 '64
Fenin, G.   The face of '63--United States.   Films &
    Filming 9-6:55 Mr '63
Sarris, A.   Minor disappointments; filmog.   Film Culture
    28:41 Spg '63
Kramer, S.   How I learned to stop worrying and love the
    cinema.   Films & Filming 8-9:12 Je '63
The directors choose the best films.   Cinema (BH) 1-5:14
    Ag/S '63
Tornabene, L.   Contradicting the Hollywood image.   Sat
    R 46:19 D 28 '63
Direct hit.   Newsweek 63:79 F 3 '64
Lyon, P.   Astonishing Stanley Kubrick.   Holiday 35:101
    F '64
Burgess, J.   The anti-militarism of Stanley Kubrick.
    Film Q 18-1:4 Fall '64
Beyond the stars.   New Yorker 41:38 Ap 24 '65
Director of the year; filmog.   International Film G 2:26
    '65
Alpert, H.   Offbeat director in outer space.   N.Y. Times
    Mag p14 Ja 16 '66
To prepare a man for the extraordinary.   Esquire 65:117
    My '66
Kubrick, farther out.   Newsweek 68:106 S 12 '66
Bernstein, J.   Profiles.   New Yorker 42:70 N 12 '66
Spinrad, N.   Stanley Kubrick in the 21st Century.   Cinema
    (BH) 3-4:4 D '66
Gilliatt, P.   Current cinema.   New Yorker 44:150 Ap 13
    '68
Take One talks with Wally Gentleman.   Take One 1-11:18
    My/Je '68
Gasser, H. M.   2001: a space odyssey.   Cineaste 2-1
    Sum '68
Crowdus, G.   A tentative for the viewing of 2001.
    Cineaste 2-1 Sum '68
Barker, C.   Is 2001 worth seeing twice?   Cineaste 2-1
    Sum '68
Becker, M.   2004?   Cineaste 2-1 Sum '68
Kubrick reveals all.   Cineaste 2-1 Sum '68
Quotemanship.   Action 3-3:20 Jl/Ag '68
Bernstein, J.   Books: 2001: a space odyssey.   New
    Yorker 44:180 S 21 '68
Playboy interview.   Playboy 15-9:85 S '68
A talk with Stanley Kubrick.   Action 4-1:15 Ja/F '69
James, C.   2001: Kubrick vs. Clarke.   Cinema (Lon)
    2:18 Mr '69

What directors are saying.  Action 6-1:30 Ja/F '71
Robinson, W. R.   The movies as a revolutionary moral
   force (2001).   Contempora 1-6:15 My/Ag '71
What directors are saying.   Action 6-6:22 N/D '71
Phillips, G.   Kubrick; interview; filmog.   Film Comment
   7-4:30 Win '71/72
Stick, P.   Kubrick's horrorshow.   Sight & Sound 41-1:45
   Win '71/72
Kubrick's brilliant vision.   Newsweek 79-1:28 Ja 3 '72
Weinrub, B.   Kubrick tells what makes Clockwork orange
   tick.   N. Y. Times Bio Ed Ja 4 '72
What directors are saying.   Action 7-1:36 Ja/F '72
McGregor, C.   Nice boys from the Bronx.   N. Y. Times
   Bio Ed Ja 30 '72
Strick, P. & Houston, P.   Interview.   Sight & Sound
   41-2:62 Spg '72
Boyers, R.   Kubrick's A clockwork orange: some obser-
   vations.   Film Heritage 7-4:1 Sum '72
Walker, B.   From novel to film: Kubrick's Clockwork
   orange.   Women & Film 2:4 '72

KUCHAR, GEORGE
   George Kuchar speaks on films and truth.   Film Culture
      33:14 Sum '64
   Listing of films.   Film Culture 37:7 Sum '65
   Renan, S.   Interview.   Film Culture 45:47 Sum '67
   Chomont, T. S.   Interview.   Film Culture 45:50 Sum '67
   Weiner, P.   New American cinema; filmog.   Film 58:22
      Spg '70

KUCHAR, MIKE
   Listing of films.   Film Culture 37:7 Sum '65
   Weiner, P.   New American cinema; filmog.   Film 58:22
      Spg '70
   Renan, S.   Interview.   Film Culture 45:47 Sum '70
   Chomont, T. S.   Interview.   Film Culture 45:50 Sum '70

KUNN, RODOLFO
   Cobos, J.   The face of '63--Spain.   Films & Filming
      10-1:39 O '63

KULESHOV, LEV
   Hill, S. P.   Prophet without honor?   Film Culture 44:1
      Spg '67
   Lev Kuleshov: 1899-1970.   Afterimage 1:no p# Ap '70
   Taylor, R.   Lev Kuleshov 1899-1970.   Silent Pic 8:28
      Aut '70

Levace, R. Kuleshov. Sight & Sound 40-2:86 Spg '71
Selections from Lev Kuleshov's Art of the cinema.
  Screen 12-4:103 Win '71/72

## KUMEL, HARRY
  Biographical note. International Film G 7:70 '70

## KUPERMAN, MARIO
  Lucchetti, R. F. Interview. CTVD 8-1(29):2 Spg '71

## KURI, YOJI
  K. is for Kuri and Kristl. Film 42:36 Win '64
  Listing of films. Film Culture 37:7 Sum '65
  Edera, B. A survey; filmog. International Film G
    4:203 '67
  Clemente, J. L. Yoji Kuri. CTVD 7-4:27 Win '70/71

## KURKVAARA, MAUNU
  Biographical note. International Film G 9:128 '72

## KUROSAWA, AKIRA
  Leyda, J. The films of Kurosawa. Sight & Sound
    24-2:74 O/D '54
  Personality of the month. Films & Filming 4-2:5 N '57
  McVay, D. The rebel in a kimono. Films & Filming
    7-10:9 Jl '61
  McVay, D. Samurai--and small beer. Films & Filming
    7-11:15 Ag '61
  Foster, N. G. Japan: the peculiar films. Holiday
    30:112 O '61
  Richie, D. Dostoevsky with a Japanese camera. Horizon
    4:42 Jl '62
  West, A. The art of Akira Kurosawa. Show 2-7:58
    Jl '62
  Japanese apocalypse. Time 80:90 S 21 '62
  Gentleman of Japan. Time 81:42 Ja 25 '63
  Richie, D. The face of '63--Japan. Films & Filming
    9-10:15 Jl '63
  Interview. Cinema (BH) 1-5:27 Ag/S '63
  Iida, S. Kurosawa. Cinema (BH) 1-5:28 Ag/S '63
  Seven bullets. Newsweek 63:84 Mr 9 '64
  Biography. Current Biography 26:27 Ap '65
    Same. Current Biography Yearbook 1965:239 '65
  Probing for Kurosawa's secret; symposium. Atlas 9:299
    My '65
  Higham, C. Kurosawa's humanism. Kenyon R 27:737
    Aut '65

Ortelani, B.   Films & Faces of Akira Kurosawa.
    America 113:368 O 2 '65
Alpert, H.   Japanese screen.   Sat R 48:35 D 25 '65
Note.   International Film G 2:34 '65
Director of the year; filmog.   International Film G 3:13
    '66
Pinto, A.   Akira Kurosawa; filmog.   Films In Review
    18-4:255 Ap '67
Epic vision.   Time 93:67 Ja 17 '69
Kurosawa, A.   Why Mifune's beard won't be red; state-
    ment on color.   Cinema (BH) 2-2:40 '69
Chekhonin, B.   Kurosawa's troubles in big bad Hollywood.
    Atlas 19:59 Mr '70
Mellen, J.   The epic cinema of Kurosawa; filmog.   Take
    One 3-4:16 Mr/Ap '71
Interview.   Cinema (BH) 7-2:14 Spg '72
Director's decline.   Japanese Fantasy #9 '72


KUTZ, KAZIMIERZ
    The Polish cinema.   Film 31:26 Spg '62

## LA CAVA, GREGORY
Thorp, D. Sketch. Motion Pic Classic 23:62 My '26
Gregory La Cava. Cinema Digest 2-6:9 Ja 16 '33
Men behind megaphones. Cue 4-12:3 Ja 18 '36
Reynolds, Q. Give me real people. Colliers 101:18
    Mr 26 '38
Spotlight on Hollywood. Arts & Decoration 51:24 D '39
Biographical note; filmog. Movies & People 2:43 '40
Biography. Current Biography '41
Obit. Current Biography 13:25 Ap '52
    Current Biography Yearbook 1952:321 '53
    N. Y. Times p92 Mr 2 '52
    Newsweek 39:70 Mr 10 '52
    Screen World 4:176 '53
    Time 59:98 Mr 10 '52
Biography. National Cylopaedia 40:575 '55
Sarris, A. Esoterica; filmog. Film Culture 28:22
    Spg '63

## LACHMAN, HARRY
Harry Lachman, Chevalier of the legion of honor, director
    of Dante's inferno. Cue 3-40:3 Ag 3 '35
Herrmann, D. U. You throw it out the back door, he
    brings it in the front door. House Beautiful 87:56
    Ag '47
Woodson, W. Harry Lachman, a link with the impres-
    sionists. American Artist 26:20 O '62

## LAINE, EDVIN
Biographical note. International Film G 9:128 '72

## LALOUX, RENE
Granja, V. Rene Laloux. CTVD 4-2:4 Spg '66
Laloux, R. The animation cinema needs thinking. CTVD
    4-2:4 Spg '66
Laloux, R. A hunger for the future. CTVD 5-3:18 Win
    '67/68

## LAMAC, CARL
Obit. N. Y. Times p61 Ag 3 '52

## LAMAČ, KAREL
Dewey, L. Czechoslovakia: silence into sound Film 60:5
    n. d.

LAMONT, CHARLES
    Photographing children.  Popular Science 141:144 O '42
    Putting laughs in your home movies.  Popular Science
        143:24 S '43

LAMORISSE, ALBERT
    Lamorisse's new balloon.  Time 76:65 O 24 '60
    Biography.  Current Biography 24:24 Je '63
        Same.  Current Biography Yearbook 1963:229 '64
    Obit.  Current Biography 31:47 Jl '70
        Current Biography Yearbook 1970:465 '71
        Film R p19 '71/72
        N. Y. Times p43 Je 4 '70
        Time 95:54 Je 15 '70

LAMOTHE, ARTHUR
    Biographical note; filmog.  Cahiers (Eng) 4:46 '66

LANDAU, HERMAN
    Listing of films.  Film Culture 37:7 Sum '65

LANDOW, GEORGE
    Listing of films.  Film Culture 37:7 Sum '65
    Sitney, P. A.  Interview.  Film Culture 47:10 Sum '69
    Sitney, P. A.  Avant garde film.  Afterimage 2:22 Aut '70

LANFIELD, SIDNEY
    Earhart, D.  The helper upper.  Silver Screen 8-2:47 D
        '37

LANG, FRITZ
    Fraenkel, H.  His story.  Motion Pic Classic 23:38
        Mr '26
    Bagai, R.  Fritz Lang--master of mood.  Cinema Prog-
        ress 3-2:10 My/Je '38
    Snyder, W. L.  Cinema and stage.  Cinema Progress
        4-1/2:11 Je/Jl '39
    Biographical note; filmog.  Movies & People 2:43 '40
    Jacobs, L.  Film directors at work.  Theatre Arts
        25:229 Mr '41
    Ferguson, O.  Behind the camera.  New Republic 104:887
        Je 30; 105:21 Jl 7 '41
    Biography.  Current Biography '43
    Weinberg, H. G.  An index to the creative work of Fritz
        Lang.  Sight & Sound (Special sup) Index Series #5
        F '46
    Freedom of the screen.  Theatre Arts 31:52 D '47

Lambert, G.   Fritz Lang's America.   Sight & Sound
    25-1:15 Spg; 25-2:92 Sum '55
Hart, H.   Fritz Lang today.   Films In Review 7-6:261
    Je/Jl '56
Bachmann, G.   The impact of television on motion pic-
    tures; interview.   Film Culture 3-2(12):5 '57
Taylor, J. R.   The nine lives of Doctor Mabuse.   Sight
    & Sound 31-1:43 Win '61/62
Fritz Lang who in 1925 dreamed of the future talks about
    the problems of life today.   Films & Filming 8-9:20
    Je '62
Bartlett, N.   The dark struggle.   Film 32:11 Sum '62
Fritz Lang talks about Dr. Mabuse.   Movie 4:4 N '62
Sarris, A.   Second line; filmog.   Film Culture 28:11
    Spg '63
Madson, A.   Interview.   Sight & Sound 36-3:108 Sum '67
Berg, G.   Fritz Lang.   Take One 2-2:12 N/D '68
Chamberlain, P.   The films of Fritz Lang; filmog.
    Cinema (BH) 5-3:38 Fall '69
The films of Fritz Lang at the Los Angeles county mu-
    seum.   Cinema (BH) 5-3:38 Fall '69
What directors are saying.   Action 4-6:28 N/D '69
Joannides, P.   Aspects of Fritz Lang.   Cinema (Lon)
    6/7:5 Ag '70
What directors are saying.   Action 5-6:22 N/D '70
Jensen, P. M.   Fritz Lang and reflections of present-day
    moods.   Filmograph 1-3:21 '70
What directors are saying.   Action 7-3:28 My/Je '72
Lyons, B.   Fritz Lang and the film noir.   Mise-En-Scene
    1:11 n. d.


LANG, WALTER
    Parsons, L. O.   Cosmopolitan's citation for the best
        direction of the month.   Cosmop 120:61 Ap '46
    Parsons, L. O.   Cosmopolitan's citation for the best
        direction of the month.   Cosmop 124:13 Ap '48
    Obit.   Classic Film Collector 34:X-3 Spg '72 (reprint
        from N. Y. Times) N. Y. Times F 8 '72
        Same.   N. Y. Times Bio Ed F 8 '72


LANGESTRATT, BOB
    Biographical note.   International Film G 9:199 '72


LANGLEY, NOEL
    Filmography.   Film 14:8 N/D '57
    British feature directors; an index to their work.   Sight &
        Sound 27-6:298 Aut '58

LANTZ, WALTER
  Irwin, W.   Walter Lantz.   Films In Review 22-4:211
    Mr '71

LARKIN, JOHN
  Obit.   Screen World 17:238 '66

LASSEBY, STIG
  Pensel, H.   Animated animator on Swedish animation;
    interview.   CTVD 4-4:11 Win '66/67

LATTUADA, ALBERTO
  Lattuada, A.   Adventures among masterpieces.   Inter-
    national Film A 1:36 '57
  Lattuada, A.   We took the actors into the streets.   Films
    & Filming 5-7:8 Ap '59

LAUNDER, FRANK
  Filmography.   Film 14:8 N/D '57
  British feature directors; an index to their work.   Sight
    & Sound 27-6:298 Aut '58

LEACOCK, PHILIP
  Leacock, P.   Fact and ... fiction.   Films & Filming
    3-7:16 Ap '57
  Filmography.   Film 14:8 N/D '57
  British feature directors; an index to their work.   Sight
    & Sound 27-6:298 Aut '58

LEACOCK, RICHARD
  Leacock, R.   To far places with camera and sound-track.
    Films In Review 1-2:3 Mr '50
  Bell, H.   Richard Leacock tells how to boost available
    light.   Popular Photo 38:104 F '56
  Weddings and babies.   Harper 217:86 S '58
  The work of Ricky Leacock; interview.   Film Culture
    22/23:12 '61
  Leacock, R.   For an uncontrolled cinema.   Film Culture
    22/23:23 '61
  Mekas, J.   Notes on the new American cinema.   Film
    Culture 24:8 Spg '62
  Shivas, M.   Interview.   Movie 8:16 Ap '63
  Blue, J.   One man's truth; interview.   Film Culture
    3-2:15 Spg '65
  Christgau, R.   The MGM of the underground?   Show
    1-1:34 Ja '70
  Leacock, R.   On filming the dance.   Filmmakers News-
    letter 4-1:34 N '70

LEAN, DAVID
Biography.   Current Biography 14:44 My '53
Same.   Current Biography Yearbook 1953:347 '53
Holden, J.   A study of David Lean.   Film Journal (Aus)
# 1 Ap '56
Filmography.   Film 14:8 N/D '57
Reynolds, C.   What you can learn from movies; inter-
view.   Popular Photo 42:108 Mr '58
British feature directors; an index to their work.   Sight
& Sound 27-6:298 Aut '58
Watts, S.   David Lean.   Films In Review 10-4:245 Ap '59
McVay, D.   Lean--lover of life.   Films & Filming 5-11:
9 Ag '59
Lean, D.   Out of the wilderness.   Films & Filming 9-4:
12 Ja '63
Sarris, A.   Fallen idols; filmog.   Film Culture 28:30
Spg '63
Alpert, H.   David Lean recipe: a whack in the guts.
N. Y. Times Mag p32 My 23 '65
Stewart, R. S.   Dr. Zhivago: the making of a movie.
Atlantic 216:58 Ag '65
Oscar bound.   Time 86:44 D 24 '65
Epic of beauty and terror: Dr. Zhivago with report by
Richard Schickel.   Life 60:48 Ja 21 '66
Quotemanship.   Action 3-3:20 Jl/Ag '68
What directors are saying.   Action 4-6:28 N/D '69
Alpert, H.   David Lean's big gamble.   Sat R 53:53 N 14
'70
Kael, P.   Current cinema.   New Yorker 46:116 N 21 '70
Westerbeck, C. L. Jr.   Lean years.   Commonweal 93:32
D 18 '70
Blume, M.   A brief encounter with David Lean.   After
Dark 13-8:18 D '70
What directors are saying.   Action 6-1:30 Ja/F '71
Furniss, C.   Lean at San Francisco.   Films In Review
22-4:237 Ap '71
British cinema filmography.   Film 65:10 Spg '72

LEARNER, KEITH
Interview.   International Film G 3:191 '66

LEBRECQUE, JEAN-CLAUDE
Interview; filmog.   Take One 1-2:13 N/D '66

LEDERBERG, DOV
Listing of films.   Film Culture 37:7 Sum '65

LEDERER, CHARLES
  New faces among MGM directors too.   Lions Roar 1-11/
    12:no p# Jl/Ag '42
  Filmography.   Film Comment 6-4:101 Win '70/71

LEE, FRANCIS
  Survey among unsuccessful applicants for the Ford
    Foundation film grants.   Film Comment 2-3:10 Sum '64
  Filmography.   Film Culture 29:75 Sum '63
  Listing of films.   Film Culture 37:7 Sum '65

LEE, JACK
  Filmography.   Film 14:8 N/D '57
  British feature directors; an index to their work.   Sight
    & Sound 27-6:298 Aut '58
  A free hand.   Sight & Sound 28-2:60 Spg '59

LEE, ROWLAND V.
  Biographical note; filmog.   Movies & People 2:43 '40

LEE-THOMPSON, J.
  (See: THOMPSON, J. LEE)

LEENHARDT, ROGER
  Marcorelles, L.   Interview with Roger Leenhardt and
    Jacques Rivette.   Sight & Sound 32-4:168 Aut '63

LEFEBVRE, JEAN-PIERRE
  Biographical note; filmog.   Cahiers (Eng) 4:49 '66
  La Rochelle, R. & Maggi, G.   Political situation of
    Quebec cinema.   Cineaste 5-3:4 Sum '72
  Fraser, G.   The gentle revolutionary.   Take One 1-7:10
    n. d.

LeGRICE, MALCOLM
  Dawson, J. & Johnston, C.   More British sounds.
    Sight & Sound 39-3:144 Sum '70

LEHRMAN, HENRY
  Obit.   N. Y. Times p17 N 9 '46

LEIGH, MIKE
  Armitage, P.   The director.   Film 65:7 Spg '72

LEISEN, MITCHELL
  Westgate, H. Jr.   Routine of a director.   Cinema Progress
    4-1/2:8 Je/Jl '39

Superman. American 133:76 My '42

Wilson, E. Pecularities of glamour girls. Silver Screen 14-5:24 Mr '44

Leisen, M. You women won't like this. Silver Screen 16-7:40 My '46

Sarris, A. Likable but elusive; filmog. Film Culture 28:35 Spg '63

Greenberg, J. Mitchell Leisen. Films In Review 17-3:198 Mr '66

Maltin, L. A visit with Mitchell Leisen. Action 4-6:7 N/D '69

Filmography. Films In Review 20-10:645 D '69

Maltin, L. Film Fan Monthly interviews Mitchell Leisen; filmog. Film Fan Mo 103:3 Ja '70

Owen, D. Letter. Films In Review 21-3:189 Mr '70

## LEISER, ERWIN

Leiser, E. Germany awake! Film Comment 3-4:40 Fall '65

## LEITE, MAURICIO GOMES

Viany, A. Who's who in the cinema novo. CTVD 5-4:26 Sum '68

Round table on the cinema novo. Cinema (Lon) 5:15 F '70

## LELOUCH, CLAUDE

Lerman, L. International movie report. Mademoiselle 64:119 F '67

What directors are saying. Action 6-6:22 N/D '71

## LENICA, JAN

Jan Lenica. Film 36:10 Sum '63

Animation quartet. International Film G 3:175 '66

Artist and animator; filmog. Film 65:35 Spg '72

## LEONARD, ROBERT Z.

Willis, R. Robert Z. Leonard--the inexhaustible youth. Photoplay 6-2:113 Jl '14

Leonard, R. Z. Memoirs of a veteran Hollywood director. Screen Book 19-3:54 O; 19-4:46 N '37

Biographical note; filmog. Movies & People 2:43 '40

Back to entertainment. Lions Roar 1-6:no p# F '42

A director goes down to the sea. Lions Roar 2-3:no p# D '42

The man from up here. Lions Roar 3-1:no p# S '43

MGM's directors range from pioneers to newcomers.

    Lions Roar 3-4:no p# Jl '44
Mr. Leonard sees stars! Lions Roar 3-5:no p# D '44
Obit.   Classic Film Collector 22:56 Fall/Win '68 (re-
    print from Los Angeles Times)
N. Y. Times p35 Ag 29 '68
Screen World 30:236 '69

## LEONE, SERGIO
    Hi-Ho, denaro! Time 90:56 Ag 4 '67
    Frayling, C.  Sergio Leone.  Cinema (Lon) 6/7:35 Ag
      '70

## LERNER, CARL
    Odyssey from Hollywood to New York; filmog.  Film
      Comment 2-4:2 Fall '64
    Lerner turns teacher.  Film Comment 4-1:42 Fall '66
    (Carl Lerner was a frequent contributor to Film Comment
      during the 1960's)

## LERNER, IRVING
    Knight, A.  Sleeping beauties.  Sat R 42:27 Ja 31 '59
    Johnson, A.  Irving Lerner.  Sight & Sound 29-4:173
      Aut '60
    Fenin, G.  The face of '63--United States.  Films &
      Filming 9-6:55 Mr '63
    Sarris, A.  Oddities and one shots.  Film Culture 28:45
      Spg '63

## LERNER, JOSEPH
    Lerner, J.  Only one at a time.  Making Films 2-3:32
    Je '68

## LEROUX, JACQUES
    Granja, V.  Interview.  CTVD 6-2:29 Win '68/69

## LeROY, MERVYN
    What's wrong with the movies?  Motion Pic 46:42 S '33
    Mervyn LeRoy, Warner Bros' ace.  Cue 3-18:3 Mr 2 '35
    Reynolds, Q.  Shooting stars.  Colliers 95:12 F 9 '35
    Sher, J.  His ability to recognize talent.  Movie Classic
      10:51 Ap '36
    Norberg, G.  Sketch.  Motion Pic 51:62 My '36
    Straight-shooter.  Lit Digest 123:20 F 13 '37
    Work of.  Motion Pic 53:14 F '37
    Eveleve, A.  Sock! interview.  Silver Screen 7-12:47
      D !37
    Beatty, J.  Mervyn of the movies.  American 126:32 Jl '38

Hall, J. Wizard of Oz. Good Housekeeping 109:40
   Ag '39
Biographical note; filmog. Movies & People 2:44 '40
Front page staff. Lions Roar 1-3:no p# N '41
Spotting stars. Lions Roar 1-5:no p# Ja '42
It's their baby. Lions Roar 2-3:no p# D '42
How he transforms unknowns into movie stars. Cosmop
   114:38 Mr '43
Just what the doctor ordered. Lions Roar 3-2:no p# Ja
   '44
Of romance and radium. Lions Roar 3-2:no p# Ja '44
MGM's directors range from pioneers to newcomers.
   Lions Roar 3-4:no p# Jl '44
LeRoy, M. He lived for them.... Lions Roar 3-5:no
   p# D '44
Confucius said it. Lions Roar 3-5:no p# D '44
Parsons, L. O. Cosmopolitan's citation for the best
   direction of the month. Cosmop 120:71 My '46
Rosten, L. Dance of the reels. Sat R 36:24 My 30 '53
LeRoy, M. The making of Mervyn LeRoy. Films In
   Review 4-5:220 My '53
Motion pictures and pay TV. Atlantic 200:84 D '57
Sarris, A. Likable but elusive; filmog. Film Culture
   28:35 Spg '63
Should directors produce? Action 3-4:10 Jl/Ag '68
Hudson, P. Look and listen. Senior Scholastic 96:8
   Mr 16 '70
What directors are saying. Action 5-3:30 My/Je '70

LESLIE, ALFRED
   Mekas, J. Notes on the new American cinema. Film
      Culture 24:6 Spg '62
   Listing of films. Film Culture 37:7 Sum '65
   Return to the challenge. Time 91:30 Ja 12 '68
   Davis, D. Return of the real. Newsweek 75:105 F 23
      '70

LESTER, RICHARD
   Lester, R. In search of the right knack. Films &
      Filming 11-10:14 Jl '65
   Carthew, A. Knack of being Richard Lester. N. Y.
      Times Mag p16 Ag 8 '65
   French, P. Richard Lester. Movie 14:5 Aut '65
   People are talking about. Vogue 146:112 S 15 '65
   Bluestone, R. Lunch with Lester. Film Q 19-4:12
      Sum '66
   Alpert, H. New faces. Sat R 49:21 D 24 '66

Biography.   British Book Year 1966:140 '66
And the art of comedy.   Film 48:16 Spg '67
Richard, L.   Interview.   New Yorker 43:50 O 28 '67
Schwalberg, C.   Minute that took fifteen hours.   U. S.
    Camera 30:66 O '67
Vaudeville of the absurd.   Time 90:105 N 17 '67
Gilliatt, P.   Current cinema.   New Yorker 44:87 Je 15
    '68
Cameron, I. & Shivas, M.   Interview with Richard
    Lester; filmog.   Movie 16:16 Win '68/69
Lester, R.   What I learned from commercials.   Action
    4-1:32 Ja/F '69
Prelutsky, B.   What's Richard Lester trying to do?
    Holiday 45:82 Ap '69
Biography.   Current Biography 30:25 Ap '69
    Same.   Current Biography Yearbook 1969:253 '70
What directors are saying.   Action 5-1:28 Ja/F '70
Lester, R.   What I learned from commercials. Making
    Films 4-1:9 F '70
Richardson, B.   Dick Lester.   Take One 1-8:4 n. d.


LETHEM, ROLAND
    Wallington, M.   Roland Lethem; filmog.   Cinema (Lon)
    8:20 '71


LEVIN, ARNOLD
    Profile.   Making Films 2-5:38 O '68


LEVINE, CHARLES
    Listing of films.   Film Culture 37:7 Sum '65


LEVINE, NAOMI
    Listing of films.   Film Culture 37:7 Sum '65


LEVINSON, FRED
    Is New York developing new techniques for film industry?
    Making Films 2-5:18 O '68
    Interview.   Making Films 3-6:28 D '69


LEVY, DON
    Gillett, J.   Happening here.   Sight & Sound 34-3:138
    Sum '65
    Interview; filmog.   Cinema (Lon) 2:14 Mr '69
    British cinema filmography.   Film 65:10 Spg '72


LEVY, RALPH
    Young pro.   Newsweek 41:56 Ap 13 '53

LÉVY, RAOUL, J.
About the producer.   Newsweek 57:96 My 1 '61
The hallucinogenic hotel room.   Playboy 13-11:110 O '66
Come to me, baby.   Time 89:42 Ja 13 '67
Obit.   Newsweek 69:72 Ja 16 '67
    Time 89:68 Ja 13 '67

LEWIN, ALBERT
True confessions of a movie producer.   Theatre Arts
    25:659 S '41
MGM's directors range from pioneers to newcomers.
    Lions Roar 3-4:no p# Jl '44
Parsons, L. O.   Cosmopolitan's citation for the best
    direction of the month.   Cosmop 122:67 Mr '47
Sarris, A.   Likable but elusive; filmog.   Film Culture
    28:35 Spg '63
Arkadin.   Film Clips.   Sight & Sound 37-1:47 Win '67/68
Obit.   N. Y. Times p44 Mr 10 '68
    Screen World 20:236 '69
Homage to Albert Lewin.   Action 3-4:4 Jl/Ag '68

LEWIS, EDGAR
Sketch.   Theatre 28:249 O '18
Harrington, H.   A genius of the screen.   Theatre 31:414
    My '20

LEWIS, JAY
Attuned to the cadence of quality.   Sat R 32:16 Ja 29 '49

LEWIS, JERRY
New voices, old gags.   Newsweek 33:61 Ap 18 '49
Talk of show business.   Time 53:57 My 23 '49
Parsons, L. O.   Cosmopolitan's citation for the best
    newcomer of the month.   Cosmop 127:12 O '49
The riot started in Atlantic City.   TV Guide 3-45:8 N 11
    '50
Davidson, B.   Anything for a laugh.   Colliers 127:30
    F 10 '51
Jeffers, W.   Investigating Martin and Lewis.   TV Guide
    4-25:24 Je 23 '51
Hard work.   Time 58:82 Jl 23 '51
Free show; Paramount Theatre.   New Yorker 27:16 Jl 28
    '51
Crackpots hit jackpot.   Life 31:57 Ag 13 '51
Lewis, Mrs. J.   I married a madman!   American 153:22
    Ja '52
Edwards, J.   Martin and Lewis: to ps in comedy.   Coro-

net 31:85 F '52

Martin and Lewis marathon.   TV Guide 5-11:6 Mr 14 '52

Funny men Dean Martin and Jerry Lewis.   Sight & Sound 22-1:30 Jl/S '52

Lewis, J.   I'm in love with my best friend's wife.   Photoplay 42-2:58 Ag '52

Zeitlin, I.   Behind the riot act.   Photoplay 42-3:56 S '52

Lewis, Mrs. J.   How I trained my husband.   Photoplay 43-3:52 Mr '53

Kass, R.   Jerry Lewis analyzed.   Films In Review 4-3: 119 Mr '53

Armstrong, G.   Time to part?   Photoplay 43-5:31 My '53

Martin and Lewis' backyard movies.   TV Guide 1-10:4 Je 5 '53

Bailey, C.   Mayhem, unlimited.   Photoplay 44-4:46 O '53

Clouse, B.   Jerry Lewis, movie maker; hints to fellow amateurs.   Photography 33:87 D '53

Jerry's jitterbug.   Look 18:107 Mr 9 '54

Taurog, N.   It really happened.   Photoplay 45-4:36 Ap '54

Rogow, L.   Making sows' ears from silk purses.   Sat R 37:35 Jl 31 '54

Arnold, M.   Are Martin and Lewis breaking up?   Photoplay 46-1:50 Jl '54

It's not love, Chum.   Newsweek 46:81 Ag 15 '55

Arnold, M.   Are they heading for the big split-up?   Photoplay 48-3:31 S '55

Zolotow, M.   Martin and Lewis feud.   Cosmop 139:62 O '55

To the rescue.   Time 67:74 Ja 9 '56

Wood, C.   TV personalities biographical sketchbook.   TV Personalities p64 '56

The birth of Jerry Lewis' new career.   TV Guide 5-3:17 Ja 12 '57

Davidson, B.   I've always been scared.   Look 21:51 F 5 '57

Taylor, T.   New soloist in town.   Cue 26-6:12 F 9 '57

Eustis, H.   McCalls visits.   McCalls 84:22 Mr '57

Thomas, B.   Has Jerry fooled the critics?   Photoplay 52-3:62 S '57

Nine-channel spectacular.   TV Guide 6-7:4 F 15 '58

Hoffman, J.   Hollywood's funniest feud is on.   Photoplay 53-6:42 Je '58

Hoffman, J.   I'm not Jerry Lee Lewis.   Photoplay 54-4: 29 O '58

Taves, I.   Always in a crowd--always alone.   Look 22:83 D 23 '58

Talk with a star. Newsweek 52:64 D 29 '58

Phillips, D. Jerry Lewis helps answer a little boy's prayer. Photoplay 55-1:42 Ja '59

Hoffman, J. Jerry Lewis: this thermometer tastes awful. Photoplay 55-3:50 Mr '59

Wolters, L. Jerry Lewis: what makes him tick? Todays Health 37:24 Je '59

School for comedy. TV Guide 7-35:14 Ag 29 '59

The day the undertaker called--for me. Photoplay 57-3:36 Mr '60

Exit Jerry, enter Danny. Newsweek 56:69 S 5 '60

Lewis, C. I always play with daddy. Photoplay 58-3:58 S '60

Jean, G. Nobody knows about me and Jerry. Photoplay 59-2:54 F '61

Triple-decker bachelor's paradise for Jerry Lewis. Life 50:12 Mr 3 '61

Jerry Lewis spoofs the world's great lovers. Look 25:51 My 9 '61

Miller, E. Frantic world of Jerry Lewis. Seventeen 20:100 Je '61

Ardmore, J. L. I'm nutty about my kids; interview. Parents 36:48 Jl '61

Bogdanovich, P. Mr. Lewis is a pussycat. Esquire 58:136 N '62

Biography. Current Biography 23:10 N '62
Same. Current Biography Yearbook 1962:252 '63

Fenin, G. The face of '63--United States. Films & Filming 9-6:55 Mr '63

Sarris, A. Oddities and one shots. Film Culture 28:45 Spg '63

Gehman, R. That kid. TV Guide 11-24:20 Je 15 '63

Linn, E. Search for Jerry Lewis. Sat Evening Post 236:83 O 12 '63

Gehman, R. What happened to Jerry Lewis. TV Guide 11-50:18 D 14 '63

Hill, L. Nutty professor contest winners. Photoplay 65-1:84 Ja '64

Public loves him. Newsweek 63:92 F 17 '64

Taylor, J. R. Jerry Lewis. Sight & Sound 34:82 Spg '65

Alpert, H. France is made for ... Jerry Lewis? N. Y. Times Mag p28 F 27 '66

Schickel, R. Jerry Lewis retrieves a lost ideal. Life 61:10 Jl 15 '66

Hanson, C. L. Point of view. Cinema (BH) 3-4:50 D '66

Madsen, A. Interview. Cahiers (Eng) 4:27 '66

His threatened marriage.   Photoplay 73-4:60 Ap '68
Manes, S.   Jerry Lewis as auteur.   Focus 3/4:21 '68
Behn, A.   Big daddy.   Photoplay 75-5:56 My '69
What directors are saying.   Action 4-5:32 S/O '69
Lewis, J.   Five happy moments.   Esquire 74:137 D '70
What directors are saying.   Action 6-1:30 Ja/F '71
Newsmakers.   Newsweek 77:63 My 10 '71
Camper, F.   Essays in visual style.   Cinema (Lon)
   8:32 '71
What directors are saying.   Action 7-1:36 Ja/F '72
Comedy is the mirror we hold up to life; interview.
   Focus 7:4 Spg '72


LEWIS, JOSEPH H.
   Sarris, A.   Esoterica; filmog.   Film Culture 28:22
      Spg '63
   Schrader, P.   Joseph H. Lewis.   Cinema (BH) 7-1:43
      Fall '71
   Mundy, R.   Joseph H. Lewis; filmog.   Cinema (BH)
      7-1:45 Fall '71
   Bogdanovich, P.   Interview.   Cinema (BH) 7-1:47 Fall
      '71
   Thompson, R.   Joseph H. Lewis.   Cinema (BH) 7-1:46
      Fall '71


LEWIS, ROBERT
   Director at work.   Cue 19-52:10 D 30 '50
   Point of view and a place to practice it.   Theatre Arts
      44:62 Ap '60
   Dance magazine awards.   Dance 36:38 My '62


LEWTON, VAL
   Farber, M.   Sketch.   New Republic 111:339 S 18 '44
   Sketch.   Time 44:56 S 25 '44
   Producer of bedlam specializes in terror.   Life 20:123
      F 25 '46
   Wechsberg, J.   Story of.   Liberty 23:31 Ag 24 '46
   Obit.   N. Y. Times p29 Mr 15 '51
      Time 57:82 Mr 26 '51
   Farber, M.   Films.   Nation 172:353 Ap 14 '51
   Bodeen, D.   Val Lewton; filmog.   Films In Review
      14-4:210 Ap '63
   Arkadin.   Film clips.   Sight & Sound 35-1:46 Win '65/66
   Ellison, H.   A theory of film horror from the works of
      Val Lewton.   Cinema (BH) 3-2:4 Mr '66
   Bodeen, D.   Three faces of fear; letter.   Cinema (BH)
      3-4:23 D '66

Siegel, J. E.   Val Lewton.   Films In Review 21-3:188
   Mr '70

LEYNSE, HUMPHREY W.
   Where are the days of Nanook of the North?   Making
      Films 3-4:12 Ag '69

L'HERBIER, MARCEL
   The big screens.   Sight & Sound 24-4:209 Spg '55
   Roud, R.   Memories of Resnais.   Sight & Sound 38-3:124
      Sum '69
   Blumer, R. H.   The camera as snowball: France 1918-
      1927.   Cinema J 9-2:31 Spg '70

LIMA, WALDEMAR
   Viany, A.   Who's who in the cinema novo.   CTVD 5-4:26
      Sum '68

LIMA, WALTER, JR.
   Viany, A.   Who's who in the cinema novo.   CTVD 5-4:26
      Sum '68

LINDBERG, PER
   Cozarinsky, E.   Adventures in style: the films of Per
      Lindberg; filmog.   Focus On Film 11:48 Aut '72

LINDER, CARL
   Linder, C.   Notes and writings.   Film Culture 35:29
      Win '64/65
   Filmography.   Film Culture 35:50 Win '64/65
   Linder, C.   San Francisco letter.   Film Culture 35:65
      Win '64/65
   Listing of films.   Film Culture 37:7 Sum '65
   Linder, C.   Notes and writings.   Film Culture 44:62
      Spg '67
   Alexander, T. K.   San Francisco's hipster cinema.
      Film Culture 44:70 Spg '67
   Letter exchange with Paul Sharits.   Filmmakers News-
      letter 1-6:17 Ap '68
   Barries, G.   The films of Carl Linder.   Film Q 22-1:41
      Fall '68

LINDON, KEN
   Film Comment announces the recipients of the 1964 an-
      niversary awards.   Film Comment 2-3:3 Sum '64

LITTIN, MIGUEL
    Film in Chile; interview.    Cineaste 4-4:4 Spg '71

LITTLEWOOD, JOAN
    Strasberg-on-Avon.    Time 76:62 O 31 '60
    Fay, G.    London panorama.    Theatre Arts 46:68 Ja '62
    Cowie, P.    The face of '63--Great Britain.    Films &
        Filming 9-5:19 F '63
    Brien, A.    Openings, London.    Theatre Arts 47:31 Je '63
    Opening the old kit bag.    Time 82:64 Jl 5 '63
    Bailey, A.    Would little Joan Littlewood were here!
        Esquire 61:113 Ja '64
    Brien, A.    Joan Littlewood.    Vogue 144:160 S 15 '64
    Littlewood's war.    Newsweek 64:104 O 12 '64
    Rogoff, G.    Joan and the good guys.    Reporter 31:52
        N 19 '64
    Howard, J.    Merry, angry mother hen.    Life 57:59 N 27
        '64
    Tynan, K.    Joan of Cockaigne.    Holiday 36:113 N '64
    Fun palace.    Drama R 12:130 Spg '68

LITVAK, ANATOLE
    Biographical note; filmog.    Movies & People 2:44 '40
    Story of his production of The snake pit.    Time 52:44
        D 20 '48
    Eyles, A. & Pattison, B.    A cutter at heart; interview.
        Films & Filming 13-5:16 F '67
    Nolan, J. E.    Anatole Litvak; filmog.    Films In Review
        18-9:548 N '67

LIZZANI, CARLO
    New names.    Sight & Sound 25-3:120 Win '55/56
    Lane, J. F.    The face of '63--Italy.    Films & Filming
        9-7:11 Ap '63

LLOYD, FRANK
    Service, F.    Interview.    Classic 16:42 Je '23
    Frank Lloyd, celluloid animal.    Cue 4-5:3 N 30 '35
    Condon, F.    Mutiny on the set.    Colliers 97:10 My 2 '36
    Penfield, C.    Work of.    Stage 13:52 My '36
    Sharpe, H. Work of.    Photoplay 50:70 N '36
    Messenger, D.    From A to Z with cinema magicians.
        Christian Science Mon Mag p14 Ja 27 '37
    Millions for movie ideas.    Popular Mechanics 70:514
        O '38
    Biographical note; filmog.    Movies & People 2:44 '40
    Obit.    British Book Year 1961:516 '61

N. Y. Times p18 Ag 11 '60
Newsweek 56:61 Ag 22 '60
Screen World 12:222 '61

## LOACH, KENNETH
Kael, P.   Current cinema.   New Yorker 43:92 F 3 '68
Robinson, D.   Case histories of the next renasence.
    Sight & Sound 38:39 Win '68
Bream, P.   Spreading wings at Kestrel; interview.   Films
    & Filming 18-6:36 Mr '72
British cinema filmography.   Film 65:10 Spg '72

## LOGAN, JOSHUA
Houghton, N.   Bretaigne Windust and Joshua L. Logan.
    Theatre Arts 31:31 Ap '47
Director-co-author.   Time 51:63 Mr 1 '48
Co-author of new drama tells how bestselling novel
    Mr. Roberts was made into Broadway hit.   Cue
    17-10:12 Mr 6 '48
On fire.   New Yorker 25:22 Ap 16 '49
Barnett, L.   Josh Logan.   Life 26:102 My 9 '49
Biography.   Current Biography O '49
Brown, J. M.   Louisiana Chekhov.   Sat R 33:36 Ap 15
    '50
Long, long ago.   Theatre Arts 34:38 S '50
MacKaye, M.   Broadway says he's a genius.   Sat
    Evening Post 224:44 O 20 '51
Keating, J.   Josh Logan turns "tummeler."   Cue 21-24:
    15 Je 14 '52
Lochheim, A. B.   Director, having wonderful time.
    N. Y. Times Mag p22 Je 15 '52
Kah, E. J.   Profiles.   New Yorker 29:38 Ap 4; 29:37
    Ap 11 '53
Joshua fit de battle ob video.   Life 34:73 Je 1 '53
Joshua and the Midas touch.   Look 17:61 N 17 '53
Get off the beaten path; interview.   Theatre Arts 37:76
    D '53
Zolotow, M.   Josh-of-all-theatre-trades.   Theatre Arts
    38:18 O '54
Virtuoso director.   Theatre Arts 39:68 F '55
Davidson, B.   Fear is my enemy..   Look 22:70 Jl 22 '58
Davidson, B.   My greatest crisis.   Look 22:54 Ag 5 '58
Davidson, B.   Recovery from fear.   Look 22:20 Ag 19
    '58
What's right, what's wrong.   Theatre Arts 45:8 My '61
My invasion of Marseilles.   Harper 223:14 Jl '61
Caron, L.   Making the might three-in-one into Logan's

Fanny.    Films & Filming 7-10:7 Jl '61
House is us, and we're it.    Vogue 138:120 Ag 1 '61
Personality of the month.    Films & Filming 8-1:5 O '61
Miller, B.    Josh Logan--watermelons and sex.    Vision
    1-1:11 Spg '62
Talese, G.    Soft psyche of Joshua Logan.    Esquire
    59:82 Ap '63
Sarris, A.    Minor disappointments; filmog.    Film Culture
    28:41 Spg '63
The directors choose the best films.    Cinema (BH) 1-5:
    14 Ag/S '63
Should directors produce?    Action 3-4:10 Jl/Ag '68
Gold diggers of 1969: Joshua Logan talks to Gordon Gow.
    Films & Filming 16-3:12 D '69
What directors are saying.    Action 5-2:16 Mr/Ap '70
Logan, J.    Fonda memories.    Show 1-4:6 Ap '70
Drake, R.    South Pacific background.    TV Guide 19-47:18
    N 20 '71
Logan, J.    Salute to a cockeyed optimist:  Oscar Ham-
    merstein II.    TV Guide 20-27:30 Jl 1 '72
Logan, J.    A memory of Marilyn Monroe the actress.
    Show 2-6:25 S '72


LOGAN, STANLEY
    Obit.    N. Y. Times p88 F 1 '53


LOPES, FERNANDO
    Granja, V.    Fernando Lopes' next film.    CTVD 6-2:31
    Win '68/69

---

LORENTZ, PARE
    Stillborn art.    Forum 80:364 S '28
    Medicine men.    Forum 81:sup34 Ap '29
    Moral racketeering in the movies.    Scribner 88:256 S '30
    Young man goes to work.    Scribner 89:205 F '31
    Go home, young man, go home!  New Outlook 161:26
        Je '33
    Movie platform.    Lit Digest 124:23 Ag 7 '37
    Impresario.    American 125:109 My '38
    Award to Pare Lorentz.    Mag Art 31:424 Jl '38
    White, W. L.    Head man of government motion pictures.
        Scribner 105:7 Ja '39
    Black, C. M.    He serves up America.    Colliers 106:22
        Ag 3 '40
    McEvoy, J. P.    Young man with a camera.    Reader
        Digest 37:73 Ag '40
    Biography.    Current Biography '40

Fight for survival.  McCalls 84:28 Ja '57
The River--21 years after.  Film Journal (Aus) # 12 F
    '59
Rare treat.  Newsweek 58:100 S 25 '61
Conscience of the 30's.  Newsweek 72:6 Ag 5 '68

LOSEY, JOSEPH
    Losey, J.  Mirror to life.  Films & Filming 5-9:7 Je '59
    Houston, P. & Gillett, J.  Conversations with Nicholas
        Ray and Joseph Losey.  Sight & Sound 30-4:157 Aut
        '61
    The British cinema.  Movie 1:7 Je '62
    Joseph Losey.  Films & Filming 8-11:5 Ag '62
    Losey: Eve and the damned; interview.  Movie 6:20 Ja
        '63
    Sarris, A.  Third line; filmog.  Film Culture 28:18 Spg
        '63
    Desert island films.  Films & Filming 9-11:11 Ag '63
    Brunius, J.  Joseph Losey and The servant; interview.
        Film 38:27 Win '63
    Losey, J.  The monkey on my back.  Films & Filming
        10-1:11 O '63
    Who is the master.  Newsweek 63:96 Mr 23 '64
    Durgnat, R.  Losey: Modesty and Eve.  Films & Film-
        ing 12-7:26 Ap '66
    Durgnat, R.  Losey: Puritan maids.  Films & Filming
        12-8:28 My '66
    Ross, T. J.  Notes on an early Losey.  Film Culture
        40:35 Spg '66
    Jacob, G.  Joseph Losey, or the camera calls.  Sight &
        Sound 35-3:142 Sum '66
    Houston, P.  Losey's paper handkerchief.  Sight & Sound
        35-3:142 Sum '66
    Joseph Losey and Accident.  Cahiers (Eng) 9:5 Mr '67
    Durgnat, R.  The cubist puritanism of Joseph Losey.
        Film 50:10 Win '67
    Directors of the year; filmog.  International Film G 4:15
        '67
    Phillips, G. D.  The critical camera of Joseph Losey.
        Cinema (BH) 4-1:22 Spg '68
    Arkadin.  Losey on location.  Sight & Sound 37-3:127
        Sum '68
    Quotemanship.  Action 3-3:20 Jl/Ag '68
    Interview.  Cinema (Lon) 3:17 Je '69
    Biography.  Current Biography 30:23 D '69
        Same.  Current Biography Yearbook 1969:265 '70
    Jerome, R. L.  The disappearance of The damned.

Cinefantastique 1-1:21 Fall '70

Losey, J. Speak, think, stand up. Film Comment 50/
51:53 Fall/Win '70

Losey on McCarthyism. Film Comment 50/51:61 Fall/
Win '70

Salute of the week. Cue 40-33:1 Ag 14 '71

Gow, G. Weapons; interview. filmog. Films & Filming
18-1:36 O '71

Guerin, A. From The go-between to Trotsky. Show
2-8:46 O '71

British cinema filmography. Film 65:10 Spg '72

Hale, W. Fellini's Rome and Losey's Trotsky. N.Y.
Sun News sec3:7 O 8 '72

LOURIE, GENE (Eugene)
Lourie, G. A background to horror. Films & Filming
6-5:14 F '60

LOVI, STEPHEN
Listing of films. Film Culture 37:7 Sum '65

LOW, COLIN
Biographical note. International Film G 2:60 '65

LOY, NANNI
Lane, J. F. The face of '63--Italy. Films & Filming
9-7:11 Ap '63

LUBIMOV, PAUL
A Russian six. Films & Filming 13-12:27 S '67

LUBIN, ARTHUR
The incredible Mr. Lubin. Castle of Frankenstein 5:45
n. d.

LUBITSCH, ERNST
Lewisohn, L. Interview. Nation 114:76 Ja 18 '22
Smith, F. J. Interview. Motion Pic Classic 14:34
Ap '22
Carr, H. Sketch. Motion Pic 25:27 Jl '23
Work of. Classic 18:24 N '23
Smith, A. Sketch. Classic 19:38 Mr '24
My two years in America. Motion Pic 28:24 D '24
Green, E. Interview. Motion Pic 30:34 Je '26
Tully, J. Interview. Vanity Fair 27:82 D '26
Cruikshank, H. Sketch. Motion Pic Classic 28:33 O '28
Orme, M. Sketch. London News 178:160 Ja 31 '31

Birrell, F.   Famous directors.   New Statesman 4:833
D 24 '32
Quirk, M. A.   Interview.   Photoplay 44:58 Ag '33
What's wrong with the movies?   Motion Pic 46:42 S '33
Cheatham, M.   They have something different.   Silver
Screen 4-10:23 Ag '34
Sketch.   Time 25:72 F 18 '35
The famed Lubitsch touch.   Cue 3-39:3 Jl 27 '35
Jones, G.   Movie magician.   Colliers 96:26 S 21 '35
Versatility of Mr. Lubitsch.   Living Age 350:325 Je '36
Biographical note; filmog.   Movies & People 2:44 '40
Huff, T.   An index to the films of Ernst Lubitsch.   Sight
& Sound (special sup) Index Series # 9 Ja '47
Obit.   N. Y.   Times p21 D '47
Newsweek 30:44 D 8 '47
Time 50:100 D 8 '47
Wollenberg, H. H.   Two masters.   Sight & Sound 17-65:
46 Spg '48
Weinberg, H. G.   A tribute to Lubitsch.   Films In Re-
view 2-7:3 Ag/S '51
Eisner, L.   Origins of the Lubitsch style; letter.   Film
Journal (Aus) 15:62 Mr '60
Weinberg, H. G.   Ernst Lubitsch.   Film Culture 25:37
Sum '62
Sarris, A.   Second line; filmog.   Film Culture 28:11
Spg '63
Auriol, J-G.   Chez Ernst.   Cahiers (Eng) 9:54 Mr '67
A tribute to Lubitsch.   Action 1-6:14 N/D '67
Maltin, L.   Lubitsch.   Film Fan Mo 90:3 D '68
Everson, W. K.   The Lubitsch legend.   Film Library
Q 2-2:40 Spg '69
Weinberg, H. G.   Ernst Lubitsch; a parallel to George
Feydeau.   Film Comment 6-1:62 Spg '70
Baxter, J.   Some Lubitsch silents.   Silent Pic 11/12:no
p# Sum/Aut '71
Sarris, A.   Lubitsch in the thirties.   Film Comment
7-4:55 Win '71/72
Sarris, A.   Lubitsch in the thirties.   Film Comment
8-2:20 Sum '72
Barry, J. K.   Ernst Lubitsch and the comedy of the
thirties.   Mise-En-Scene 1:7 n. d.

LUCAS, GEORGE
Fensch, T.   Amateurs on the campus make professional
films.   Making Films 5-2:12 Ap '71

LUCAS, JOHN MEREDYTHE
Nolan, J. E.   Films on TV.   Films In Review 22-10:
629 D '71

LUDWIG, EDWARD
Biographical note; filmog.   Movies & People 2:44 '40

LUMET, SIDNEY
Minoff, P.   Danger is his business.   Cue 20-29:13
Jl 21 '51
Lumet, S.   Notes on TV.   Cue 21-29:6 Jl 19 '52
Director participation.   Life 34:103 Je 8 '53
Good men and true and all angry.   Life 42:137 Ap 22 '57
Personality of the month.   Films & Filming 6-11:5 Ag
'60
Bogdanovich, P.   Interview.   Film Q 14-2:18 Win '60
Why am I happy?   Newsweek 57:94 Je 12 '61
Economy class journey.   Time 79:50 Je 1 '62
Fenin, G.   The face of '63--United States.   Films &
Filming 9-6:55 Mr '63
Sarris, A.   Likable but elusive; filmog.   Film Culture
28:35 Spg '63
Lumet, S.   Keep them on the hook.   Films & Filming
11-1:17 O '64
Bean, R.   The insider.   Films & Filming 11-9:9 Je '65
Casty, A.   The pawnbroker and the new direction in
film realism; filmog.   Film Heritage 1-3:3 Spg '66
Benchley, P.   Group embalmed.   Holiday 39:155 My '66
Why I like it here; a statement by Sidney Lumet.   Making
Films 1-1:17 Mr '67
Bravo, Braverman!   Making Films 1-2:16 My/Je '67
Biography.   Current Biography 28:26 S '67
Same.   Current Biography Yearbook 1967:258 '68
Petrie, G.   The films of Sidney Lumet.   Film Q 21-2:9
Win '67/68
Director of the year; filmog.   International Film G 5:20
'68
Farber, S.   Lumet in '69.   Sight & Sound 38-4:190
Aut '69
What directors are saying.   Action 4-6:28 N/D '69
What directors are saying.   Action 5-3:30 My/Je '70

LUMIÈRE, AUGUSTE
Sadoul, G.   The last interview.   Sight & Sound 17-66:68
Sum '48
Obit.   Screen World 6:224 '55

LUMIÈRE, LOUIS
  Browne, M. Artisan in light. Christian Science Mon
    Mag p3 Ag 7 '35
  Obit. Time 51:87 Je 14 '48


LUPINO, IDA
  Sketch. Photoplay 44:60 N '33
  Goldbeck, E. Sketch. Movie Classic 6:52 My '34
  Hall, G. Interview. Motion Pic 52:37 O '36
  Small, F. It was hate at first sight. Photoplay 50-4:66
    O '36
  Crichton, K. Career girl. Colliers 99:20 Je 26 '37
  Castle, M. Story of. Motion Pic 54:45 N '37
  Hamilton, S. & Morse, W. Jr. Sketch. Photoplay
    54:21 Mr '40
  Sketch. Newsweek 16:36 Jl 29 '40
  Rhea, M. The lady has character. Photoplay 54-8:31
    Ag '40
  Service, F. She's as crazy as a fox. Silver Screen
    11-1:24 N '40
  Mulvey, K. Sketch. Womans Home Companion 68:27
    Mr '41
  How Mr. and Mrs. Hayward live. Photoplay 20-1:48
    D '41
  Sharpe, H. Ida, the mad Lupino. Photoplay 20-2:52
    Ja; 20-3:50 F '42
  Vallee, W. L. Hostess extraordinary. Silver Screen
    12-5:38 Mr '42
  Hopper, H. Sketch. Photoplay 21:28 Ag '42
  St. Johns, A. R. Story of. Cosmop 114:46 Ja '43 and
    following issues.
  Trotter, M. Her horoscope. Photoplay 22:30  F '43
  Lupino, I. to Dorothy Haas. Wives should have war
    dates. Photoplay 22-4:40 Mr '43
  Embarrassing moment. Photoplay 23:59 S '43
  My secret dream. Photoplay 23:54 O '43
  Biography. Current Biography '43
  Should a girl propose? Photoplay 24:43 F '44
  My faith. Photoplay 24:48 My '44
  Perkins, D. W. Perpetual emotion. American 138:28
    S '44
  Bangs, B. Ida with a lilt. Silver Screen 15-4:42 F '45
  Hall, G. Ida Lupino reads her tea leaves. Silver
    Screen 16-1:30 N '45
  Lupino, I. My fight for life. Photoplay 28-3:58 F '46
  Lupino, I. The trouble with men is women. Silver
    Screen 17-6:36 Ap '47

Lupino, I.   Who says men are people?   Silver Screen
    18-8:22 Je '48
Nelson, K.   Keep it simple!   Silver Screen 18-12:44
    O '48
Waterbury, R.   Home of.   Photoplay 34:56 F '49
Lupino, I.   I cannot be good!   Silver Screen 19-8:42
    Je '49
Keats, P.   Ida takes over in no-woman's land.   Silver
    Screen 20-8:36 Je '50
Lupino, I.   New faces in new places.   Films In Review
    1-9:17 D '50
Holiday awards for 1950.   Holiday 9:79 Ja '51
Hill, G.   Hollywood's beautiful bulldozer.   Colliers
    127:18 My 12 '51
Shane, D.   Who's boss--Ida or Howard?   Silver Screen
    23-10:36 Ag '53
The director and the public; a symposium.   Film Culture
    1-2:15 Mr/Ap '55
A fourth for TV.   TV Guide 3-49:16 D 3 '55
Bartlett, M.   Howard Duffs set their own stage.   Ameri-
    can Home 56:72 N '56
Minoff, P.   Non-private lives?   Cue 26-3:12 Ja 19 '57
Mr. Duff and Ida.   TV Guide 5-22:17 Je 1 '57
A new twist.   TV Guide 5-28:28 Jl 13 '57
Wood, C.   TV personalities biographical sketchbook.
    TV Personalities p16 '57
Vermilye, J.   Ida Lupino; filmog.   Films In Review
    10-5:266 My '59
Motion Lupino.   Time 81:42 F 8 '63
Sarris, A.   Oddities and one shots.   Film Culture 28:45
    Spg '63
Nolan, J. E.   Ida Lupino.   Films In Review 16-1:61
    Ja '65
Whitney, D.   Follow Mother, here we go kiddies.   TV
    Guide 14-41:14 O 8 '66
Lupino, I.   Me, mother directress.   Action 2-3:14
    My/Je '67
Nolan, J. E.   Ida Lupino, director; directing filmog.
    Film Fan Mo 89:8 N '68
What directors are saying.   Action 4-5:32 S/O '69
Catching up with Ida Lupino.   Modern Screen 66-11:68
    N '72

LUFTI, DIB
    Viany, A.   Who's who in the cinema movo.   CTVD
    5-4:26 Sum '68

LYE, LEN
Forms in air; tangibles.   Time 74:56 Ag 24 '59
Dandignac, P.   Visionary art of Len Lye.   Craft
    Horizons 21:30 My '61
Lye, L.   Is film art?   filmog.   Film Culture 29:38 Sum
    '63
Weinberg, G.   Interview.   Film Culture 29:40 Sum '63
Survey among unsuccessful applicants for the Ford
    Foundation film grants.   Film Comment 2-3:10 Sum '64
Timehenge.   Newsweek 65:94 Mr 22 '65
Johnson, C. B.   Gallery for young people.   School Arts
    65:46 Ja '66
Mancis, A. & Van Dyke, W.   Artist as filmmaker.
    Art In America 54:98 Jl '66
Len Lye speaks at the filmmakers' cinematheque.   Film
    Culture 44:48 Spg '67

LYON, FRANCIS D.
Two cameras shooting can cut costs.   Making Films
    5-1:18 F '71

## MAAS, WILLARD

Tyler, P. Willard Maas. Film Culture 20:53 n. d.

Mass, W. The Gryphon yaks; filmog. Films Culture 29:46 Sum '63

Poetry and the film: a symposium. Film Culture 29:55 Sum '63

Sensel, G. Interview; filmog. Film Comment 7-3:60 Fall '71

Obit. N. Y. Times p42 Ja 13 '71

## McBRIDE, JIM

Carson, L. M. K. Interview. Interview 2-6:25 O '71

## McCAREY, LEO

Conlon, S. Sketch. Motion Pic 50:54 S '35

Work of. Time 33:45 Mr 20 '39

Biographical note; filmog. Movies & People 2:44 '40

Underhill, D. Funny money. Colliers 110:19 D 12 '42

Biography. Current Biography 7:32 Jl '46

　Same. Current Biography Yearbook 1946:360 '47

Martin, P. Going his way. Sat Evening Post 219:14 N 30 '46

Rhodes, K. Work of. Photoplay 30:86 Ap '47

McCarey, L. What makes a box office hit? Cinema (Hollywood) 1-1:5 Je '47

Religion, greater accent on, needed in movies. Photoplay 33:33 S '48

Sarris, A. Third line; filmog. Film Culture 28:18 Spg '63

Daney, S. & Noames, J-L. Interview. Cahiers (Eng) 7:43 Ja '67

Obit. Classic Film Collector 24:14 Sum '69
　Current Biography 30:46 S '69
　Current Biography Yearbook 1969:469 '70
　Film R p17 '70/71
　N. Y. Times p45 Jl 6 '69
　Newsweek 74:92 Jl 21 '69
　Screen World 20:239 '69
　Time 94:68 Jl 18 '69

Crosby, B. & Butler, D. Remembering Leo McCarey. Action 4-5:11 S/O '69

Lloyd, P. Some affairs to remember: the style of Leo McCarey. Monogram 4:17 '72

O'Brien, G. An appreciation. On Film 1-0:29 n. d.

McCLOY, MICHAEL
McCloy, M. Catch ... as catch ... can! Movie Maker
6-9:610 S '72

McDERMOTT, GERALD
McDermott, G. Anansi the spider. Sightlines 2-6:6
Jl/Ag '69

McDERMOTT, JOHN W.
Donnell, D. Home of. Motion Pic Classic 25:24 Jl '27

MacDONALD, DAVID
British feature directors; an index to their work. Sight
& Sound 27-6:299 Aut '58

McDONELL, FERGUS
Filmography. Film 14:12 N/D '57

McGOWAN, JOHN P.
The girl on the cover and her daughter. Photoplay
7-4:53 Mr '15
Corliss, A. "Let's go" McGowan. Photoplay 10-5:135
O '16
Gaddis, P. Sketch. Motion Pic 13:102 Mr '17
Obit. N. Y. Times p30 Mr 27 '52

McGRATH, JOE
British cinema filmography. Film 65:10 Spg '72

MACHATY, GUSTAV
Sarris, A. Beyond the fringe. Film Culture 28:29
Spg '63

MACIAN, FRANCISCO
Gasca, L. Francisco Macian's new technique for fantastic film. CTVD 6-2:13 Win '68/69

MACK, RUSSELL
Obit. Classic Film Collector (reprint N. Y. Times) 36:
extra 2 Fall '72
N. Y. Times Bio Ed Je 3 '72

MACKANE, DAVID
Filmography. Film 14:8 N/D '57

MacKAY, TANYA BALLANTYNE
Women on women in films. Take One 3-2:10 N/D '70

MACKENDRICK, ALEXANDER
  Cutts, J.   Mackendrick finds sweet smell of success.
    Films & Filming 3-9:8 Je '57
  Filmography.   Film 14:8 N/D '57
  British feature directors; an index to their work.   Sight
    & Sound 27-6:299 Aut '58
  Alexander Mackendrick. Films & Filming 9-4:7 Ja '63
  Sarris, A.   Oddities and one shots.   Film Culture 28:45
    Spg '63
  American Film Institute University advisory committee
    seminar.   Dialogue On Film 2-1:entire issue '72

MACKENZIE, JOHN
  British cinema filmography.   Film 65:10 Spg '72

MACKENZIE, KENT
  A discussion: personal creation in Hollywood, can it be
    done?   Film Q 15-3:16 Spg '62

MacLAINE, CHRISTOPHER
  Listing of films.   Film Culture 37:7 Sum '65

McLAREN, NORMAN
  Sabin, R.   New sound recording process seen by League
    of composers.   Musical America 69:12 Ja 15 '49
  Hen tracks on sound tracks.   Popular Mechanics 91:168
    Ap '49
  Sketch.   Vogue 114:132 Ag 15 '49
  Guitar, M. A.   Facts on film.   Nation 171:194 Ag 26 '50
  Movies without a camera, music without instruments.
    Theatre Arts 36:16 O '52
  Starr, C.   Animation: abstract and concrete.   Sat R
    35:47 D 13 '52
  McLaren, N.   Notes on animated sound.   Q Film Radio
    TV 7-3:223 Spg '53
  Jordan, W. E.   Norman McLaren:   his career and
    techniques.   Q Film Radio TV 8-1:1 Fall '53
  McLaren, N.   Making films on small budgets.   Film
    6:15 D '55
  Larkin, T.   Art films.   School Arts 57:48 O '57
  The craft of Norman McLaren.   Film Q 16-2:17 Win
    '62/63
  MacDermot, A.   Etchcraft on celluloid.   UNESCO Courier
    17:20 Ja '64
  A survey; filmog.   International Film G 1:161 '64
  Davis, E.   Paint a movie on film!   Popular Photo 56:120
    My '65

Multi-McLaren.  Take One 1-1:19 S/O '66
Burns, D.  Pixillation.  Film Q 22-1:36 Fall '68
Interview.  Film Library Q 3-2:13 Spg '70

McLEOD, NORMAN Z.
    Biographical note; filmog.  Movies & People 2:44 '40
    McLeod's madness.  Lions Roar 1-11/12:no p# Jl/Ag '42
    Quiet, please.  Lions Roar 2-1:no p# S/O '42
    Sound stage diplomat.  Lions Roar 2-5:no p# Jl '43
    MGM's directors range from pioneers to newcomers.
        Lions Roar 3-4:no p# Jl '44
    Crichton, K.  Gamble with music.  Colliers 117:22
        Mr 23 '46
    Obit.  Film R p45 '64/65
        N. Y. Times p31 Ja 28 '64
        Screen World 16:224 '65

McLUCAS, LEROY
    Listing of films.  Film Culture 37:7 Sum '65

McNAUGHT, BOB
    Filmography.  Film 14:8 N/D '57

MacPHERSON, JEANIE
    Martin, A.  From "wop" parts to bossing the job.
        Photoplay 10-5:95 O '16

MacRAE, HENRY
    Biography.  National Cylopaedia 33:576 '47

MADDOW, BEN
    Screenwriters symposium; filmog.  Film Comment
        6-4:86 Win '70/71

MAETZIG, KURT
    Bean, R.  The face of '63--Germany.  Films & Filming
        9-9:41 Je '63

MAJDAK, NIKOLA
    Biographical note.  International Film G 7:248 '70

MAKAVEJEV, DUSAN
    Sarris, A.  Movers.  Sat R 50:16 D 23 '67
    Kaufmann, S.  Ahmed and Isabella.  New Republic 158:24
        F 17 '68
    Sketch.  Film 51:33 Spg '68
    Biographical note.  International Film G 5:169 '68

Crick, P.   Three East European directors.   Screen
    11-2:64  Mr/Ap '70
Oppenheim, O.   Makavejev in Montreal.   Sight & Sound
    39-2:72  Spg '70
Makavejev and The mysteries of the organism.   Film
    63:17  Aut '71
Robinson, D.   The films of Dusan Makavejev.   Sight &
    Sound 40-4:177  Aut '71
Sitton, R.; MacBean, J. R.; Callenbach, E.   Interview.
    Film Q 25-2:3  Win '71/72
Colaciello, R.   Interview.   Interview 19:30  F '72
MacBean, J. R.   Sex and politics.   Film Q 25-3:2
    Spg '72

MÄKINEN, AITO
    Biographical note.   International Film G 8:143 '71

MAKK, KÁROLY
    Listing of films.   Film Culture 37:7  Sum '65
    Malanga, G.   Letter.   Film Culture 46:20 O '68

MALANGA, GERARD
    Listing of films.   Film Culture 37:7  Sum '65
    Malanga, G.   Letter.   Film Culture 46:20 O '68

MALLE, LOUIS
    Biographical note.   Unifrance 45:10 D '57
    Spotlights five young Frenchmen who are giving French
        cinema a new look.   Films & Filming 5-3:18 D '58
    Meeting La nouvelle vague; conversation.   Films &
        Filming 6-1:7 O '59
    Billard, G.   The men and their work.   Films & Filming
        6-1:7 O '59
    Hartung, P. T.   Screen.   Commonweal 71:265 N 27 '59
    Kauffmann, S.   New directors, old directions.   New Re-
        public 141:21 D 7 '59
    Talk with the director.   Newsweek 58:88 N 27 '61
    Graham, P.   The face of '63--France.   Films & Filming
        9-8:13 My '63
    Strick, P.   Louis Malle.   Film 35:9 Spg '63
    Interview.   Film 39:12 Spg '64
    Director of the year; filmog.   International Film G 2:24
        '65
    Grenier, C.   There's more to Malle than sex, sex, sex.
        N. Y. Times Bio Ed F 6 '72
    Pasquariello, N.   Louis Malle, murmuring of the heart.
        Interview 23:18 Jl '71

MAMOULIAN, ROUBEN
   Merrick, M.   Personalities prominent in the press.
     Cinema Digest 1-6:4 Jl 25 '32
   Birrell, F.   Art of Mamoulian.   New Statesman & Nation
     4:657 N 26 '32
   They stand out from the crowd.   Lit Digest 117:11 Mr
     '34
   Nicolai, B.   Marriage rumors.   Movie Classic 6:22
     Mr '34
   Sarris, A.   Fallen idols; filmog.   Film Culture 28:30
     Spg '63
   The directors choose the best films.   Cinema (BH) 1-5:14
     Ag/S '63
   Shatouni the magnificent.   Reader Digest 87:170 Jl '65
   What directors are saying.   Action 5-3:30 My/Je '70
   Mamoulian on his Dr. Jekyll and Mr. Hyde.   Cinefan-
     tastique 1-3:36 Sum '71
   Summers, M.   Rouben Mamoulian and his Dr. Jekyll
     and Mr. Hyde today.   Filmograph 2-2:45 '71
   Rouben Mamoulian: style is the man; interview; bibli-
     ography; filmog; list of stage productions.   Discussion
     2:entire issue '71

MANKIEWICZ, JOSEPH L.
   Biography.   Current Biography S '49
     Same.   Current Biography Yearbook 1949:396 '50
   Alpert, H.   Case of Joseph L. Mankiewicz.   Sat R
     33:31 O 21 '50
   Holiday awards for 1950.   Holiday 9:79 Ja '51
   Coughlan, R.   Fifteen authors in search of a character
     named Joseph L. Mankiewicz.   Life 30:158 Mr 12 '51
   Nugent, F. S.   All about Joe.   Colliers 127:24 Mr 24 '51
   Biographical note.   Newsweek 38:82 Ag 27 '51
   Alpert, H.   Golden touch of Mankiewicz.   Sat R 35:32
     Mr 8 '52
   Munsel, P.   Mankiewicz at the Met.   Cue 21-52:13 D 27
     '52
   Biography.   Colliers Yearbook 1952:507 '52
   Houseman, J.   Julius Caesar: Mr. Mankiewicz's shooting
     script.   Q Film Radio TV 8-2:109 Win '53
   Rogow, L.   Hollywood oasis.   Sat R 37:31 O 16 '54
   Runyonland revisited.   Cue 24-42:15 O 22 '55
   Shoot it in Tanganyika.   Sat R 40:14 D 21 '57
   Personality of the month.   Films & Filming 4-8:5 My '58
   Conrad, D.   Putting on the style.   Films & Filming
     6-4:9 Ja '60
   Alpert, H.  Joseph and Cleopatra.   Sat R 45:20 Ag 18 '62

Love is a sometime thing.   Time 80:47 N 2 '62

Kurnitz, H.   Mankiewicz the great.   Holiday 33:93 Ja '63

Fenin, G.   The face of '63--United States.   Films &
     Filming 9-6:55 Mr '63

Cleopatra barges in at last.   Life 54:72 Ap 19 '63

Sarris, A.   Fallen idols; filmog.   Film Culture 28:30
     Spg '63

Numb; writing and directing Cleopatra.   New Yorker
     39:27 Je 15 '63

Just one of those things.   Time 81:90 Je 21 '63

Great ideas that never got filmed.   Show 3-8:59 Ag '63

Reid, J. H.   Cleo's Joe.   Films & Filming 9-11:44
     Ag; 9-12:13 S '63

Bontemps, J. & Overstreet, R.   Interview.   Cahiers
     (Eng) 8:28 F '67

Brion, P.   Biofilmography.   Cahiers (Eng) 8:28 F '67

Sarris, A.   Mankiewicz of the movies.   Show 1-3:27
     Mr '70

What directors are saying.   Action 5-2:16 Mr/Ap '70

Williams, J.   Mankiewicz in London.   Sight & Sound
     39-4:185 Aut '70

Gow, G.   Cocking a snook; interview; filmog.   Films &
     Filming 17-2:18 N '70

Filmography.   Film Comment 6-4:101 Win '70/71

What directors are saying.   Action 6-1:30 Ja/F '71

Springer, J.   The films of Joseph L. Mankiewicz; filmog
     (writing and directing).   Films In Review 22-3:153
     Mr '71

---

MANN, ANTHONY

Parsons, L. O.   Cosmopolitan's citation for the best
     direction of the month.   Cosmop 124:13 Mr '48

Personalities of the month.   Films & Filming 5-11:5
     Ag '59

Reid, J. H.   Mann and his environment.   Films &
     Filming 8-4:11 Ja '62

Reid, J. H.   Tension at twilight.   Films & Filming
     8-5:19 F '62

Sarris, A.   Esoterica; filmog.   Film Culture 28:22 Spg
     '63

Mann, A.   Empire demolition.   Films & Filming 10-6:7
     Mr '64

Obit.   Film R p32 '66/68
     Illustrated London N 250:13 My 6 '67
     N. Y. Times p86 Ap 30; p37 My 1 '67
     Newsweek 69:71 My 15 '67
     Screen World 19:236 '68
     Time 89:98 My 5 '67

A lesson in cinema; interview; filmog.   Cahiers (Eng)
    12:45 D '67
Quotemanship.   Action 3-3:20 Jl/Ag '68
Wicking, C. & Pattison, B.   Interview.   Screen 10-4/5:
    32 Jl/O '69


MANN, DANIEL
    Gehman, R. B.   Staged by Daniel Mann.   Theatre Arts
        35:24 N '51
    Ardmore, J. K.   I'm a family man.   Parents 31:46
        D '56
    Personalities of the month.   Films & Filming 5-11:15
        Ag '59
    Reid, J. H.   Portraying life with dignity.   Films &
        Filming 8-6:19 Mr '62
    The directors choose the best films.   Cinema (BH)
        1-5:14 Ag/S '63


MANN, DELBERT
    Early arrivals.   Vogue 126:232 D 1 '55
    Personalities of the month.   Films & Filming 5-11:5
        Ag '59
    Reid, J. H.   Marty and other squares.   Films & Film-
        ing 8-7:20 Ap '62
    What is a Mann?   Action 2-4:9 Jl/Ag '67
    Should directors produce?   Action 3-4:10 Jl/Ag '68


MANUPELLI, GEORGE
    When a painter tries sculpture.   School Arts 61:13
        My '62
    Photograms: creative control of light.   School Arts
        62:17 O '62
    Films and photography.   School Arts 62:28 Mr '63
    Drawing on film.   School Arts 63:10 F '64
    Weiner, P.   New American cinema; filmog.   Film 58:22
        Spg '70


MARCIN, MAX
    Sketch.   Theatre 22:228 N '15
    Marcin, M.   How I sold my plays.   Theatre 24:268 N '16
    Bird, C.   Sketch.   Theatre 40:12 Mr '25
    Obit.   Wilson Library B 22:650 My '48


MARCORELLES, LOUIS
    Marcorelles, L.   The Eastern challenge.   International
        Film A 2:62 '58
    Marcorelles, L.   Making it short.   International Film A
        3:55 '59

MARIN, EDWIN L.
Obit. N.Y. Times p29 My 3 '51

MARINELLI, LAWRENCE
Listing of films. Film Culture 37:7 Sum '65

MARINS, JOSE MOJICA
Lucchetti, R. F. Brazil's terrorist director. CTVD
6-1:29 Fall '68

MARKER, CHRIS
Billard, G. The men and their work. Films & Filming
6-1:7 O '59
Lyrical French documentarist. CTVD 1-2:8 Sum '62
Graham, P. The face of '63--France. Films & Filming
9-8:13 My '63
Jacob, G. Chris Marker and the mutants. Sight &
Sound 35-4:164 Aut '66
Cameron, I. Cuba si! censor no! Movie 3:14 n. d.

MARKOPOULOS, GREGORY
Tyler, P. Two down and one to go? Film Culture 21:33
Sum '60
Markopoulos, G. The erasing influence. Vision 1-1:24
Spg '62
Markopoulos, G. Beyond audio visual space. Vision
1-2:52 Sum '62
Markopoulos, G. The golden poet. Film Culture 27:20
Win '62/63
Markopoulos, G. Letters. Film Culture 29:81 Sum '63
Markopoulos, G. Statement concerning cinema; filmog.
Film Culture 29:73 Sum '63
Markopoulos, G. Toward a new narrative form in mo-
tion pictures. Film Comment 1-6:46 Fall '63
Markopoulos, G. Towards a new narrative film form.
Film Culture 31:11 Win '63/64
Markopoulos, G. Projection of thoughts. Film Culture
32:3 Spg '64
Brown, R. Interview. Film Culture 32:6 Spg '64
Markopoulos, G. Innocent revels. Film Culture 33:41
Sum '64
Survey among unsuccessful applicants for the Ford
Foundation film grants. Film Comment 2-3:10 Sum '64
Markopoulos, G. Random notes during a two week
lecture tour of the U.S. Film Comment 2-4:54 Fall '64
Markoupolos, G. Three filmmakers. Film Culture 35:23
Win '64/65

Listing of films.   Film Culture 37:7 Sum '65

Kevles, B. L.   Interview.   Film Culture 38:43 Fall '65

Markopoulos, G.   The driving rhythm.   Film Culture 40:31 Spg '66

Markopoulos, G.   From Fanshawe to Swain.   Film Culture 41:17 Sum '66

Eighth independent film award.   Film Culture 42:1 Fall '66

Christopoulos, G.   Cinemaportraits--Markopoulos galaxie. Film Culture 42:2 Fall '66

Markopoulos, G.   Galaxie (production and critical notes). Film Culture 42:5 Fall '66

Markopoulos, G.   The filmmaker as physician of the future.   Film Culture 44:60 Spg '67

Markopoulos, G.   Free association.   Film Culture 45:52 Sum '67

Markopoulos, G.   Correspondences of smells and visuals. Film Culture 46:35 O '68

Markopoulos, G.   The adamantine bridge; Love's task. Film Culture 53/54/55:84 Spg '72

Markopoulos, G.   Triumph of the symbol.   Film Comment 1-3:19 n. d.

Markopoulos, G.   The museum of modern art.   Film Comment 1-3:41 n. d.

Jurors named anniversary awards.   Film Comment 2-2: 49 n. d.


MARKSON, MORLEY
  Interview.   Finders Keepers 1:24 Win '72


MARSHALL, GEORGE
  Parsons, L. O.   Cosmopolitan's citation for the best direction of the month.   Cosmop 124:13 My '48

  Parsons, L. O.   Cosmopolitan's citation for the best direction of the month.   Cosmop 125:13 Jl '48

  Movies.   Christian Century 85:297 Mr 6 '68

  Marshall, G.   55 years in movies.   Action 5-6:3 N/D '70

  Marshall, G.   Making Murder.   Film Fan Mo 117:20 Mr '71


MARTON, ANDREW
  Marton, A.   Ben-Hur's chariot race.   Films In Review 11-1:27 Ja '60


MARZANO, JOSEPH
  Listing of films.   Film Culture 37:7 Sum '65

MASELLI, FRANCESCO
New names.   Sight & Sound 25-3:121 Win '55/56

MASON, BILL
Thorvaldson, P.   Who's who in filmmaking; interview.
Sightlines 5-2:5 N/D '71

MASON, RICHARD
Peavy, C. D.   The films of Richard Mason.   Cineaste
2-4:4 Spg '69

MASSIMINO-GARNIER, MAX
Granja, V.   Paul Campini and Max Massimino-Garnier
alive and well!   CTVD 6-3:9 Spg '69

MASSINGHAM, RICHARD
Richard Massingham.   Film 4:4 Mr '55

MASUMURA, YASUZO
Richie, D.   The face of '63--Japan.   Films & Filming
9-10:15 Jl '63

MATÉ, RUDOLPH
Everson, W.   Rudy Mate: his work with Carl Dreyer.
Films & Filming 2-2:7 N '55
Luft, M. G.   Rudolph Mate.   Films In Review 15-8:480
O '64
Filmography (as cinematographer and director).   Film
Comment 8-2:45 Sum '72

MATHIS, JUNE
Sketch.   Photoplay 24:63 O '23
Home of.   Classic 18:52 F '24
Hall, G.   Sketch.   Classic 19:22 Mr '24
Sketch.   Photoplay 30:46 O '26
Feldman, J. & H.   Women directors.   Films In Review
1-8:9 N '50

MATTSON, ARNE
Note.   International Film G 2:41 '65

MAYER, GERALD
American motion pictures in world trade.   Annals
American Academy 254:31 N '47

MAYO, ARCHIE
Work of.   Motion Pic 53:66 Jl '37

MAYSLES, ALBERT
Reynolds, C.   Focus on Albert Maysles.   Popular Photo
54:128 My '64
Film Comment announces the recipients of the 1964 an-
niversary awards.   Film Comment 2-3:3 Sum '64
(See also:  MAYSLES BROTHERS)

MAYSLES, DAVID
O'Brien, G.   Interview.   Interview 2-4:28 Jl '71
(See also:  MAYSLES BROTHERS)

MAYSLES BROTHERS (Albert and David)
Shivas, M.   Interview.   Movie 8:19 Ap '63
Survey among unsuccessful applicants for the Ford
Foundation film grants.   Film Comment 2-3:10 Sum '64
Blue, J.   Thoughts on cinema verite and a discussion
with the Maysles Brothers.   Film Comment 2-4:22
Fall '64
Maysles Brothers.   Film Culture 42:114 Fall '66
The amazing Maysles exhibit The salesman.   Making
Films 3-2:27 Ap '69
Sitton, B.   Interview.   Film Library Q 2-3:13 Sum '69
The Rolling Stones' Gimme shelter obituary for Wood-
stock nation.   Show 2-1:49 Mr '71
Kolker, R. P.   Interview.   Sight & Sound 40-4:183
Aut '71
Maysles, A. & D.   Gimme shelter: production notes.
Filmmakers Newsletter 5-2:28 D '71

MAZURSKY, PAUL
Greenfield, J.   Paul Mazursky in wonderland.   Life
69:51 S 4 '70
What directors are saying.   Action 5-6:22 N/D '70
Cocks, J.   Portrait of the artisan.   Time 97:75 Ja 18 '71

MEAD, TAYLOR
Survey among unsuccessful applicants for the Ford
Foundation film grants.   Film Comment 2-3:10 Sum '64
Listing of films.   Film Culture 37:7 Sum '65

MEADER, ABBOTT
Listing of films.   Film Culture 37:7 Sum '65

MEKAS, JONAS
Mekas, J.   N. Y. letter.   Sight & Sound 28-3/4:118
Sum/Aug '59
Cinema underground; Filmmakers' cooperative.   New

Yorker 39:16 Jl 13 '63

Hamill, P.   Explosion in the movie underground.   Sat
Evening Post 236:82 S 28 '63

Mekas, J.   Statement.   Film Comment 2-1:28 Win '64

Private.   New Yorker 40:27 Ja 16 '65

Listing of films.   Film Culture 37:7 Sum '65

Levy, A.   Voice of the underground cinema.   N. Y.
Times Mag p70 S 19 '65

Kevles, B. L.   Interview.   Film Culture 38:36 Fall '65

Weiner, P.   New American cinema; filmog.   Film 58:22
Spg '70

(Jonas Mekas is Editor of FILM CULTURE)


MELFORD, GEORGE
Owen, K.   Uncle George.   Photoplay 16-1:42 Je '19


MÉLIÈS, GEORGES
Melies, G.   The silver lining.   Sight & Sound 7-25:7
Spg '38

Sadoul, G.   An index to the creative work of Georges
Melies.   Sight & Sound (special sup) Index Series # 11
Ag '47

Stephenson, R.   Commemorating Melies.   Sight & Sound
30-4:174 Aut '61

Stephenson, R.   A film a day.   Films & Filming 8-3:19
D '61

Haleff, M.   An interview.   Film Culture 48/49:60 Win/
Spg '70

Hammond, P.   A Georges Melies scrapbook.   Cinema
(Lon) 9:4 n. d.


MELVILLE, JEAN-PIERRE
Melville, J-P.   Finding the truth without faith.   Films &
Filming 8-6:9 Mr '62

Graham, P.   The face of '63--France.   Films & Filming
9-8:13 My '63

Breitbart, E.   Jean-Pierre Melville.   Film Culture 35:15
Win '64/65

Filmography.   Film Culture 35:43 Win '64/65

Nogueira, R. & Truehaud, F.   A samurai in Paris.
Sight & Sound 37-3:119 Sum '68

Eyles, A.   Jean-Pierre Melville; filmog.   Focus On
Film 4:6 S/O '70

Jean-Pierre Melville talks to Rui Nogueira.   Sight &
Sound 40-4:181 Aut '71

Armes, R.   Director of the year; filmog.   International
Film G 8:33 '71

MENKEN, MARIE
    Mekas, J.  Notes on the new American cinema.  Film
       Culture 24:6 Spg '62
    Maas, W.  The Gryphon yaks; filmog.  Film Culture
       29:46 Sum '63
    Listing of films.  Film Culture 37:7 Sum '65
    Myers, L. B.  Marie Menken herself.  Film Culture
       45:37 Sum '67
    Weiner, P.  New American cinema; filmog.  Film 58:22
       Spg '70
    Pyros, J.  Notes on women directors.  Take One 3-2:7
       N/D '70
    Obit.  N. Y. Times p26 D 31 '70
       Same.  N. Y. Times Bio Ed D 31 '70

MENZEL, JIŘÍ
    Sarris, A.  Movers.  Sat R 50:41 D 23 '67
    Kolodny, I.  The man who made Closely watched trains;
       interview.  Action 3-3:13 My/Je '68
    Levy, A.  Czech Jiri Menzel directs a movie.  N. Y.
       Times Mag p28 F 9 '69
    Crick, P.  Three East European directors.  Screen
       11-2:64 Mr/Ap '70

MENZIES, WILLIAM CAMERON
    Birdwell, R.  Painting with a punch.  Cinema Progress
       3-3/4:21 Ja '39
    Obit.  N. Y. Times p29 Mr 7 '57
       Screen World 9:225 '58
    Leading film designers.  International Film G 5:36 '68

MEREDITH, CHARLES H.
    Obit.  Screen World 16:224 '65

MÉSZÁROS, MÁRTA
    Biographical note.  International Film G 7:137 '70

METZGER, RADLEY
    Brown, R.  Radley Metzger: auteur of the erotic. Todays
       Filmmaker 1-1:26 Ag '71
    Brode, D.  Master of the erotic on film.  Show 2-2:42
       S '71

MEYER, ANDREW
    Markopoulos, C.  Three filmmakers.  Film Culture
       35:23 Win '64/65
    Listing of films.  Film Culture 37:7 Sum '65

MEYER, RUSS
    Mister X.   Newsweek 75:83 Ja 19 '70
    What directors are saying.   Action 5-1:28 Ja/F '70
    Our man in Beyond the valley of the dolls.   Show 1-5:69
        My '70
    Schickel, P.   Porn and man at Yale.   Harper 241:34
        Jl '70
    The remarkable Russ Meyer.   Show 2-4:42 Je '72
    Koch, M.   Interview.   Interview 19:22 F '72

MEZL, ZDENEK
    Fiala, V.   Mezl's graphic art for TV.   CTVD 8-2:15
        Fall '71

MICHEAUX, OSCAR
    Black film; God's step children, filmed in 1938, black
        director.   New Yorker 46:34 Ap 18 '70

MIDEKE, MICHAEL
    Listing of films.   Film Culture 37:7 Sum '65

MIGLIACCIO, FLAVIO
    Viany, A.   Who's who in the cinema novo.   CTVD 6-1:25
        Fall '68

MIHIC, GORDAN
    Biographical note.   International Film G 8:281 '71

MILES, BERNARD
    Miles, B.   The minority audience.   Film 9:16 S/O '56
    Filmography.   Film 14:8 N/D '57
    Lampe, D.   Mermaid at Puddle dock.   Reporter 23:48
        Jl 7 '60
    Fay, G.   London panorama.   Theatre Arts 46:68 Ja '62

MILES, CHRISTOPHER
    Cohn, N.   Virgin and the gypsy rescued him.   N. Y.
        Times Bio Ed Ag 23 '70
    Williams, J.   All that sparkles is not champagne; inter-
        view; filmog.   Films Illustrated 1-6:30 D '71
    British cinema filmography.   Film 65:10 Spg '72

MILESTONE, LEWIS
    Reynolds, Q.   That's how pictures are born.   Colliers
        105:14 Ja 6 '40
    Goodman, E.   Directed by Lewis Milestone.   Theatre
        Arts 27:111 F '43

Work of.   Newsweek 27:98 Ja 21 '46
First aid for a sick giant.   New Republic 120:15 Ja 31
    '49
The big screens.   Sight & Sound 24-4:209 Spg '55
McCarten, J.   Current cinema.   New Yorker 35:117
    Je 13 '59
Personality of the month.   Films & Filming 5-10:5 Jl '59
Young, C.   The old dependables.   Film Q 13-1:2 Fall '59
Lewis Milestone.   Films & Filming 903:7 D '62
Sarris, A.   Fallen idols; filmog.   Film Culture 28:30
    Spg '63
Feinstein, H.   Interview.   Film Culture 34:25 Fall '64
Should directors produce?   Action 3-4:10 Jl/Ag '68
Diehl, D.   Directors go to their movies; interview. Action
    7-4:2 Jl/Ag '72

MILLARDE, HARRY WILLIAMS
    Sketch.   Motion Pic 9:94 Jl '15
    Obit.   N.Y. Times p37 S 5 '69

MILLER, DAVID
    New feature directors.   Lions Roar 1-9:no p# My '42
    New faces among MGM directors too.   Lions Roar 1-11/
        12:no p# Jl/Ag '42
    Gray, M.   Without a formula.   Films & Filming 3-5:6
        F '57
    Sarris, A.   Minor disappointments; filmog.   Film Culture
        28:41 Spg '63

MILLER, JONATHAN
    Hill, V.   Directing isn't surgery.   Show 1-2:63 F '70
    Biography.   Current Biography 31:24 O '70
        Same.   Current Biography Yearbook 1970:294 '71

MILLER, ROBERTO
    Lucchetti, R. F.   Roberto Miller on the experimental
        cinema; filmog.   CTVD 6-3:2 Spg '69

MILTON, ROBERT
    Sketch.   Theatre 37:12 Ap '23
    The man behind the actors.   Theatre 39:9 Ag '24
    Sketch.   Theatre 43:30 F '26

MIMICA, VATROSLAV
    Nogeira, R. & Zalaffi, N.   All men are filmmakers;
        interview.   Film 53:32 Win '68/69

MINNELLI, VINCENT
  Work of.   Theatre Arts 20:37 Ja '36
  Houghton, N.   Work of.   Theatre Arts 20:783 O '36
  Sketch.   American 122:90 O '36
  Perelman, S. J.   Sketch.   Stage 14:66 Ap '37
  Hollywood tent show.   Lions Roar 2-4:no p# Ap '43
  Interpreter of fantasy.   Lions Roar 3-1:no p# S '43
  Minnelli from Broadway.   Lions Roar 4-1:no p# F '44
  MGM's directors range from pioneers to newcomers.
      Lions Roar 3-4:no p# Jl '44
  St. Johns, A. R.   His engagement to Judy Garland.
      Photoplay 26:28 Ap '45 and following issues.
  Director Minnelli's talents.   Time 45:93 My 14 '45
  Farber, M.   A skillful director.   New Republic 112:709
      My 21 '45
  Ormiston, R.   His honeymoon.   Photoplay 27:34 O '45
  Harcourt-Smith, S.   Vincent Minnelli.   Sight & Sound
      21-3:115 Ja/Mr '52
  Minnelli, V.   So we changed it.   Films & Filming 5-2:7
      N '58
  Johnson, A.   The films of Vincent Minnelli.   Film Q
      12-2:21 Win '58; 12-3:32 Spg '59
  McVay, D.   The magic of Minnelli.   Films & Filming
      5-9:11 Je '59
  Minnelli, V.   The rise and fall of the musical; interview.
      Films & Filming 8-4:9 Ja '62
  Shivas, M.   Minnelli's method.   Movie 1:17 Je '62
  Talking about people.   Film 32:6 Sum '62
  Reynolds, C.   Interview.   Popular Photo 51:106 Jl '62
  Mayersberg, P.   The testament of Vincent Minnelli.
      Movie 3:10 O '62
  Fenin, G.   The face of '63--United States.   Films &
      Filming 9-6:55 Mr '63
  Sarris, A.   Third line; filmog.   Film Culture 28:18
      Spg '63
  Serebrinsky, E. & Garaycochea, O.   Interview in
      Argentina; filmog.   Movie 10:23 Je '63
  Galling, D. L.   Vincent Minnelli; filmog.   Films In Re-
      view 15-3:129 Mr '64
  Letters.   Films In Review 15-4:250 Ap '64
  The sandpiper; interview.   Cinema (BH) 2-6:7 Jl/Ag '65
  Elsaesser, T.   Vincent Minnelli.   Brighton 15:11 D '69
  Elsaesser, T.   Vincent Minnelli.   Brighton 18:20 Mr '70
  Diehl, V.   Vincent Minnelli and Gigi; interview.   Action
      7-5:2 S/O '72

MITCHELL, DENIS
  Reisz, K. On the outside looking in.  International Film
    A 3:50 '59

METROTTI, MARIO
  Biographical note.  International Film G 9:281 '72

MITCHELL, HOWARD
  Sketch.  Motion Pic 10:109 Ag '15

MIZOGUCHI, KENJI
  Richie, D. & Anderson, J. L. Kenji Mizoguchi. Sight
    & Sound 25-2:76 Aut '55
  Cameron, I. Kenji Mizoguchi.  Movie 5:36 D '62
  Note.  International Film G 2:34 '65
  Mizoguchi spectrum; filmog.  Cinema (BH) 6-3:12 Spg '71
  Belton, J. The crucified lovers of Mizoguchi.  Film Q
    25-1:15 Fall '71

MIZRAHI, MOSHE
  Mizrahi, M. Les stances a' Sophie.  American Cinema-
    tographer 52-8:776 Ag '71

MOCKY, JEAN-PIERRE
  Graham, P. The face of '63--France.  Films & Film-
    ing 9-8:13 My '63

MOLANDER, GUSTAF
  Note.  International Film G 2:41 '65

MOLINARO, ÉDOUARD
  Spotlights five young Frenchmen who are giving French
    cinema a new look.  Films & Filming 5-3:18 D '58
  Meeting La nouvelle vague: conversation.  Films &
    Filming 6-1:7 O '59
  Three directors.  Films & Filming 7-1:12 O '60

MOLLO, ANDREW
  Gillett, J. Happening here.  Sight & Sound 34-3:138
    Sum '65

MOORSE, GEORGE
  Dictionary of young German filmmakers.  CTVD 4-2:11
    Spg '66
  Portrait of an American as a young German filmmaker.
    CTVD 5-3:6 Win '67/68

MORANAN, CHRISTOPHER
  British cinema filmography.   Film 65:10 Spg '72

MORE-O'FERRALL, GEORGE
  (See: O'FERRALL, GEORGE MORE)

MORLEY, PETER
  Morley, P.   On changing mediums.   Film 24:29 Mr/Ap
    '60

MORRISSEY, PAUL
  Listing of films.   Film Culture 37:7 Sum '65
  Raynes, T.   Interview.   Cinema (Lon) 6/7:42 Ag '70
  Kael, P.   Current cinema.   New Yorker 46:132 O 10 '70
  Howton, F. W.   Filming Andy Warhol's Trash; interview.
    Filmmakers Newsletter 5-8:24 Je '72

MOXEY, JOHN LLEWELLYN
  Interview.   Cinema (BH) 4-4:8 D '68
  Films on TV; filmog.   Films In Review 22-5:299 My '71

MULLIGAN, ROBERT
  Sarris, A.   Minor disappointments; filmog.   Film Culture
    28:41 Spg '63
  Godfrey, L.   Flavored genius.   Films & Filming 13-4:47
    Ja '67
  Castell, D.   Small comings and goings; filmog.   Films
    Illustrated 1-1:11 Jl '71
  Mercer, J.   A loss of innocence.   Film 63:20 Aut '71
  Taylor, J. R.   Inside Robert Mulligan.   Sight & Sound
    40-4:215 Aut '71

MUNIZ, SERGIO
  Viany, A.   Who's who in the cinema novo.   CTVD 6-1:25
    Fall '68

MUNK, ANDRZEJ
  Munk, A.   National character and the individual.   Films
    & Filming 8-2:15 N '61

MURAKAMI, TERU
  Crick, P.   Notes on Jimmy Murakimi.   Film 43:34 Aut
    '65

MURNAU, F. W.
  Interview.   Motion Pic Classic 22:24 Ja '26
  Josephson, M. Interview. Motion Pic Classic 24:16 O '26

Thompson, P.   Work of.   Motion Pic Classic 25:36 Jl '27

The ideal picture needs no titles.   Theatre 47:41 Ja '28

Cruikshank, M.   Interview.   Motion Pic Classic 27:38
   Jl '28

Appreciation.   Lit Digest 99:28 O 20 '28

South Sea tragedy is Murnau's epitaph.   Lit Digest 109:37
   Ap 4 '31

Black, M.   Sketch.   Motion Pic Classic 33:28 Je '31

Huff, T.   An index to the films of F. W. Murnau.   Sight
   & Sound (special sup)   Index Series #15 Ag '48

Jones, D. B.   Sunrise; a Murnau masterpiece.   Q Film
   Radio TV 9:238 Spg '55

Sarris, A.   Pantheon directors; filmog.   Film Culture
   28:2 Spg '63

Estes, O. Jr.   F. W. Murnau and his world famous
   classic The last laugh.   8mm Collector 13:18 Fall/Win
   '65

Astruc, A.   Fire and ice.   Cahiers (Eng) 1:69 Ja '66

Guillerme, G. P.   Shadow and substance.   Sight & Sound
   36-3:150 Sum '67

Henderson, B.   The long take.   Film Comment 7-2:6
   Sum '71

Guillerme, G. P.   F. W. Murnau; filmog.   Film Comment 7-2:13 Sum '71

Flaherty, D.   A few reminiscences.   Film Culture 20:14
   n. d.


MUTRUX, FLOYD

   Benoit, S.   Dusty and Sweets McGee: the making of a
      movie.   Show 2-3:40 My '71

   What did he say?   Show 2-8:6 O '71

NAKAHIRA, YASUSHI
    Richie, D. Japan: the younger talents. Sight & Sound
        29-2:78 Spg '60

NAKAMURA, NOBORU
    Toshiyama, T. Japanese film director; interview. CTVD
        4-4:15 Win '66/67

NAM, VU
    Hitchens, G. Filmmaking under the bomb. Film Com-
        ment 5-2:86 Spg '69

NARIZZANO, SILVIO
    David Austen talks to Silvio Narizzano about a movie
        called Blue. Films & Filming 14-11:5 Ag '68
    British cinema filmography. Film 65:10 Spg '72
    Phillips, G. Portrait of a filmmaker. Take One 1-9:6
        n. d.

NARUSAWA, MASAHIGE
    Richie, D. The face of '63--Japan. Films & Filming
        9-10:15 Jl '63

NARUSE, MIKIO
    Richie, D. The face of '63--Japan. Films & Filming
        9-10:15 Jl '63
    Note. International Film G 2:35 '65

NEAME, RONALD
    Filmography. Film 14:8 N/D '57
    British feature directors; an index to their work. Sight
        & Sound 27-6:300 Aut '58
    British cinema filmography. Film 65:10 Spg '72

NEGULESCO, JEAN
    Director-artist. Life 16:65 Je 19 '44

NEILAN, MARSHALL (Mickey)
    Cohn, A. A. Director "Mickey." Photoplay 12-4:67
        S '17
    Naylor, H. S. Sketch. Motion Pic 15:34 S '18
    Peltret, E. Interview. Motion Pic Classic 10:20 Ap/My
        '20

McGaffey, K. Interview. Motion Pic Classic 13:50
  D '21
St. Johns, A. R. Sketch. Photoplay 23:39 Mr '23
Home of. Classic 20:32 O '24
Obit. N. Y. Times p35 O 28 '58
  Newsweek 52:66 N 10 '58
  Time 72:88 N 10 '58
Gribbel, J. Marshall Neilan. Films In Review 11-3:190
  Mr '60


NELSON, GENE
Dancer acts out bedtime story. Life 27:14 Ag 15 '49
Nelson, G. The girl in row four. Silver Screen 21-4:24
  F '51
Nelson, Mrs. G. How I pursued my husband. Photoplay
  40-1:40 Jl '51
Nelson, M. I married a serviceman. Photoplay 41-2:46
  F '52
MacDonald, E. It couldn't have worked out better.
  Silver Screen 22-10:42 Ag '52
Knight, A. Gene Nelson, Agnes DeMille and Oklahoma!
  Dance 29:28 Jl '55
Gene, Nelson: working Hollywood. Dance 30:24 My '56


NELSON, GUNVOR
Richardson, B. Interview. Film Q 25-1:34 Fall '71


NELSON, RALPH
Casty, A. A story about people, that's my clay; inter-
  view. Film Comment 3-3:2 Sum '65
Symposium: adding to the director's tools. Action 3-6:26
  N/D '68
What directors are saying. Action 5-1:28 Ja/F '70
Nelson, R. Massacre at Sand Creek; interview. Films
  & Filming 16-6:26 Mr '70
Nelson, R. Impressions of Russia. Action 6-4:10 Jl/Ag
  '71
American directors visit Moscow. Making Films 5-4:30
  O '71


NELSON, ROBERT
Listing of films. Film Culture 37:3 Sum '65
Alexander, T. K. San Francisco's hipster cinema.
  Film Culture 44:70 Spg '67
Bodien, E. The films of Robert Nelson. Film Q 20-3:
  50 Spg '67
Dale, R. C. Interview. Filmmakers Newsletter 2-12:4 O '69

Robert Nelson on Robert Nelson.　Film Culture 48/49:23
　　Win/Spg '70

NÉMEC, JAN
　　Director of the year; filmog.　International Film G 5:25
　　　'68

NEVES, DAVID
　　Viany, A.　Who's who in the cinema novo.　CTVD 6-1:25
　　　Fall '68

NEWMAN, JOSEPH M.
　　New faces among MGM directors too.　Lions Roar
　　　1-11/12:no p# Jl/Ag '42
　　Young veteran.　Lions Roar 2-3(sup):no p# Ja '43
　　Newman, J.　Directors are businessmen.　Films In Re-
　　　view 2-7:24 Ag/S '51

NIBLO, FRED
　　His best lines.　Everybodys 34:502 Jl '16
　　Cheatham, M.　Interview.　Motion Pic Classic 10:32
　　　Jl '20
　　McGaffey, K.　Sketch.　Motion Pic Classic 13:60 O '21
　　Home of.　Classic 16:34 Ap '23
　　Home of.　Photoplay 24:54 O '23
　　Screen actresses--what makes them stars?　Photoplay
　　　24:48 N '23
　　Americanizing American films.　Theatre 47:32 My '28
　　The perfect voice does not emerge from Hollywood, but
　　　from the New York speaking stage.　Theatre 50:39
　　　Ag '29
　　Home of.　Architecture 14:307 Je '30
　　Obit.　N. Y. Times p23 N 12 '48
　　　Times 52:98 N 22 '48
　　Biography.　National Cylopaedia 38:264 '53
　　Route, W. D.　Buried directors.　Focus 7:9 Spg '72

NICHOLS, MIKE
　　Watt, D.　Tables for two.　New Yorker 33:46 D 21 '57
　　Success story.　Newsweek 51:64 Ja 27 '58
　　People are talking about.　Vogue 131:91 Ap 1 '58
　　Fresh eggheads.　Time 71:53 Je 2 '58
　　Scott, J. A.　How to be a success in show business.
　　　Cosmop 145:68 N '58
　　Cotler, G.　For the love of Mike and Elaine.　N. Y.
　　　Times Mag p71 My 24 '59
　　TV gets laugh from its griefs.　Life 48:106 F 15 '60

Wool, R.   Mike and Elaine: Mirrors to our madness.
    Look 24:46 Je 21 '60
Two characters in search.   Time 76:61 S 26 '60
McCarten, J.   Theatre.   New Yorker 36:74 O 15 '60
Evening with Mike Nichols and Elaine May.   Time 76:73
    O 24 '60
Brustein, R.   Comedians from underground.   New Re-
    public 143:28 O 31 '60
Mike Nichols and Elaine May at the photographer's.
    Theatre Arts 44:59 O '60
Nichols, May and horses.   New Yorker 36:44 N 12 '60
Fun with human foibles.   Life 49:65 N 21 '60
Evening with Mike Nichols and Elaine May.   Theatre Arts
    44:12 D '60
Nichols, M.   Theatre.   Coronet 49:22 F '61
Markel, H.   Mike Nichols and Elaine May.   Redbook
    116:32 F '61
Hip comics and the new humor; discussion.   Playboy 8:35
    Mr '61
Biography.   Current Biography 22:37 Mr '61
    Same.   Current Biography Yearbook 1961:345 '62
Comics take a long hard look at the art of conversation.
    Living for Young Homemakers 14:88 Mr '61
Rice, R.   Profiles.   New Yorker 37:47 Ap 15 '61
Broadway's top comedy team takes up bowling.   Good
    Housekeeping 152:32 My '61
Save my seat.   New Yorker 37:57 N 18 '61
Hamblin, D. J.   Comic catapults to higher stage.   Life
    56:100 Mr 20 '64
Mike and Max.   New Yorker 40:32 Ap 11 '64
People are talking about.   Vogue 144:142 O 15 '64
Hammel, F.   Director at work.   Cue 33-45:12 N 7 '64
Lifferts, B.   Now the Nichols touch.   N. Y. Times Mag
    p34 N 22 '64
Nichols touch.   Time 84:86 N 27 '64
On the scene.   Playboy 12-2:136 F '65
Mike Nichols and the Midas touch.   Show 5-2:32 Mr '65
View from the penthouse.   Newsweek 65:89 Ap 5 '65
Jennings, C. R.   All for the love of Mike.   Sat Evening
    Post 238:83 O 9 '65
Lewis, E.   Manhattan Merlin.   Cue 35-1:13 Ja 1 '66
Roddy, J.   Elizabeth Taylor and Richard Burton, the
    night of the brawl.   Look 30:42 F 8 '65
Interview.   Playboy 13-6:63 Je '66
Gussow, M.   Mike Nichols director as star.   Newsweek
    68:95 N 14 '66
Alpert, N.   New faces.   Sat R 49:12 D 24 '66

Biography.   British Book Year 1966:143 '66

Thompson, T.   Whatever happened to Elaine May?   Life
63:54 Jl 28 '67

Rollin, B.   Mike Nichols: wizard of wit.   Look 32:71
Ap 2 '68

Brackman, J.   Onward and upward with the arts.   New
Yorker 44:34 Jl 27 '68

Day, B.   It depends on how you look at it; interview.
Films & Filming 15-2:4 N '68

Sokolov, R. A.   There's a catch: Catch-22.   Newsweek
73:52 Mr 3 '69

Ephron, N.   Yossarian is alive and well in the Mexican
desert.   N. Y. Times Mag p30 Mr 16 '69

What directors are saying.   Action 4-5:32 S/O '69

Gelmis, J.   Mike Nichols talks about his films; interview.
Atlantic 225:71 F '70

Jeremial.   The stars' stars: astrology.   Show 1-3:16
Mr '70

What directors are saying.   Action 5-3:30 My/Je '70

Henry, B.   Frantic filming of a crazy classic.   Life
Je 12 '70

Some things are more Yossarian than others.   Time
95:66 Je 15 '70

Kauffmann, S.   Films.   New Republic 163:32 Jl 4 '70

Thegze, C.   I see everything twice.   Film Q 24:7 Fall
'70

Goldsmith, B.   Grass, women and sex; interview.
Harper Bazaar 104:142 N '70

What directors are saying.   Action 5-6:22 N/D '70

Was this man a Svengali who changed the lives of Candice
Bergen and Ann-Margret?   Modern Screen 65-12:26
D '71

Brown, J. L.   Pictures of innocence.   Sight & Sound
41-2:101 Spg '72


NIGH, WILLIAM
Gibson, M.   He's seen them all.   Silver Screen 8-3:47
Ja '38


NILSSON, LEOPOLDO TORRE
(See:  TORRE-NILSSON, LEOPOLDO)


NORDSTROM, KRISTINA
Bless Kristina Nordstrom.   Show 2-6:12 S '72


NORMAN, LESLIE
Filmography.   Film 14:8 N/D '57

British feature directors; an index to their work.    Sight
     & Sound 27-6:300 Aut '58

NORONHA, LINDUARTE
     Viany, A.   Who's who in the cinema novo.    CTVD 6-1:25
     Fall '68

NORTON, BILL
     I had never worked with a big crew or actors like Gene
     Hackman.    Action 7-1:21 Ja/F '72

NOVAK, VLADO
     Survey among unsuccessful applicants for the Ford
     Foundation film grants. Film Comment 2-3:10 Sum '65

NOWLAND, EUGENE
     Craig, J.   The virtuoso who plays on a camera.   Photo-
     play 8-4:28 S '15

NUCHTERN, SIMON
     A feature film in Super 16.   Making Films 5-6:11 D '71

NUGENT, ELLIOTT
     Gray, C.   Sketch.   Motion Pic 39:42 Mr '30
     Fender, R.   Sketch.   Motion Pic Classic 32:63 D '30
     The versatile Nugent.   Cue 13-16:9 Ap 15 '44
     Isaacs, H. R.   Featuring the voice of the turtle.
        Theatre Arts 28:280 My '44
     Biography.   Current Biography Jl '44
     Hollywood's favorite rebel.   Sat Evening Post 222:25
        Jl 23 '49
        Same, abridged.   Reader Digest 55:53 O '49
     How to stay young.   American 154:49 O '52
     Wild ride.   Newsweek 66:110 D 13 '65
     Hutchens, J. K.   Days of roses followed by rain.   Sat R
        49:35 Mr 5 '66

NYBY, CHRISTIAN
     Sarris, A.   Oddities and one shots.   Film Culture 28:45
        Spg '63

OBOLER, ARCH
   Genius's hour.   Time 54:30 S 4 '39
   Oboler, one-man script mill, tries venture with Nazimova.
      Newsweek 14:38 S 4 '39
   Allen, L.   Literary light of radio.   Christian Science
      Mon Mag p5 Ag 31 '40
   Busy wunderkind.   Time 36:56 D 2 '40
   Biography.   Current Biography '40
   Wunderkind out.   Time 37:87 Mr 17 '41
   Oboler's free world.   Newsweek 21:74 Mr 1 '43
   Matthews, W.   The literary value of his radio plays.
      Hollywood Q 1:44 O '45
   Dialogue between you and Oboler.   Scholastic 48:22
      Mr 18 '46
   Rughum.   Time 47:71 Ap 8 '46
   Thoughts on radio playwriting.   Writer 60:131 Ap '47
   Interview.   Focus 1:10 '67

O'FERRALL, GEORGE MORE
   Filmography.   Film 14:8 N/D '57
   British feature directors; an index to their work.   Sight
      & Sound 27-6:299 Aut '58

OGAWA, SHINSUKE
   Biographical note.   International Film G 8:193 '71

O'HARA, GERALD (Gerry)
   British cinema filmography.   Film 65:10 Spg '72

OLCOTT, SIDNEY
   Gaddis, P.   Blazing a trail in the movies; interview.
      Photoplay 6-4:104 S '14
   Obit.   N.Y. Times p88 D 18 '49
      Screen World 1:234 '47
      Time 54:50 D 26 '49
   Mitchell, G.  Sidney Olcott.  Films In Review 5-4:175 Ap
      '54
   Geltzer, G.   Sidney Olcott: letter.   Films In Review
      5-5:151 My '54
   Mitchell, G.   Geltzer on Olcott; letter.   Films In Re-
      view 5-6:315 Je/Jl '54

OLIVEIRA, DOMINGOS
  Viany, A.  Who's who in the cinema novo.   CTVD 6-1:26
    Fall '68

OLIVIER, LAURENCE
  Goldbeck, E.   Interview.   Motion Pic 43:66  F '32
  Churchill, E.   He got the habit.   Silver Screen 2-5:20
    Mr '32
  Maxwell, V.   Interview.   Photoplay 45:32 Ja '34
  Sketch.   Theatre World 21:270 Je '34
  Crichton, K.   Hollywood doesn't doubt.   Colliers 103:15
    Je 10 '39
  Sketch.   Life 6:31 Je 26 '39
  Schrott, G.   A new kind of lover.   Silver Screen 9-10:36
    Ag '39
  Wallace, G.   Comedy can wait.   Screen Book 22-4:70
    N '39
  Waterbury, R.   A love worth fighting for.   Photoplay
    53-12:18 D '39
  Busch, N. F.   Story of.   Life 8:74 My 20 '40
  Harris, R.   Star-cross'd lovers.   Photoplay 54-10:28
    O '40
  Mulvey, K.   Sketch.   Womans Home Companion 68:28
    Ap '41
  Letter to Douglas Fairbanks.   Photoplay 20:22 Ja '42
  Stokes, S.   Oliviers.   Theatre Arts 29:711 D '45
  Masterpiece: Olivier's Henry V.   Time 47:56 Ap '46
  Schwarz, D.   Present and future of Shakespeare.   N. Y.
    Times Mag p22 My 12 '46
  Brown, J. M.   Seeing things.   Sat R 29:46 Je 8 '46
  Biography.   Current Biography 7:28 Je '46
    Same.   Current Biography Yearbook 1946:433 '47
  Laurence Olivier and wife Vivien Leigh.   Time 48:40
    Jl 1 '46
  The Cosmopolite of the month.   Cosmop 121:8 S '46
  Olivier's Lear.   Time 48:56 O 7 '46
  Olivier as Henry V.   Senior Scholastic 49:6T O 14 '46
  Harris, R.   A knight and his lady.   Photoplay 29-5:36
    O '46
  Hall, G.   Those amazing Oliviers.   Silver Screen 16-12:
    30 O '46
  Stokes, S.   English spotlight; Old Vic production of King
    Lear.   Theatre Arts 30:702 D '46
  Knighted.   Newsweek 29:52 Je 23 '47
  Made a knight by George VI.   Time 49:40 Je 23 '47
  Olivier as Hamlet.   N. Y. Times Mag p15 Ag 10 '47
  Speaking of pictures.   Life 23:18 N 24 '47

English star makes film of Hamlet. Cue 17-8:14 F 21
'48

Herlie, E. As I know Laurence Olivier. Silver Screen
18-4:40 F '48

Olivier's Hamlet. Time 51:54 Je 28 '48

Laurence Olivier and Vivien Leigh in Australia with the
Old Vic company in repertory. Theatre World 44:20
Ag '48

Kobler, J. Sir Laurence Olivier. Life 25:129 O 18 '48

Lejeune, C. A. The Bard competes with the body.
N. Y. Times Mag p24 D 12 '48

Scores triumph in his last regular season at the Old Vic.
Time 53:57 F 28 '49

Oscar awards. Illustrated London N 214:435 Ap 2 '49

Cobb, J. Promise and the achievement. Theatre Arts
33:95 Je '49

Assumes management of St. James's theatre. Illustrated
London N 215:870 D 3 '49

Hill, G. Oliviers in Hollywood. N. Y. Times Mag p24
O 22 '50

Canfield, A. A lady in love. Silver Screen 21-3:36
Ja '51

Venzky, A. Enter the Oliviers. Cue 20-49:10 D 8 '51

Watts, S. Enter the Oliviers (diffidently). N. Y. Times
Mag p15 D 16 '51

Newman, J. L. Cleopatra and friends. Colliers 128:21
D 22 '51

Morehouse, W. King of the thespians. American
Mercury 74:116 Ja '52

Hewes, H. Olivier and his green umbrellas. Sat R
35:29 Mr 8 '52

Encrusted. New Yorker 28:24 Mr 22 '52

Nathan, G. J. Two Cleopatras. Theatre Arts 36:18
Mr '52

Gehman, R. Oliviers live their own love story. Coronet
33:131 Ja '53

Bentley, E. I hear Olivier singing. New Republic 128:
20 Jl 20 '53

Knight, A. Sir Laurence's opus 3: Beggar's opera. Sat R
36:28 Ag 15 '53

Peck, S. Now Olivier acts a Shakespeare villain:
Richard III on the screen. N. Y. Times Mag p24
Ja 30 '55

Blakelock, D. Larry the lamb. Plays & Players 2-6:8
Mr '55

Heroic hypnotist. Plays & Players 2-9:9 Je '55

Shakespeare by the Oliviers. N. Y. Times Mag p16 Jl 10 '55

Olivier as Titus.  N. Y.  Times Mag p20 S 4 '55
Panter-Downes, M.  Letter from London; Richard III.
  New Yorker 31:49 D 31 '55
Trewin, J. C.  Olivier at Stratford-upon-Avon.  World
  Theatre 5-1:51 '55
Co-stars.  Time 67:94 F 20 '56
Peck, S.  Sir Laurence again widens his range.  N. Y.
  Times Mag p28 F 26 '56
Knight, A. ; Hewes, H. ; Seldes, G.  Sir Laurence and
  The Bard.  Sat R 39:26 Mr 10 '56
New pictures.  Time 67:112 Mr 12 '56
Sir Laurence Olivier; triumph in Shakespeare's great
  year.  Newsweek 47:105 Mr 19 '56
At home and abroad with Richard III.  Theatre Arts 40:22
  Mr '56
Amour and the man.  Sat R 39:29 O 13 '56
Harvey, E.  TV imports.  Colliers 136:37 O 14 '56
Olivier and Monroe.  Look 20:44 O 30 '56
Knightly entertainer.  Plays & Players 4-8:5 My '57
Unlikely pair make great match.  Life 42:80 Je 3 '57
Supreme player of many parts.  Illustrated London N
  231:37 Jl 6 '57
Barker, F. G.  Knight at the music hall.  Plays &
  Players 5-1:7 O '57
Directing filmography.  Film 14:8 N/D '57
British feature directors; an index to their work.  Sight
  & Sound 27-6:300 Aut '58
Case of TV fright.  Newsweek 52:84 D 1 '58
First knight.  Time 74:70 Jl 20 '59
Hewes, H.  Gems from Coriolanus.  Sat R 42:26 Jl 25
  '59
$100,000 TV debut for Olivier.  Life 47:55 N 2 '59
Gelman, M.  Sir Laurence Olivier.  Theatre 2-2:17
  F '60
Bester, A.  Sir Larry.  Holiday 27:119 F '60
Knight, A.  Many faces of Sir Laurence.  Sat R 43:31
  O 1 '60
Olivier--from holy man to hoofer.  Life 49:95 O 24 '60
Garbo chill.  Newsweek 57:79 Ja 16 '61
Pryce-Jones, A.  Sir Laurence & Larry.  Theatre Arts
  45:14 F '61
Hewes, H.  Awake at the switch.  Sat R 44:26 My 27 '61
Clurman, H.  Theatre.  Nation 192:467 My 27 '61
Herndon, B.  The power and the glory.  TV Guide 9-43:
  17 O 28 '61
Robin, A.  Living legends.  Todays Health 40:84 Ja '62
Laurence Olivier.  Plays & Players 9-10:7 Jl '62

McVay, D.   Hamlet to clown.   Films & Filming 8-12:16
     S '62
Panter-Downes, M.   Letter from London.   New Yorker
     38:80 D 22 '62
Brien, A.   Openings: London.   Theatre Arts 46:57 D '62
Cowie, P.   The face of '63--Great Britain.   Films &
     Filming 9-5:19 F '63
Definitive Moor.   Time 83:80 My 1 '64
Tynan, K.   In his talent, Shakespeare summoned up.
     Life 56:101 My 1 '64
The great Sir Laurence.   Life 56:80A My 1 '64
Trewin, J. C.   Laurence Olivier: a profile.   Plays &
     Players 11-8:8 My '64
Panter-Downes, M.   Letter from London.   New Yorker
     40:98 Je 13 '64
Rogoff, G.   Olivier's Othello, coiling power and wounded
     majesty.   Hi Fi 14:34 D '64
Personalities of the week.   Illustrated London N 247:12
     Jl 17 '65
Kallet, N.   Olivier and the Moor.   Holiday 39:143 Ap '66
Tynan, K.   The actor and the moor.   Plays & Players
     13-11:47 Ag '66
Coward, N.   Laurence Olivier.   McCalls 94:103 O '66
Tynan, K.   Interview.   Tulane Drama R 11:71 Win '66
Tynan, K.   Interview.   World Theatre 16:67 Ja '67
Panter-Downes, M.   Performance of Strindberg's Dance
     of death at the Old Vic.   New Yorker 43:158 Ap 15 '67
Clurman, H.   Theatre in Europe.   Nation 204:797 Je 19
     '67
Hewes, H.   Olivier triumphant.   Sat R 50:36 Jl 1 '67
Best of breed.   Time 90:64 N 3 '67
Hart, H.   Laurence Olivier.   Films In Review 18-10:593
     D '67
Roman, R. C.   Filmography.   Films In Review 18-10:
     610 D '67
Miller, E.   Hollywood scene.   Seventeen 27:48 Ag '68
Ehrlich, H.   Sir says; interview.   Look 34:22 Ja 27 '70
Sir Laurence.   Newsweek 75:57 F 2 '70
Michell, K.   Cue salutes.   Cue 39-13:22 Mr 28 '70
Newsmakers.   Newsweek 75:49 Je 22 '70
Newsmakers.   Newsweek 76:69 O 12 '70
People.   Time 96:36 O 12 '70
Jeremiah.   The stars' stars; astrology.   Show 1-6:15
     O '70
Coleman, T.   Olivier now.   Show 1-6:43 O '70
Newsmakers.   Newsweek 77:49 Ap 5 '71

OLMI, ERMANNO
Lane, J. F.   The triumph of Italy's realism.   Films &
  Filming 8-3:38 D '61
Houston, P.   Ermanno Olmi in London.   Sight & Sound
  31-1:16 Win '61/62
Solomos, G. P.   Ermanno Olmi.   Film Culture 24:35
  Spg '62
Kauffmann, S.   Fine Italian hand.   New Republic 150:34
  F 15 '64
Bachmann, G.   Interview.   Nation 198:542 My 25 '64
Bachmann, G.   The new Italian films.   Nation 198:540
  My 25 '64
Ermanno Olmi, a conversation with John Francis Lane.
  Sight & Sound 39-3:148 Sum '70
Filmography.   Monogram 2:19 Sum '71
Walsh, M.   Ermanno Olmi.   Monogram 2:25 Sum '71

O'NEILL, PATRICK
Swarthout, M.   Interview; filmog.   Film Culture 53/54/
  55:126 Spg '72

OPHULS, MAX
Koval, F.   Interview.   Sight & Sound 19-5:192 Jl '50
Archer, E.   Ophuls and the romantic tradition.   Yale
  French Studies 17:3 '56
Obit.   N. Y. Times p31 Mr 27 '58
Mason, J.; Matras, C.; Natanson, J.; Ustinov, P.   Max
  Ophuls.   Sight & Sound 27-1:49 Sum '57
Sarris, A.   Pantheon directors; filmog.   Film Culture
  28:2 Spg '63
Olmi, E.   My experience.   Cahiers (Eng) 1:63 Ja '66
Gilliatt, P.   Current cinema.   New Yorker 45:137 My 3
  '69
Schickel, R.   Artist risking all, a film to remember.
  Life 66:9 My 23 '69
Williams, F.   The mastery of movement; an appreciation.
  Film Comment 5-4:71 Win '69
Koch, H.   Script to screen with Max Ophuls.   Film
  Comment 6-4:40 Win '70/71
Henderson, B.   The long take.   Film Comment 7-2:6
  Sum '71
Sarris, A.   Max Ophuls; filmog.   Film Comment 7-2:57
  Sum '71

ORLOFF, JOHN
Gelman, M.   Hollywood's young lions.   Television 24:21
  Jl '67

OSHIMA, NAGISA
  Iwabutchi, M.  Japanese cinema 1961.  Film Culture
    24:85 Spg '62
  Cameron, I.  Interview; filmog.  Movie 17:7 Win '69/70
  Oshima.  Film 58:4 Spg '70
  Johnston, C.  Director of the year; filmog.  International
    Film G 8:39 '71

OSWALD, GERD
  Sarris, A.  Esoterica; filmog.  Film Culture 28:22
    Spg '63
  Nolan, J. E.  Films on TV.  Films In Review 19-3:164
    Mr '68
  Greenberg, J.  Additional filmog.  Films In Review
    19-6:386 Je/Jl '68

OSWALD, RICHARD
  Luft, H. G.  Richard Oswald.  Films In Review 9-8:443
    O '58
  Tozzi, R.  Richard Oswald; letter.  Films In Review
    11-6:379 Je/Jl '60

OTERO, MANUEL
  Granja, V.  Interview.  CTVD 6-2:29 Win '68/69

OTTO, HENRY
  Obit.  N. Y. Times p19 Ag 5 '52

OWEN, CLIFF
  British cinema filmography.  Film 65:10 Spg '72

OWEN, DON
  Adrift in a sea of mud.  Take One 1-6:4 n. d.

OZEROV, YURI
  The coming of the Russians.  Action 6-2:4 Mr/Ap '71
  The Russians are here.  Making Films 5-3:10 Je '71

OZU, YASUJIRO
  Richie, D.  The later films of Yasujiro Ozu.  Film Q
    13-1:18 Fall '59
  Yasujiro Ozu; filmog.  Film 36:8 Sum '63
  Richie, D.  The face of '63--Japan.  Films & Filming
    9-10:15 Jl '63
  Milne, T.  Flavour of green tea over rice.  Sight &
    Sound 32-4:182 Aut '63
  Richie, D.  The syntax of his films.  Film Q 17-2:11
    Win '63/64

Hatch, R.   Family of Ozu.   Nation 198:638 Je 22 '64
Ryu, C.   Yasujiro Ozu.   Sight & Sound 33:92 Spg '64
Note.   International Film G 2:35 '65
Ozu, Y.   Abusing the star system.   Cinema (BH) 6-1:8
    '70
A talk with Ozu; interview.   Cinema (BH) 6-1:7 '70
Schrader, P.   Ozu spectrum.   Cinema (BH) 6-1:2 '70
Ryu, C.   Ozu.   Cinema (BH) 6-1:6 '70
Ozu on Ozu; interview.   Cinema (BH) 6-1:3 '70
Richie, D.   A biographical filmography.   Film Comment
    7-1:4 Spg '71
Zeman, M.   The zen artistry of Ozu; filmog. & bibli-
    ography.   Film Journal 1-3/4:62 Fall/Win '72

PABST, G. W.   (George Wilhelm)
  Potamkin, H. A.   A review of his work.   Creative Art
    9:74 Jl '31
  Orme, M.   A screen psychologist.   London News 180:398
    Mr 12 '32
  Birrell, F.   Famous directors.   New Statesman 4:833
    D 24 '32
  Rotha, P.   Pabst, Pudovkin and the producers.   Sight &
    Sound 2-6:50 Sum '33
  Pabst, G. W.   Censor the censor!   Sight & Sound 7-28:
    149 Win '38/39
  Kracauer, S.   Analysis of Pabst.   Sight & Sound 16-61:
    21 Spg '47
  Sarris, A.   Beyond the fringe.   Film Culture 28:29 Spg
    '63
  Luft, H. G.   G. W. Pabst; filmog.   Films In Review
    15-2:93 F '64
  Brooks, L.   Pabst and Lulu.   Sight & Sound 34-3:123
    Sum '65
  Paul Rotha on Pabst.   Films & Filming 13-5:66 F '67
  Luft, H. G.   G. W. Pabst.   Films & Filming 13-7:18
    Ap '67
  Obit.   N. Y.   Times p43 My 31 '67
    Screen World 19:237 '68
    Sight & Sound 36:209 Aut '67
    Time 89:96 Je 9 '67
  Eisner, L.   Meetings with Pabst.   Sight & Sound 36-4:
    209 Aut '67
  Luft, H. G.   G. W. Pabst.   Cinema (BH) 3-6:14 Win '67
  Stuart, J.   Working with Pabst.   Silent Pic 8:25 Aut '70
  Brooks, L.   Actors and the Pabst spirit.   Focus On
    Film 8:45 n. d.

PAGNOL, MARCEL
  Rx for Hollywood.   N. Y. Times Mag p37 N 21 '48
  Alpert, H.   Homage a Pagnol.   Sat R 38:27 D 24 '55
  Biography.   Current Biography 17:45 Mr '56
    Same.   Current Biography Yearbook 1956:477 '57
  Ford, C.   Marcel Pagnol; filmog.   Films In Review
    21-4:197 Ap '70
  Nolan, J. E.   Letter.   Films In Review 21-5:316 My '70

PAINLEVÉ, JEAN
  Maddison, J.   The world of Jean Painleve.   Sight &

Sound 19-6:249 Ag '50

PAKULA, ALAN J.
What directors are saying. Action 5-2:16 Mr/Ap '70
Alan Pakula, Jane Fonda, Klute. Films Illustrated 1-8:4
F '72
Alan Pakula talks to Tom Milne. Sight & Sound 41-2:89
Spg '72

PAKZAD, CYRUS
Schreiber, M. Interview. Todays Filmmaker 2-1:30
Ag '72

PAL, GEORGE
Seton, M. George Pal. Sight & Sound 5-18:13 Sum '36
Work of George Pal. Castle of Frankenstein 4:52 My '64
Johnson, D. S. The five faces of George Pal. Cinefan-
tastique 1-4:10 Fall '71

PANAMA, NORMAN
Panama, N. Comedy at the crossroads. Films & Filming 8-8:25 My '62
Panama, N. Why directors criticize critics. Action
4-1:13 Ja/F '69

PANDOLFI, VITO
Callenbach, E. Natural exchange. Tulane Drama R
11:137 Fall '66

PANFILOV, GLEB
Vronskaya, J. Recent Russian cinema. Film 62:5
Sum '71

PAPIC, KRSTO
Biographical note. International Film G 8:282 '71

PARAJANOV, SERGE (Paradjanov, Sergei)
Parajanov, S. Shadows of our forgotten ancestors.
Film Comment 5-1:39 Fall '68
Parajanov, S. Perpetual motion. Film Comment 5-1:40
Fall '68

PARK, IDA MAY
Denton, F. Lights! Camera! Quiet! Ready! Shoot!
Photoplay 13-3:48 F '18

## PARKER, ALBERT

Shannon, B. Interview. Photoplay 18:92 Je '20
Redway, S. Wants more adventure and fewer sex dramas on the screen. Motion Pic 31:26 Je '26

## PARKS, GORDON

Freedom's fearful foe. Life 50:86 Je 16 '61
Anniversary portfolio. Popular Photo 50:69 My '62
What their cry means to me. Life 54:31 My 31 '63
Subdued light for color beauty. U. S. Camera 26:66 Je '63
How it feels to be black. Life 55:72 Ag 16 '63
Long search for pride. Life 55:80 Ag 16 '63
Paris. Life 56:62 Ap 10 '64
Flight over Africa. Vogue 144:8 Jl '64
I was a zombie then; like all Muslims, I was hypnotized. Life 58:28 Mr 5 '65
I make my choice of weapons; excerpt from Choice of weapons. Life 60:62 Ja 28 '66
Through a lens darkly. Newsweek 67:86 F 7 '66
Yoder, E. M. Jr. No catch for the hawk. Sat R 49:40 F 12 '66
Armed with a camera. Time 87:102 F 18 '66
Stackpole, P. Camera as a sociological weapon. U. S. Camera 29:16 My '66
Redemption of a champion. Life 61:76 S 9 '66
Bodyguard of young cats. Life 62:76B My 19 '67
Harlem family. Life 64:48 Mr 8; 23 Mr 29 '68
The weapons of Gordon Parks. Sightlines 1-4:28 Mr/Ap '68
Man who tried to love somebody. Life 64:29 Ap 19 '68
Heller, F. Color-blind camera. Newsweek 71:84 Ap 29 '68
Interview. Mademoiselle 67:367 Ag '68
Biography. Current Biography 29:33 O '68
Same. Current Biography Yearbook 1968:300 '69
Moore, G. Return of the prodigy. Life 65:116 N 15 '68
Moore, G. Suddenly doors open. Life 65:123 N 15 '68
Cherry, R. The many worlds of Gordon Parks. Action 4-2:12 My/Ap '69
Morgenstern, J. Boy's life. Newsweek 74:74 Ag 11 '69
What directors are saying. Action 4-5:32 S/O '69
What directors are saying. Action 6-4:20 Jl/Ag '71
The professional director speaks. Making Films 5-4:40 Ag '71
Gordon Parks, director of Shaft. Making Films 5-4:42 Ag '71

Brown, R.  Shooting Shaft; photos.  Todays Filmmaker
1-1:48 Ag '71
Gordon Parks directing second Shaft film.  Making Films
6-2:40 Ap/My '72
Thomas, B.  A talk with Gordon Parks.  Action 7-4:15
Jl/Ag '72
Eyles, A.  Biographical sketch.  Focus On Film 8:7 n. d.

PARRISH, ROBERT
Sarris, A.  Minor disappointments; filmog.  Film Culture
28:41 Spg '63

PARRY, GORDON
British feature directors; an index to their work.  Sight
& Sound 27-6:300 Aut '58

PASCAL, GABRIEL
Condon, F.  Shaw man.  Colliers 103:48 Ap 29 '39
Sketch.  Fortune 19:170 Ap '39
Watts, S.  Promoter of Pygmalion.  Living Age 356:245
My '39
Biographical note; filmog.  Movies & People 2:45 '40
Shaw's disciple.  New Yorker 17:12 My 31 '41
Biography.  Current Biography '42
Jacobson, S.  Androcles in Hollywood.  Theatre Arts
36:66 D '52
Obit.  Americana Annual 1955:574 '55
Current Biography 15:59 S '54
Current Biography Yearbook 1954:501 '54
Illustrated London N 255:109 Jl 17 '54
N. Y.  Times p31 Jl 7 '54
Newsweek 44:61 Jl 19 '54
Screen World 6:224 '55
Time 65:66 Jl 19 '54
Delacorte, V.  G. B. Shaw in filmland.  Esquire 62:150
D '64

PASINETTI, FRANCESCO
Obit.  N. Y.  Times p23 Ap 4 '49

PASOLINI, PIER PAOLO
Lane, J. F.  The triumph of Italy's realism.  Films &
Filming 8-3:38 D '61
Murray, W.  Letter from Rome.  New Yorker 38:167
Ap 21 '62
Pasolini, P. P.  Cinematic and literary stylistic figures.
Film Culture 24:42 Spg '62

Renton, B.   No joy for Pasolini.   New Statesman 64:769
    N 30 '62
Lane, J. F.   The face of '63--Italy.   Films & Filming
    9-7:11 Ap '63
Pasolini queried.   CTVD 3-2:12 Win '64
Pasolini--an epical-religious view of the world.   Film Q
    18-4:31 Sum '65
Kumlien, G. D.   Marxist's Christ.   Commonweal 82:471
    Jl 2 '65
Pier Paolo Pasolini and the art of directing.   Film Com-
    ment 3-4:20 Fall '65
Blue, J.   Interview.   Film Comment 3-4:25 Fall '65
Walsh, M.   Gospel according to St. Matthew.   America
    114:307 F 26 '66
Kauffmann, S.   Pasolini's passion.   New Republic 154:33
    Mr 22 '66
Press conference New York film festival, 1966.   Film
    Culture 42:101 Fall '66
Bragin, J.   A conversation in Rome, June 1966.   Film
    Culture 42:102 Fall '66
Pasolini, P. P.   The cinema of poetry.   Cahiers (Eng)
    6:34 D '66
Kauffmann, S.   Poet and the pimp.   New Republic 158:
    22 Ap 6 '68
Gervais, M.   Pier Paolo Pasolini.   Sight & Sound 38-1:2
    Win '68/69
Grazzini, G.   Falling in live with Eros--that's the hell
    of it.   Atlas 17:60 Ja '69
Berry, L. J.   According to Pasolini.   Commonweal
    89:706 Mr 7 '69
Pasolini's Teorema.   America 120:518 My 3 '69
Pasolini: rebellion, art and a new society.   Screen
    10-3:19 My/Je '69
Wallington, M.   Pasolini: structuarlism and semiology.
    Cinema (Lon) 3:5 Je '69
Buckley, J.   An ancient woman.   Opera News 34:8 D 13
    '69
Biography.   Current Biography 31:36 Jl '70
    Same.   Current Biography Yearbook 1970:345 '71
Cruck, P.   Pasolini: philosophy of cinema.   Cinema
    (Lon) 6/7:13 Ag '70
Purdon, N.   Pasolini: the film of alienation.   Cinema
    (Lon) 6/7:14 Ag '70
Director of the year; filmog.   International Film G p31
    '70
Armes, R.   Pasolini.   Films & Filming 17-9:55 Je '71
Elsaesser, T.   Eric Rohmer vs. Pasolini.   Monogram 2:6
    Sum '71

Ingrid Thulin comments on Pasolini. Dialogue on Film
3:16 '72

PASSER, IVAN
Gerard, L. N. A quiet day in Czechoslovakia. Film
Library Q 4-4:18 Fall '71
What directors are saying. Action 7-1:36 Ja/F '72

PATRICK, NIGEL
Filmography. Film 14:8 N/D '57

PATTON, RICHARD
Listing of films. Film Culture 37:7 Sum '65

PAVLOVIĆ, ŽIVOJIN
Biographical note. International Film G 5:169 '68

PEARSON, GEORGE
Honri, B. George Pearson remembered. Silent Pic
2:3 Spg '69
Dickinson, T. Working with Pearson. Silent Pic 2:5
Spg '69
Balcon, M. One professional survivor to another. Silent
Pic 2:8 Spg '69
George Pearson: the man, his art. Silent Pic 2:15 Spg
'69

PECKINPAH, SAM
Sarris, A. Oddities and one shots. Film Culture 28:45
Spg '63
Wanted: Sam Peckinpah; interview. Cinema (BH) 1-4:5
Je/Jl '63
Silke, J. R. War: a film critic's first hand report on
the making of Sam Peckinpah's Major Dundee. Cinema
(BH) 2-3:4 O/N '64
Callenbach, E. A conversation with Sam Peckinpah.
Film Q 17-2:3 Win '63/64
Madsen, A. Pin from the cold. Sight & Sound 36-3:123
Sum '67
McArthur, C. Sam Peckinpah's West. Sight & Sound
36-4:180 Aut '67
Medjuck, J. Sam Peckinpah lets it all hang out. Take
One 2-3:18 Ja/F '69
Man and myth. Time 93:85 Je 20 '69
Farber, S. Peckinpah's return. Film Q 23-1:2 Fall '69
Whitehall, R. Talking with Peckinpah. Sight & Sound
38-4:172 Aut '69

Schrader, P.  Sam Peckinpah going to Mexico.  Cinema
    (BH) 5-3:18 Fall '69
What directors are saying.  Action 4-5:32 S/O '69
Cutts, J.  Shoot! Interview.  Films & Filming 16-1:4
    O '69
McCarty, J. A.  Sam Peckinpah and The wild bunch.
    Film Heritage 5-2:1 Win 69/70
Knight, A.  Unkindest cut.  Sat R 53:42 Ap 11 '70
Reisner, J & Kane, B.  Sam Peckinpah.  Action 5-3:24
    My/Je '70
Brackman, J.  Films.  Esquire 73:68 Je '70
Moss, R. F.  Peckinpah's ballad.  Film Heritage 6-3:15
    Spg '71
Yergin, D.  Peckinpah's progress.  N. Y. Times Mag p16
    O 31 '71
    Same.  N. Y. Times Bio Ed O 31 '71
What directors are saying.  Action 7-1:36 Ja/F '72
Charlton Heston comments on Peckinpah.  Dialogue on
    Film 1:10 '72
Blevins, W.  The artistic vision of Sam Peckinpah. Show
    2-1:37 Mr '72
Interview.  Playboy 19-8:65 Ag '72


PÉLISSIER, ANTHONY
    Filmography.  Film 14:8 N/D '57


PENN, ARTHUR
    New successes.  Vogue 125:171 F 1 '55
    Brothers Penn.  Vogue 140:186 S 1 '62
    Brower, B.  Untheatrical director takes the stage. N. Y.
        Times Mag p32 My 20 '62
    Sarris, A.  Esoterica; filmog.  Film Culture 28:22 Spg
        '63
    Towne, R.  A trip with Bonnie and Clyde.  Cinema (BH)
        3-5:4 Sum '67
    Penn, A.  Attention Harlan Ellison; letter.  Cinema (BH)
        3-2:32 Sum '67
    Interview.  Cinema (BH) 3-5:11 Sum '67
    Medjuck, J.  Penn; interview.  Take One 2-1:6 S/O '68
    Heller, J.  Arthur Hill.  Screen 10-1:5 Ja/F '69
    Bolas, T.  The left handed gun of Arthur Penn.  Screen
        10-1:15 Ja/F '69
    Stickney, J.  Alice's family of folk song fame becomes a
        family.  Life 66:43 Mr 28 '69
    Van Der Bergh, L.  Alice's restaurant.  Sight & Sound
        38-2:66 Spg '69
    Lindsay, M.  Interview.  Cinema (BH) 5-3:32 Fall '69

What directors are saying.   Action 4-5:32 S/O '69

Weinraub, B.   Director Arthur Penn takes on General
    Custer.   N. Y. Times Mag p10 D 21 '69

Director of the year; filmog.   International Film G 6:21
    '69

What directors are saying.   Action 5-2:16 Mr/Ap '70

Wood, P.   Arthur Penn in Canada; interview.   Movie
    18:26 Win '70/71

Kael, P.   Current cinema.   New Yorker 46:50 D 26 '70

Salute of the week.   Cue 40-2:1 Ja 9 '71

What directors are saying.   Action 6-3:28 My/Je '71

Milne, T.   Biographical note; filmog.   Focus On Film
    6:6 Spg '71

Gow, G.   Metaphor; interview; filmog.   Films & Filming
    17-10:17 Jl '71

The professional director speaks.   Making Films 5-4:40
    Ag '71

Fisher, J.   Savage child and grieving witness; myth and
    vision in Arthur Penn's films.   Contempora 2-2:34 Mr/Jl '72

Penn, A.   Bonnie and Clyde, private morality and public
    violence.   Take One 1-6:20 n. d.

Bell, W.   Arthur Penn directing films and plays.   Mise-
    En-Scene 1:62 n. d.


PENNEBAKER, DONN ALAN
    Survey among unsuccessful applicants for the Ford
        Foundation film grants.   Film Comment 2-3:10 Sum '64
    Christgau, R.   The MGM of the underground.   Show
        1-1:34 Ja '70


PEREIRA, WILLIAM LEONARD
    William the conqueror swings a double-edged career of
        blueprints and movie film.   Architectural Forum
        85:114 S '46
    Architect of success.   Time 48:94 O 14 '46


PERIES, LESTER
    Peries, L.   A filmmaker in Ceylon.   Sight & Sound
        27-2:99 Aut '57


PERRAULT, PIERRE
    La Rochelle, R. & Maggi, G.   Political situation of
        Quebec cinema.   Cineaste 5-3:7 Sum '72


PERRY, FRANK
    Hard way.   Time 81:59 Ja 25 '63
    Bayer, W.   Interview.   Film Comment 1-5:15 Sum '63

Small  stars  spoof  the  boss.    Life  55:133  O  4  '63
Hammel,  F.    Filmmakers  at  home.    Cue  32-51:11  D  21
   '63
Boeth,  R.    New  face,  old  pro.    Sat  R  46:21  D  28  '63
Salute  of  the  week.    Cue  38-34:1  Ag  23  '69
Nirenberg,  S.    Collaboration  also  sets  the  scene  at
   home.    House  Beautiful  112:72  Ag  '70
People  are  talking  about.    Vogue  156:374  S  1  '70
Guerin,  A.    Play  it  as  it  lays--from  novel  to  film;  in-
   terview.    Show  2-8:32  N  '72


PERRY,  WILLIS  II
Conversations  with  myself;  filmog.    Sightlines  4-3:7
   Ja/F  '71


PERSON,  LUIS  SERGIO
Viany,  A.    Who's  who  in  the  cinema  novo.    CTVD  6-1:26
   Fall  '68


PETERSON,  SIDNEY
Peterson,  S.    A  note  on  comedy  in  experimental  film;
   filmog.    Film  Culture  29:27  Sum  '63
Tyler,  P.    Sidney  Peterson.    Film  Culture  19:38  n. d.


PETRI,  ELIO
Lane,  J.  F.    The  face  of  '63--Italy.    Films  &  Filming
   9-7:11  Ap  '63


PETROVIC,  ALEKSANDAR
Biographical  note.    International  Film  G  6:191  '69


PEVNEY,  JOSEPH
The  director  and  the  public;  a  symposium.    Film  Culture
   1-2:15  Mr/Ap  '55


PICHEL,  IRVING
Service,  F.    Sketch.    Movie  Classic  2:26  Mr  '32
Sketch.    Photoplay  46:45  Jl  '34
Pichel,  I.    Creativeness  cannot  be  diffused.    Hollywood
   Q  1-1:20  O  '45
Pichel,  I.    Seeing  with  the  camera.    Hollywood  Q  1-2:138
   Ja  '46
Pichel,  I.    Character,  personality,  and  image;  a  note  on
   screen  acting.    Hollywood  Q  2-1:25  O  '46
Pichel,  I.    Areas  of  silence.    Hollywood  Q  3-1:51  Fall
   '47
Service,  F.  Modern  Pied  Piper.  Silver  Screen  17-4:53  F  '47

Pichel, I.   Stills in motion.   Hollywood Q 5-1:8 Fall '50
Pichel, I.   A long rope.   Hollywood Q 3-4:416 Sum '48
Pichel, I.   Crisis and incantation.   Hollywood Q 5-3:213
    Spg '51
Pichel, I.   Films for television.   Hollywood Q 5-4:363
    Sum '51
Pichel, I.   In defense of virtuosity.   Q Film Radio TV
    6-3:228 Spg '51
Pichel, I.   Revivals, reissues, remakes and A place in
    the sun.   Q Film Radio TV 6-4:388 Sum '51
Pichel, I.   Martin Luther; the problem of documentation.
    Q Film Radio TV 8-2:172 Win '53
Pichel, I.   College courses on filmmaking.   Films In Re-
    view 4-10:523 D '53
Obit.   N. Y. Times p27 Jl 14 '54
    Screen World 6:225 '55
    Time 64:75 Jl 26 '54
Luft, H. G.   Irving Pichel; letter.   Films In Review
    5-8:442 O '54
MacGowan, K.; Seldes, G.; Hume, S. J.; Brown, G.;
    Glass, E.; Moise, N.; Muni, P.; Nichols, D.; von
    Sternberg, J.; Sproul, R. C.; Freud, R.   Irving
    Pichel (1891-1954) Wonderful to have had you with us.
    Q Film Radio TV 9-2:109 Win '54


PIERSON, FRANK R.
    What directors are saying.   Action 4-6:28 N/D '69


PIKE, ROBERT
    Pike, R.   The growth of independent filmmaking.   Film-
    makers Newsletter 4-9/10:26 Jl/Ag '71


PINE, WILLIAM HOY
    Show business; Pine-Thomas pictures.   Time 46:82
        Ag 6 '45
    English, R.   Gaudiest producers in Hollywood.   Sat
        Evening Post 225:22 Ja 3 '53
    Obit.   N. Y. Times p17 Ap 30 '55


PINTOFF, ERNEST
    Who da hell is dot?   Newsweek 62:79 S 2 '63
    Weinberg, G.   Interview.   Film Culture 31:54 Win '63/64
    Macdonald, D.   Complete works of Ernest Pintoff.
        Esquire 61:16 Ap '64
    Innocent fireman.   Newsweek 63:110 My 25 '64
    Selby, S. A.   Ernest Pintoff, fireman; filmog.   Film
        Comment 2-3:4 Sum '64

Wild, wild East.　Newsweek 65:58 Je 21 '65
Weinberg, G.　The 6th Montreal film festival.　Film
　Heritage 1-2:35 Win '65/66

## PIRÈS, GÉRARD
Eyles, A.　Gerard Pires; filmog.　Focus On Film 4:9
　S/O '70

## PIRES, ROBERTO
Viany, A.　Who's who in the cinema novo.　CTVD 6-1:26
　Fall '68

## PLATTS-MILLS, BARNEY
British cinema filmography.　Film 65:10 Spg '72
Elsaesser, T.　Interview.　Monogram 3:39 '72

## PÖHLAND, HANSJÜRGEN
Mclean, K.　Hansjurgen Pohland.　Film 35:15 Spg '63
Bean, R.　The face of '63--Germany.　Films & Filming
　9-9:41 Je '63
Three enterprising filmmakers.　International Film G 1:96
　'64

## POLAC, MICHEL
Interview.　CTVD 8-1(29):11 Spg '71

## POLANSKI, ROMAN
Weinberg, G.　Interview.　Sight & Sound 33:32 Win '63
Alpert, H.　Headstrong directors.　Sat R 48:63 O 16 '65
Bucher, F.　Questions to Roman Polanski.　Camera
　45:50 Mr '66
On the scene.　Playboy 13-10:162 O '66
Kahan, S.　Transylvania: Polanski style.　Cinema (BH)
　3-4:7 D '66
Delahaye, M. & Fieschi, J-A.　Interview.　Cahiers
　(Eng) 3:29 '66
Lerman, L.　International movie report.　Mademoiselle
　64:119 F '67
Directors of the year; filmog.　International Film G 4:22
　'67
Gilliatt, P.　Current cinema. New Yorker 44:87 Je 15 '68
Hamilton, J.　Rosemary's baby.　Look 32:91 Je 25 '68
Engle, H.　Roman Polanski in New York; interview.
　Film Comment 5-1:14 Fall '68
Polanski biography; filmog.　Film Comment 5-1:10 Fall
　'68
McArthur, C.　Polanski.　Sight & Sound 38-1:14 Win '68/69

Ross, T. J.   Roman Polanski, Repulsion and the new
   mythology.   Film Heritage 4-2:1 Win '68/69
Gow, G.   Satisfaction--a most unpleasant feeling.   Films
   & Filming 15-7:15 Ap '69
McCarty, J. A.   The Polanski puzzle.   Take One 2-5:18
   My/Je '69
Nairn, T.   Roman Polanski; filmog.   Cinema (Lon) 3:22
   Je '69
Biography.   Current Biography 30:39 Je '69
   Same.   Current Biography Yearbook 1969:347 '70
Nothing but bodies.   Time 94:24 Ag 15 '69
Hollywood murders.   Newsweek 74:28 Ag 18 '69
Night of horror.   Time 94:16 Ag 22 '69
Tate set.   Newsweek 74:24 Ag 25 '69
Thompson, T.   Tragic trip to the house on a hill.   Life
   67:42 Ag 29 '69
Reisner, J. & Kane, B.   Interview.   Cinema (BH) 5-2:11
   Sum '69
Interview.   Cinema (BH) 5-2:10 Sum '69
Macbeth by daylight.   Time 97:45 Ja 25 '71
Cook, J. & Canham, K.   Interview.   Film Society R
   6-8:36 Ap '71
Freud, C.   An odyssey in Wales; Roman Polanski's
   Macbeth.   Show 2-4:24 Je '71
Vronskaya, J.   Polanski's Macbeth and its antecedents.
   Film 62:23 Sum '71
Weinraub, B.   If you don't show violence the way it is,
   says Roman Polanski, I think that's immoral and
   harmful.   N. Y. Times Mag p36 D 12 '71
   Same.   N. Y. Times Bio Ed D 12 '71
What directors are saying.   Action 7-1:36 Ja/F '72
The making of Macbeth.   Playboy 19-2:77 F '72
British cinema filmography.   Film 65:10 Spg '72

POLLACK, SYDNEY
   Harmetz, A.   Sydney didn't want to shoot "Horses" N. Y.
      Times Bio Ed Mr 8 '70
   Eyles, A.   Biographical note; filmog.   Focus On Film
      3:5 My/Ag '70

POLLARD, HARRY
   Barry, R. H.   Harry Pollard: writer, director, actor.
      Photoplay 6-1:80 Je '14
   How he became a photoplayer.   Motion Pic 9:111 F '15

POLLET, JEAN-DANIEL
   Billard, G.   The men and their work.   Films & Filming
      6-1:7 O '59

Meeting La nouvelle vague; conversation.   Films &
  Filming 6-1:7 O '59


POLONSKY, ABRAHAM
  Polonsky, A.   The case of David Smith.   Hollywood Q
    1-2:185 Ja '46
  Pechter, W.   Abraham Polonsky and Force of evil.
    Film Q 15-3:47 Spg '62
  Sarris, A.   Oddities and one shots.   Film Culture 28:45
    Spg '63
  Pechter, W.   Parts of some times spent with Abraham
    Polonsky.   Film Q 22:14 Win '68/69
  Nolan, J. E.   Films on TV; TV filmog.   Films In Re-
    view 20-4:241 Ap '69
  Wolf, W.   Abraham Polonsky; a voice from the past with
    talent for the present.   Cue 38-52:7 D 27 '69
  Canham, K.   Polonsky; back into the light; filmog.   Film
    58:12 Spg '70
  Polonsky, A.   How the blacklist worked in Hollywood.
    Film Comment 50/51:41 Fall/Win '70
  Filmography.   Film Comment 50/51:49 Fall/Win '70/71
  Polonsky, A.   Making movies.   Sight & Sound 40-2:101
    Spg '71


PONTECORVO, GILLO
  Lane, J. F.   Is Marlon Brando really necessary?   Show
    1-1:46 Ja '70
  Mellen, J.   Interview.   Film Q 26-1:2 Fall '72


POOLE, WAKEFIELD
  Buckley, P.   A dirty movie is a dirty movie is a dirty
    movie is a....   Films & Filming 18-11:27 Ag '72


PORTER, EDWIN S.
  Obit.   Current Biography '41
  Sadoul, G.   English influences on the work of E. S.
    Porter.   Hollywood Q 3-1:41 Fall '47
  Drum, D.   Porter and Griffith.   Films In Review 7-3:
    138 Mr '56
  Gessner, R.   Moving image.   American Heritage 11:30
    Ap '60
  Spears, J.   ESP.   Films In Review 21-6:327 Je/Jl '70
  Letters.   Films In Review 21-7:447 Ag/S '70


POST, TED
  Winogura, D.   Dialogues on apes, apes and more apes.
    Cinefantastique 2-2:22 Sum '72

POTTER, HENRY C.
  Reed, E.  Roster of new faces.  Theatre Arts 18:59
    Ja '34
  Talmey, A.  Sketch.  Stage 11:21 Jl '34
  Stage to film.  Action 3-5:12 S/O '68
  Hollywood haywire.  Film Fan Mo 133/134:43 Jl/Ag '72

POWELL, DICK
  Sketch.  Motion Pic 44:42 O '32
  Sketch.  Photoplay 42:70 N '32
  Manners, D.  Sketch.  Motion Pic 44:58 D '32
  Manners, D.  Interview.  Motion Pic 46:56 O '33
  Gwin, J.  All good but the feet.  Silver Screen 3-12:29
    O '33
  Sketch.  Photoplay 45:87 Mr '34
  Harper, S.  Would you girls marry Dick Powell?  Photo-
    play 46-1:48 Je '34
  Harrison, H.  Interview.  Movie Classic 7:42 Ja '35
  Tully, J.  Biographical sketch.  Movie Classic 8:32 My
    '35
  Sher, J. J.  Interview.  Motion Pic 49:30 Jl '35
  English, R.  Interview.  Movie Classic 9:32 N '35
  Mook, D.  Story of.  Motion Pic 51:41 F '36
  Dick Powell as a host.  Photoplay 49:78 Ap '36
  Anthony, W.  Interview.  Movie Classic 10:35 Ap '36
  Ramsey, W.  Dick Powell admits he's in love.  Photo-
    play 49-5:21 My '36
  Liza.  The eligible heart-breakers.  Silver Screen 6-9:51
    Jl '36
  Ramsey, W.  Dick Powell lost his voice, and discovered
    his soul.  Photoplay 50-1:34 Jl '36
  Reid, J.  Sketch.  Motion Pic 52:38 O '36
  Mook, S. R.  The Dick Powells' honeymoon.  Photoplay
    51-1:21 Ja '37
  McHenry, M.  His love story.  Movie Classic 11:20 Ja
    '37
  Crichton, K.  Double star; story of Dick Powell and
    Joan Blondell.  Colliers 99:22 F 20 '37
  Darnton, C.  In search of his age.  Silver Screen 7-7:32
    My '37
  Mook, D.  I have no regrets.  Screen Book 20-6:32 Jl
    '38
  Wilson, E.  Don't get these Powells wrong.  Silver
    Screen 10-10:26 Ag '40
  Biographical note; filmog.  Movies & People 2:30 '40
  This is Dick Powell.  Lions Roar 3-3:no p# Ap '44
  Pine, D.  Breakup.  Photoplay 24-5:65 Ap '44

Exit Dimples Dick--enter Gumshoe Powell.　Cue 14-9:10
Mr 3 '45

Mook, D.　A star is reborn.　Silver Screen 15-7:50
My '45

Waterbury, R.　They're Mr. and Mrs. Dick Powell.
Photoplay 27-6:32 N '45

St. Johns, E.　Corner on happiness.　Photoplay 28-6:38
My '46

Marsh, P.　Still newlyweds.　Silver Screen 16-8:37 Je '46

Downing, H.　Dick Powell.　Photoplay 32-1:56 D '47

Biography.　Current Biography F '48
Same revised.　Current Biography Yearbook 1948:502
'49

Graham, S.　The A-P puzzle.　Photoplay 34:46 D '48

Allyson, J.　Lady with a past.　Photoplay 36-1:46 Je '49

Powell, D.　Mr. and Mrs. Mike.　Photoplay 36-4:50
S '49

Dreier, H.　Welcome home.　Photoplay 37-5:60 My '50

Powell, D.　I never had so much fun.　Silver Screen
20-8:30 Je '50

Arnold, M.　The best years of our lives.　Photoplay
38-1:44 Jl '50

Arnold, M.　The happy heart.　Photoplay 38-5:36 N '50

Engstead, J.　I was there.　Photoplay 38-6:36 D '50

Martin, P.　Hollywood's child bride.　Sat Evening Post
223:34 Ja 20 '51

Zeitlin, I.　Hollywood's first family.　Photoplay 40-5:46
N '51

Powell's progress.　Life 34:62 Je 8 '53

Powell, D.　as told to J. Hyams.　Me and the mutiny.
Cue 23-3:14 Ja 16 '54

Backstage mutiny; Caine mutiny courtmartial.　Newsweek
43:83 Ja 25 '54

Voight, R. D.　June Allyson says: Our adopted child
taught us family love.　Womans Home Companion
81:18 F '54

Another project for Powell.　TV Guide 2-40:10 O 2 '53

Ott, B.　Rumor's targets.　Photoplay 48-6:50 D '55

Here comes the heroes.　TV Guide 4-37:28 S 15 '56

Man in the middle.　TV Guide 5-7:4 F 16 '57

Too many bears.　Outdoor Life 119:48 F '57

Harrison, J.　The three weeks we'd like to forget.
Photoplay 52-1:48 Jl '57

Allyson, J.　Let's be frank about me.　Sat Evening Post
230:17 D 14; 20 D 21 '57

Wood, C.　TV personalities biographical sketchbook.　TV
Personalities p121 '57

We start with the character.   TV Guide 7-17:8 Ap 25 '59
Tornabene, L.   Lunch date with Dick Powell.   Cosmop
150:11 Ja '61
Thomas, A.   Dick Powell.   Films In Review 12-5:267
My '61
Roman, R. C.   An index of Dick Powell's films.   Films
In Review 12-5:27 My '61
J. Pierpont Powell.   Time 79:40 Ja 5 '62
Davidson, B.   Deadeye Dick from Little Rock.   TV
Guide 10-12:6 Mr 24; 10-13:22 Mr 31; 10-14:15 Ap 7
'62
Torre, M.   Much-mended marriage of Dick Powell and
June Allyson.   McCalls 89:94 Je '62
James, E. H.   Boss is his brightest star.   Television
19:50 S '62
Obit.   Americana Annual 1964:743 '64
British Book Year 1964:632 '64
Broadcasting 64:74 Ja 7 '63
Current Biography 24:31 F '63
Current Biography Yearbook 1963:343 '64
Illustrated London N 242:63 Ja 12 '63
Newsweek 61:49 Ja 14 '63
Screen World 15:224 '64
Time Ja 11 '63
O'Hara, J.   Egos and actors.   Holiday 40:34 O '66
The love teams.   Screen Greats 1-2:10 Sum '71
Corneau, E.   Dick Powell, the crooner who turned tough
guy.   Classic Film Collector 36:41 Fall '72

POWELL, MICHAEL
Gibbs, P.   An analysis of his work.   World R p60 Ap
'47
Powell, M.   Four powers in waltz time.   Films &
Filming 2-2:5 N '55
Filmography.   Film 14:8 N/D '57
British feature directors; an index to their work.   Sight
& Sound 27-6:300 Aut '58
Green, O. O.   Michael Powell; filmog.   Movie 14:17
Aut '65
Nolan, J. E.   Films on TV.   Films In Review 19-5:303
My '68
Collins, R. & Christie, I.   Interview.   Monogram 3:32
'72

POWELL, PAUL MAHLON
Biographical note.   Photoplay 9-4:42 My '16
Biography.   National Cylopaedia 33:340 '47

POWERS, BILLY
  Listing of films.  Film Culture 37:7 Sum '65

PRAŽSKÝ, PRĚMYSL
  Dewey, L.  Czechoslovakia; silence into sound.  Film
    60:5 n. d.

PRELORAN, JORGE
  Suber, H.  Jorge Preloran; interview; filmog.  Film
    Comment 7-1:43 Spg '71

PREMINGER, OTTO
  Vallee, W. L.  The villainous Mr. Four-In-One.  Silver
    Screen 13-6:44 Ap '43
  Preminger's inferno.  Newsweek 46:66 D 26 '55
  Hartung, P. T.  Screen.  Commonweal 63:332 D 30 '55
  Set free; auditioning for movie version of Saint Joan.
    New Yorker 32:38 S 22 '56
  Minoff, P.  Search for a saint.  Cue 25-38:12 S 22 '56
  Dragnet for Saint Joan.  Life 41:119 O 29 '56
  Charmer on the set.  Newsweek 49:113 Ap 8 '57
  Bachmann, G.  The impact of television on motion pic-
    tures; interview.  Film Culture 3-2(12):20 '57
  Whitcomb, J.  Bonjour tristesse on location.  Cosmop
    144:76 Mr '58
  Personality of the month.  Films & Filming 4-7:5 Ap '58
  Biography.  Current Biography 20:39 Jl '59
  Same.  Current Biography Yearbook 1959:369 '60
  Preminger, O.  Your taste, my taste ... and the
    censor's.  Films & Filming 6-2:7 N '59
  Peter Baker makes the pilgrimage to Israel to see the
    making of Preminger's Exodus.  Films & Filming
    6-12:28 S '60
  Zunser, J.  Israel reborn on film.  Cue 29-47:13 N 19
    '60
  Whitcomb, J.  Sage of Exodus.  Cosmop 149:12 N '60
  Gehman, R.  Otto Preminger.  Theatre Arts 45:60 Ja '61
  Glinn, A.  How to get along with Otto Preminger.
    Esquire 55:120 Mr '61
  Reid, J. H.  Fabulous saints and sinners.  Films &
    Filming 7-6:31 Mr '61
  Sex and censorship in literature and the arts; discussion.
    Playboy 13:27 Jl '61
  Advise and consent.  Time 78:69 S 29 '61
  The screen answers back.  Films & Filming 8-8:12 My
    '62
  Talk with a moviemaker.  Newsweek 59:100 Je 11 '62

Bunzel, P.	Patriotic movie or not.	Life 53:73 Jl 6 '62
Drury, A.	Based on the novel Advise and consent.
	McCalls 89:12 Jl '62
Why Preminger? (with comments on his films by various
	writers).	Movie 2:11 S '62
Mayersburg, P.	Interview; filmog.	Movie 4:18 N '62
John Huston, actor.	Newsweek 61:102 Mr 18 '63
Fenin, G.	The face of '63--United States.	Films &
	Filming 9-6:55 Mr '63
Sarris, A.	Second line; filmog.	Film Culture 28:11
	Spg '63
Preminger and company.	Show 3-9:88 S '63
Preminger, O.	The cardinal and I.	Films & Filming
	10-2:11 N '63
Silke, J. R.	Three directors in danger; Otto the great.
	Cinema (BH) 1-6:4 N/D '63
Walsh, M.	Otto Preminger looks at the Catholic church.
	Catholic World 198:365 Mr '64
How to rate a critic.	Sat R 47:16 D 26 '64
Lawrenson, H.	Is it true what they say about Otto?
	McCalls 92:106 Mr '65
Preminger, O.	Keeping out of harm's way.	Films &
	Filming 11-9:6 Je '65
Cameron, I.; Shivas, M.; Mayersberg, P.	Otto; inter-
	view.	Movie 13:14 Sum '65
Sarris, A.	Preminger's two periods.	Film Comment
	3-3:12 Sum '65
Ross, L.	Profiles.	New Yorker 41:42 F 19 '66
Meehan, T.	Otto the terrible.	Sat Evening Post 240:26
	Ap 8 '67
Excerpt from statement before Communication subcom-
	mittee, Oct. 10, 1967.	Congressional Digest 46:304
	D '67
Interview.	Focus 3/4:9 '68
Otto Preminger, the New York filmmaker.	Making Films
	5-4:36 Ag '71
Grubman, L.	Such good friends "a unique shot."	Film-
	makers Newsletter 4-12:19 O '71
Not all such good friends.	Films Illustrated 1-11:8 My
	'72
Lyons, D.	Otto Preminger auteur de force.	Interview
	23:14 Jl '72
Noqueira, R.	Writing for the movies; interview with
	Walter Newman.	Focus On Film 11:40 Aut '72
Loney, G. M.	Interview.	Interview 2-3:32 n. d.
Bogdanovich, P.	Interview.	On Film 1-0:37 n. d.

PREOBRASHENSKAIA,  OLGA
(Preobrazhenskaya,  Preobrajenska,  Preobrashenskaya)
Feldman,  J.  &  H.   Women  directors.   Films  In  Review
    1-8:9  N  '50
Tugal,  P.   A  witness  of  a  glorious  past.   Dancing Times
    500:469  My  '52
Clandon,  L.   Olga  Preobrashenskaia  at  86.   Dance 32:48
    F  '58
Pyros,  J.   Notes  on  women  directors.   Take  One  3-2:7
    N/D  '70


PRESSBURGER,  EMERIC
Filmography.   Film  14:8  N/D  '57
British  film  directors;  an  index  to  their  work.   Sight  &
    Sound  27-6:301  Aut  '58


PRESTON,  RICHARD
Preston,  R.   The  deep-frozen  eye  of  God.   Film  Culture
    24:17  Spg  '62
Mekas,  J.   Notes  on  the  new  American  cinema.   Film
    Culture  24:6  Spg  '62
Listing  of  films.   Film  Culture  37:7  Sum  '65


PREVERT,  PIERRE
Taylor,  J.  R.   Surrealist  admen.   Sight  &  Sound  40-4:187
    Aut  '71


PRIVETT,  R.  E.
R.  E.  Privett  considers  Us  and  U. P. A.   Film  4:16  Mr
    '55


PTUSKO,  ALEXANDER
Ptusko,  A.   Stepping  out  of  the  Soviet.   Films  &  Filming
    6-4:29  Ja  '60


PUDOVKIN,  VSEVELOD
Lozowick,  L.   Soviet  cinema.   Theatre  Arts  13:664  S  '29
Seton,  M.   A  conversation  with  Vsevelod  I.  Pudovkin.
    Sight  &  Sound  2-5:13  Spg  '33
Rotha,  P.   Pabst,  Pudovkin  and  the  producers.   Sight  &
    Sound  2-6:50  Sum  '33
Lania,  L.   Films  in  birth.   Living  Age  351:251  N  '36
Pudovkin,  V.   The  global  film.   Hollywood  Q  2-4:327
    Jl  '47
Waddington,  C.  H.   Two  conversations  with  Pudovkin.
    Sight  &  Sound  17-68:159  Win  '48/49
Pudovkin,  V.   Stanislavsky's  system  in  the  cinema.  Sight

& Sound 22-3:115 Ja/Mr '53
Weinberg, H. G.    Vsevelod Pudovkin.    Films In Review
   4-7:325 Ag/S '53
Wright, B.    Homage to Pudovkin.    Sight & Sound 23-2:
   105 O/D '53

PUERILESCU, PIERRE
Tellig, J.    A new name.    Sight & Sound 29-4:172 Aut '60

PUTNAM, MICHAEL
Listing of films.    Film Culture 37:7 Sum '65

PYRIEV, IVAN ALEXANDROVICH
Pyriev, I.    From the book.    Films & Filming 6-8:29
   My '60
Donskoy, M.    While his heart beat; a tribute to Ivan
   Pyriev.    Film Comment 5-1:34 Fall '68

## QUINE, RICHARD

Two babes from Broadway.  Lions Roar 1-5:no p# Ja '42
Stars of tomorrow.  Lions Roar 1-11/12:no p# Jl/Ag '42
Bentley, J.  Out of this dream.  Photoplay 24-3:67 F '44
Parsons, L. O.  Courage is a girl named Susan.
    Photoplay 26-6:28 My '45
Quine, R.  The bravest girl in town.  Photoplay 32-5:38
    Ap '48
Stanbrook, A.  Ya gotta have heart.  Films & Filming
    6-12:6 S '60
Richard Quine.  Film 31:7 Spg '62
Sarris, A.  Minor disappointments; filmog.  Film
    Culture 28:41 Spg '63

## QUITTNER, ROBERT M.

Survey among unsuccessful applicants for the Ford
    Foundation film grants.  Film Comment 2-3:10
    Sum '64

RADEMAKERS, FONS
Talking about people. Film 31:6 Spg '63
Biographical note. International Film G 2:118 '65

RAFELSON, ROBERT (Bob)
Bob Rafelson; interview. New Yorker 46:41 O 24 '70
What directors are saying. Action 6-1:30 Ja/F '71

RANODY, LASZLO
Biographical note. International Film G 4:101 '67

RATOFF, GREGORY
Cohen, H. Praising players of minor importance.
    Cinema Digest 3-6:12 Ap 24 '33
Biographical note; filmog. Movies & People 2:45 '40
Biography. Current Biography '43
Ratoff: the man with the talking stick. Lions Roar 3-2:
    no p# Ja '44
Obit. Americana Annual 1961:848 '61
    British Book Year 1961:519 '61
    Current Biography 22:42 F '61
    Current Biography Yearbook 1961:384 '62
    Illustrated London N 237:1154 D 24 '60
    Newsweek 56:41 D 26 '60
    Opera News 25:34 F 4 '61
    Screen World 12:225 '61
    Time 76:49 D 26 '60

RAVN, JENS
Adams, S. Four Dane directors; interview. CTVD
    7-2:26 Spg '70
Biographical note. International Film G 7:90 '70

RAY, CHARLES
Martin, M. The young and debonair Charles Ray.
    Photoplay 6-5:46 O '14
The biography of Charles Ray. Feature Movie 2-7:44
    Jl 10 '15
O'Hara, K. Ince's new wonder boy. Photoplay 9-2:106
    Ja '16
Obit. Current Biography '44
    Newsweek 22:10 D 6 '43
    Time 42:76 D 6 '43

311

Bodeen, D.   Charles Ray; filmog.   Films In Review
19-9:548 N '68

RAY, NICHOLAS
Ray, N.   Story into script.   Sight & Sound 26-2:70 Aut
'56
Houston, P. & Gillett, J.   Conversations with Nicholas
Ray and Joseph Losey.   Sight & Sound 30-4:182 Aut
'61
The screen answers back.   Films & Filming 8-8:12
My '62
Perkins, V. F.   The cinema of Nicholas Ray; filmog.
Movie 9:4 My '63
Interview.   Movie 9:14 My '63
Sarris, A.   Second line; filmog.   Film Culture 28:11
Spg '63
Gomery, D.   Nicholas Ray's They live by night.   Velvet
Light Trap 5:25 Sum '72
Noqueira, R.   Writing for the movies; interview with
Walter Newman.   Focus on Film 11:43 Aut '72
Canby, V.   Nicholas Ray: still a rebel with a cause.
N. Y. Times sec2:1 S 24 '72

RAY, SATYAJIT
Ray, S.   A long time on the little road.   Sight & Sound
26-4:203 Spg '57
Personality of the month.   Films & Filming 4-3:5 D '57
Gray, H.   The growing edge: Satyajit Ray.   Film Q
12-2:4 Win '58
Ray, S.   Problems of a Bengal filmmaker.   International
Film A 2:50 '58
McVay, D.   The Ray trilogy.   Film 24:20 Mr/Ap '60
Grimes, P.   Indian movie maker who flees escape. N. Y.
Times Mag p42 Je 26 '60
Talk with the director.   Newsweek 56:118 S 26 '60
Biography.   Current Biography 22:41 Mr '61
Same.   Current Biography Yearbook 1961:384 '62
Rhode, E.   Satyajit Ray: a study.   Sight & Sound 30-3:
132 Sum '61
Portrait of a man.   UNESCO Courier 14:5 D '61
Seton, M.   Satyajit Ray at work on his film Kanchenjunga.
Sight & Sound 31-2:73 Spg '62
Malik, A.   Toughs and taxi drivers.   Sight & Sound
31-4:179 Aut '62
Satyajit Ray on himself; interview.   Cinema (BH) 2-6:41
Jl/Ag '65
Malik, A.   Reluctant God.   Sight & Sound 35-1:21 Win '65/66

Stanbrook, A.   The world of Ray.   Films & Filming
   12-2:55 N '65
Director of the year; filmog.   International Film G 2:14
   '65
Hayeem, B.   Satyajit soap operas.   CTVD 4-2:6 Spg '66
Ivory, J.   Music of Satyajit Ray.   American Record G
   32:1109 Ag '66
Ray, S.   Healthy flicker.   Atlas 12:54 O '66
Hrusa, B.   Satyajit Ray; genius behind the man.   Film
   47:8 Win '66
Das Gupta, C.   Ray and Tagore.   Sight & Sound 36-1:30
   Win '66/67
Ray, S.   From film to film; filmog.   Cahiers (Eng) 3:12
   '66
Maestro.   New Yorker 43:25 Jl 22 '67
Malik, A.   Satyajit Ray and The alien.   Sight & Sound
   37-1:20 Win '67/68
Blue, J.   I have the whole thing in my head at all
   times--the whole sweep of the film; interview; filmog.
   Film Comment 4-4:4 Sum '68
Raha, K.   Lethal Ray.   Atlas 15:54 F '68
Taper, B.   At home in Calcutta.   Harper 239:40 D '69
Mehta, V.   Profiles.   New Yorker 46:87 Mr 21 '70
Isaksson, F.   Conversation with Satyajit Ray.   Sight &
   Sound 39-3:114 Sum '70
Pechter, W. S.   India's Chekhov.   Commonweal 93:71
   O 16 '70
The Oriental master.   Film 57:7 Win '70

RAYMOND, JACK
   Obit.   N. Y. Times p17 Mr 21 '53

RAYNS, TOM
   Dawson, J. & Johnston, C.   More British sound.   Sight
   & Sound 39-3:144 Sum '70

READ, JOHN
   Hayman, P.   Art films of John Read.   Sight & Sound
   26-4:216 Spg '57
   Read, J.   The film on art as documentary; filmog.
   Film Culture 3-3(13):6 O '57

REED, CAROL
   Goodman, E.   Carol Reed.   Theatre Arts 31:57 My '47
   Breit, H.   I give the public what I like.   N. Y. Times
   Mag p18 Ja 15 '50
   Biography.   Current Biography 11:40 Mr '50

Same. Current Biography Yearbook 1950:480 '51

Sarris, A. Carol Reed in the context of his time. Film Culture 2-4(10):14 '56; 3-1(11):11 '57

Sarris, A. First of the realists. Films & Filming 3-12:9 S '57

Sarris, A. The stylist goes to Hollywood. Films & Filming 4-1:11 O '57

Filmography. Film 14:8 N/D '57

British feature directors; an index to their work. Sight & Sound 27-6:301 Aut '58

Fawcett, M. Sir Carol Reed. Films In Review 10-3:134 Mr '59

Sarris, A. Fallen idols; filmog. Film Culture 28:30 Spg '63

Kael, P. Current cinema. New Yorker 44:193 D 14 '68

British cinema filmography. Film 65:10 Spg '72


REED, LUTHER

Obit. Screen World 13:225 '62


REED, MAX

Obit. N.Y. Times p89 Mr 8 '53


REEVES, MICHAEL

Wood, R. In memoriam: Michael Reeves. Movie 17:2 Win '69/70

British cinema filmography. Film 65:10 Spg '72


REICHENBACH, FRANÇOIS

Biographical note. Unifrance 48:14 O '58

Billard, G. The men and their work. Films & Filming 6-1:7 O '59

Meeting La nouvelle vague; conversation. Films & Filming 6-1:7 O '59

Visual De Tocqueville. Time 76:54 D 19 '60


REICHER, FRANK

Obit. Screen World 17:240 '66


REINER, CARL

Second bananas. Look 17:17 My 5 '53

Wood, C. TV personalities biographical sketch book. TV Personalities p83 '56

New creative writers. Library J 83:489 F 1 '58

Delbier, M. Two TV stars on the printed page. N.Y. Herald Tribune Book R p2 My 4 '58

Biography. Current Biography 22:34 Ap '61

Same.   Current Biography Yearbook 1961:386 '62

View from the lively minority.   Life 53:74 O 19 '62

Kael, P.   Current cinema.   New Yorker 45:190 D 6 '69

Homecoming; interview.   New Yorker 45:47 D 13 '69

The director-actor: a conversation.   Action 5-1:21 Ja/F
    '70

Rob Reiner: I was 21 and ready for the rubber-padded
    room.   TV Guide 20-16:18 Ap 15 '72

Eyles, A. & Billings, P.   Biographical sketch; filmog.
    Focus On Film 8:6 n. d.


REINHARDT, GOTTFRIED
    Ross, L.   Onward and upward with the arts.   New
        Yorker 28:32 My 24; 29 My 31; 32 Je 7; 39 Je 14;
        31 Je 21 '52


REINHARDT, JOHN
    Obit.   N. Y. Times p31 Ag 12 '53


REINIGER, LOTTE
    White, E. W.   Lotte Reiniger and her art.   Horn Book
        15:45 Ja '39
    The films of Lotte Reiniger.   Film Culture 2-3(9):20 '56
    Gelder, P.   Lotte Reiniger, figures in silhouette.   Film
        59:9 Sum '70
    Reiniger, L.   The adventures of Prince Achmed.   Silent
        Pic 8:2 Aut '70


REIS, IRVING
    Obit.   N. Y. Times p11 Jl 4 '53
        Screen World 5:209 '54


REISZ, KAREL
    Seton, M. ; Reisz, K. ; McLeod, L.   Unfair to Eisenstein.
        Sight & Sound 20-2:54 Je '51
    Reisz, K.   Interview with John Huston.   Sight & Sound
        21-3:130 Ja/Mr '52
    Reisz, K.   Hollywood's anti-red boomerang.   Sight &
        Sound 22-3:132 Ja/Mr '53
    Reisz, K.   Stroheim in London.   Sight & Sound 23-4:172
        Ap/Je '54
    Reisz, K.   Experiment at Brussels.   Sight & Sound
        27-5:231 Sum '58
    Reisz, K.   Experiment at Brussels.   International Film
        A 2:131 '58
    Reisz, K.   On the outside looking in.   International Film
        A 3:50 '59

Karel Reisz and experimenters; an exchange of correspondence. Films & Filming 8-3:41 D '61

Cowie, P. The face of '63--Great Britain. Films &
Filming 9-5:19 F '63

How to get into films, by the people who got in themselves. Films & Filming 9-10:11 Jl '63

Desert island films. Films & Filming 9-11:11 Ag '63

Interview. Cinema (BH) 4-2:53 Sum '68

British cinema filmography. Film 65:10 Spg '72


REITZ, EDGAR
Dictionary of young German filmmakers. CTVD 4-2:11
Spg '66


RELPH, MICHAEL
British film directors; an index to their work. Sight &
Sound 27-6:301 Aut '58


RENOIR, JEAN
Renoir, J. Farthingales and facts. Sight & Sound
7-26:51 Sum '38

Plant, R. R. Jean Renoir. Theatre Arts 23:429 Je '39

Note. Harper Bazaar 83:71 Jl '49

Knight, A. Renoir in India. Sat R 34:40 Ag 4 '51

Allison, G. He calls himself a filmmaker. Theatre
Arts 35:18 Ag '51

Hatch, R. Renoir in India. New Republic 125:22 S 10
'51

Renoir on the movies. Coronet 31:14 F '52

Renoir, J. I know where I'm going. Films In Review
3-3:97 Mr '52

Renoir, J. Personal notes. Sight & Sound 21-4:152
Ap/Je '52

My memories of Renoir. Life 32:90 My 19 '52

Rivette, J. & Truffaut, F. Renoir in America. Sight
& Sound 24-1:12 Jl/S '54

Biographical note. Unifrance 32:3 O/N '54

Rivette, J. & Truffaut, F. Renoir in America. Films
In Review 5-9:449 N '54

French can-can. N. Y. Times Mag p39 D 19 '54

The big screens. Sight & Sound 24-4:209 Spg '55

La Chienne. Film 9:8 S/O '56

Garey, H. B.; Beranger, J. Illustrious career of Jean
Renoir. Yale French Studies 17:27 '56

Gow, G. The quest for realism; discussion. Films &
Filming 4-3:13 D '57

Bazin, A. Cinema and television; interview. Sight &

Sound 28-1:26 Win '58/59

Renoir, J.   Devil of the new world.   International Film
    A 2:91 '58

6 films 6 faces.   Unifrance 50:25 Jl/S '59

Bob; a conversation.   Film 21:25 S/O '59

Biography.   Current Biography 20:18 D '59
    Same.   Current Biography Yearbook 1959:381 '60

Roud, R.   The naturalness of Renoir.   International
    Film A 3:105 '59

Whitehall, R.   Painting life with movement.   Films &
    Filming 6-9:13 Je '60

Whitehall, R.   The screen is his canvas.   Films &
    Filming 6-10:29 Jl '60

Dyer, P. J.   Renoir and realism.   Sight & Sound 29-3:
    105 Sum '60

Callenbach, E. & Schuldenfrei, R.   The presence of
    Jean Renoir.   Film Q 14-2:8 Win '60

The French film; discussion.   Film 26:10 N/D '60

Maynard, V.   Rehearsal of Jean Renoir.   Educational
    Theatre J 13:92 My '61

Marcorelles, L.   Conversation with Jean Renoir.   Sight
    & Sound 31-2:78 Spg '62

Renoir; excerpt from Renoir, my father.   Look 26:50
    N 6 '62

Jean Renoir.   Films & Filming 9-2:7 N '62

Children of the famous.   Show 3-2:92 F '63

Sarris, A.   Pantheon directors; filmog.   Film Culture
    28:2 Spg '63

Incident and sequel; excerpt from Renoir, my father.
    Reader Digest 82:55 My '63

Cry of love; excerpt from Renoir, my father.   Reader
    Digest 83:86 Ag '63

Interview.   Cinema (BH) 2-1:12 F/Mr '64

Various.   Jean Renoir: the spirit and the style.   Film
    Journal (Aus) 23:34 Jl '64

Milne, T.   Love in three dimensions.   Sight & Sound
    34-2:71 Spg '65

Nichols, L.   First novelist.   N. Y. Times Book R p8
    O 30 '66

Delahaye, M.   & Fieschi, J-A.   Interview.   Cahiers
    (Eng) 9:41 Mr '67

Joly, J.   Between theater and life.   Film Q 21-2:2
    Win '67/68

Sketch.   Film 51:33 Spg '68

Nogueira, R. & Truchaud, F.   Interview.   Sight &
    Sound 37-2:57 Spg '68

Renoir in London.   Sight & Sound 37-2:60 Spg '68

Millar, D.   The Autumn of Jean Renoir.   Sight & Sound
   37-3:136 Sum '68
Gilliatt, P.   The Current cinema.   New Yorker 44:54
   Ag 31 '68
Gilliatt, P.   Profiles.   New Yorker 45:34 Ag 23 '69
Gilliatt, P.   Leading back to Renoir; Lincoln Center
   festival.   New Yorker 45:96 S 6 '69
What directors are saying.   Action 5-1:28 Ja/F '70
What directors are saying.   Action 5-4:30 Jl/Ag '70
Gilliatt, P.   Current cinema.   New Yorker 46:58 Ag 8
   '70
Sesenski, A.   Renoir, a progress report.   Cinema (BH)
   6-1:16 '70
Diehl, D.   Directors go to their movies; interview.
   Action 7-3:3 My/Je '72
Bachmann, G.   Interview.   Film Journal (Aus) # 7 n. d.
Interview.   Take One 1-7:4 n. d.


RESNAIS, ALAIN
   6 films 6 faces.   Unifrance 50:25 Jl/S '59
   Billard, G.   The men and their work.   Films & Filming
      6-1:7 O '59
   Sadoul, G.   Notes on a new generation.   Sight & Sound
      28-3/4:111 Sum/Aut '59
   Marcorelles, L. ; Colpi, H. ; Roud, R.   Alain Resnais
      and Hiroshima mon amour.   Sight & Sound 29-1:12
      Win '59/60
   Burch, N.   A conversation with Alain Resnais.   Film Q
      13-3:27 Spg '60
   Top drop.   Time 78:76 S 15 '61
   Grenier, C.   Explorations in the unconscious.   Sat R
      44:37 D 23 '61
   Resnais, A.   Trying to understand my own film.   Films
      & Filming 8-5:9 F '62
   All things to all men.   Time 79:56 Mr 16 '62
   Archer, E.   Director of enigmas.   N. Y. Times Mag p54
      Mr 18 '62
   Last words on Last year; discussion with Alain Resnais
      and Alain Robbe-Grillet.   Films & Filming 8-6:39
      Mr '62
   Excerpt from interview with Gideon Bachmann.   Film
      31:19 Spg '62
   Graham, P.   The face of '63--France.   Films & Filming
      9-8:13 My '63
   Cowie, P.   Interview.   International Film G 1:35 '64
   Biography.   Current Biography 26:30 F '65
      Same.   Current Biography Yearbook 1965:339 '65

Jacob, G. & Clouzot, C.   Letter from Paris.   Sight & Sound 34-4:160 Aut '65

Maben, A.   Alain Resnais: the war is over; interview. Films & Filming 13-1:40 O '66

Alpert, H.   Strain of genius.   Sat R 50:55 F 4 '67

Lacassin, F.   Dick Tracy meets Muriel.   Sight & Sound 36-2:101 Spg '67

Roud, R.   Memories of Resnais.   Sight & Sound 38-3:124 Sum '69

Tuten, F.   Films of Alain Resnais.   Vogue 154:24 Jl '69

Armes, R.   Resnais and reality.   Films & Filming 16-8:12 My '70

Ingrid Thulin comments on Resnais.   Dialogue on Film 3:16 '72

RÉVÉSZ, GYÖRGY
Biographical note.   International Film G 2:96 '65

RHODES, NELSON
The rise of a young filmmaker.   Making Films 4-1:32 F '70

RICARDO, SERGIO
Viany, A.   Who's who in the cinema novo.   CTVD 6-1:26 Fall '68

RICE, RON
Mekas, J.   Notes on the new American cinema.   Film Culture 24:6 Spg '62

Rice R.   A statement.   Film Culture 25:71 Sum '62

Rice, R.   Dazendada works.   Film Culture 29:10 Sum '63

Survey among unsuccessful applicants for the Ford Foundation film grants. Film Culture 2-3:10 Sum '64

Listing of films.   Film Culture 37:7 Sum '65

Rice, R.   Diaries, notebooks, scripts, letters, documents.   Film Culture 39:87 Win '65

Weiner, P.   New American cinema; filmog.   Film 58:22 Spg '70

Batten, M.   Ron Rice and his work; interview.   Film Comment 1-3:30 n. d.

RICH, JOHN
Sawyer, P.   John Rich; a biographical sketch.   Theatre A 15:55 '59

Rich, J.   High-flying films are for the birds.   Action 2-1:22 Ja/F '67

All's fair for youth at Expo '70.   Seventeen 29:146 Mr
'70
Kasindorf, M.   Award winner: John Rich.   Action
7-3:12 My/Je '72

## RICHARDS, DICK
I found myself totally alone ... living with my commit-
ments.   Action 7-1:30 Ja/F '72
What directors are saying.   Action 7-3:28 My/Je '72

## RICHARDS, PENNINGTON
Filmography.   Film 14:8 N/D '57

## RICHARDSON, TONY
Richardson, T.   The films of Luis Bunuel.   Sight &
Sound 23-3:125 Ja/Mr '54
Richardson, T.   The metteur en scene.   Silght & Sound
24-2:62 O/D '54
Richardson, T.   London letter.   Film Culture 2-2(8):16
'56
Richardson, T.   The method and why: an account of the
Actor's studio.   Sight & Sound 26-3:132 Win '56/57
Richardson, T.   The man behind an angry young man.
Films & Filming 5-5:9 F '59
A free hand.   Sight & Sound 28-2:60 Spg '59
Young, C.   Tony Richardson; an interview in Los
Angeles.   Film Q 13-4:10 Sum '60
Britain's angry young director.   Sat R 43:48 D 24 '60
Richardson, T.   The two worlds of the cinema.   Films
& Filming 7-9:7 Je '61
The cost of independents.   Sight & Sound 30-3:110 Sum
'61
The screen answers back.   Films & Filming 8-8:12 My
'62
Entertainer.   Time 81:36 Ja 18 '63
People are talking about.   Vogue 141:78 F 15 '63
Cowie, P.   The face of '63--Great Britain.   Films &
Filming 9-5:19 F '63
Director.   New Yorker 39:47 O 12 '63
Biography.   Current Biography 24:11 D '63
Same.   Current Biography Yearbook 1963:360 '64
Lukas, M.   Tom Jones.   Show 4-4:60 Ap '64
Moller, D.   Britain's busiest angry young man.   Film
Comment 2-1:3 Win '64
Durgent, R.   Loved one.   Films & Filming 12-5:19 F;
12-6:37 Mr '66
Tom Jones meets Goldfinger.   Time 90:57 Ag 4 '67

Lellis, G.   Recent Richardson ... cashing the blank
   check.   Take One 2-1:10 S/O '68
Gill, B.   Production of Hamlet.   New Yorker 45:121
   My 10 '69
Kael, P.   Current cinema.   New Yorker 45:66 Ja 17 '70
British cinema filmography.   Film 65:10 Spg '72

RICHTER, HANS
   Harro is dead.   Christian Century 61:875 Jl 26 '44
   Richter, H.   The avant-garde film seen from within.
      Hollywood Q 4-1:34 Fall '49
   Weinberg, H. G.   30 years of experimental film.   Films
      In Review 2-10:22 D '51
   Easel, scroll, film.   Mag Art 45:78 F '52
   Boyle, K.   Evidence of conscience.   Nation 182:316
      Ap 14 '56
   Mekas, J.   Hans Richter on the nature of film poetry;
      interview.   Film Culture 3-1(11):5 '57
   Clowning out of the void.   Sat R 41:20 F 1 '58
   Habasque, G.   Hans Richter.   Quandrum 13:61 '62
   From interviews with Hans Richter during the last ten
      years.   Film Culture 31:26 Win '63/64
   Mussman, T.   Early surrealist expression in the film.
      Film Culture 41:8 Sum '66
   Gray, C.   Portrait: Hans Richter.   Art In America 56:48
      Ja '68
   Fascination with rhythm.   Time 91:54 F 16 '68
   In memory of a friend.   Art In America 57:40 Jl '69

RIEFENSTAHL, LENI
   Hitler's dictator.   Newsweek 4:16 S 15 '34
   Schulberg, B.   Nazi pin-up girl; Hitler's No. 1 movie
      actress.   Sat Evening Post 218:11 Mr 30 '46
   Feldman, J. & H.   Women directors.   Films In Review
      1-8:9 N '50
   Admired by Adolf.   Time 59:40 My 5 '52
   The case of Leni Riefenstahl.   Sight & Sound 29-2:68
      Spg '60
   Gunston, D.   Leni Riefenstahl.   Film Q 14-1:4 Fall '60
   Muller, R.   Romantic Miss Riefenstahl.   Spectator (Lon)
      206:179 F 10 '61
   Berson, A. & Keller, J.   Shame and glory in the movies.
      National R 16:17 Ja 14 '64
   Berson, A.   The truth about Leni.   Films & Filming
      11-7:15 Ap '65
   Various letters.   Film Comment 3-3:82 Sum '65

Letters. Film Comment 3-4:84 Fall '65

Hitchens, G. Interview with a legend. Film Comment 3-1:4 Win '65

Biographical sketch. Film Comment 3-1:12 Win '65

Gregor, U. A comeback for Leni Riefenstahl? Film Comment 3-1:24 Win '65

Gardner, R. Can the will triumph? Film Comment 3-1:28 Win '65

Arkadin. Film clips. Sight & Sound 35-1:46 Win '65/66

Brownlow, K. Leni Riefenstahl. Film 47:14 Win '66

Delahaye, M. Leni and the wolf; interview. Cahiers (Eng) 5:49 '66

Rotha, P. Reply to Brownlow. Film 48:12 Spg '67

Brownlow, K. Reply to Rotha. Film 48:14 Spg '67

Riefenstahl, L. Letter. Film Comment 4-2/3:126 Fall/ Win '67

Where are they now? Newsweek 72:26 O 28 '68

Corliss, R. Leni Riefenstahl; a bibliography. Film Heritage 5-1:27 Fall '69

Richards, J. Leni Riefenstahl: style and structure. Silent Pic 8:17 Aut '70

Pyros, J. Notes on women directors. Take One 3-2:7 N/D '70

RIESNER, CHARLES

And he's seen battling ever since. Lions Roar 1-7:no p# Mr '42

From gags to nags. Lions Roar 2-4:no p# Ap '43

The punch that counts. Lions Roar 3-3:no p# Ap '44

MGM's directors range from pioneers to newcomers. Lions Roar 3-4:no p# Jl '44

RILLA, WOLF

Rilla, W. Pattern of a film. Film 8:9 Mr/Ap '56

Rilla, W. The danger of playing safe. Film 14:11 N/D '57

Filmography. Film 14:8 N/D '57

British feature directors; an index to their work. Sight & Sound 27-6:301 Aut '68

RIMMER, DAVID

Nordstrom, K. The films of David Rimmer. Film Library Q 5-3:28 Sum '72

Greenspun, R. Quick--who are David Rimmer and James Herbert? N.Y. Times sec2:17 O 8 '72

RIPLEY, ARTHUR
  Towers, R.  Arthur Ripley; letter.  Films In Review
    12-4:255 Ap '61
  Sarris, A.  Esoterica; filmog.  Film Culture 28:22 Spg '63

RISKIN, ROBERT
  Awarded prize by the Academy of motion picture arts and
    sciences.  Time 25:52 Mr 11 '35
  Lewis, J. D.  Top story man.  Colliers 107:21 Mr 29 '41
  Obit.  N. Y. Times p31 S 22 '55
    Newsweek 46:80 O 3 '55
    Time 66:94 O 3 '55
  Filmography.  Film Comment 6-4:101 Win '70/71

RITCHIE, MICHAEL
  What directors are saying.  Action 5-3:30 My/Je '70
  Ritchie, M.  Snow job.  Action 5-5:4 S/O '70
  Mori, S. Y.  The making of The candidate.  Todays
    Filmmaker 2-1:44 Ag '72

RITT, MARTIN
  Gray, M.  He wrote it five times.  Films & Filming
    5-8:17 My '59
  Personality of the month.  Films & Filming 6-7:3 Ap '60
  Talk with the director.  Newsweek 58:86 O 2 '61
  McVay, D.  The best and worst of Martin Ritt.  Films
    & Filming 11-3:43 D '64
  Field, S.  Outrage.  Film Q 18-3:34 Spg '65
  Godfrey, L.  Tall when they're small.  Films & Filming
    14-11:42 Ag '68
  Campbell, R.  Biographical note; filmog.  Focus On Film
    3:10 My/Ag '70
  Martin Ritt: conversation.  Action 6-2:27 Mr/Ap '71

RITTER, KARL
  Altmann, J.  Karl Ritter and his early films.  Hollywood
    Q 4-4:385 Sum '50
  Altmann, J.  Karl Ritter's "soldier" films.  Hollywood
    Q 5-1:61 Fall '50

RIVETTE, JACQUES
  Rivette, J. & Truffaut, F.  Renoir in America.  Sight
    & Sound 34-1:12 Jl/S '54
  Marcorelles, L.  Interview with Roger Leenhardt and
    Jacques Rivette.  Sight & Sound 32-4:168 Aut '63
  Stein, E.  Suzanne Simonin, Diderot's nun.  Sight &
    Sound 35-3:130 Sum '66

Lloyd,  P.   Jacques  Rivette  and  l'amour  fou.   Monogram
2:10  Sum  '71

ROBBE-GRILLET,  ALAIN
Weightman,  J.  G.   French  neo-realists.   Nation  188:381
Ap  25  '59
Last  word  on  Last  year;  a  discussion.   Films  &  Filming
8-6:39  Mr  '62
New-realists.   Time  80:80  Jl  20  '62
Alain  Robbe-Grillet.   Vogue  141:124  Ja  1  '63
Graham,  P.   The  face  of  '63--France.   Films  &  Filming
9-8:13  My  '63
Robbe-Grillet.   New  Yorker  40:24  Ja  9  '65
McCann,  B.   Alain  Robbe-Grillet.   Film  51:22  Spg  '68
Ward,  J.   The  novelist  as  director.   Sight  &  Sound
37-2:86  Spg  '68
Gilliatt,  P.   Current  cinema.   New  Yorker  44:153  My  18
'68
Alain  Robbe-Grillet  and  modern  cinema;  filmog.   Kinema
1:entire  issue  Je  '68
Thomaier,  W.   Alain  Robbe-Grillet.   Sight  &  Sound
37-3:160  Sum  '68
Meades,  J.   Alain  Robbe-Grillet.   Sight  &  Sound  37-3:161
Sum  '68
Roud,  R.   Memories  of  Resnais.   Sight  &  Sound  38-3:124
Sum  '69
Crick,  P.   Trans-Europ  express.   Cinema  (Lon)  5:21
F  '70
Bersani,  L.   Narrative  murder.   Yale  R  59:376  Mr  '70

ROBERTSON,  JOHN  S.
Sketch.   Photoplay  20:25  O  '21
Obit.   N. Y.  Times  p88  N  8  '64
Screen  World  16:225  '65

ROBINSON,  CASEY
Filmography.   Film  Comment  6-4:101  Win  '70/71

ROBINSON,  RICHARD
Improve  your  frames  with  inserts.   Design  56:33  S  '54

ROBSON,  MARK
Why  you  hear  what  you  hear  at  the  movies.   Good
Housekeeping  141:99  Jl  '55
Wald,  J.  &  Robson,  M.   The  code  doesn't  stultify.  Films
In  Review  8-10:503  D  '57
Personality  of  the  month.   Films  &  Filming  4-6:5  Mr  '58

Director's way.    Sat R 41:12 D 20 '58
Robson, M.    Nine hours of my life.    Films & Filming
    9-2:47 N '62
Fenin, G.    The face of '63--United States.    Films &
    Filming 9-6:55 Mr '63
Luft, H. G.    Mark Robson; filmog.    Films In Review
    19-5:288 My '68
Special report.    Action 4-3:22 My/Je '69
What directors are saying.    Action 5-1:28 Ja/F '70

ROCCOS, STELIOS
Who's who in filmmaking.    Sightlines 1-3:4 Ja/F '68

ROCHA, GLAUBER
    Rocha's violence.    CTVD 4-2:18 Spg '66
    Viany, A.    Who's who in the cinema novo.    CTVD
        6-1:26 Fall '68
    Round table on the cinema novo.    Cinema (Lon) 5:15 F
        '70
    Interview.    Afterimage 1:no p# Ap '70
    Rocha, G.    The aesthetics of violence.    Afterimage 1:no
        p# Ap '70
    Interview.    Cineaste 4-1:2 Sum '70
    Hitchens, G.    Interview.    Filmmakers Newsletter 3-11:20
        S '70
    Hitchens, G.    The way to make a future; conversation
        with Glauber Rocha.    Film Q 24-1:27 Fall '70
    Rocha, G.    Beginning at zero: notes on cinema and
        society.    Drama R 14:144 Win '70
    Fisher, J.    Politics by magic; filmog.    Film Journal
        1-1:32 Spg '71
    Viani, E.    Interview.    Afterimage 3:68 Sum '71
    MacBean, J. R.    At the crossroads.    Sight & Sound
        40-3:144 Sum '71
    Quote on film importation.    Cineaste 5-1:30 Win '71/72
    Malanga, G.    Interview.    Interview 1-7:16 n. d.
    O'Brien, G.    Interview.    Interview 2-3:24 n. d.

ROCHLIN, DIANE
    Listing of films.    Film Culture 37:7 Sum '65

ROCHLIN, SHELDON
    Listing of films.    Film Culture 37:7 Sum '65

RODAKIEWICZ, HENWAR
    Rodakiewicz, H.    Documentary: a personal retrospect.
        Film Library Q 2-3:33 Sum '69

RODRIGUEZ-SOLTERO, JOSE
    Listing of films.　Film Culture 37:7 Sum '65

ROEG, NICOLAS
    Survival in itself is brutal; filmog.　Films Illustrated
        1-4:26 O '71
    Gow, G.　Identify; interview; filmog.　Films & Filming
        18-4:18 Ja '72
    British cinema filmography.　Film 65:10 Spg '72

ROEMER, MICHAEL
    Kurosawa's way of seeing.　Reporter 22:36 Mr 17 '60
    Three hours in hell.　Reporter 24:40 Mr 30 '61
    New wave and old rock.　Reporter 25:45 O 26 '61
    Bergman's bag of tricks.　Reporter 26:37 F 15 '62
    Survey among unsuccessful applicants for the Ford
        Foundation film grants. Film Comment 2-3:10 Sum '64
    Cohen, S.　Filmmakers of Nothing but a man; filmog.
        Film Comment 3-2:8 Spg '65
    Widmark, A.　Conversation with Michael Roemer.　Film
        Heritage 3-2:29 Win '67/68

ROGERS, MACLEAN
    British feature directors; an index to their work.　Sight
        & Sound 27-6:301 Aut '58

ROGOSIN, LIONEL
    Compulsion.　New Yorker 36:30 Je 18 '60
    Rogosin, L.　Interpreting reality (notes on the esthetics
        and practices of improvisational acting).　Film Culture
        21:20 Sum '60
    Davis, P.　Rogosin and documentary.　Film Culture
        24:25 Spg '62
    Mekas, J.　Lionel Rogosin: social engagement.　Film
        Culture 24:7 Spg '62

ROHMER, ERIC
    Eric Rohmer.　Film 51:27 Spg '68
    Clarens, C.　L'amour sage.　Sight & Sound 39-1:6 Win
        '69/70
    Cowie, P.　Eric Rohmer; filmog.　Focus On Film 1:13
        Ja/F '70
    Salute of the week.　Cue 40-18:1 My 1 '71
    Mystifier.　Newsweek 77:100 My 3 '71
    Adams, S.　Eric Rohmer in conversation.　CTVD 8-1(29):
        29 Spg '71
    Petrie, G.　Interview.　Film Q 24-4:34 Sum '71

Nogueira, R.  Interview.  Sight & Sound 40-3:119 Sum '71
Elsaesser, T.  Eric Rohmer vs. Pasolini.  Monogram
  2:6 Sum '71
Mellen, J.  The moral psychology of Rohmer's tales.
  Cinema (BH) 7-1:17 Fall '71
Rossell, D.  Interview.  Cinema (BH) 7-1:21 Fall '71
Eric Rohmer in conversation.  CTVD 8-2:30 Fall '71
Davis, M. S.  Boy talks with girl, boy argues with girl,
  boy says....  N. Y. Times Bio Ed N 21 '71
Eric Rohmer in conversation.  CTVD 8-3:30 Win '71/72
Canby, V.  From Maud to Claire to Chloe.  N. Y. Times
  sec 2:1 O 8 '72
Simon, J.  Why do they rave so over Rohmer.  N. Y.
  Times sec 2:1 O 29 '72
Chase, D. & Feiden, R.  Eric Rohmer talks about Chloe
  in the afternoon.  Interview 27:20 N '72
Director of the year; filmog.  International Film G p28
  '72


ROMERS, GEORGE
  Block, A. B.  Filming Night of the living dead; interview.  Filmmakers Newsletter 5-3:19 Ja '72


ROMM, MIKHAIL I.
  Russian art and anti-Semitism; address.  Commentary
  36:435 D '63
  Obit.  Classic Film Collector 34:X-2 Spg '72
  N. Y. Times Bio Ed N 3 '71


ROOKS, CONRAD
  Knight, A.  New film vocabulary.  Sat R 50:50 F 11 '67
  Self as hero.  Time 90:166 N 17 '67
  McDonald, R.  The elusiveness of Conrad Rooks.  Take
  One 3-5:5 My/Je '71
  Gow, G.  Up from the underground.  Films & Filming
  17-11:24 Ag '71


ROOS, OLE
  Adams, S.  Four Dane directors; interview.  CTVD
  7-2:26 Spg '70
  Biographical note.  International Film G 7:90 '70


ROSEN, STEVE
  Rosen, S.  SOS--save our sea.  American Cinematographer
  52-9:888 S '71

## ROSI, FRANCESCO

These faces will win top places during 1959. Films &
Filming 5-7:18 Ap '59

Lane, J. F. The face of '63--Italy. Films & Filming
9-7:11 Ap '63

Interview. Film 39:12 Spg '64

Lane, J. F. Moments of truth. Films & Filming 11-3:5
D '64

Bachmann, G. Francesco Rosi; interview. Film Q
18-3:50 Spg '65

Director of the year; filmog. International Film G 3:18
'66

Lane, J. F. Moments of truth; interview. Films &
Filming 16-12:6 S '70

## ROSS, ARTHUR R.

Ross, A. R. About the process of creativity. Making
Films 3-6:16 D '69

## ROSS, HERBERT

Clandon, L. Meet Herbert Ross. Dance 32:28 Ja '58

Choreographers make good film directors; interview.
Films & Filming 15-12:52 S '69

What directors are saying. Action 4-6:28 N/D '69

Joel, L. Dancer-choreographer-show doctor now film
director. Dance 41:42 D '69

## ROSSELLINI, ROBERTO

Note. Vogue 112:170 O 1 '48

Ordway, P. Prophet with honor. Theatre Arts 33:49
Ja '49

Monsey, D. A meeting with Rossellini. World R p58
Ja '49

Life in a sausage factory. Time 53:84 F 7 '49

Rossellini. New Yorker 24:25 F 19 '49

Rossellini. Cue 18-8:17 F 19 '49

Strombolian idyl. Life 26:48 My 2 '49

Fantasy on the black island. Time 53:102 My 16 '49

Biography. Current Biography 10:50 Jl '49

Same. Current Biography Yearbook 1949:532 '50

Venturi, L. Roberto Rossellini. Hollywood Q 4-1:1
Fall '49

Weller, G. Ingrid's Rossellini. Colliers 124:14 N 12
'49

Difficulties in his romance. Time 54:51 D 26 '49

Ingrid Bergman has a baby. Life 28:42 F 13 '50

Basket of ricotta. Time 55:86 F 13 '50

Stomboli bambino. Newsweek 35:32 F 13 '50

Kobler, J. Tempest on the Tiber. Life 28:115 F 13 '50

Roberto and the Rota. Newsweek 35:72 F 27 '50

Harcourt-Smith. The stature of Rossellini. Sight &
Sound 19-2:86 Ap '50

Senor y senora. Time 55:86 Je 5 '50

Koval, F. Interview. Sight & Sound 19-10:393 F '51

Murray, W. Man who knows no rules. U. N. World
7:44 My '53

Good old Roberto. Newsweek 43:52 Je 28 '54

Scherer, M. & Truffaut, F. Interview. Film Culture
1-2:12 Mr/Ap '55

Joan at the stake. Theatre Arts 39:30 My '55

Rossellini story. Newsweek 49:41 Je 3 '57

Not forever after. Newsweek 50:65 N 18 '57

Gow, G. The quest for realism; discussion. Films &
Filming 4-3:13 D '57

Davidson, B. Ingrid Bergman. Look 22:20 S 16; 29 S
22; 47 O 14 '58

Bazin, A. Cinema and television; interview. Sight &
Sound 28-1:26 Win '58/59

Cosulich, C. Rossellini's India. Films & Filming 5-7:12
Ap '59

Lane, J. F. The face of '63--Italy. Films & Filming
9-7:11 Ap '63

Sarris, A. Beyond the fringe. Film Culture 28:29 Spg
'63

Sarris, A. Rossellini rediscovered. Film Culture 32:60
Spg '64

Casty, H. The achievement of Roberto Rossellini. Film
Culture 2-4:17 Fall '64

Weinberg, G. The sixth Montreal international film
festival. Film Heritage 1-2:34 Win '65/66

Mardore, M. Age of iron. Cahiers (Eng) 3:47 '66

Gilliatt, P. Current cinema. New Yorker 46:58 Ap 22
'70

Adams, S. Rossellini and Socrates. CTVD 8-1(29):9
Spg '71

Rossellini, R. Roberto Rossellini. Cinema (BH) 7-1:14
Fall '71

MacBean, J. R. Rossellini's materialist mise-en-scene.
Film Q 25-2:20 Win '71/72

Canby, V. If Elsa could see Roberto now. N. Y. Times
Bio Ed D 12 '71

O'Connor, J. J. Could Rossellini work here? N. Y.
Times sec2:17 Ap 30 '72

Shedlin, M. Love, estrangement and coadunation in

Rossellini's Voyage to Italy.   Women & Film 2:46 '72
Keller, J. & O'Brien, G.   Interview.   Interview 2-2:30
   n. d.
Camper, F.   Voyage to Italy.   Cinema (Lon) 9:36 n. d.

ROSSEN, ROBERT
   His new fangled techniques.   Time 54:102 D 5 '49
   Biography.   Current Biography 11:48 O '50
      Same.   Current Biography Yearbook 1950:506 '51
   Hart, H.   Notes on Robert Rossen.   Films In Review
      13-6:333 Je/Jl '62
   Burton, H.   Notes on Rossen films.   Films In Review
      13-6:335 Je/Jl '62
   Springer, J.   A Rossen index; filmog.   Films In Review
      13-6:341 Je/Jl '62
   Robert Rossen on The face of independence.   Films &
      Filming 8-11:7 Ag '62
   Sarris, A.   Minor disappointments; filmog.   Film Culture
      28:41 Spg '63
   Cohen, S. B.   Robert Rossen and the filming of Lilith.
      Film Comment 3-2:3 Spg '65
   Obit.   Current Biography 27:42 Mr '66
      Current Biography Yearbook 1966:470 '67
      N. Y. Times p27 F 19 '66
      Newsweek 67:63 F 28 '66
      Screen World 18:240 '67
      Time 87:104 F 25 '66
   Casty, A.   The films of Robert Rossen.   Film Q 20-2:3
      Win '66/67
   Lessons learned in combat; interview.   Cahiers (Eng)
      7:21 Ja '67
   Biofilmography.   Cahiers (Eng) 7:38 Ja '67
   Casty, A.   Retrospective study of his films.   Cinema (BH)
      4-3:18 Fall '68
   Dark, C.   Reflections of Robert Rossen.   Cinema (Lon)
      6/7:57 Ag '70
   Wald, M.   Robert Rossen.   Films In Review 13-7:446
      Ag/S '72

ROSSI, FRANCO
   New names.   Sight & Sound 25-3:121 Win '55/56
   Lane, J. F.   The face of '63--Italy.   Films & Filming
      9-7:11 Ap '63
   Oh, the smog bites; interview.   Cinema (BH) 1-4:16
      Je/Jl '63

ROSSON, ARTHUR H.
  Obit.   Screen World 12:225 '61

ROSSON, RICHARD
  No feeling!  modern movie thrills are real.   Popular
    Science 129:38 N '36
  Obit.   N.Y. Times p13 Je 1 '53
    Screen World 5:209 '54

ROSTOTSKY, STANISLAV
  The coming of the Russians.   Action 6-2:4 Mr/Ap '71
  The Russians are here.   Making Films 5-3:10 Je '71

ROTHA, PAUL
  An interview with Paul Rotha.   Sight & Sound 2-5:9 Spg
    '33
  Rotha, P.   Pabst, Pudovkin and the producers.   Sight &
    Sound 2-6:50 Sum '33
  Ferguson, O.   Home truths from abroad; English social
    films.   New Republic 93:171 D 15 '37
  Making facts dramatic.   Scholastic 31:35S Ja 15 '38
  Films of fact and fiction.   Theatre Arts 22:186 Mr '38
  Rotha, P.   The lament.   Sight & Sound 7-27:120 Aut '38
  Paul Rotha on documentary.   Film 2:12 D '54; 3:12 F '55
  Rotha, P.   Television and the future of documentary.
    Q Film Radio TV 9-4:366 Sum '55
  Luft, H. G.   Rotha and the world.   Q Film Radio TV
    10-1:89 Fall '55
  Rotha, P.   Hard lines for the British films.   Film 5:11
    S/O '55
  Rotha, P.   Presenting the world to the world.   Films &
    Filming 2-7:8 Ap '56
  Biography.   Current Biography 18:46 Ap '57
    Same.   Current Biography Yearbook 1957:475 '58
  An industry geared to routine production.   Film 14:7 N/D
    '57
  Filmography.   Film 14:8 N/D '57
  Rotha, P.   On collecting old stills.   Film 15:19 Ja/F '58
  Pardoe, F. E.   Rotha on the film.   Film 16:21 Mr/Ap '58
  British feature directors; an index to their work.   Sight &
    Sound 27-6:301 Aut '58
  The critical issue; discussion.   Sight & Sound 27-6:270
    Aut '58
  Rotha, P.   The small budget film.   International Film A
    2:137 '58
  Rotha and the Abbey.   Sight & Sound 28-2:67 Spg '59
  A free hand.   Sight & Sound 28-2:60 Spg '59

Rotha, P.   Through the eye of the lens.   International
Film A 3:121 '59
Cowie, P.   The face of '63--Great Britain.   Films &
Filming 9-5:19 F '63
The directors choose the best films.   Cinema (BH) 1-5:14
Ag/S '63


ROTHCHILD, AMALIE
Kaplan, D.   Selected short subjects.   Women & Film
2:37 '72


ROTHMAN, STEPHANIE
Women on women in films.   Take One 3-2:10 N/D '70


ROUCH, JEAN
Sadoul, G.   Notes on a new generation.   Sight & Sound
28-3/4:111 Sum/Aut '59
Sandall, R.   The films of Jean Rouch.   Film Q 15-2:57
Win '61/62
Awakening African cinema.   UNESCO Courier 15:10 Mr
'62
Interview.   Movie 8:21 Ap '63
Graham, P.   The face of '63--France.   Films & Filming
9-8:13 My '63
Blue, J.   The films of Jean Rouch.   Film Comment
4-2/3:82 Fall/Win '67
Blue, J.   Jean Rouch in conversation.   Film Comment
4-2/3:84 Fall/Win '67
Veuve, J.   Jean Rouch in conversation.   Film Comment
4-2/3:90 Fall/Win '67


ROVENSKÝ, JOSEF
Dewey, L.   Czechoslovakia; silence into sound.   Film
60:5 n. d.


ROWLAND, ROY
Hollywood's youngest pioneer.   Lions Roar 2-4:no p#
Ap '43
Tricks in the directing trade.   Lions Roar 3-2:no p#
Ja '44
MGM's directors range from pioneers to newcomers.
Lions Roar 3-4:no p# Jl '44
Rowland, R.   The western as history.   Films In Review
3-5:220 My '52


ROY, BIMEL
Ray, S. K.   New Indian directors.   Film Q 14-1:63 Fall '60

ROZIER, JACQUES
Interview. Movie 8:23 Ap '63

RUBEN, JOSE
Obit. N. Y. Times p47 Ap 30 '69

RUBIN, BARBARA
Listing of films. Film Culture 37:7 Sum '65

RUGGLES, WESLEY
Cruikshank, H. Sketch. Motion Pic Classic 29:33 Jl '29
His marriage. Movie Classic 1:35 Ja '32
Brown, B. Interview. Photoplay 45:62 Ap '34
Earhart, D. Star builder. Silver Screen 8-1:51 N '37
Biographical note; filmog. Movies & People 2:45 '40
Genius at work. Lions Roar 2-1:no p# S/O '42
Ruggles, W. Prop laughs. Lions Roar 2-4:no p# Ap '43
Autobiographical. American 137:60 Mr '44
Ruggles, W. Tickling the army's funny-bone. Lions
    Roar 3-3:no p# Ap '44
MGM's directors range from pioneers to newcomers.
    Lions Roar 3-4:no p# Jl '44
Obit. Classic Film Collector 34:X-2 Spg '72 (reprint
    N. Y. Times D 29 '71) N. Y. Times D 29 '71
    N. Y. Times Bio Ed Ja 10 '72

RUSH, RICHARD
Goodwin, M. & Wise, N. Getting Richard Rush straight.
    Take One 2-8:17 N/D '69
Roberts, J. Making it as a film director. Action 5-2:31
    Mr/Ap '70
Roberts, J. Rush's progress. Making Films 4-3:29
    Je '70
What directors are saying. Action 5-6:22 N/D '70
Geist, K. Interview. Interview 1-9:28 n. d.

RUSSELL, KEN
Russell, K. Ideas for films. Film 19:13 Ja/F '59
Kael, P. Current cinema. New Yorker 46:97 Mr 28 '70
Oakes, P. Ken and Glenda and Peter and Nina. Show
    1-3:57 Mr '70
Salute of the week. Cue 39-22:1 My 30 '70
Futures, great. Vogue 156:92 Jl '70
Gow, G. Shock treatment; filmog. Films & Filming
    16-10:8 Jl '70
Phillips, G. D. Interview; filmog. Film Comment 6-3:10
    Fall '70

Langley, L. A director who demands the right to be outrageous. Show 2-8:34 O '71

Ken Russell films The boy friend. Films & Filming 18-1:34 O '71

Luft, H. G. Letter. Films In Review 22-9:580 N '71

What directors are saying. Action 7-1:36 Ja/F '72

Ken Russell writes on Raising Kane. Films & Filming 18-8:16 My '72

Castell, D. Always new continents to conquer. Films Illustrated 1-11:4 My '72

What directors are saying. Action 7-3:28 My/Je '72

Dempsey, M. The world of Ken Russell. Film Q 25-3: 13 Spg '72

British cinema filmography. Film 65:10 Spg '72

Rose, T. Interview. Movie Maker 6-9:616 S '72

Flatley, G. I'm surprised my films shock people. N. Y. Times sec2:15 O 15 '72

Buckley, P. Savage saviour; interview. Films & Filming 19-1:13 O '72

O'Brien, G. Ken Russell in the port of New York; interview. Interview 27:9 N '72

RYDELL, MARK
Murder necessitated. Time 80:56 Ag 24 '62
Cherry, R. Jazz to acting to directing: Mark Rydell. Action 5-1:25 Ja/F '70

RYSSACK, EDDY
Granja, V. Eddy Ryssack said; interview. CTVD 4-3:15 Fall '66

SAGAN, LEONTINE
   Orme, M. Work of. Illustrated London N 180:780
     My 7 '32.
   Corathiel, E. Interview. Theatre World 18:295 D '32
   Johns, E. Interview. Theatre World 22:38 Jl '34
   Richards, H. Interview. Theatre World 30:129 S '38
   Feldman, J. & H. Women directors. Films In Review
     1-8:9 N '50

SAGAR, RAMANAND
   Biographical note. International Film G 6:100 '69

ST. CLAIR, MALCOLM
   Waterbury, R. Sketch. Photoplay 30:42 S '26
   Weinberg, H. G. Malcolm St. Clair; letter. Films In
     Review 3-7:366 Ag/S '52
   Obit. Screen World 4:178 '53
   Geltzer, G. Malcolm St. Clair. Films In Review
     5-2:56 F '54

SAKS, GENE
   Saks, G. Well, how do you like directing movies?
     Action 2-2:10 Mr/Ap '67
   Stage to film. Action 3-5:12 S/O '68

SALE, RICHARD
   Sale, R. They built the sea. Films & Filming 3-5:14
     F '57

SAMPSON, PADDY
   Interview. Take One 2-5:4 Je '67

SAMSONOV, SAMSON
   Hill, S. P. Interview; filmog. Film Culture 42:118
     Fall '66

SANDERS, DENIS
   Sanders, D. & T. Small films can have big themes.
     Films & Filming 2-9:13 Je '56
   Young, C. & Bachmann, G. New wave--or gesture?
     Film Q 14-3:6 Spg '61
   Young, C. West Coast report. Sight & Sound 30-3:137
     Sum '61

SANDRICH, MARK
    Work of.    Motion Pic 51:62 Jl '36
    Biographical note; filmog.    Movies & People 2:45 '40

SANGSTER, JIMMY
    British cinema filmography.    Film 65:10 Spg '72

SANJINES, JORGE
    A talk with Jorge Sanjines.    Cineaste 4-3:12 Win '70/71
    Interview.    Afterimage 3:40 Sum '71
    The courage of the people; interview.    Cineaste 5-2:18
        Spg '72

SANTELL, ALFRED
    Squier, E. L.    Interview.    Photoplay 18:76 Jl '20
    Sketch.    Photoplay 30:88 O '26
    Cruikshank, H.    Sketch.    Motion Pic Classic 29:35 Je '29
    Biographical note; filmog.    Movies & People 2:45 '40
    Cort, R. F.    Berkeley and Santell; letter.    Films In Re-
        view 8-6:30 Je/Jl '57
    Letters.    Films In Review 8-7:362 Ag/S '57
    Dyer, E. V.    Stroheim and Santell; letter.    Films In
        Review 9-3:158 Mr '58

SANTOS, ROBERTO
    Viany, A.    Who's who in the cinema novo.    CTVD 6-1:27
        Fall '68

SÁRA, SÁNDOR
    Biographical note.    International Film G 9:164 '72

SARACENI, PAULO CESAR
    Viany, A.    Who's who in the cinema novo.    CTVD 6-1:28
        Fall '68

SARGENT, JOSEPH
    What directors are saying.    Action 5-6:22 N/D '70
    Sargent, J.    First feature: Colossus.    Action 6-3:23
        My/Je '71
    Nolan, J. E.    Films on TV.    Films In Review 23-3:178
        Mr '72

SARKISIAN, PAUL
    Survey among unsuccessful applicants for the Ford
        Foundation film grants.    Film Comment 2-3:10 Sum '64

SARNE, MIKE
    Sarne, M.   How to handle directors.   Films & Filming
       11-7:41 Ap '65
    Sarne, M.   The other side of the camera.   Films &
       Filming 12-10:36 Jl '66
    Sarne, M.   For love of Myra.   Films & Filming 17-5:26
       F '71
    British cinema filmography.   Film 65:10 Spg '72
    Sarne, M.   Knight in the big apple.   Films & Filming
       19-1:22 O '72

SARNO, GERALDO
    Viany, A.   Who's who in the cinema novo.   CTVD 6-1:29
       Fall '68

SAROFF, RAYMOND
    Listing of films.   Film Culture 37:7 Sum '65

SASDY, PETER
    Andrews, E.   I won't go back to television without attain-
       ing my goals in the cinema.   Films Illustrated 1-10:14
       Ap '72
    British cinema filmography.   Film 65:10 Spg '72

SAUNDERS, CHARLES
    British feature directors; an index to their work.   Sight
       & Sound 27-6:302 Aut '58

SAURA, CARLOS
    Eder, R.   Saura describes film Spain banned.   N. Y.
       Times Bio Ed O 27 '71

SAVILLE, PHILIP
    British cinema filmography.   Film 65:10 Spg '72

SAVILLE, VICTOR
    British feature directors; an index to their work.   Sight
       & Sound 27-6:302 Aut '58

SCARDON, PAUL
    Baremore, R. W.   A stage-struck director.   Photoplay
       16-4:69 S '19
    Obit.   N. Y. Times p27 Ja 20 '54

SCHAEFER, GEORGE
    Schaefer, G.   The director's ballpark.   Action 4-2:37
       Mr/Ap '69

What directors are saying.   Action 4-5:32 S/O '69
Biography.   Current Biography 31:36 F '70
    Same.   Current Biography Yearbook 1970:373 '71
What directors are saying.   Action 5-4:30 Jl/Ag '70
What directors are saying.   Action 6-3:28 My/Je '71
The professional director speaks.   Making Films 5-4:40
    Ag '71


SCHAFFNER, FRANKLIN J.
    Schaffner, F.   The best and the worst of it.   Films &
        Filming 11-1:9 O '64
    Wilson, D.   Franklin Schaffner.   Sight & Sound 35-2:73
        Spg '66
    Should directors produce?   Action 3-4:10 Jl/Ag '68
    Kaufman, S. L. Jr.   The early Franklin J. Schaffner;
        interview.   Films In Review 20-7:409 Ag/S '69
    Sarris, A.   Director of the month.   Show 1-4:23 Ap '70
    Eyles, A.   Biographical note; filmog.   Focus On Film
        3:15 My/Ag '70
    Munroe, D.   Director Franklin Schaffner; from Planet of
        the apes to Patton.   Show 1-10:16 Ag 6 '70
    What directors are saying.   Action 5-6:22 N/D '70
    Award winner.   Action 6-3:13 My/Je '71
    Michael Jayston on Nicholas and director Franklin
        Schaffner.   Show 2-11:35 Ja '72
    Charlton Heston comments on Schaffner.   Dialogue On
        Film 1:9 '72
    Winogura, D.   Dialogues on apes, apes and more apes;
        interview.   Cinefantastique 2-2:19 Sum '72
    Geist, K.   Chronicler of power; interview; filmog.   Film
        Comment 8-3:29 S/O '72
    Feiden, R.   Interview.   Interview 20:30 n. d.


SCHAMONI, PETER
    Dictionary of young German filmmakers.   CTVD 4-2:11
        Spg '65


SCHAMONI, ULRICH
    Dictionary of young German filmmakers.   CTVD 4-2:11
        Spg '66


SCHILLER, LAWRENCE
    Everyone's doing it.   Show 2-6:6 Ag '71


SCHLESINGER, JOHN
    John Schlesinger.   Films & Filming 8-9:5 Je '62
    Cowie, P.   The face of '63--Great Britain.   Films &

Filming 9-5:19 F '63

Blessed Isle or fool's paradise; interview.    Films &
Filming 9-8:8 My '63

How to get into films by the people who got in themselves.    Films & Filming 9-10:11 Jl '63

His father's son.    Time 82:64 Ag 2 '63

Weinberg, G.    John Schlesinger at the 6th Montreal International film festival.    Film Heritage 1-1:42 Fall
'65

Lerman, L.    International movie report.    Mademoiselle
64:119 F '67

Vivid victoriana.    Time 40:102 O 27 '67

Weaver, N.    John Schlesinger, a British director talks
about making films in the United States.    After Dark
11-5:26 S '69

A buck for Joe; Schlesinger talks to Gordon Gow about
his Midnight cowboy.    Films & Filming 16-2:4 N '69

Phillips, G.    John Schlesinger, social realist; filmog.
Film Comment 5-4:58 Win '69

Hall, H.    Award winner; interview.    Action 5-4:4 Jl/Ag
'70

Biography.    Current Biography 31:30 N '70

Same.    Current Biography Yearbook 1970:377 '71

Schlesinger's formula for winning top awards; interview.
Making Films 4-6:30 D '70

What directors are saying.    Action 6-6:22 N/D '71

Biography.    British Book Year 1971:157 '71

British cinema filmography.    Film 65:10 Spg '72

Loney, G. M.    Making it in films.    Interview 1-7:11 n. d.


SCHLÖNDORFF, VOLKER
Dictionary of young German filmmakers.    CTVD 4-2:11
Spg '66
Volker Schlondorff the rebel.    Film 55:26 Sum '69


SCHNEIDER, IRA
Listing of films.    Film Culture 37:7 Sum '65


SCHNITZER, GERALD
Schnitzer, G.    The third happiest day.    Action 2-4:22
Jl/Ag '67


SCHOEDSACK, ERNEST B.
Warriors of the desert.    Travel 61:4 Ag '33


SCHROEDER, BARBET
Gray, P.    Cinema verite; interview.    Tulane Drama R
11:130 Fall '66

SCHOENDOERFFER, PIERRE
   Biographical note.   Unifrance 48:12 O '58

SCHORM, EVALD
   Holloway, R.   Director of the year; filmog.   Inter-
      national Film G 8:47 '71

SCHWARTZ, ZACHARY
   Hubley, J. & Schwartz, Z.   Animation learns a new
      language.   Hollywood Q 1-4:360 Jl '46

SCHWERIN, JULES VICTOR
   Survey among unsuccessful applicants for the Ford
      Foundation grants.   Film Comment 2-3:10 Sum '64

SCOTT, PETER GRAHAM
   British feature directors; an index to their work.   Sight
      & Sound 27-6:302 Aut '58

SCULLY, WILLIAM J.
   Obit.   N.Y. Times p25 My 3 '49

SEASTROM, VICTOR
   (See:  SJOSTROM, VICTOR)

SEATON, GEORGE
   Seaton, G.   A comparison of the playwright and the
      screen writer.   Q Film Radio TV 10-3:217 Spg '56
   Quotes from address at presentation of Samuel Goldwyn
      Creative writing awards.   Writer 71:17 Ag '58
   Seaton, G.   Getting out on a limb.   Films & Filming
      7-7:9 Ap '61
   Quotemanship.   Action 3-3:20 Jl/Ag '68
   Brown, V.   George Seaton.   Action 5-4:21 Jl/Ag '70
   What directors are saying.   Action 5-6:22 N/D '70
   Simon, J. S.   George Seaton; filmog.   Films In Review
      22-9:521 N '71
   American Film Institute University advisory committee
      Seminar.   Dialogue on Film 2-1:entire issue '72

SÉCHAN, EDMOND
   Meeting La nouvelle vague; conversation.   Films & Film-
      ing 6-1:7 O '59

SEDGWICK, EDWARD
   Hynd, A.   Sketch.   Motion Pic 34:50 D '27
   30 years of laughter.   Lions Roar 2-4:no p# Ap '43

Obit.    N. Y.  Times  p25  My  8  '53
Newsweek 41:76  My  18  '53
Screen World 5:209  '54

SEITER, WILLIAM A.
Sketch.    Motion Pic 33:98  F  '27
Cruikshank, H.    Sketch.    Motion Pic Classic 27:33
Ag '28
Cosmopolitan's citation for the best direction of the
month.    Cosmop 121:67  Jl '46
The director and the public; a symposium.    Film Culture
1-2:15  Mr/Ap '55
Obit.    Screen World 16:225  '65

SEITZ, GEORGE B.
Mille, B.    Sketch.    Motion Pic Classic 9:28  D '19
Biographical note; filmog.    Movies & People 2:45  '40
His famous family.    Lions Roar 1-7:no p#  Mr '42
Seitz visualizes thrills.    Lions Roar 1-11/12:no p#  Jl/Ag
'42
Americana, Hardy trademark.    Lions Roar 2-3:no p#
D '42
MGM's directors range from pioneers to newcomers.
Lions Roar 3-4:no p#  Jl '44
Obit.    Current Biography '44
Smith, F. L.    The man who made serials.    Films In
Review 7-8:375  O '56

SELANDER, LESLEY
Selander, L.    Up from assistant director.    Action 6-1:25
Ja/F '71

SEMBÈNE, OUSMANE
Bery, J. L.    Simply the idea of money.    Atlas 17:64
Ap '69
What directors are saying.    Action 5-1:28  Ja/F '70

SEN, MRINAL
Williams, F.    The art film in India.    Film Culture 48/49
Win/Spg '70

SENFT, HARO
Dictionary of young German filmmakers.    CTVD 4-2:11
Spg '66

SENNETT, MACK
Carr, H. C.    Mack Sennett--laugh tester.    Photoplay
7-6:71  My '15

Hewston, E. W.   Sketch.   Motion Pic Classic 1:47 Ja '16
The split reel.   Film Players Herald & Movie Pictorial
    2-7:28 F '16
Lindsay, F. Movie spirit of the Keystone comedies.
    Sunset 39:34 D '17
The psychology of film comedy.   Motion Pic Classic 7:20
    N '18
Carr, H.   Interview.   Motion Pic 23:20 Je '22
Carr, H.   Interview.   Motion Pic 28:37 Ag '24
Carr, H.   Secret of making film comedies.   Motion Pic
    Classic 22:18 O '25
Tully, J.   Maker of comedies.   Vanity Fair 26:64 My '26
Wagner, R.   Dean of custard college; interview.   Colliers
    80:8 O 29; 13 N 5 '27
Dreiser, T.   Interview.   Photoplay 34:32 Ag '28
To produce talking pictures.   Photoplay 38:10 Ag '30
Manners, D. Defense of low-brow comedy.   Motion Pic
    Classic 32:36 O '30
Beatty, J.   Anything for a laugh; interview.   American
    111:40 Ja '31
Inside story told by Mack Sennett's rise to fame.   News-
    week 4:26 O 27 '34
Pie in art.   Nation 139:524 N 7 '34
Tully, J.   Sketch.   Motion Pic 49:33 Mr '35
Custard-pie classics.   N. Y. Times Mag p28 Je 8 '47
Mack Sennett, 1949.   Cue 18-33:10 Ag 13 '49
Agee, J.   Comedy's greatest era.   Life 27:70 S 5 '49
Pryor, T. M.   Then and now.   N. Y. Times Mag p27
    F 22 '53
Custard pies.   Newsweek 44:106 D 6 '54
Knight, A.   Era of the great comedians.   Sat R 37:20
    D 18 '54
Mack Sennett's at it.   Newsweek 52:90 O 6 '58
Galaxy of present-day stars in a classic Mack Sennett
    chase.   Life 45:148 D 22 '58
Obit.   Americana Annual 1961:663 '61
    British Book Year 1961:520 '61
    8mm Collector 15:13 Sum '66
    Illustrated London N 237:859 N 12 '60
    N. Y. Times p1 N 6 '60
    Newsweek 56:28 N 14 '60
    Screen World 12:225 '61
    Time 76:104 N 14 '60
Maltin, L.   Mack Sennett.   8mm Collector 9:25 S '64
Sennett comedies available on 8mm market.   8mm Collec-
    tor 9:25 S '64
Kearns, M. More Mack Sennett. 8mm Collector 10:11 Win
    '64

Giroux, R.  Mack Sennett.  Films In Review 19-10:593
D '68

Giroux, R.  Mack`Sennett.  Films In Review 20-1:1 Ja
'69

Hoffner, J. R. Jr.  King of Keystone.  Classic Film
Collector 31:22 Sum '71

SEWELL, VERNON
British feature directors; an index to their work.  Sight
& Sound 27-6:302 Aut '58

SHAH, KRISHNA
Shah, K.  First feature; conversation with myself.
Action 7-4:20 Jl/Ag '72

SHAINDLIN, JACK
The promised land.  Making Films 1-1:14 Mr '67
Sound and fury adding up to zero.  Making Films 1-4:31
O '67

SHANTARAM, V.
Ray, S. K.  New Indian directors.  Film Q 14-1:63
Fall '60

SHARITS, PAUL J.
Listing of films.  Film Culture 37:7 Sum '65
Letter exchange with Carl Linder.  Filmmakers News-
letter 1-6:17 Ap '68

SHARP, DON
How to get into films, by the people who got in them-
selves.  Films & Filming 9-10:11 Jl '63
Clarke, F. S.  Rasputin on film.  Cinefantastique 1-1:6
Fall '70
British cinema filmography.  Film 65:10 Spg '72

SHARPE, ROBERT K.
Sharpe, R. K.  Filming before the mountain was moved.
Filmmakers Newsletter 5-1:24 O '71

SHAUGNESSY, ALFRED
British feature directors; an index to their work.  Sight
& Sound 27-6:302 Aut '58

SHAVELSON, MELVILLE
Viva Italian flim flam!  Film 53:19 N 9 '62
Gow, G. Tightrope; interview;filmog.  Films & Filming
19-1:29 O '72

SHAYE, ROBERT
    Listing of films.    Film Culture 37:7 Sum '65

SHEBIB, DONALD
    McLuhan's child.   New Yorker 46:47 N 21 '70

SHERIFF, PAUL
    Obit.   N. Y. Times p35 S 29 '60

SHERIN, EDWIN
    In the words of Edwin Sherin.   Cue 38-21:15 My 24 '69
    What directors are saying.   Action 5-3:30 My/Je '70

SHINDO   KANETO
    About the moviemaker.   Newsweek 60:104 S 10 '62
    Note.   International Film G 2:35 '65

SHINODA, MASAHIRO
    Svensson, A.   Masahiro Shinoda; filmog.   Focus On Film
        2:6 Mr/Ap '70

SHUKSHIN, VASSILI
    A Russian six.   Films & Filming 13-12:27 S '67
    Vronskaya, J.   Recent Russian cinema.   Film 62:5 Sum
        '71

SHUVAL, MENAKHEIM
    Listing of films.   Film Culture 37:7 Sum '65

SIANI, TONI
    Listing of films.   Film Culture 37:7 Sum '65

SIDNEY, GEORGE
    Like grandfather ... like grandson.   Lions Roar 1-10:no
        p# Je '42
    New faces among MGM directors too.   Lions Roar 1-11/
        12:no p# Jl/Ag '42
    Star tester.   Lions Roar 2-5:no p# Jl '43
    Let there be music.   Lions Roar 3-2:no p# Ja '44
    MGM's directors range from pioneers to newcomers.
        Lions Roar 3-4:no p# Jl '44
    Hep cat by proxy.   Lions Roar 3-4:no p# Jl '44
    O'Leary, D.   T. N. T. means Tracy 'n' Turner.   Silver
        Screen 18-2:24 D '47
    Hints from a Hollywood pro.   Popular Mechanics 89:164
        Ja '48
    Sidney, G. The director's art. Films In Review 2-6:9 Je/Jl
        '51

Are you a director.   Popular Photo 39:95 Ag '56
Sarris, A.   Likable but elusive; filmog.   Film Culture
    28:35 Spg '63
Sidney, G.   A message from the president.   Action
    1-1:2 S/O '66
Arkadin.   Film clips.   Sight & Sound 36-2:98 Spg '67
Sidney, G.   The three ages of the musical.   Films &
    Filming 14-9:4 Je '68


SIDNEY, SCOTT
    Biographical note.   Photoplay 9-4:42 Mr '16


SIEGEL, DON
    Sarris, A.   Esoterica; filmog.   Film Culture 28:22 Spg
        '63
    Bogdanovich, P.   Interview; filmog.   Movie 15:1 Spg '68
    Austin, D.   Out for the kill.   Films & Filming 14-8:4
        My; 14-9:10 Je '68
    Quotemanship.   Action 3-3:30 Jl/Ag '68
    Interview.   Cinema (BH) 4-1:4 S '68
    Siegel, D.   The anti-heroes.   Films & Filming 15-4:22
        Ja '69
    No time to waste; the recent work of Don Siegel.
        Kinema 2:no p# Je '69
    What directors are saying.   Action 5-1:28 Ja/F '70
    Mundy, R.   Don Siegel: time and motion, attitudes and
        genre.   Cinema (Lon) 5:10 F '70
    Kaminsky, S.   Don Siegel; filmog.   Take One 3-4:8
        Mr/Ap '71
    Maltin, L.   Conversation with Don Siegel.   Action 6-4:22
        Jl/Ag '71
    Higham, C.   Suddenly, Don Siegel's high camp-us.   N. Y.
        Times Bio Ed Jl 25 '71
    Fuller, S.   Don Siegel.   Interview 21:11 My '72
    Gardner, P.   Siegel at 59: director, rebel, 'star.'   N. Y.
        Times Bio Ed My 31 '72


SIERCK, DETLEF HANS
    (See: SIRK, DOUGLAS)


SILANO, GEORGE
    The right role of the director/cameraman.   Making Films
        3-5:42 O '69


SILVERSTEIN, ELLIOT
    Knight, A.   New faces.   Sat R 49:22 D 24 '66
    What directors are saying.   Action 5-6:22 N/D '70

SILVERSTEIN, MORTON
    Rosenthal, A.    Interview.    Film Library Q 4-2:9 Spg '71
    Interview on Banks of the poor.    Film Library Q 4-2:17
        Spg '71

SIMMONS, ANTHONY
    Gillett, J.    Happening here.    Sight & Sound 34-3:138 Sum
        '65

SIMON, FRANK
    The Queen, interview.    Cinema (BH) 4-3:2 Fall '68

SIMON, S. SYLVAN
    Simon, S. S.    Art and the box office.    Cinema Progress
        4-1/2:9 Je/Jl '39
    Director gets action when he asks army.    Lions Roar
        1-5:no p# Ja '42
    A career in comedy.    Lions Roar 1-9:no p# My '42
    Simon, S. S.    He keeps 'em laughing.    Lions Roar 2-3:
        no p# D '42
    Simon, S. S.    A salute to the marines.    Lions Roar 3-1:
        no p# S '43
    Comedy on the cuff.    Lions Roar 3-1:no p# S '43
    MGM's directors range from pioneers to newcomers.
        Lions Roar 3-4:no p# Jl '44
    Obit.    N. Y. Times p15 My 19 '51

SINCLAIR, ANDREW
    British cinema filmography.    Film 65:10 Spg '72

SINCLAIR, ROBERT B.
    Eustis, M.    Interview.    Theatre Arts 20:216 Mr '36
    Sinclair, R.    The director salutes.    Lions Roar 1-1:no
        p# S '41
    Man who made Weekey.    Lions Roar 1-5:no p# Ja '42
    Miracle of television may be that it hasn't yet made the
        family obsolete.    Sat Evening Post 227:12 Ap 23 '55
    Obit.    N. Y. Times Bio Ed Ja 5 '70
        Newsweek 75:95 Ja 19 '70
        Screen World 22:240 '71
    The making of Sinclair.    Films Illustrated 1-9:32 Mr '72

SINGER, ALEXANDER
    Vallance, T. & Eyels, A.    Alexander Singer.    Film 38:4
        Win '63

SIODMAK, CURT
> Taylor, J. R.   Encounter with Siodmak.   Sight & Sound 28-3/4:180 Sum/Aut '59
> Siodmak, C.   Filming behind the iron curtain.   Action 1-2:16 N/D '66

SIODMAK, ROBERT
> (Also: SIODMARK, ROBERT)
> Parsons, L. O.   Cosmopolitan's citation for the best direction of the month.   Cosmop 120:55 Ja '46
> Marshman, D.   Mister See-odd-mack.   Life 23:100 Ag 25 '47
> Higham, C.   Robert Siodmak in America.   Film Journal (Aus) #9 F '58
> Siodmak, R.   Hoodlums; the myth or the reality.   Films & Filming 5-9:10 Ja '59
> Sarris, A.   Esoterica; filmog.   Film Culture 28:22 Spg '63
> Nolan, J. E.   Robert Siodmak; filmog.   Films In Review 20-4:218 Ap '69

SIRK, DOUGLAS
> (Also: SIERCK, DETLEF HANS)
> The man who outwitted Hitler.   Lions Roar 2-5:no p# Jl '43
> Parsons, L. O.   Cosmopolitan's citation for the best direction of the month.   Cosmop 123:170 N '47
> Sarris, A.   Second line; filmog.   Film Culture 28:11 Spg '63
> Coulson, A. A.   Letter; filmog.   Films In Review 19-2: 121 F '68
> Nolan, J. E.   Partial filmog.   Films In Review 19-3:186 Mr '68
> Joannides, P.   Two films by Douglas Sirk.   Cinema (Lon) 6/7:57 Ag '70
> Keneshea, E.   The not so tender trap.   Women & Film 2:51 '72

SJÖBERG, ALF
> Note.   International Film G 2:41 '65

SJÖMAN, VILGOT
> Note.   International Film G 2:41 '65
> Sjoman, V.   From L 136; a diary of Ingmar Bergman's Winter light.   Lit R 9:257 Win '65/66
> Krohn, S.   Convention be damned.   Atlas 12:55 Ag '66
> Gray, P.   Catching the rare moment. Tulane Drama R 11:102 Fall '66

Theren, U. Of no interest. Atlas 15:53 F '68
Edstrom, M. Savage, shameless. Atlas 15:52 F '68
Morgenstern, J. Curiouser and curiouser. Newsweek
73:114 Mr 24 '69
Gross, L. After nudity, what, indeed? Look 33:80
Ap 29 '69
Holloway, R. We are playing with reality; a conversa-
tion; filmog. Film Journal 1-1:5 Spg '71
Filmmaking in Sweden. Interview 1-10:24 n. d.


SJÖSTRÖM, VICTOR
(Also: SEASTROM, VICTOR)
Smith, A. Sketch. Classic 19:38 Mr '24
Tully, J. The greatest director in the world. Classic
19:17 Ap '24
Vaughan, D. Victor Sjostrom and D. W. Griffith. Film
15:13 Ja/F '58
Shibuk, C. Letter. Films In Review 10-5:313 My '59
Obit. Americana Annual 1961:850 '61
American Scandinavian R 48:87 Mr '60
N. Y. Times p29 Ja 4 '60
Screen World 12:225 '61
Sight & Sound 29:97 Spg '60
Time 75:92 Ja 18 '60
Duncan, C. The magic of two heroes. Film Journal
(Aus) 15:57 Mr '60
Becker, J. Bergman on Victor Sjostrom. Sight & Sound
29-2:96 Spg '60
Turner, C. L. Victor Sjostrom; filmog. as actor.
Films In Review 11-5:266 My '60
Turner, C. L. Victor Sjostrom; filmog. as director.
Films In Review 11-6:343 Je/Jl '60
Fleisher, F. Victor Sjostrom, pioneer of the Swedish
film. American Scandinavian R 48:250 S '60
Note. International Film G 2:42 '65
Sjostrom, V. As I remember him (Mauritz Stiller).
Film Comment 6-2:48 Sum '70
Richards, J. 16mm discovery: Under the red robe.
Focus On Film 9:57 Spg '72


SKOLIMOWSKI, JERZY
Situation of the new cinema; interview. Cahiers (Eng)
7:55 Ja '67
Toeplitz, K. Portrait of a debutant director. Film Q
21:1:25 Fall '67
Sarris, A. Movers. Sat R 50:39 D 23 '67
Delahaye, M. Interview. Cahiers (Eng) 12:5 D '67

Thomsen, C. B.   Skolimowski.  Sight & Sound 37-3:142
Sum '68
Jerzy Skolimowski; interview.   Film Comment 5-1:12
Fall '68
Skolimowski, biography and filmog.   Film Comment
5-1:17 Fall '68
Director of the year; filmog.   International Film G p37
'70

SKOLIMOWSKI, YUREK
Bean, R.   Adventures of Yurek; interview.   Films &
Filming 15-3:57 D '68

SLOMAN, EDWARD
Brownlow, K.   The lost work of Edward Sloman.   Film
48:8 Spg '67

SMALLMAN, KIRK
Survey among unsuccessful applicants for the Ford
Foundation film grants.   Film Comment 2-3:10 Sum '64
Smallman, K.   Toward visual cinema.   Film Comment
2-3:44 Sum '64

SMIGHT, JACK
Knight, A.   New faces.   Sat R 49:19 D 24 '66
Smight, J.   Why directors criticize critics.   Action
4-1:14 Ja/F '69

SMITH, CLIFFORD S.
Smith, C.   My gang!   Photoplay 15-2:30 Ja '19

SMITH, HARRY
Seventh independent film award.   Film Culture 37:1 Sum
'65
Berge, C.   The work of Harry Smith.   Film Culture
37:2 Sum '65
Sitney, P. A.   Harry Smith interview.   Film Culture
37:4 Sum '65
Listing of films.   Film Culture 37:7 Sum '65

SMITH, JACK
Heroes every day.   Time 64:52 Jl 26 '54
Cult of the kitchen sink.   Life 40:163 Ap 23 '56
Non Boob.   Newsweek 56:85 Ag 29 '60
Why San Franciscans really don't like us.   Sat Evening
Post 235:73 N 3 '62
Kelman, K.   Smith myth; filmog. Film Culture 29:4 Sum '63

Smith, J. Red orchids. Film Culture 33:19 Sum '64
Survey among unsuccessful applicants for the Ford
  Foundation film grants. Film Comment 2-3:10 Sum '64
Listing of films. Film Culture 37:7 Sum '65
Malanga, G. Interview. Film Culture 44:12 Sum '67

SMITH, JUDY
  Interview. Women & Film 1:30 n. d.

SMITH, PERCY
  A memoir. Sight & Sound 14-53:6 Ap '45

SMITH, PETE
  Victorek, D. Pete Smith; filmog. Films In Review
    21-7:411 Ag/S '70

SNOW, MICHAEL
  Mekas, J. & Sitney, P. A. Conversation with Michael
    Snow. Film Culture 46:1 O '68
  Snow, M. Letter. Film Culture 46:4 O '68
  Sitney, P. A. Avant garde film. Afterimage 2:13
    Aut '70
  Medjuck, J. The life and times of Michael Snow. Take
    One 3-3:6 Ja/F '71
  Mekas, J. A note on Michael Snow written in a Minne-
    sota snowstorm. Take One 3-3:12 Ja/F '71

SOBILOFF, HYMAN
  Obit. N. Y. Times Bio Ed Ag 13 '70

SOCIN, JAY
  Listing of films. Film Culture 37:7 Sum '65

SOLANAS, FERNANDO
  Fernando Solanas; interview. Film Q 24-1:37 Fall '70
  MacBean, J. R. Interview. Film Q 24:37 Fall '70
  MacBean, J. R. La Hora de les lornos. Film Q 24:31
    Fall '70

SOLÁS, HUMBERTO
  Douglas, M. E. The Cuban cinema; filmog. Take One
    1-12:6 Jl/Ag '68
  Engel, A. Solidarity and violence. Sight & Sound 38-4:
    196 Aut '69
  Interview. Atlas 19:64 Ap '70

SOLDATI, MARIO
 Jarratt, V.   Mario Soldati.   Sight & Sound 17-66:71
  Sum '48
 Mith, H.   Book of three differences.   Sat R 36:65 O 24
  '53
 Milan, P.   New Italian writing.   New Republic 131:16
  D 13 '54
 Lemon, R.   Biographical sketch.   Sat R 39:14 F 11 '56
 Biography.   Current Biography 19:35 Ap '58
  Same.   Current Biography Yearbook 19:35 Ap '58

SONTAG, SUSAN
 Kent, L.   What makes Susan Sontag make movies.   N. Y.
  Times Bio Ed O 11 '70
 Filmmaking in Sweden.   Interview 1-7:24 n. d.

SPERLING, KAREN
 Buchanan, J.   I'll keep on persisting.   After Dark 4-8:26
  D '71

SPIEKER, FRANZ-JOSEF
 Bean, R.   The face of '63--Germany.   Films & Filming
  9-9:41 Je '63

SPOTTISWOODE, RAYMOND
 Biographical note.   Sat R 31:32 Ag 14 '48
 World of witness.   Sat R 32:32 Ap 9 '49
 Grass roots films.   Sat R 32:60 My 14 '49
 Spottiswoode, R.   The Friese-Greene controversy; the
  evidence reconsidered.   Q Film Radio TV 9-3:217
  Spg '55
 Obit.   Publisher W 198:38 S 7 '70

SPRING, SYLVIA
 Women on women in films.   Take One 3-2:10 N/D '70

STAHL, JOHN M.
 Work of.   Motion Pic 54:72 N '37
 Obit.   N. Y. Times p15 Ja 14 '50
  Screen World 2:235 '51
 Sarris, A.   Esoterica; filmog.   Film Culture 28:22
  Spg '63

STANGERUP, HENRIK
 Biographical note.   International Film G 8:117 '71

STAPP, PHILIP
    Stapp, P. Technique vs. content as medium becomes
      message. Film Library Q 1-3:31 Sum '68

STAREVITCH, LADISLAS
    (Also: STAREWITCH, LADISLAS)
    Ford, C. Ladislas Starevitch. Films In Review 9-4:190
      Ap '58
    Estes, O. G. Jr. The master of animation. Classic
      Film Collector 17:11 Win/Spg '67

STAUDTE, WOLFGANG
    Bean, R. The face of '63--Germany. Films & Filming
      9-9:41 Je '63
    Bachmann, J. Wolfgang Staudte; filmog. Film 36:12
      Sum '63

STAUFFACHER, FRANK
    Richter, H. Frank Stauffacher. Film Culture 1-5/6:4
      Win '55

STENBAEK, KIRSTEN
    Sketch. Film 51:33 Spg '68

STERN, GERD
    Listing of films. Film Culture 37:7 Sum '65

STERNBURG, JANET
    Sternburg, J. Revealing herself. Film Library Q 5-1:7
      Win '71/72

STEVENS, GEORGE
    Biographical note; filmog. Movies & People 2:46 '40
    Best director in Hollywood. Time 39:84 F 16 '42
    Director Stevens. Lions Roar 1-6:no p# F '42
    Sketch. American 135:126 My '43
    Biography. Current Biography 13:48 Ap '52
      Same. Current Biography 1952:558 '53
    Shane. Time 61:104 Ap 13 '53
    Martin, B. Man who made the hit called Shane. Sat
      Evening Post 226:32 Ag 8 '53
    Houston, P. Shane and George Stevens. Sight & Sound
      23-2:71 O/D '53
    Cecil, N. George Stevens; letter. Films In Review
      5-2:105 F '54
    New pictures. Time 68:110 O 22 '56
    Houston, P. A place in the sun. Sight & Sound 35-1:23

Win '65/66

Archer, E.   George Stevens and the American dream; filmog.   Film Culture 3-1(11):2 '57

Stang, J.   Stevens relives Anne Frank's story.   N. Y. Times Mag p14 Ag 3 '58

Luft, H. G.   George Stevens; filmog.   Films In Review 9-9:486 N '58

Great director, great story, filming The diary of Anne Frank.   Life 45:444 D 22 '58

Personality of the month.   Films & Filming 5-3:5 D '58

Letters.   Films In Review 10-1:60 Ja '59

Stang, J.   Hollywood romantic.   Films & Filming 5-10:9 Jl '59

George who?   Atlantic 205:99 Mr '60

Faster, faster.   Sat R 44:22 Ag 26 '61

Cut!   Newsweek 58:77 S 18 '61

Modest professional.   Sat R 45:18 S 8 '62

Forget the incense; filming of The greatest story ever told.   Time 80:34 S 28 '62

Fenin, G.   The face of '63--United States.   Films & Filming 9-6:55 Mr '63

The Biblical then and now.   Show 3-4:115 Ap '63

Sarris, A.   Third line; filmog.   Film Culture 28:18 Spg '63

Trombley, W.   Greatest story ever told; filming in Utah desert.   Sat Evening Post 236:34 O 19 '63

Silke, J. R.   The costumes of George Stevens.   Cinema (BH) 1-6:17 N/D '63

America's ten outstanding young men of 1963.   Look 28:63 Ja 28 '64

Bartlett, N.   Sentiment and humanism.   Film 39:26 Spg '64

Silke, J. R.   A monography of George Stevens' films.   Cinema (BH) 2-4:8 D '64/Ja '65

Heston, C.   Greatest story diaries.   Cinema (BH) 2-4:4 D '64/Ja '65

Interview.   Cinema (BH) 2-4:17 D '64/Ja '65

Silke, J. R.   The picture.   Cinema (BH) 2-4:26 D '64/Ja '65

McVay, D.   Greatest Stevens.   Films & Filming 11-7:10 Ap '65

McVay, D.   Giant Stevens.   Films & Filming 11-8:16 My '65

Very model of a modern intellectual.   Sat R 52:27 F 22 '69

Beresford, B.   George Stevens.   Film 59:12 Sum '70

Maltin, L.   George Stevens; shorts to features; interview.   Action 5-6:12 N/D '70

Spies, J.   Letter regarding film festival in Dallas.  Films
In Review 22-5:318 My '71
American Film Institute University advisory committee
seminar.   Dialogue On Film 2-1:entire issue '72

STEVENSON, ROBERT
Nolan, J. E.   Films on TV.   Films In Review 20-7:432
Ag/S '69

STEWART, BHOB
Listing of films.   Film Culture 37:7 Sum '65

STILLER, MAURITZ
Bainbridge, J.   Great Garbo; excerpts from Garbo.
Life 38:76 Ja 17 '55
Idestam-Almquist, B.   The man who found Garbo.  Films
& Filming 2-11:10 Ag '56
Gronowicz, A.   Greta Garbo and my book.   Contem-
porary R 198:679 D '60
Note.   International Film G 2:42 '65
Sjostrom, V.   As I remember him.   Film Comment
6-2:48 Sum '70

STONE, ANDREW L.
Campbell, A.   Farcial finish of a famous old ship.
Life 47:86 S 7 '59
Andrew and Virginia Stone.   Film 33:14 Aut '62
Stone, A.   A method of making films.   Movie 4:28 N '62
Sarris, A.   Likable but elusive; filmog.   Film Culture
28:35 Spg '63
What directors are saying.   Action 6-3:28 My/Je '71
The professional director speaks.   Making Films 5-4:40
Ag '71

STONE, EZRA
Chrichton, K.   Story of.   Colliers 105:11 Ap 27 '40
Scheuer, P. K.   Directing radio comedy.   Action 4-6:16
N/D '69

STONE, JEROME
Man in the shadow.   Sat R 39:25 O 27 '56

STONE, GEORGE
New films on mental health.   Survey 87:136 Mr '51
New opportunity in a new South.   Survey 87:148 Ap '51
Doctors in Washington.   Survey 87:227 My '51
Sword and the heart, impact of defense.   Survey 87:279 Je '51

Weapon of shame.   Survey 87:391 S '51
Films about getting well.   Survey 87:504 N '51

STOUMEN, LOUIS CLYDE
Naked eye makes still pictures move.   Popular Photo
40:116 Ap '57
Kevles, B. L.   Interview.   Film Culture 38:44 Fall '65

STRAUB, JEAN-MARIE
Dictionary of young German filmmakers.   CTVD 4-2:11
Spg '66
Baxter, B.   Jean-Marie Straub.   Film 54:35 Spg '69

STREIT, DAVID
Streit, D.   Filming at 21,000 feet.   Filmmakers Newsletter 5-4:19 F '72

STRICK, JOSEPH
Fenin, G.   The face of '63--United States.   Films &
Filming 9-6:55 Mr '63
Joy censors beware.   Newsweek 68:110 S 19 '66
Things I am here to read.   Life 62:58 Mr 31 '67
Arkadin.   Film clips.   Sight & Sound 36-2:100 Spg '67
Rhode, E.   Strick's Ulysses.   Encounter 29:51 Ag '67
On the scene.   Playboy 15-9:177 S '68
Loney, G.   I can be pretty insulting!   After Dark 12-3:47
Jl '70

STROBEL, HANS ROLF
Dictionary of young German filmmakers.   CTVD 4-2:11
Spg '66

STROMBERG, HUNT
MGM producer.   Cue 3-13:3 Ja 26 '35
Biographical note; filmog.   Movies & People 2:46 '40
Beatty, J.   Star maker.   American 139:46 Ja '45

STROYEVNA, VERA
Feldman, J. & H.   Women directors.   Films In Review
1-8:9 N '50

STUART, MEL
Margulies, L.   In the documentary you cannot comment
on love and sex.   Action 7-1:9 Ja/F '72

STURGEON, ROLLIN
Wing, W. E. Sketch.   N. Y. Dramatic Mirror 69:42 Ja 15 '13

Colwell, M.   Work of.   Motion Pic 12:89 N '16

STURGES, JOHN
    Anderson, J. L.   When the twain meet:  Hollywood's
      remake of The seven samurai.   Film Q 15:55 Spg '62
    Sturges, J.   How the west was lost.   Films & Filming
      9-3:9 D '62
    Fenin, G.   The face of '63--United States.   Films &
      Filming 9-6:55 Mr '63
    Sarris, A.   Minor disappointments; filmog.   Film
      Culture 28:41 Spg '63
    Cherry, R.   Capsule of John Sturges.   Action 4-6:9 N/D
      '69
    Noqueira, R.   Writing for the movies; interview with
      Walter Newman.   Focus On Film 11:44 Aut '72

STURGES, PRESTON
    Biography.   Current Biography 2:844 '41
    King, A.   Biographical sketch.   Vogue 104:156 Ag 15 '44
    Busch, N. F.   Preston Sturges.   Life 20:85 Ja 7 '46
    Parsons, L. O.   Cosmopolitan's citation for the best di-
      rection of the month.   Cosmop 121:72 N '46
    Life looks at the habits of U. S. executives.   Life 24:112
      Je 28 '48
    Kracauer, S.   Preston Sturges on laughter betrayed.
      Films In Review 1-1:11 F '50
    Innovation by Sturges.   Newsweek 37:84 My 7 '51
    Conversation with Preston Sturges.   Sight & Sound 25-4:
      182 Spg '56
    Carey, A. L.   Then and now.   N. Y. Times Mag p94
      D 2 '56
    King, N. & Stonier, G. W.   Preston Sturges.   Sight &
      Sound 28-3/4:185 Sum/Aut '59
    Filmography.   Film 21:32 S/O '59
    Obit.   Americana Annual 1960:860 '60
      British Book Year 1960:515 '60
      Current Biography 20:42 O '59
      Current Biography Yearbook 1959:434 '60
      Film 21:32 S/O '59
      Illustrated London N 235:90 Ag 22 '59
      N. Y. Times p32 Ag 7; p88 Ag 9 '59
      Newsweek 54:66 Ag 17 '59
      Screen World 11:224 '60
    Farber, M. & Poster, W. S.   Preston Sturges: success
      in movies.   Film Culture 26:9 Fall '62
    Jensson, E.   Preston Sturges and the theory of decline.
      Film Culture 26:17 Fall '62

Sarris, A.   Third line; filmog.   Film Culture 28:18 Spg
'63

Houston, P.   Preston Sturges.   Sight & Sound 34-3:130
Sum '65

Downey, R.   Past master.   New York 3-33:46 Ag 17 '70

Sarris, A.   Preston Sturges in the thirties; filmog.   Film
Comment 6-4:81 Win '70/71

Zucker, P.   List of screenplays.   Films In Review 22-3:
184 Mr '71

Corliss, R.   Preston Sturges; filmog.   Cinema (BH)
7-2:25 Spg '72


SUCKSDORFF, ARNE
Hardy, F.   The films of Arne Sucksdorff.   Sight & Sound
17-66:60 Sum '48

Ulrichsen, E.   Arne Sucksdorff.   Films In Review 4-8:441
O '53

de la Roche, C.   Arne Sucksdorff's adventure.   Sight &
Sound 23-2:83 O/D '53

Biography.   Current Biography 17:61 Ap '56
Same.   Current Biography Yearbook 1956:612 '57

Starr, C.   Paradise regained on home movies.   House
Beautiful 99:100 F '57

Arne Sucksdorff; interview.   Cinema (BH) 2-6:39 Jl/Ag
'65

Note.   International Film G 2:42 '65


SUFRIN, MARK
Journey to Masada.   Commentary 19:568 Je '55

Sufrin, M.   Filming a skid row.   Sight & Sound 25-3:133
Win '55/56

Case of the disappearing cook.   American Heritage 21:37
Ag '70


SUGHRUE, JOHN J.
Sughrue, J. J.   What's a documentary?   Action 1-1:6
S/O '66

Sughrue, J. J.   One frame at a time.   Action 2-4:14
Jl/Ag '67


SULLIVAN, MARK
Sullivan, M.   Holographic movies.   Filmmakers Newsletter 4-6:39 Ap '71


SUMMER, EDWARD T.
Demby, B. J.   Filming sci-fi: Item 72-D.   Filmmakers
Newsletter 5-12:32 O '72

SUTHERLAND, A. EDWARD (Eddie)
    Harden, D.   Sketch.   Photoplay 29:66 My '26
    Black, C. M.   Man with a megaphone.   Colliers 102:17
        Jl 16 '38

SUTTON, HOWARD
    Sutton, H.   The practical animator.   Todays Filmmaker
        1-1:50 Ag '71

SWIKARD, CHARLES
    Biographical note.   Photoplay 9-4:42 Mr '16

SZABO, ISTVAN
    Sarris, A.   Movers.   Sat R 50:21 D 23 '67
    Hungarian director Szabo discusses his Father.   Film
        Comment 5-1:59 Fall '68
    Biographical note.   International Film G 5:100 '68

TABOAS, FRANK
  Film Comment announces the recipients of the 1964 anni-
    versary awards.  Film Comment 2-3: Sum '64

TALBOT, LINDA
  Listing of films.  Film Culture 37:7 Sum '65

TASHLIN, FRANK
  Bogdanovich, P.  Frank Tashlin; interview and an appre-
    ciation; filmog.  Film Culture 26:21 Fall '62
  Bogdanovich, P. Tashlin! Interview.  Movie 7:14 F/Mr '63
  Cameron, I.  Frank Tashlin and the new world; filmog.
    Movie 7:16 F/Mr '63
  Filmography.  Film Comment 6-4:101 Win '70/71
  Obit.  N. Y. Times Bio Ed  My 9 '72
  Bogdanovich, P.  Frank Tashlin.  N. Y. Times Bio Ed
    May 28 '72
  Funeral.  (Reprint L. A. Times)  Classic Film Collector
    36:extra 2  Fall '72

TATI, JACQUES
  Knight, A.  One man's movie.  Sat R 37:30 Je 19 '54
  Mr. Hulot.  New Yorker 30:20 Jl 17 '54
  Mayer, A. C.  The art of Jacques Tati.  Q Film Radio
    TV 10-1:19 Fall  '55
  Jacques Tati.  Film 17:10 S/O '58
  Talk with Tati.  Newsweek 52:98 N 10 '58
  Torment of Mr. Tati.  Life 45:20 N 17 '58
  The French film; discussion.  Film 26:10 N/D '60
  Biography.  Current Biography 22:40 F '61
    Same.  Current Biography Yearbook 1961:443 '62
  Lachize, S.  Close to a masterpiece.  Atlas 15:55 Mr '68
  Chapier, H.  Gauche and ridiculous.  Atlas 15:56 Mr '68
  Maelstaf, R.  Interview.  CTVD 5-4:8 Sum '68
  Director of the year; filmog.  International Film G 6:25
    '69
  Armes, R.  The comic art of Jacques Tati.  Screen
    11-1:68 F '70
  What directors are saying.  Action 5-6:22 N/D '70
  Eyles, A.  Biographical sketch; filmog.  Focus On Film
    8:8 n. d.

## TAUROG, NORMAN

Comedy relief artists who saw pictures by making people laugh. Photoplay 46:67 Je '34

Courtney, W. B. His success with child actors. Colliers 96:14 O 12 '35

Biographical note; filmog. Movies & People 2:46 '40

He looked at himself. Lions Roar 1-4:no p# D '41

Uncle Norm. Lions Roar 2-1:no p# S/O '42

He raises stars. Lions Roar 2-4:no p# Ap '43

Hot show: 109 in the shade. Lions Roar 3-1:no p# S '43

MGM's directors range from pioneers to newcomers. Lions Roar 3-4:no p# Jl '44

The directors choose the best films. Cinema (BH) 1-5:14 Ag/S '63

## TAYLOR, DONALD F.

Obit. Screen World 18:240 '67

## TAYLOR, RAY

Malcomson, R. M. The sound serial. Views & Reviews 3-1:13 Sum '71

## TAYLOR, SAM

Shales, T. From Woodville to Greystone: the odyssey of a young, black filmmaker. AFI Report 3:9 N '72

## TAYLOR, SAMUEL

Obit. Screen World 10:226 '59

## TAYLOR, WILLIAM DESMOND

How he became a photoplayer. Motion Pic 8:78 Ja '15

Willis, R. William Desmond Taylor. Movie Pictorial 2-6:8 D '15

Taylor, W. D. An explanation of some of the studio terms. Film Players Herald & Movie Pictorial 2-7:24 F '16

Obit. N. Y. Clipper 70:30 F 8 '22

Chrisman, J. E. The Taylor murder case as a fiction thriller. Motion Pic 42:32 Ag '31

District attorney exonerates Mary Miles Minter of Taylor death. Lit Digest 123:10 F 13 '37

Hynd, A. Murder in Hollywood. American Mercury 69:594 N '49

The William Desmond Taylor mystery. Show 1-12:18 S 3 '70

## TERRISS, TOM

Grayson, C. Sketch. Motion Pic Classic 33:65 Ap '31

Bravest of the bulls.   Coronet 35:78 F '54
Obit.   Screen World 16:225 '65

TERRY, PAUL H.
Obit.   Classic Film Collector 33:46 Win '71 (reprint N.Y.
Times)  N.Y. Times O 26 '71
Same.   N.Y. Times Bio Ed O 26 '71

TESHIGAHARA, HIROSHI
Documentary fantasist.   New Yorker 41:35 Ap 10 '65

TETZLAFF, TED
Parsons, L. O.   Cosmopolitan's citation for the best director of the month.   Cosmop 127:13 Jl '49

THIELE, ROLF
Bean, R.   The face of '63--Germany.   Films & Filming
9-9:41 Je '63

THOMAS, GERALD
Filmography.   Film 14:8 N/D '57
British cinema filmography.   Film 65:10 Spg '72

THOMAS, RALPH
Filmography.   Film 14:8 N/D '57
British feature directors; an index to their work.   Sight
& Sound 27-6:303 Aut '58
British cinema filmography.   Film 65:10 Spg '72

THOMAS, WILLIAM C.
Show business; Pine-Thomas pictures.   Time 46:82 Ag 6
'45
English, R.   Gaudiest producers in Hollywood.   Sat Evening Post 225:22 Ja 3 '53

THOMPSON, HUGH
Listing of films.   Film Culture 37:7 Sum '65

THOMPSON, J. LEE
Filmography.   Film 14:8 N/D '57
British feature directors; an index to their work.   Sight &
Sound 27-6:299 Aut '58
Personality of the month.   Films & Filming 5-5:5 F '59
Movie viewer; interview.   Modern Photo 25:28 N '61
Fenin, G.   The face of '63.   Films & Filming 9-6:55
Mr '63
Thompson, J. L.   The still small voice of truth.  Films
& Filming 8-7:5 Ap '63

British cinema filmography.　Film 65:10 Spg '72
Winogura, D.　On the filming of Conquest of the planet of
　the apes.　Cinefantastique 2-2:32 Sum '72
Winogura, D.　Dialogues on apes, apes and more apes;
　interview.　Cinefantastique 2-2:23 Sum '72

THOMSEN, KNUD LEIF
　Biographical note.　International Film G 6:63 '69

THORNBY, ROBERT T.
　Sketch.　N. Y. Dramatic Mirror 75:33 Je 10 '16

THORPE, RICHARD
　Work of.　Motion Pic 54:64 Ag '37
　Biographical note; filmog.　Movies & People 2:46 '40
　The screen's challenge.　Lions Roar 1-6:no p# F '42
　Tarzan for escape.　Lions Roar 1-10:no p# Je '42
　The world's his stage.　Lions Roar 2-2:no p# N '42
　Jungle to penthouse.　Lions Roar 2-3(sup):no p# Ja '43
　To the ladies.　Lions Roar 2-5:no p# Jl '43
　60 days in a Hollywood harem.　Lions Roar 3-2:no p# Ja
　　'44
　Two towns and a director.　Lions Roar 3-3(sup):no p#
　　Ap '44
　MGM's directors range from pioneers to newcomers.
　　Lions Roar 3-4:no p# Jl '44
　Quiet, please.　Lions Roar 4-1:no p# F '45
　Richard Thorpe.　Film 33:10 Aut '62
　Brion, P.　Filmography.　Films In Review 17-7:463 Ag/S
　　'66

TILDEN, MILANO C.
　Obit.　N. Y. Times p28 O 2 '51

TORRE-NILSSON, LEOPOLDO
　Trajtenberg, M.　Torre-Nilsson and his double.　Film Q
　　15-1:34 Fall '61
　DiNubila, D.　An Argentine partnership.　Films & Filming
　　7-12:17 S '61
　The screen answers back.　Films & Filming 8-8:12 My '62
　Torre-Nilsson, L.　How to make a new wave.　Films &
　　Filming 9-2:19 N '62
　Betsford, K.　Leopoldo Torre-Nilsson; the underside of
　　the coin.　Show 2-11:84 N '62
　Cobos, J.　The face of '63--Spain.　Films & Filming
　　10-1:39 O '63
　Interview.　CTVD 2-3:9 Win '63/64

Director of the year; filmog.   International Film G 4:31
'67

TORRICELLI, UGO
Davis, H.   Inside the mind of a communications philoso-
pher; interview.   Filmmakers Newsletter 4-12:31 O '71

TOURNEUR, JACQUES
Stylization in motion picture direction.   Motion Pic 15:101
S '18
Haskins, H.   Work of.   Motion Pic Classic 7:16 S '18
Cheatham, M. S.   Interview.   Motion Pic Classic 9:34
F '20
Handy, T. B.   Interview.   Motion Pic 20:40 N '20
Goldbeck, W.   Interview.   Motion Pic 24:25 Ja '23
Sarris, A.   Esoterica; filmog.   Film Culture 28:22
Spg '63
Tourneur, J.   Taste without cliches.   Films & Filming
12-2:9 N '65
Wood, R.   The shadow world of Jacques Tourneur.
Film Comment 8-2:64 Sum '72

TOURNEUR, MAURICE
Tourneur.   Photoplay 9-2:139 Ja '16
Nutting, D.   Monsieur Tourneur.   Photoplay 14-2:55
Jl '18
Geltzer, G.   Maurice Tourneur; filmog.   Films In Re-
view 12-4:193 Ja '61
Obit.   Screen World 13:226 '62

TOWNSEND, GORDON
Listing of films.   Film Culture 37:7 Sum '65

TOYE, WENDY
Personality of the month.   Films & Filming 3-5:3 F '57
Filmography.   Film 14:8 N/D '57
British feature directors; an index to their work.   Sight
& Sound 27-6:303 Aut '58

TRACHTENBERG, LEO
Films owe responsibility to society.   Making Films
3-2:32 Ap '69

TREMPER, WILL
Bean, R.   The face of '63--Germany.   Films & Filming
9-9:41 Je '63
Three enterprising filmmakers.   International Film G 1:96
'64

## TRESS, ARTHUR
Listing of films. Film Culture 37:7 Sum '65
Scully, J. Usual subjects; unusual images. Modern Photo 33:72 Ap '69
Urban meadows; photographs. Sat R 53:56 Mr 7 '70

## TRESSLER, GEORG
Bean, R. The face of '63--Germany. Films & Filming 9-9:41 Je '63
Streibig, D. Children's game. Popular Photo 54:141 Ja '64

## TRIMBLE, LAWRENCE (Larry)
Sumner, K. This man trained Strongheart, the wonder dog. American 95:8 Mr '23
Motion picture dogs and others. Sat Evening Post 201:8 F 2 '29
Obit. N.Y. Times p29 F 10 '54
Screen World 6:225 '55

## TRINTIGNANT, NADINE
Talks on her movie, It only happens to others. Show 2-10:36 D '71

## TRIVAS, VICTOR
Obit. N.Y. Times p41 Ap 13 '70

## TRNKA, JIŘÍ
Metzl, E. Four European illustrators. American Artist 19:34 D '55
Broz, J. Interview. Film 7:16 Ja/F '56
Trnkaland. Newsweek 67:99 Mr 28 '66
Obit. Graphic 25-146:574 '69/70
N.Y. Times p23 D 31 '69
Newsweek 75:45 Ja 12 '70

## TROELL, JAN
Director of the year; filmog. International Film G p35 '72
Filmmaking in Sweden. Interview 1-7:27 n.d.

## TRUFFAUT, FRANÇOIS
Rivette, J. & Truffaut, F. Renoir in America. Sight & Sound 24-1:12 Jl/S '54
Scherer, M. & Truffaut, F. Interview with Roberto Rossellini. Film Culture 1-2:12 Mr/Ap '55
Grenier, C. New wave at Cannes. Reporter 21:39 Jl 23 '59

6 films 6 faces. Unifrance 50:24 Jl/S '59

Sadoul, G. Notes on a new generation. Sight & Sound 28-3/4:111 Sum/Aut '59

Meeting La nouvelle vague; conversation. Films & Filming 6-1:7 O '59

Billard, G. The men and their work. Films & Filming 7-1:7 O '59

Hartung, P. T. Screen. Commonweal 71:265 N 27 '59

On film. New Yorker 36:36 F 20 '60

Tomorrow the artists. Films & Filming 7-1:17 O '60

The French film; discussion. Film 26:10 N/D '60

Marcorelles, L. Interview. Sight & Sound 31-3:35 Win '61/62

Franchi, R. M. & Lewis, M. Conversation with Truffaut. Film Journal (Aus) 19:37 Ap '62

Truffaut, F. Jules & Jim, sex and life. Films & Filming 8-10:19 Jl '62

Graham, P. The face of '63--France. Films & Filming 9-8:13 My '63

Shatnoff, J. Francois Truffaut--the anarchist imagination. Film Q 16-3:3 Spg '63

Ronder, P. Interview. Film Q 17-1:3 Fall '63

Truffaut, F. Skeleton keys (Hitchcock). Film Culture 32:63 Spg '64

Meanwhile ... action! Film 39:24 Spg '64

Truffaut. New Yorker 40:45 O 31 '64

Director of the year; filmog. International Film G p19 '64

Klein, M. The literary sophistication of Francois Truffaut. Film Comment 3-3:24 Sum '65

Billiard, P. From critic to director. Atlas 10:178 S '65

Truffaut, F. A certain tendency of the French cinema. Cahiers (Eng) 1:31 Ja '66

Genet. Letter from Paris. New Yorker 42:182 O 1 '66

Truffaut, F. Skeleton keys (Hitchcock). Cahiers 2:61 '66

Truffaut, F. Journal of Fahrenheit 451. Cahiers (Eng) 5:11 '66; 6:11 D '66; 7:9 Ja '67

Jacob, G. Holloywood sur Seine. Sight & Sound 36-4:162 Aut '67

Morgenstern, J. MacGuffin man. Newsweek 71:59 Ja 1 '68

Biography. Time 92:54 Jl 5 '68

Sklar, R. Two masters of the cinema. Reporter 38:48 F 8 '68

Cinema. Time 92:54 Jl 5 '68

Braudy, L. Hitchcock, Truffaut, and the irresponsible audience. Film Q 21-4:21 Sum '68

Jacob, G. The 400 blows of Francois Truffaut. Sight & Sound 37-4:190 Aut '68

Biography.   Current Biography 30:39 Ja '69
   Same.   Current Biography Yearbook 1969:428 '70
Jacob, G.   Miraculous and inspired.   Atlas 17:64 F '69
Schickel, R.   Monsieur Truffaut makes it look so easy.
   Life 66:18 Mr 7 '69
Kael, P.   Current cinema.   New Yorker 45:114 Mr 8 '69
Morgenstern, J.   Ten years of Truffaut.   Newsweek
   73:99 Mr 10 '69
Millar, G.   Hitchcock versus Truffaut.   Sight & Sound
   38-2:82 Spg '69
DeGramont, S.   Life style of homo cinematius.   N. Y.
   Times Mag p12 Je 15 '69
Wood, R.   Chabrol and Truffaut.   Movie 17:16 Win
   '69/70
Elsaesser, T.   Truffaut.   Brighton 21:17 Mr '70
Is Truffaut the happiest man on earth?   Esquire 74:66
   Ag '70
Gilliatt, P.   Current cinema.   New Yorker 46:67 S 12 '70
Flatley, G.   So Truffaut decided to work on his own
   miracle.   N. Y. Times Bio Ed S 27 '70
Interview.   New Yorker 46:35 O 17 '70
O'Connor, J. J.   Will the real Francois Truffaut please
   stand up.   Making Films 4-5:41 O '70
Bordwell, D.   Francois Truffaut; a man can serve two
   masters.   Film Comment 7-1:18 Spg '71
Cast, D.   Style without style.   Film Heritage 7-2:10
   Win '71/72
Gerlach, J.   Truffaut and Itard.   Film Heritage 7-3:1
   Spg '72
Gow, G.   Interview; filmog.   Films & Filming 8-10:18
   Jl '72
Jebb, J.   Truffaut: the educated heart.   Sight & Sound
   41-3:144 Sum '72

TRUMAN, MICHAEL
   Filmography.   Film 14:8 N/D '57

TRUMBULL, DOUGLAS
   Thomas, B.   First feature.   Action 7-3:17 My/Je '72
   Anderson, K. & Meech, S.   Silent running; interview.
      Cinefantastique 2-2:8 Sum '72

TRYON, GLENN
   Standish, B.   Interview.   Motion Pic Classic 26:42 F '28
   Reay, N.   Interview.   Photoplay 35:56 D '28
   Calhoun, D.   Sketch.   Motion Pic 38:78 D '29
   Walker, H. L.   Interview.   Motion Pic 40:42 Ag '30

TSUCHIMOTO, NORIAKI
  Biographical note.   International Film G 9:185 '72

TUCKER, GEORGE LOANE
  Saga of Singing pine.   Better Home & Garden 15:24 Mr
    '37

TULLY, MONTGOMERY
  British feature directors; an index to their work.   Sight
    & Sound 27-6:303 Aut '58

TURMAN, LAWRENCE
  What directors are saying.   Action 6-3:28 My/Je '71
  Turman, L.   The marriage of a young stockbroker.
    Action 6-4:17 Jl/Ag '71
  The professional director speaks.   Making Films 5-4:40
    Ag '71

TUTTLE, FRANK
  Truck driver becomes a star.   Cue 13-44:13 O 28 '44
  Obit.   Screen World 15:226 '64

TWIST, DEREK
  Filmography.   Film 14:8 N/D '57
  British feature directors; an index to their work.   Sight
    & Sound 27-6:303 Aut '58

ULMER, EDGAR G.
   Sarris, A.   Esoterica; filmog.   Film Culture 28:22
      Spg '63
   Belton, J.   Prisoners of paronoia; filmog.   Velvet Light
      Trap 5:17 Sum '72

UNCLE, ARTY
   Listing of films.   Film Culture 37:7 Sum '65

USTINOV, PETER
   Ustinov, P.   Extra weight.   Sight & Sound 18-71:14
      Aut '49
   Johns, E.   A phenomenal exception.   Theatre World p33
      S '49
   Unquenchable Ustinov.   Life 34:101 F 2 '53
   One-man band.   New Statesman 47:407 Mr 27 '54
   Runswick, J.   Journey with Ustinov.   Plays & Players
      2-8:21 My '55
   Biography.   Current Biography 16:46 D '55
      Same.   Current Biography Yearbook 1955:618 '56
   Hobson, L. Z.   Trade winds.   Sat R 39:6 Jl 21 '56
   Barker, F. G.   Sugar-coated satirist.   Plays & Players
      3-10:5 Jl '56
   People are talking about.   Vogue 130:171 O 1 '57
   Ustinov, P.   Max Ophuls.   Sight & Sound 27-1:49 Sum
      '57
   New perspective for playwrights   Theatre Arts 41:21
      O '57
   Directing filmography.   Film 14:8 N/D '57
   Ustinov, P.   Tiring, wearing, infuriating--but great fun.
      International Film A 1:66 '57
   Busting out all over.   Time 71:59 Mr 10 '58
   Everything's his line.   Newsweek 51:80 Mr 10 '58
   Stanley, J. P.   Television.   America 98:733 Mr 22 '58
   Eleven fine actors get their dream roles.   Life 44:76
      Ap 14 '58
   Schickel, R.   Country called Ustinov.   Look 22:86 Ap 29
      '58
   By the beard of the prophet.   TV Guide 6-18:12 My 3 '58
   Bester, A.   Loveable egghead.   Holiday 24:99 Jl '58
   McCalls visits.   McCalls 86:8 N '58
   Brandon, H.   America's quest for culture; interview.
      New Republic 139:13 D 8 '58

Salute to Ustinov. Christian Century 76:5 Ja 7 '59

Ustinov, P. Doing it all at once. Films & Filming 6-8:5 My '60

Millstein, G. Cartel called Ustinov. N. Y. Times Mag p18 Ja 29 '61

Peter, the great showman. Life 50:81 My 19 '61

Bachmann, G. Ustinov; interview. Film 30:18 Win '61

Peter Ustinov. Film 34:14 Win '62

Cowie, P. The face of '63--Great Britain. Films & Filming 9-5:19 F '63

Alive and kicking. Life 54:53 Ap 19 '63

Ustinov writes of the days when he was a roadster. Life 54:56 Ap 19 '63

Peter Ustinov. Plays & Players 11-4:9 Ja '64

Brandon, H. Peter Ustinov speaking. Atlantic 214:29 Jl '64

Lyon, N. Peter Ustinov: I like what tempts my eye. Vogue 144:223 O 1 '64

Art of asking questions; adaptation of address. Sat R 48:22 D 25 '65

Politics and the arts; excerpt from address. Atlantic 218:44 Jl '66

Polymorph. Newsweek 68:99 O 10 '66

Higgins, R. Nobody has ever called him dull. TV Guide 14-45:38 N 5 '66

Atlantic report. Atlantic 218:16 N '66

Ustinov. New Yorker 43:23 Jl 15 '67

Luxury. Vogue 150:147 N 1 '67

Art and artlessness. Films & Filming 15-1:4 O '68

Ustinov on tennis. Sports Illustrated 30:40 Je 23 '69

Motor trend; interview. Motor Trend 22:98 My '70

Levy, A. Peter Ustinov plays Santa to the children of many nations. Good Housekeeping 171:38 D '70

Musel, R. Peter Ustinov, one-man show. TV Guide 19-11:20 Mr 13 '71

Knapp, D. On location in Mexico. Show 2-7:18 S '71

What directors are saying. Action 7-1:36 Ja/F '72

VADIM, ROGER
    Biographical note.  Unifrance 45:11 D '57
    Schneider, P. E.  France's fabulous young five.  N. Y.
        Times Mag p12 Mr 30 '58
    Which is which?  Look 23:62 Mr 31 '59
    Chapsal, M.  Sins out of context.  Reporter 21:31
        N 12 '59
    Billard, G.  Ban on Vadim.  Films & Filming 6-2:29
        N '59
    Pygmalion of sex.  New Statesman 60:295 S 3 '60
    Personality of the month.  Films & Filming 8-5:7 F '62
    Graham, P.  The face of '63--France.  Films & Filming
        9-8:13 My '63
    The French Fonda.  Playboy 13-8:66 Ag '66
    Blonde black panther.  Time 88:76 S 9 '66
    Maben, A.  Vadim and Zola.  Films & Filming 13-1:58
        O '66
    The night Jane Fonda's husband flew off with another
        woman.  Photoplay 77-5:38 My '70
    Harmetz, A.  In Vadim's garden--Pretty maids all in a
        row.  N. Y. Times Bio Ed S 6 '70
    What directors are saying.  Action 6-1:30 Ja/F '71
    Vadim, R.  Pretty maids.  Playboy 18-4:153 Ap '71

VAIL, LESTER
    Obit.  Screen World 11:225 '60

VALCROZE, DONIOL
    Billard, G.  The men and their work.  Films & Filming
        6-1:7 O '59

VALÈRE, JEAN
    Meeting La nouvelle vague; conversation.  Films & Film-
        ing 6-1:7 O '59

VAN BRAKEL, NOUCHKA
    Biographical note.  International Film G 8:208 '71

VanDerBEEK, STAN
    VanDerBeek, S.  If the actor is the audience.  Film
        Culture 24:92 Spg '62
    Mekas, J.  Notes on the new American cinema.  Film
        Culture 24:6 Spg '62

VanDerBeek, S.  Anti-dotes for poisoned movies.   Film
    Culture 25:71 Sum '62
Listing of films.   Film Culture 38:7 Sum '65
Christgau, R.   Master of animation.   Popular Photo
    57:106 S '65
Weinberg, G.   The sixth Montreal international film
    festival.   Film Heritage 1-2:35 Win '65/66
VanDerBeek, S.   Culture: intercom and expanded cinema.
    Film Culture 40:15 Spg '66
VanDerBeek, S.   Re: vision.   American Scholar 35:335
    Spg '66
Culture: intercom.   Tulane Drama R 11:38 Fall '66
Manica, A. & Van Dyke, W.   Four artists as filmmakers.
    Art In America 55:71 Ja '67
Disposable art--synthetic media-- and artificial intelligence.
    Take One 2-3:14 Ja/F '69
New talent: the computer.   Art In America 58:86 Ja '70
Weiner, P.   New American cinema; filmog.   Film 58:22
    Spg '70
VanDerBeek, S.   Movies: disposable art.   Filmmakers
    Newsletter 3-9/10:4 Sum '70
VanDerBeek, S.   Media wrap-around.   Filmmakers News-
    letter 4-5:20 Mr '71


van der HEYDE, NIKOLAI
    Biographical note.   International Film G 5:118 '68
    Biographical note.   International Film G 8:209 '71


van der HEYDEN, JEF
    Biographical note.   International Film G 5:118 '68


VAN der HORST, HERMAN
    Biographical note.   International Film G 2:117 '65
    Biographical note.   International Film G 8:209 '71


VAN DER KEUKEN, JOHAN
    Biographical note.   International Film G 7:166 '70


van der LINDEN, CHARLES
    Biographical sketch.   International Film G 3:117 '66
    Biographical note.   International Film G 8:209 '71


VAN DER LINDEN, RUPERT
    Biographical note.   International Film G 8:209 '71


VAN DYKE, W. S. (Woodbridge Strong)
    Cruikshank, H.   Sketch.   Motion Pic 36:72 Ja '29

Tilden, G.   The story of filming Eskimo.   Movie
    Classic 5:34 N '33
Beatty, J.   The most interesting man in Hollywood.
    American 118:76 Ag '34
W. S. Van Dyke, from horse opera to epic.   Cue 3-20:3
    Mr 16 '35
Condon, F.   Choice locations.   Colliers 95:18 My 18 '35
Penfield, C.   Sketch.   Stage 13:62 Ap '36
Lee, S.   Interview.   Movie Classic 10:43 Jl '36
Sharpe, H.   Work of.   Photoplay 50:71 D '36
Russell, F.   A short-short visit.   Silver Screen 7-10:55
    Ag '37
Rodgers, B.   Van Dyke, the unorthodox.   Cinema
    Progress 2-3:14 Ag '37
Biographical note; filmog.   Movies & People 2:46 '40
Everybody loves a fight.   Lions Roar 1-2:no p# O '41
W. S. Van Dyke II, vigorous romantic.   Lions Roar
    1-3:no p# N '41
He sees stars.   Lions Roar 1-5:no p# Ja '42
Mr. Van at work.   Lions Roar 1-8:no p# Ap '42
Mr. Van.   Lions Roar 2-1:no p# S/O '42
It made him mad.   Lions Roar 2-3:no p# D '52
Obit.   Current Biography '43
    Newsweek 21:6 F 15 '43
    Time 41:58 F 15 '43
Riggan, B.   Damn the crocodiles, keep the camera
    rolling!  American Heritage 18:38 Je '68
Canaba, R. Jr.   Concerning Trader Horn.   Views &
    Reviews 3-1:35 Sum '71
Tuska, J.   Trader Horn.   Views & Reviews 3-1:51
    Sum '71

VAN DYKE, WILLARD
    Group f 64.   Scribner 103:55 Mr '38
    Take a camera and find out.   Scholastic 36:14T My 20
    '40
    Van Dyke, W.   The interpretive camera in documentary
        films.   Hollywood Q 1-4:405 Jl '46
    Director on location.   Sat R 32:45 S 10 '49
    Mekas, J. & Lauret, E.   Interview.   Film Culture
        2-3(9):6 '56
    Focus on Willard Van Dyke.   Popular Photo 56:118
        Ap '65
    Engle, H.   Thirty years of social inquiry; interview;
        filmog.   Film Comment 3-2:24 Spg '65
    Van Dyke, W.   Letters.   Film Comment 3-2:38 Spg '65
    Kevles, B. L.   Interview.   Film Culture 38:41 Fall '65

Van Dyke, W.   The role of the Museum of modern art in
     motion pictures.   Film Library Q 1-1:36 Win '67/68
Hays, L.   Glancing backward ... without nostalgia.   Film
     Library Q 4-3:16 Sum '71

van GASTEREN, LOUIS A.
     Biographical sketch.   International Film G 3:118 '66
     Biographical note.   International Film G 8:208 '71

van GELDER, HAN
     Biographical note.   International Film G 9:200 '72

van HAREN NOMAN, THEO
     Biographical note.   International Film G 5:119 '68

VAN METER, BEN
     Alexander, T. K.   San Francisco's hipster cinema.
     Film Culture 44:70 Spg '67

VAN NIE, RENE
     Biographical note.   International Film G 8:208 '71

VAN PEEBLES, MELVIN
     Alpert, H.   Van Peebles story.   Sat R 51:55 Ag 3 '68
     Story of a three-day pass.   Ebony 23:54 S '68
     What directors are saying.   Action 5-2:16 Mr/Ap '70
     On the scene.   Playboy 17-9:195 S '70
     Sweet song of success.   Newsweek 77:89 Je 21 '71
     Rubine, M.   The decolonizer of the black mind.   Show
          2-5:27 Jl '71

VARDA, AGNÈS
     Billard, G.   The men and their work.   Films & Filming
          6-1:7 O '59
     Shivas, M.   Cleo de 5 a 7. and Agnes Varda.   Movie
          3:32 O '62
     Graham, P.   The face of '63--France.   Films & Filming
          9-8:13 My '63
     Strick, P.   Agnes Varda.   Film 35:7 Spg '63
     Gill, B.   Current cinema.   New Yorker 42:113 My 28 '66
     Plants and animals.   Newsweek 67:117 Je 13 '66
     Varda, A.   Le Bonheur.   Cinema (BH) 3-4:48 D '66
     Gow, G.   The underground river.   Films & Filming
          16-6:6 Mr '70
     Biography.   Current Biography 31:40 Jl '70
        Same.   Current Biography Yearbook 1970:424 '71

VASAN, S. S.
Ray, S. K.   New Indian directors.   Film Q 14-1:63
Fall '60

VÉDRÈS, NICOLE
Knight, A.   Paris 1900.   Theatre Arts 34:36 D '50
Knight, A.   La vie commence demain.   Theatre Arts
35:38 S '51
Obit.   Sight & Sound 35:100 Spg '66

VEHR, WILLIAM
Listing of films.   Film Culture 37:7 Sum '65

VENGHEROV, VLADIMIR
Vengherov, V.   Give me actors--not stars.   Films &
Filming 7-6:12 Mr '61

VENTURI, LAURO
Venturi, L.   Roberto Rossellini.   Hollywood Q 4-1:1
Fall '49
Venturi, L.   Films on art: an attempt at classification.
Q Film Radio TV 7-4:385 Sum '53

VERONA, STEPHEN F.
A filmmaker works. . . .   Making Films 5-1:24 F '71

VERSTAPPEN, WIM
Biographical note.   International Film G 6:125 '69
Biographical note.   International Film G 8:208 '71

VERTOV, DZIGA
The writings of Dziga Vertov.   Film Culture 25:50 Sum
'62
Dziga Vertov.   Afterimage 1:no p# Ap '70
The Vertov papers.   Film Comment 8-1:46 Spg '72
Bordwell, D.   Dziga Vertov; an introduction; filmog.
Film Comment 8-1:38 Spg '72
MacBean, J. R.   Godard and the Dziga Vertov group;
film and dialectics.   Film Q 26-1:30 Fall '72
Vertov, D.   Film directors, a revolution.   Cinema (Lon)
9:25 n. d.

VESELY, HERBERT
Dictionary of young German filmmakers.   CTVD 4-2:11
Spg '66

VIANY, ALEX
Viany, A.  Who's who in the cinema novo.  CTVD 6-1:29
Fall '68

VICARIO, JOHN M.
Listing of films.  Film Culture 37:7 Sum '65

VIDOR, CHARLES
Gray, M.  No swansong for director Charles Vidor.
Films & Filming 2-9:12 Je '56
Obit.  British Book Year 1960:516 '60
N. Y. Times p27 Je 5 '59
Newsweek 53:70 Je 15 '59
Screen World 11:226 '60
Time 73:84 Je 15 '59

VIDOR, KING
St. Johns, A. R.  A young crusader.  Photoplay 17-1:64
D '19
Early steps to success.  Motion Pic Classic 8:24 Ag '19
Cheatham, M.  Interview.  Motion Pic Classic 10:22
Je '28
Mulligan, W. E.  Work of.  National R 49:163 Jl '28
Beach, B.  Interview.  Motion Pic 21:57 Mr '21
Home of.  Photoplay 22:48 O '22
Home of.  Classic 15:42 N '22
St. Johns, A. R.  Story of.  Photoplay 24:28 Ag '23
Smith, F. J.  Tells how The big parade was made.
Motion Pic Classic 23:26 My '26
Tully, J.  Interview.  Vanity Fair 26:46 Je '26
Hynd, A.  Work of.  Motion Pic 34:46 S '27
Weller, S. M.  Interview.  Motion Pic Classic 26:23 S '27
Marriage and a screen career hazardous.  Theatre 46:26
N '27
Braver-Mann, B. G.  Widor and evasion.  Experimental
Cinema 1-3 F '31
Orme, M.  Genius of realism.  Illustrated London N
180:12 Ja 2 '32
Wingate, R.  Separation from Eleanor Boardman.  Movie
Classic 3:28 S '32
Trumbo, D.  Stepchild of the muses.  North American
R D '33
Vidor, K.  Rubber stamp movies.  New Theatre S '34
Troy, W.  Collectivism more or less.  Nation 139:488
O 24 '34
Work of.  Motion Pic 52:62 N '36
Vidor, K.  Director's notebook--why teach cinema?

Cinema Progress 4-1/2:2 Je/Jl '39
Biographical note; filmog. Movies & People 2:46 '40
Vidor, K. Bringing Pulham to the screen. Lions Roar
1-4:no p# D '41
Daugherty, F. Steel comes to the films; Vidor's film
America. Christian Science Mon Mag p8 My 8 '43
King Vidor's America. Lions Roar 3-4:no p# Jl '44
MGM's directors range from pioneers to newcomers.
Lions Roar 3-4:no p# Jl '44
Art vs. stocks and bonds. House Beautiful 87:102 D '45
Parsons, L. O. Cosmopolitan's citation as one of the
best directors of the month. Cosmop 122:98 Ja '47
Knight, A. 1929: year of great transition. Theatre
Arts S '49
Arnheim, R. From flickers to Fischinger. Sat R F
18 '50
Vidor, K. The story conference. Films In Review
3-6:266 Je/Jl '52
Vidor, K. & Brooks, R. Two story conferences. Sight
& Sound 22-2:85 O/D '52
Harrington, C. King Vidor's Hollywood progress. Sight
& Sound 22-4:179 Ap/Je '53
Griffith, R. Sovereign audience. Sat R 36:23 O 24 '53
The big screens. Sight & Sound 24-4:209 Spg '55
Man who did it. Newsweek 48:53 Jl 30 '56
Biography. Current Biography 18:50 F '57
Same. Current Biography Yearbook 1957:567 '58
Vidor, K. Me ... and my spectacle. Films & Filming
6-1:6 O '59
Brownlow, K. King Vidor. Film 34:19 (Lon) Win '62
Sarris, A. Second line; filmog. Film Culture 28:11
Spg '63
Perkins, V. F. & Shivas, M. Interview. Movie 11:7
Jl/Ag '63
The directors choose the best films. Cinema (BH) 1-5:14
Ag/S '63
Mitchell, G. J. King Vidor. Films In Review 15-3:179
Mr '64
Higham, C. King Vidor. Film Heritage 1-4 Sum '66
Godard in Hollywood. Take One 1-10:13 Je '68
King Vidor at New York University; discussion. Cineaste
1-4 Spg '68
Greenberg, J. War, wheat and steel; interview. Sight
& Sound 37-4:192 Aut '68
Barr, C. King Vidor. Brighton 21:22 Mr '70
Luft, H. G. A career that spans half a century. Film
Journal 1-2:27 Sum '71

Higham, C.   Long live Vidor, a Hollywood King.   N. Y.
Times Sec 2:1 S 3 '72
Lyons, D. & O'Brien, G.   King Vidor; filmog.   Interview
26:12 O '72

VIGNOLA, ROBERT G.
Poland, J. F.   Sketch.   Motion Pic 15:86 Jl '18

VIGO, JEAN
Kracauer, S.   Jean Vigo.   Hollywood Q 2-3:261 Ap '47
Agee, J.   Life and work of.   Nation 165:51 Jl 12 '47
Weinberg, H. G.   The films of Jean Vigo.   Cinema
(Hollywood) 1-2:17 Jl '47
Isaacs, H. R.   Films in review.   Theatre Arts 31:13
Ag '47
Zilzer, G.   Remembrances of Jean Vigo.   Hollywood Q
3-2:125 Win '47/48
Ashton, D. S.   Portrait of Vigo.   Film 6:20 D '55
The French film; discussion.   Film 26:10 N/D '60
Rhode, E.   Jean Vigo.   Encounter 26:37 F '66
Mills, B.   Anarchy, surrealism and optimism in Zero
de conduite.   Cinema (Lon) 8:24 '71

VINCENT, JAMES
Obit.   N. Y. Times p72 Jl 14 '57
Screen World 9:226 '58

VISCONTI, LUCHINO
Castello, G. C.   Luchino Visconti.   Sight & Sound 25-4:
184 Spg '56
Lane, J. F.   Visconti--the last decadent.   Films &
Filming 2-10:11 Jl '56
Dyer, P. J.   The vision of Visconti.   Film 12:22
Mr/Ap '57
Pepper, C. G.   Composers' director.   Theatre Arts
43:21 Mr '59
Doniol-Valcroze & Donarchi, J.   Interview.   Sight &
Sound 28-3/4:144 Sum/Aut '59
Poggi, G.   Luchino Visconti and the Italian cinema.
Film Q 13-3:11 Spg '60
Pepper, C. G.   Rebirth in Italy.   Newsweek 58:66 Jl 10
'61
Armitage, P.   Visconti and Rocco.   Film 30:28 Win '61
Ardoin, J.   Master magician.   Musical America 81:14
N '61
Colquhoun, A.   ... on safari with Visconti.   Films &
Filming 9-1:10 O '62

Minoff, L.   New old master.   Sat R 45:18 D 29 '62

Lane, J. F.   The face of '63--Italy.   Films & Filming
    9-7:11 Ap '63

People are talking about.   Vogue 142:48 Jl '63

Moravia, A.   Visconti, the leopard man.   Vogue 142:50
    Jl '63

Visconti, L.   Drama of non-existence.   Cahiers (Eng)
    2:12 '66

Hanson, W.   Leopard: interview.   Opera N 28:16 S 28 '63

Director of the year; filmog.   International Film G p11 '64

Biography.   Current Biography 26:38 Ja '65
    Same.   Current Biography Yearbook 1965:436 '65

Visconti.   New Yorker 44:25 Jl 20 '68

Seria, D. J.   Artist life.   Hi Fi 18:MA8 O '68

Roud, R.   Memories of Resnais.   Sight & Sound 38-3:124
    Sum '69

Salute of the week.   Cue 38-51:1 D 20 '69

Elsaesser, T.   Luchino Visconti.   Brighton 17:21 F '70

Sarris, A.   Director of the month.   Show 1-3:21 Mr '70

Wolf, W.   A celebrated director creates his own universe.
    Cue 39-26:7 Je 27 '70

Alpert, H.   Visconti in Venice.   Sat R 53:16 Ag 8 '70

Fischer, J.   Visconti's The damned: words, sights,
    echoes.   Contempora 1-4:2 O/N '70

Radkai, K.   Visconti.   Vogue 156:182 N 1 '70

Visconti, L.   Reply to Alpert.   Sat R 53:20 D 19 '70

Death in Venice; Mann's masterpiece becomes a film
    triumph.   Show 2-4:34 Je '71

Special issue on Death in Venice.   Interview 2-4 Jl '71

Ingrid Thulin comments on Visconti.   Dialogue on Film
    3:16 '72


VLADO, KRISTL
    Dictionary of young German filmmakers.   CTVD 4-2:11
        Spg '66


VON BAGH, PETER
    Biographical note.   International Film G 9:126 '72


von GERLACH, ARTHUR
    O'Leary, L.   Arthur von Gerlach; the unknown director.
        Silent Pic 8:23 Aut '70


von STERNBERG, JOSEF
    Tully, J.   His career.   Vanity Fair 30:66 Jl '28
    Littlejohn, J.   Interview.   Motion Pic Classic 33:50 My
        '31

Potamkin, H. A.   Field generals of the film.   Vanity
Fair 38:52 Mr '32
Hall, H.   Jo(k)e von Sternberg.   Cinema Digest 3-3:3
Ap 3 '33
Larkin, M.   Why he makes films that are different.
Movie Classic 6:48 Je '34
Hunter, L.   Sketch.   Motion Pic 48:14 Ja '35
Reynolds, Q.   Shooting stars.   Colliers 95:12 F 9 '35
Meet Josef von Sternberg: the man of many talents.
Columbia Mirror 2-5:3 N 22 '35
Creative film director.   Cue 4-7:3 D 14 '35
Lockhart, G.   Parts he's liked to play.   Stage 13:44
Ja '36
Harold, J. C.   Prodigal's return.   Cue 8-26:20 D 23 '39
Harrington, C.   His films and their anomalous position
in history of cinema.   Hollywood Q 3-4:405 '48
Harrington, C.   An index to the films of Josef von Stern-
berg.   Sight & Sound (special sup) Index Series # 17
F '49
Harrington, C.   Arrogant gesture.   Theatre Arts 34:42
N '50
von Sternberg, J.   On life and film.   Films In Review
3-8:383 O '52
Weinberg, H. G.   Has von Sternberg discovered a
Japanese Dietrich?   Theatre Arts 37:26 Ag '53
The big screens.   Sight & Sound 24-4:209 Spg '55
von Sternberg, J.   More light.   Sight & Sound 25-2:70
Fall '55
von Sternberg, J.   Acting in film and theatre.   Film
Culture 1-5/6:1 Win '55
Geltzer, E. M.   Letter concerning involvement with I
take this woman.   Films In Review 14-2:126 F '63
Sarris, A.   Pantheon directors; filmog.   Film Culture
28:2 Spg '63
von Sternberg, J.   A taste for celluloid.   Films &
Filming 9-10:40 Jl '63
von Sternberg principle.   Esquire 60:90 O '63
Smith, J.   Belated appreciation of von Sternberg.   Film
Culture 31:4 Win '63/64
Pankaka, J.   Sternberg at 70.   Films In Review 15-5:312
My '64
Peppeteer.   Newsweek 65:88B Mr 29 '65
Bogdanovich, P.   Filmography.   Movie 13:17 Sum '65
Bogdanovich, P.   Encounter with Josef von Sternberg.
Movie 13:24 Sum '65
Stein, E.   Fun in a Chinese laundry.   Sight & Sound
34-4:202 Aut '65

Weinberg, H. G. Sternberg and Stroheim. Sight &
Sound 35-1:50 Win '65/66
Macklin, F. H. Interview. Film Heritage 1-2:3 Win
'65/66
Weinberg, H. G. Josef von Sternberg. Film Heritage
1-2:13 Win '65/66
Luft, H. G. A study. Film Journal (Aus) 24:62 D '65
Higham, C. A visit to the von Sternbergs. Film
Journal (Aus) 24:76 D '65
Kevin Brownlow on Josef von Sternberg. Film 45:4
Spg '66
von Sternberg, J. Extract from Fun in a Chinese
laundry. Films & Filming 13-4:14 Ja '67
Weinberg, H. G. On Sternberg. Sight & Sound 36-3:158
Sum '67
von Sternberg by von Sternberg. Film Fan Mo 87:16 S '68
Maelstaf, R. von Sternberg in Brussels. CTVD 6-3:7
Spg '69
Obit. (reprint N. Y. Times) Classic Film Collector
26:ex2 Win '70
    Film R p16 '70/71
    N. Y. Times p31 D 23 '69
    Newsweek p31 D 23 '69
    Screen World 21:241 '70
    Time 95:43 Ja 5 '70
Jubak, J. In memoriam. Focus 6:25 Spg '70
Camper, F. Essays on visual style. Cinema (Lon) 8:16
'71
Flinn, T. Joe, where are you? Velvet Light Trap 6:9
Fall '72

von STROHEIM, ERICH
Yost, R. M. Jr. Gosh, how they hate him! Photoplay
17-1:80 D '19
Cheatham, M. Interview. Motion Pic Classic 9:34 Ja
'20
Fredericks, J. Interview. Motion Pic 20:73 Ag '20
Gassaway, G. Interview. Motion Pic 22:40 O '21
Fletcher, A. W. Interview. Motion Pic 23:28 My '22
Goldbeck, W. Interview. Classic 15:18 S '22
Gassaway, G. Interview. Motion Pic 25:36 S '23
Carr, H. As a director. Classic 18:24 N '23
Tully, J. Interview. Classic 19:20 My '24
Quirk, J. R. Estimate. Photoplay 27:27 Ja '25
Tully, J. Sketch. Vanity Fair 26:50 Mr '26
Ryan, D. The Don Quixote of pictures. Motion Pic
Classic 23:22 My '26

Leslie, A.   Interview.   Motion Pic 31:39 Ap '27
Sorensen, B.   A close-up of "Von."   Motion Pic 33:39
  Jl '27
The seamy side of directing.   Theatre 46:18 N '27
Bay, D.   Sketch.   Motion Pic Classic 26:23 D '27
Carr, H.   Sketch.   Photoplay 33:38 My '28
Welch, T.   Sketch.   Motion Pic 37:42 My '29
Gray, C. W.   Sketch.   Motion Pic Classic 30:21 S '29
Calhoun, D.   Interview.   Motion Pic Classic 31:30 Ap '30
Belfrage, C.   Charges against him and his reply.   Motion
  Pic Classic 31:36 Je '30
Hamilton, S.   Sketch.   Photoplay 54:72 Je '40
Work of.   Newsweek 21:87 My 31 '43
Erich von Stroheim plays Field Marshal Rommel.   Life
  14:47 Je 14 '43
Weinberg, H. G.   An index to the creative work of Erich
  von Sternberg.   Sight & Sound (special sup) Index
  Series #1 Je '43
Anstey, E.   Work of.   Spectator 171:59 Jl 16 '43
Noble, P.   Stroheim--his work and influence.   Sight &
  Sound 16-64:163 Win '47/48
Noble, P.   Man you love to hate.   Theatre Arts 34:22
  Ja '50
Perelman, S. J.   Cloudland revisited.   New Yorker
  28:34 S 20 '52
Lambert, G.   Stroheim revisited.   Sight & Sound 22-4:165
  Ap/Je '53
Jensen, O.   Lunch with Erich von Stroheim.   Vogue 122:
  19 O 15 '53
Stonier, G. W.   Press party.   New Statesman 47:35
  Ja 9 '54
Reisz, K.   Stroheim in London.   Sight & Sound 23-4:172
  Ap/Je '54
Obit.   Americana Annual 1958:825 '58
  Illustrated London N 230:821 My 18 '57
  Screen World 9:226 '58
  Time 69:98 My 27 '57
Everson, W. K.   Erich von Stroheim 1885-1957.   Films
  In Review 8-7:305 Ag/S '57
Mitchell, G.   Stroheim.   Films In Review 8-8:423 O '57
Curtiss, T. Q.   The last years of von Stroheim.   Film
  Culture 4-18:3 '58
Watts, R. Jr.   A few reminiscences.   Film Culture
  4-18:5 '58
Eisner, L. H.   Homage to an artist.   Film Culture
  4-18:7 '58
Arnheim, R.   Portrait of an artist.   Film Culture 4-18:11 '58

Eisner, L. H.   Notes on the style of Stroheim.   Film
  Culture 4-18:13 '58
Marion, D.   Erich von Stroheim: the legend and the fact.
  Sight & Sound 31:22 Win '61/62
Sarris, A.   Pantheon directors; filmog.   Film Culture
  28:2 Spg '63
Estes, O. Jr.   The compromised maestro of Foolish
  wives.   8mm Collector 8:14 My '64
Weinberg, H. G.   Sternberg and Stroheim.   Sight &
  Sound 35-1:50 Win '65/66
Pinto, A.   Filmography.   Films In Review 18-6:374
  Je/Jl '67
Dulaney, J.   Art and the business of art.   Classic Film
  Collector 18:13 Sum '67
Letters.   Films In Review 18-7:449 Ag/S '67
Lee, R.   Count von realism.   Classic Film Collector
  23:43 Spg '69

VORHAUS, BERNARD
  Bledsoe, R.   England vs. Hollywood.   Cinema Progress
    4-1/2:6 Je/Jl '39

VORKAPICH, SLAVKO
  Reasons of the eye.   New Yorker 40:25 F 13 '65
  Lerner, C.   The film lectures of Slavko Vorkapich.
    Film Comment 3-3:51 Sum '65
  Slavko Vorkapich on film as a visual language and as a
    form of art.   Film Culture 38:1 Fall '65
  Slavko Vorkapich on closed-eye vision.   Film Culture
    40:78 Spg '66
  Vorkapich, S.   A fresh look at ... TV commercials.
    Making Films 2-1:9 F '68
  Vorkapich, S.   How to film dance and dancers.   Making
    Films 4-3:13 Je '70
  What they say.   Making Films 4-3:46 Je '70

VUKOTIĆ, DUŠAN
  Biographical note.   International Film G 5:170 '68
  Dusan Vukotic and the Zagreb film.   Film 60:7 n. d.

WADLEIGH, MICHAEL
Bell, D. Woodstock. Making Films 4-5:9 O '70
Dawson, J. Wadleigh after Woodstock. Making Films
4-5:9 O '70
Meyer, A. Interview. Interview 1-7:3 n. d.

WAJDA, ANDRZEJ
Michalek, B. Polish notes. Sight & Sound 28-1:5 Win
'58/59
Personality of the month. Films & Filming 6-6:5 Mr '60
Wajda, A. Destroying the commonplace. Films &
Filming 8-2:9 N '61
The Polish cinema. Film 31:26 Spg '62
Director of the year; filmog. International Film G p22
'64
Higham, C. Grasping the nettle: the films of Andrzej
Wajda. Hudson R 18:408 Aut '65
Austen, D. Wajda's generation. Films & Filming
14-10:14 Jl '68
McArthur, C. Everything for sale. Sight & Sound
38-3:138 Sum '69
Toeplitz, K. Wajda redivivus. Film Q 23-3:37 Win
'69/70
Wajda play for London. Films & Filming 18-9:13 Je '72

WAKAMATSU, KOJI
Biographical note. International Film G 8:194 '71

WALKER, HAL
Parsons, L. O. Cosmopolitan's citation for the best direction of the month. Cosmop 120:71 Mr '46

WALKER, PETER
British cinema filmog. Film 65:10 Spg '72

WALKER, STUART
What does the audience want? Theatre Arts 15:170 F '31
Obit. Current Biography '41

WALLACE, RICHARD
Cruikshank, H. Sketch. Motion Pic Classic 28:33 S '28
Home of. Vogue 96:80 O 1 '40
Obit. N. Y. Times p31 N 5 '51
Screen World 3:178 '52

WALLS, TOM
Obit. Illustrated London N 215:851 D 3 '49

WALSH, RAOUL
St. Johns, I. Sketch. Photoplay 28:86 S '25
Mizner, W. Sketch. Photoplay 34:40 N '28
Parsons, L. O. Cosmopolitan's citation for the best direction of the month. Cosmop 122:65 Je '47
Sarris, A. Third line; filmog. Film Culture 28:18
Spg '63
Where are they now? Newsweek 64:18 D 14 '64
Brownlow, K. Raoul Walsh. Film 49:17 Aut '67
Lloyd, R. Raoul Walsh. Brighton 14:9 N '69; 15:8 D '69;
21:20 Je '70
Schikel, R. Good days, good years. Harper 241:48
O '70
Conley, W. Raoul Walsh--his silent films; filmog.
Silent Pic 9:2 Win '70/71
What directors are saying. Action 7-3:28 My/Je '72

WALTERS, CHARLES
Parsons, L. O. Cosmopolitan's citation for the best direction of the month. Cosmop 126:13 Ap '49
Sarris, A. Likable but elusive; fimog. Film Culture
28:35 Spg '63
Cutts, J. On the bright side; interview. Films & Filming 16-11:12 Ag '70

WARHOL, ANDY
Slice of cake school. Time 79:52 My 11 '62
Saarinen, A. B. Explosion of pop art. Vogue 141:86
Ap 15 '63
Swenson, G. R. What is pop art? Interview. Art N
62:26 N '63
Sixth independent film award. Film Culture 33:1 Sum '64
Saint Andrew. Newsweek 64:100 D 7 '64
Junker, H. Andy Warhol, movie maker. Nation 200:206
F 22 '65
Lyon, N. Second fame. Vogue 145:184 Mr 1 '65
Listing of films. Film Culture 37:7 Sum '65
Edie and Andy. Time 86:65 Ag 27 '65
Kevles, B. L. Interview. Film Culture 38:7 Fall '65
Benjamin, J. On working at Andy Warhol's "factory."
Film Culture 40:40 Spg '66
Ehronstein, D. Interview. Film Culture 40:41 Spg '66
Antin, D. Warhol: the silver tenement. Art N 65:47
Sum '66

Steller, J. Beyond cinema: notes on some films by Andy Warhol. Film Q 20-1:35 Fall '66

The playmate as fine art. Playboy 14:141 Ja '67

Wilson, J. Andy Warhol literally. Yale Lit 135:6 My '67

Berg, G. Nothing to love; interview. Cahiers (Eng) 10:39 My '67

Corliss, R. Raggedy Andy. Commonweal 86:469 Jl 28 '67

Interview. Mademoiselle 65:325 Ag '67

Whitehall, R. Whitehall with Warhol. Cinema (BH) 3-6:20 Win '67

Gill, B. Current cinema. New Yorker 43:74 Ja 6 '68

Alloway, L. More skin, more everything in movies. Vogue 151:186 F 1 '68

Castle, F. C. Cab ride with Andy Warhol. Art N 66:46 F '68

Biography. Current Biography 29:39 F '68
Same. Current Biography Yearbook 1968:414 '69

Lugg, A. W. On Andy Warhol. Cineaste 1-4 Spg '68

Felled by scum. Time 91:25 Je 14 '68

Sweet assassin. Newsweek 71:86 Je 17 '68

Britt, J. Andy Warhol superartist. Film Library Q 1-4:15 Fall '68

Schrafft's gets with it. Time 92:98 O 25 '68

Leonard, J. Return of Andy Warhol. N. Y. Times Mag p32 N 10 '68

zzzzzzzz. Time 92:63 D 27 '68

Koch, S. Warhol. New Republic 160:24 Ap 26 '69

Say hello to the dirty half dozen, Sierra bandit, the American playground and all the superstars of the new theatre. Esquire 71:144 My '69

Carroll, P. What's a Warhol? Playboy 16-9:132 S '69

Bourdon, D. Andy Warhol's exhibition. Art N 68:44 O '69

Kent, L. It's hard to be your own script; interview. Vogue 155:167 Mr 1 '70

Perreault, J. Andy Warhol disguised as Andy Warhol. Vogue 155:164 Mr 1 '70

Moore, T. W. Midnight snack of Andy Warhol. Christian Century 87:396 Ap 1 '70

Perreault, J. Andy Warhol, this is your life. Art N 69:52 My '70

Weightman, J. Flesh in the afternoon. Encounter 34:30 Je '70

Weiner, P. New American cinema; filmog. Film 58:22 Spg '70

Raynes, T.    Andy Warhol films inc. ; interview with Paul
    Morrissey and Joe d'Allesandro.    Cinema (Lon)
    6/7:42 Ag '70
Heflin, L.    Notes on seeing the films of Andy Warhol.
    Afterimage 2:30 Aut '70
Pomeroy, R.    Interview. Afterimage 2:34 Aut '70
Kael, P.    Current cinema.    New Yorker 46:132 O 10 '70
People.    Time 97:41 Ap 12 '71
Gidal, P.    Warhol; filmog.    Films & Filming 17-7:26
    Ap; 17-8:64 My '71
Hughes, R.    Man of the machine.    Time 97:80 My 17 '71
Betsch, C.    Catalogue raisonne of Warhol's gestures.
    Art In America 59:47 My '71
Davis, D.    Warhol for real.    Newsweek 77:69 Je 7 '71
Howton, F. W.    Filming Andy Warhol's Trash; interview
    with Paul Morrissey.    Filmmakers Newsletter 5-8:24
    Je '72
Cipnic, D. J.    Andy Warhol: iconographer.    Sight &
    Sound 41-3:158 Sum '72
Larson, R.    A retrospective look at the films of D. W.
    Griffith and Andy Warhol.    Film Journal 1-3/4:80
    Fall/Win '72
Berg, G.    Andy.    Take One 1-10:10 n. d.


WATERS, JOHN S.
    Obit.    Screen World 17:241 '66


WATKINS, PETER
    Peter Watkins discusses his suppressed nuclear film The
        war game.    Film Comment 3-4:14 Fall '65
    On the scene.    Playboy 15-6:157 Je '68
    Left, right and wrong; interview.    Films & Filming
        16-6:28 Mr '70
    Peter Watkins talks about the suppression of his  work
        within Britain.    Films & Filming 17-5:35 F '71
    Punishment park.    American Cinematographer 52-8:778
        Ag '71
    Interview.    Film Society R 7-7/8/9:72 Mr/Ap/My '72
    British cinema filmography.    Film 65:10 Spg '72
    Filmmaking in Sweden.    Interview 1-7:26 n. d.


WATT, HARRY
    Filmography.    Film 14:8 N/D '57
    British feature directors; an index to their work.    Sight
        & Sound 27-6:303 Aut '58
    Personality of the month.    Films & Filming 5-9:5 Je '59

WATT, REUBEN
   Batman's backstage helper.   Ebony 21:40 Ap '66

WEBB, JACK
   Detective story.   Newsweek 39:74 Ja 14 '52
   Crime pays off.   Look 17:88 S 8 '53
   Tregaskis, R.   Cops' favorite make-believe cop.   Sat
      Evening Post 226:24 S 26 '53
   Hubler, R. G.   Jack Webb: the man who makes Dragnet.
      Coronet 34:27 S '53
   Taves, I.   Nobody's man Friday.   McCalls 80:26 S '53
   Why Jack Webb wants to give up Dragnet.   TV Guide
      1-37:5 D 11 '53
   Jack be nimble!   Time 63:47 Mr 15 '54
   Jack Webb story.   Cosmop 136:127 My '54
   He taught Hollywood a lesson.   TV Guide 2-30:4 Jl 24
      '54
   Jack of all trades.   Life 37:50 Ag 30 '54
   Biography.   Current Biography 16:59 My '55
      Same.   Current Biography Yearbook 1955:636 '56
   Jack Webb gets first 9 mm Smith & Wesson.   Outdoor
      Life 115:27 Je '55
   Jack Webb's Blues.   TV Guide 3-30:4 Jl 23 '55
   Block, C. B.   Amateur motion-picture making; interview.
      Popular Photo 37:112 O '55
   Phipps, C.   Webb's electricality.   Films In Review
      6-10:539 D '55
   Wood, C.   TV personalities biographical sketchbook.
      TV Personalities p133 '56
   The house that Jack built.   TV Guide 5-5:20 F 2 '57
   TV's most misunderstood man.   TV Guide 5-12:17
      Mr 23 '57
   Jorgensen, P. A.   The permanence of Dragnet.   Film Q
      12-1:35 Fall '58
   Jack Webb revisited.   TV Guide 7-2:10 Ja 10 '59
   No future for Friday?   Newsweek 53:62 F 23 '59
   Jack Webb's blues.   TV Guide 7-18:20 My 2 '59
   Webb, J.   Facts about me: as told to D. Jennings.
      Sat Evening Post 232:15 S 5; 36 S 12; 38 S 19 '59
   Raddatz, L.   Jack Webb revisited.   TV Guide 11-5:15
      F 2 '63
   Do-it-yourself homicide.   Writer 76:17 O '63
   Jack Webb talks about the camera and cameramen.
      American Cinematographer 47-5:318 My '66
   Lewis, R. W.   Happiness is a return to the good old
      days.   TV Guide 16-42:37 O 19 '68
   Adler, D.   I've always felt that policemen have been the

underdogs.   TV Guide 20-30:24 Jl 22 '72

## WEBB, MILLARD
Cruikshank, H.   Sketch.   Motion Pic Classic 29:35
Ag '29

## WEBB, ROBERT D.
Martin, P.   Get me a volcano.   Sat Evening Post 219:22
My 31 '47

## WEBER, LOIS
Smith, B. H.   Sketch.   Sunset 32:634 Mr '14
Johnson, L. H.   A lady general of the picture army.
Photoplay 8-1:42 Je '15
Van Loan, H. H.   Sketch.   Motion Pic 11:41 Jl '16
Black, E.   Sketch.   Overland 68:198 S '16
Peltret, E.   On the lot with Lois Weber.   Photoplay
12-5:89 O '17
Remont, F.   Sketch.   Motion Pic 15:59 My '18
Carter, A.   Interview.   Motion Pic 21:62 Mr '21
Malverne, P.   Interview.   Classic 16:60 My '23
Aydelotte, W.   Her project to aid education by installing
movies in schools.   Motion Pic 47:34 Mr '34
Feldman, J. & H.   Women directors.   Films In Review
1-8:9 N '58
Pyros, J.   Notes on women directors.   Take One 3-2:7
N/D '70

## WEILL, CLAUDIA
Kaplan, D.   Selected short subjects.   Women & Film
2:37 '72

## WEISMAN, FREDERICK
Mamber, S.   The new documentaries of Frederick Weis-
man.   Cinema (BH) 6-1:33 '70
Interview.   Cinema (BH) 6-1:38 '70

## WEISS, DON
Sarris, A.   Likable but elusive; filmog.   Film Culture
28:35 Spg '63

## WEISS, JIŘÍ
Weiss, J   Czech cinema has arrived.   Films & Filming
5-6:8 Mr '59
Weiss, J.   Mixing it.   Films & Filming 11-9:46 Je '65

## WEISS, MATTIAS

Thoms, A. German underground. Afterimage 2:45 Aut '70

## WEISS, PETER

Goldman, M. Films. Nation 202:222 F 21 '66

Potter, S. Marat/Sade. American Record G 32:790 My '66

Gray, P. Living word; interview. Tulane Drama R 11:106 Fall '66

Clausen, O. Weiss, propagandist and Weiss, playwright. N. Y. Times Mag p28 O 2 '66

Dragadze, P. Scourage of the world's theater. Life 61:49 O 28 '66

People are talking about. Vogue 148:148 N 15 '66

Biography. Current Biography 29:41 Ap '68

Same. Current Biography Yearbook 1968:425 '69

Bauke, J. P. Dreamer turned realist. Sat R 51:24 Je 29 '68

Kauffmann, S. On the edge. New Republic 159:30 Jl 6 '68

## WEISS, SAM

Survey among unsuccessful applicants for the Ford Foundation film grants. Film Comment 2-3:10 Sum '64

## WEISZ, FRANS

Biographical note. International Film G 4:124 '67

Biographical note. International Film G 8:208 '71

## WELLES, ORSON

Work of. Newsweek 9:31 Ja 23 '37

Vernon, G. Age twenty-two. Commonweal 26:423 Ag 27 '37

Parker, J. R. Lighted stages: the Mercury rises. Mag Art 30:619 O '37

Taggard, E. Julius Caesar, 1937 model. Senior Scholastic 31:6 D 11 '57

Lindley, D. He has the stage. Colliers 101:14 Ja 29 '38

Marvelous boy. Time 31:27 My 9 '38

Sedgwick, R. W. Story of the Mercury theatre. Stage 15:6 My '38

Sedgwick, R. W. Appreciation. Stage 15:5 Je '38

Playboy. American 125:88 Je '38

First person singular: Welles, innovator on stage, experiments on the air. Newsweek 12:25 Jl 11 '38

Work of.    Stage 15:30 S '38
Work of.    Life 5:58 N 14 '38
Panic! This is the Orson Welles broadcast that hoaxed
    America.    Radio G p2 N 19 '38
Experiment.    American 126:162 N '38
On staging Shakespeare and on Shakespeare's stage.
    Senior Scholastic 33:19E Ja 14 '39
Biographical sketch.    Senior Scholastic 33:21E Ja 14 '39
Orson Welles begins radio book series.    Publisher W
    135:956 Mr 4 '39
Chase, F.    He scared us to death!    Radio G p15 O 27 '39
Franchey, J.    That man from Mars.    Screen Book
    22-4:76 N '39
Johnston, A.    Orson Welles.    Sat Evening Post Ja 20 '40
Johnston, A. & Smith, F.    How to raise a child.    Sat
    Evening Post 212:9 Ja 20; 24 Ja 27; 27 F 3 '40
Hearst vs. Orson Welles.    Newsweek 17:62 Ja 20 '41
Sage, M.    Hearst over Hollywood.    New Republic p270
    F 24 '41
About the moving picture industry.    Stage 1:34 F '41
Once a child prodigy, he has never quite grown up.    Life
    10:108 My 26 '41
Ferguson, O.    Welles and his wonders.    New Republic
    104:760 Je 2; 824 Je 16 '41
Man of the moment.    Photoplay 19-2:26 Jl '41
McEvoy, J. P.    Story of.    Vogue 98:66 O 15 '41
McEvoy, J. P.    Magic is the world for Orson Welles.
    Reader Digest 39:81 D '41
Biography.    Current Biography '41
Orson's alma mater: Todd school for boys in Woodstock,
    Ill.    Time 39:50 Mr 9 '42
Rio party; Orson Welles frolics at famous Mardi gras.
    Life 12:98 My 18 '42
Mulvey, K.    Keeping up with Hollywood.    Womans Home
    Companion 69:37 My '42
Welles labors over The magnificant Ambersons and
    emerges with good film but minus RKO job.    Newsweek
    20:56 Jl 20 '42
Controversy with RKO.    Time 40:44 Jl 20 '42
Welles unlimited.    Newsweek 20:84 N 16 '42
Orson at war.    Time 40:46 N 30 '42
Anstoy, E.    Work of.    Spectator 170:243 Mr 12 '43
Berch, B.    Orson the great.    N. Y. Times Mag p11
    Ag 29 '43
Denton, J. F. & Crichton, K.    Welles' wonderland.
    Colliers 112:14 S 4 '43
Talmey, A.    His magic show for servicemen.    Vogue
    102:103 O 1 '43

Hopper, H. Story of. Photoplay 24:30 D '43

Hendricks, H. Why Rita Hayworth really married Orson Welles. Silver Screen 14-2:24 D '43

Trotter, M. Prediction for 1944. Photoplay 24:27 Ja '44

Hopper, H. Orson Welles--genus genius. Photoplay 24-6:40 My '44

At democratic headquarters. Life 17:27 N 20 '44

Dedicated wunderkind. New Yorker 20:18 Ja 27 '45

Actor turns columnist. Time 45:68 Ja 29 '45

Pritchett, F. The odd Mr. Welles. Silver Screen 15-6:38 Ap '45

Wellesapoppin. Newsweek 27:87 Je 10 '46

Welles, young man of 1,000 faces. Cue 15-26:9 Je 29 '46

Beatty, J. Big show-off. American 143:38 F '47

Murder! Life 25:106 O 11 '48

Houseman, J. Man from Mars. Harper 197:74 D '48

Koval, F. Interview. Sight & Sound 19-8:314 D '50

James, E. N. Unprecedented mass panic; the night the Martians landed. Reader Digest 58:15 F '51

Kerr, W. Wonder boy Welles. Theatre Arts 35:50 S '51

Le gros legume. New Yorker 29:27 O 24 '53

Orson Welles returns. Newsweek 42:68 O 26 '53

Hamburger, P. Television: Omnibus presentation of King Lear. New Yorker 29:103 O 31 '53

Welles, O. The third audience. Sight & Sound 23-3:120 Ja/Mr '54

Russell, R. Orson. Playboy 1:15 Je '54

MacLiammoir, M. Orson Welles. Sight & Sound 24-1:36 Jl/S '54

Bentley, E. Theatre; Othello on film. New Republic 133:21 O 3 '55

Harvey, E. TV imports. Colliers 136:38 O 14 '55

Lewis, E. Return of the prodigy. Cue 25-2:15 Ja 14 '56

Winged gorilla. New Statesman 51:65 Ja 21 '56

Gibbs, W. Schizo king. New Yorker 31:89 Ja 21 '56

Old play in Manhattan. Time 67:80 Ja 23 '56

Orson Welles' Lear. Newsweek 47:57 Ja 23 '56

Lewis, T. Theatre: Welles as King Lear. America 94:485 Ja 28 '56

Kurnitz, H. Antic arts. Holiday 19:65 Ja '56

Hayes, R. Citizen Welles. Commonweal 63:568 Mr 2 '56

Taper, B. Who's who in the cast. New Yorker 32:147 Ap 28 '56

Sacher, S. New creative writers. Library J 82:437 F 1 '57

Return of the prodigy.   Newsweek 49:108 Ap 29 '57

Wood, C.   TV personalities biographical sketchbook.
   TV Personalities   p83 '57

Welles, O.   The scenario crisis.   International Film A
   1:119 '57

Return of awesome Welles.   Life 44:53 F 24 '58

Weales, G.   Movies.   Reporter 18:33 Je 26 '58

Welles, O.   Ribbon of dreams.   International Film A
   2:163 '58

Grigs, D.   Conversations at Oxford.   Sight & Sound
   29-2:82 Ap '60

Campbell, P.   Now, Orson Welles, did I tell you?
   Vogue 136:170 N 1 '60

Stanbrook, A.   The heroes of Welles.   Film 28:12
   Mr/Ap '61

Cowie, P.   Gallery of great artists.   Films & Filming
   7-7:10 Ap '61

Tynan, K.   Orson Welles.   Show 1-1:65 O '61; 1-2:60
   N '61

Prodigal revived.   Time 79:30 Je 29 '62

Orson Welles.   Film 33:12 Aut '62

Martinez, E.   The trial of Orson Welles.   Films &
   Filming 9-1:12 O '62

The day Orson Welles frightened the world.   Film Culture
   27:49 Win '62/63

Kobler, J.   Citizen Welles rides again.   Sat Evening
   Post 235:22 D 8 '62

Sarris, A.   Pantheon directors; filmog.   Film Culture
   28:2 Spg '63

Tyler, P.   Orson Welles and the big experimental film
   cult.   Film Culture 29:30 Sum '63

Macdonald, D.   Orson Welles and his magic stream
   engine.   Esquire 60:14 Jl '63

Hatch, R.   Adult prodigy.   Horizon 5:85 Jl '63

Director of the year; filmog.   International Film G p15
   '64

Biography.   Current Biography 26:42 F '65
   Same.   Current Biography Yearbook 1965:446 '65

Cobos, J. & Rubio, M.   Welles & Falstaff; interview.
   Sight & Sound 35-4:158 Aut '66

Cobos, J.; Rubio, M.; Pruneda, J. A.   A trip to Don
   Quixoteland.   Cahiers (Eng) 5:35 '66

Morgenstern, J. & Sokolov, R.   Falstaff as Orson Welles.
   Newsweek 69:96 Mr 27 '67

Interview.   Playboy 14-3:53 Mr '67

Kael, P.   Orson Welles: there ain't no way.   New Republic 156:27 Je 24 '67

Welles on Falstaff; interview.   Cahiers (Eng) 11:5 S '67
Daney, S.   Welles in power.   Cahiers (Eng) 11:17 S '67
Duboeuf, P.   The other side.   Cahiers (Eng) 11:18 S '67
Comolli, J-L.   Jack le fataliste.   Cahiers (Eng) 11:21
    S '67
Narboni, J.   Sacher & Masoch.   Cahiers (Eng) 11:23 S
    '67
Johnson, W.   Orson Welles; of time and loss.   Film Q
    21-1:13 Fall '67
Special report.   Orson Welles.   Action 4-3:23 My/Je '69
Roud, R.   Memories of Resnais.   Sight & Sound 38-3:124
    Sum '69
McBride, J.   Welles' Chimes at midnight.   Film Q 23:11
    Fall '69
Higham, C.   It's all true.   Sight & Sound 39-2:93 Spg '70
McBride, J.   Welles before Kane.   Film Q 23-3:19
    Spg '70
What directors are saying.   Action 5-4:30 Jl/Ag '70
Sokolov, R. A.   Orsonology.   Newsweek 76:64 Ag 3 '70
Beamgold, J.   I never promised you a rosebud.   New
    York 3-35:42 Ag 31 '70
McBride, J.   Welles' immortal story.   Sight & Sound
    39-4:194 Aut '70
Wilson, R.   It's not quite all true.   Sight & Sound 39-4:
    188 Aut '70
By Orson Welles, but where are we going?   Look 34-22:
    34 N 3 '70
Higham, C.   It's all true.   Sight & Sound 40-1:55 Win
    '70/71
Wilson, R.   Reply to C. Higham's It's all true.   Sight
    & Sound 40-1:55 Win '70/71
Kael, P.   Onward and upward with the arts.   New
    Yorker 47:43 F 20: 44 F 27 '41
Love is the word.   Making Films 5-2:5 Ap '71
Henderson, B.   The long take.   Film Comment 7-2:6
    Sum '71
Prokosch, M.   Orson Welles; filmog.   Film Comment
    7-2:29 Sum '71
Delson, J.   Heston on Welles; interview with Charlton
    Heston.   Take One 3-6:7 Jl/Ag '71
What directors are saying.   Action 6-4:20 Jl/Ag '71
Goldfarb, P.   Orson Welles's use of sound.   Take One
    3-6:10 Jl/Ag '71
The professional director speaks.   Making Films 5-4:40
    Ag '71
Bucher, F. & Cowie, P.   Welles and Chabrol.   Sight &
    Sound 40-4:188 Aut '71

McBride, J. First person singular. Sight & Sound
41-1:40 Win '71/72

What directors are saying. Action 7-1:36 Ja/F '72

Ingrid Thulin comments on Welles. Dialogue on Film
1:2 '72

Ken Russell writes on Raising Kane. Films & Filming
18-8:16 My '72

Gilling, T. The Citizen Kane book; interview with
George Coulouris and Bernard Herrman. Sight &
Sound 41-2:71 Spg '72

Rubin, B. Orson Welles and I. Journal Popular Film
1-2:109 Spg '72

Mills, W. E. Orson Welles and Othello. Film Journal
(Aus) 5:1 n. d.

WELLMAN, WILLIAM

Pringle, H. F. Screwball Bill. Colliers 101:26 F 26
'38

Wildman. Cue 6-35:10 Je 25 '38

Wellman, W. Director's notebook--why teach cinema?
Cinema Progress 4-1/2:3 Je/Jl '39

Biographical note; filmog. Movies & People 2:47 '40

Griffith, R. Wyler, Wellman and Huston. Films In Review 1-1:1 F '50

Biography. Current Biography 11:51 Je '50
Same. Current Biography Yearbook 1950:608 '51

Morris, J. Half a dozen aren't cheaper but are lots of
fun. Parents 25:44 Ag '50

War in Hollywood. Newsweek 50:118 S 16 '57

Miller, E. M. Yank in the black cat squadron. Flying
69:38 Ag '61

Sarris, A. Fallen idols; filmog. Film Culture 28:30
Spg '63

Brownlow, K. William Wellman. Film 44:7 Win '65/66

Thomson, B. The years "winged" by. 8mm Collector
14:15 Spg '66

A memorable visit with an elder statesman; interview.
Cinema (BH) 3-3:20 Jl '66

William Wellman, Wings and World War I. Action 3-6:14
N/D '68

Smith, J. M. The essential Wellman. Brighton 16:21
Ja '70

Wellman, W. Jr. William Wellman: director rebel.
Action 5-2:13 Mr/Ap '70

Brooks, L. On location with Billy Wellman. Film Culture 53/54/55:145 Spg '72

WENDERS, WIM
Thoms, A.   German underground.   Afterimage 2:45
Aut '70

WENDKOS, PAUL
Johnson, A.   Interview.   Film Q 15-3:39 Spg '62
Sarris, A.   Oddities and one shots.   Film Culture 28:45
Spg '63
Auston, D.   Improvisations on an original theme; inter-
view.   Films & Filming 14-4:4 Ja '68
Winogura, D.   Interview; filmog.   Cinefantastique 2-1:21
Spg '72

WERNER, GÖSTA
Note.   International Film G 2:42 '65

WERNER, PETER
Werner, P.   Frances Flaherty: hidden and seeking.
Filmmakers Newsletter 5-9/10:28 Sum '72

WEST, RAMOND B.
Biographical note.   Photoplay 9-4:42 Mr '16
Durling, E. V.   Gas meter to megaphone.   Photoplay
14-3:35 Ag '18

WEXLER, HASKELL
Wexler, H.   It's time we scrapped the ancient iron.
Action 1-3:16 Mr/Je '67
Callenbach, E. & Johnson, A.   Danger is seduction;
interview.   Film Q 21:3 Spg '68
Jones, R. B.   Haskell Wexler and the cool medium.   Take
One 2-4:5 My/Je '69
Dynamite.   Time 94:62 Ag 22 '69
Alpert, H.   Film of social reality.   Sat R 52:43 S 6  69
Salute of the week.   Cue 38-39:1 S 27 '69
Corliss, R.   Stay with us, NBC; filmog.   Film Q 23-2:47
Win '69/70
Jones, R. B.   A view of the future; interview.   Making
Films 4-3:10 Je '70
Shedlin, M.   Haskell Wexler; filmog.   As cinematographer.
Take One 3-6:15 Jl/Ag '71
Filmography (as cinematographer and director).   Film
Comment 8-2:57 Sum '72

WHALE, JAMES
Biographical note; filmog.   Movies & People 2:47 '40
Obit.   N. Y. Times p23 My 30 '57

Screen World 9:226 '58

Edwards, R.   Movie gothic--a tribute to James Whale.
Sight & Sound 27-2:95 Aut '57

Thomaier, W.   James Whale; filmog.   Films In Review
13-5:277 My '62

Arkadin.   Film clips.   Sight & Sound 37-1:48 Win '67/68

Jensen, P.   James Whale; filmog.   Film Comment
7-1:56 Spg '71


WHIPPLE, JAMES
Devensky, D.   Silent director and discoverer of stars.
Classic Film Collector 28:52 Fall '70


WHITE, BOB
Wisconsin filmmaking; visiting Bob White.   Velvet Light
Trap 6:46 Fall '72


WHITEHEAD, PETER
I destroy, therefore I am. Films & Filming 15-4:14
Ja '69

Lyle, J.   The inner space project.   Afterimage 1:no p#
Ap '70

British cinema filmography.   Film 65:10 Spg '72


WHITNEY, JOHN
Lamont, A.   Interview; filmog.   Film Comment 6-3:28
Fall '70

Brick, R.   Interview.   Film Culture 53/54/55:39
Spg '72

Excerpts of a talk.   Film Culture 53/54/55:73 Spg '72

Whitney, J.   Notes on Permutations.   Film Culture
53/54/55:78 Spg '72

Whitney, J.   Notes on Matrix.   Film Culture 53/54/55:
79 Spg '72

Whitney bibliography; filmog.   Film Culture 53/54/55:80
Spg '72


WHORF, RICHARD
Does the summer theatre do its job?   Theatre Arts
22:446 Je '38

Success story.   Cue 10-44:33 N 1 '41

Some film actors who have made themselves known this
year.   Theatre Arts 26:184 Mr '42

The persistent Mr. Whorf.   Lions Roar 2-4:no p#  Ap '43

Whorf, R.   As I see them.   Lions Roar 3-2:no p#  Ja
'44

Richard Whorf of the movies. Cue 13-50:13 D 9 '44

Versatile guy.   Lions Roar 4-1:no p# F '45
Whorf, R.   Cronyn's a character!   Lions Roar 4-1:no
    p# F '45
Shearer, L.   One family's formula for the rich, full life.
    House Beautiful 94:131 Je '52
Lavoos, J.   Richard Whorf; painter of Americana.
    American Artist 28:32 Ap '64
Obit.   N. Y.  Times p47 D 15 '66
    Newsweek 68:57 D 26 '66
    Screen World 18:241 '67
    Time 88:70 D 23 '66

## WICKI, BERNHARD
Zurbuch, W.   From actor to director.   Film Journal
    (Aus) 15:60 Mr '60
Wicki, B.   Lesson of the hate makers.   Films & Film-
    ing 8-7:11 Ap '62
Bean, R.   The face of '63--Germany.   Films & Filming
    9-9:41 Je '63
Three enterprising filmmakers.   International Film G
    1:96 '64

## WIDERBERG, BO
Director of the year; filmog.   International Film G 5:29
    '68
What directors are saying.   Action 4-6:28 N/D '69
Counting the gains; filmog.   Films Illustrated 1-4:24
    O '71
What directors are saying.   Action 6-6:22 N/D '71
Loney, G. M.   Interview.   Interview 1-7:8 n. d.
Filmmaking in Sweden.   Interview 1-7:27 n. d.

## WIEGEL, JAN
Biographical note.   International Film G 7:165 '70

## WIEST, ROLF
Thoms, A.   German underground.   Afterimage 2:45
    Aut '70

## WILBUR, CRANE
Briscoe, J.   Why famous film favorites forsook footlights
    for filmdom.   Photoplay 7-1:127 D '14
Autobiographical.   Motion Pic 10:97 O '15
How to get into moving pictures.   Motion Pic Classic
    3:57 S '16
Poppe, H.   Sketch.   Motion Pic 13:41 My '17
How to get into moving pictures.   Motion Pic 14:75 D '17

Poppe, H.   Sketch.   Motion Pic 14:38 D '17
Smith, F. J.   Interview.   Motion Pic Classic 9:25 D '19
Leon, S.   Crane Wilbur.   Films In Review 23-1:64
    Ja '72

## WILCOX, FRED
New faces among MGM directors too.   Lions Roar
    1-11/12:no p# Jl/Ag '42
Roads to fame.   Lions Roar 3-1:no p# S '43
MGM's directors range from pioneers to newcomers.
    Lions Roar 3-4:no p# Jl '44
Obit.   N. Y. Times p41 S 25 '64

## WILCOX, HERBERT
Biography.   Current Biography N '45
Filmography.   Film 14:8 N/D '57
British feature directors; an index to their work.   Sight
    & Sound 27-6:303 Aut '58

## WILDE, CORNEL
Hamilton, S.   Wilde about love.   Photoplay 26-1:59 D '44
Ames, A.   A name to remember.   Silver Screen 15-3:32
    Ja '45
Walker, H. L.   Gentle swashbuckler.   Photoplay 27-3:45
    Ag '45
Hamilton, S.   Hungarian rhapsody.   Photoplay 28-2:40
    Ja '46
Should a woman tell her age?   Photoplay 28:52 Ap '46
Arnold, M.   Gypsy cavalier.   Photoplay 29-1:41 Je '46
Perkins, L.   Photolife of Cornel Wilde.   Photoplay
    29-2:50 Jl '46
Knight, P.   It's like this to be Mrs. Cornel Wilde.
    Photoplay 29-4:39 S '46
Deere, D.   If you were the house guest of the Cornel
    Wilde's.   Photoplay 30-1:46 D '46
Parsons, L. O.   Cornel Wilde talks back.   Photoplay
    30-3:48 F '47
Maddox, B.   Success is no cinch.   Silver Screen 17-7:35
    My '47
Asher, J.   The Wilde affair.   Photoplay 31-6:42 N '47
Graham, S.   The case of Cornel Wilde.   Photoplay
    32-2:33 Ja '48
Arden, J.   I was there.   Photoplay 32-3:56 F '48
Pritchett, F.   Cornel speaks out!   Silver Screen 18-8:24
    Je '48
Asher, J.   At last I've stopped simmering.   Silver
    Screen 22-2:24 D '51

Asher, J.   I wanted revenge!   Silver Screen 23-2:26 D '52
Wilkie, J.   Too busy for love.   Photoplay 43-2:68 F '53
Guy, R.   Africa goes Wilde; interview.   Cinema (BH)
    3-1:44 D '65
Coen, J.   Producer/director Cornel Wilde; filmog.
    Film Comment 6-1:52 Spg '70
Gow, G.   Survival!   interview; filmog.   Films & Filming
    17-1:4 O '70
What directors are saying.   Action 6-3:28 My/Je '71
The professional director speaks.   Making Films 5-4:40
    Ag '71
Directing filmog.   Films & Filming 18-11:60 Ag '72


WILDE, TED
    Dyer, V.   Letter; partial filmog.   Films In Review
        22-1:52 Ja '71
    Letters.   Filmograph 2-3:50 '71


WILDER, BILLY
    Barnett, L.   Happiest couple in Hollywood: Brackett and
        Wilder.   Life 17:100 D 11 '44
    His successful collaboration with Charles Brackett.
        Newsweek 26:114 D 10 '45
    Putting life into a movie, Ace in the hole.   Life 30:57
        F 19 '51
    Biography.   Current Biography 12:56 F '51
        Same.   Current Biography Yearbook 1951:657 '52
    Luft, H. G.   A matter of decadence.   Q Film Radio TV
        7-1:58 Fall '52
    Brackett, C.   A matter of humor.   Q Film Radio TV
        7-1:66 Fall '52
    Why not be in Paris.   Newsweek 48:106 N 26 '56
    Gillett, J.   Wilder in Paris.   Sight & Sound 26-3:142
        Win '56/57
    Wilder, B.   One head is better than two.   Films & Film-
        ing 3-5:7 F '57
    Hume, R.   A sting in the tale.   Films & Filming 3-5:8
        F '57
    Bergman and Wilder.   Sight & Sound 28-3/4:134 Sum/Aut
        '59
    Young, C.   The old dependables.   Film Q 13-1:2 Fall '59
    Schumach, M.   Wilder; the funnier touch.   N. Y. Times
        Mag p30 Ja 24 '60
    McVay, D.   The eye of a cynic.   Films & Filming 6-4:11
        Ja '60
    Wilder touch.   Life 48:41 My 30 '60
    Talk with a twosome.   Newsweek 55:110 Je 20 '60

Policeman, midwife, bastard.   Time 75:75 Je 27 '60

Jungermann, J.   Billy Wilder; letter.   Films In Review
11-8:505 O '60

Gehman, R.   Charming Billy.   Playboy 7:69 D '60

One, two, three Wilder.   Show 1-2:76 D '61

Simon, J.   Belt and suspenders.   Theatre Arts 46:20
Jl '62

Fenin, G.   The face of '63--United States.   Films &
Filming 9-6:55 Mr '63

Sarris, A.   Fallen idols; filmog.   Film Culture 28:30
Spg '63

Schumach, M.   Bright diamond.   N. Y. Times Mag p80
My 26 '63

Great ideas that never got filmed.   Show 3-8:61 Ag '63

Mirisch, H. J.   Who made Irma?   Cinema (BH) 1-4:12
Je/Jl '63

Kurnitz, H.   Billy the wild.   Holiday 35:93 Je '64

Thompson, T.   Wilder's dirty-joke film stirs a furor.
Life 58:51 Ja 15 '65

Alpert, H.   Billy, Willie and Jack.   Sat R 49:30 S 24 '66

Lemon, R.   Message in Billy Wilder's Fortune cookie.
Sat Evening Post 239:30 D 17 '66

Mundy, R.   Wilder reappraised.   Cinema (Lon) 4:14
O '69

Interview.   Cinema (Lon) 4:19 O '69

Higham, C.   Meet whiplash Wilder.   Sight & Sound
37-1:21 Win '67/68

Gillett, J.   In search of Sherlock.   Sight & Sound 39-1:26
Win '69/70

Anti-casting couch.   Time 95:37 Ja 5 '70

Machlin, M.   I. A. L. Diamond--the wit of Billy Wilder?
Show 1-1:8 Ja '70

What directors are saying.   Action 5-1:28 Ja/F '70

McBride, J. & Wilmington, M.   The private life of Billy
Wilder.   Film Q 23-4:2 Sum '70

Brown, V.   Billy Wilder: broadcast to Kuala Lumpur;
interview.   Action 5-6:16 N/D '70

Filmography.   Film Comment 6-4:101 Win '70/71

Farber, S.   The films of Billy Wilder; filmog.   Film
Comment 7-4:8 Win '71/72

Onosko, T.   Billy Wilder.   Velvet Light Trap 3:29 Win
'71/72

What directors are saying.   Action 7-3:28 My/Je '72

Noqueira, R.   Writing for the movies; interview with
Walter Newman.   Focus On Film 11:39 Aut '72

WILENSKI, STEWART
    Wilenski, S.   New documentary goal: the revealed situation.   Vision 1-2:63 Sum '62
    Survey among unsuccessful applicants for the Ford
        Foundation film grants.   Film Comment 2-3:10 Sum '64

WILES, GORDON
    Wiles, G.   The main thing is to keep moving.   Action
        3-4:14 Jl/Ag '68

WILEY, DOROTHY
    Richardson, B.   Interview.   Film Q 25-1:34 Fall '71

WILLAT, IRWIN V.
    Brownlow, K.   Irvin Willat.   Film 50:18 Win '67

WILLIAMS, ELMO
    Williams, E.   ... the cowboy.   Films In Review 5-7:347
        Ag/S '54
    Williams, E.   Genius in the cutting room.   Films In
        Review 8-9:443 N '57

WILLIAMS, LLOYD MICHAEL
    On becoming a pro.   Popular Photo 52:117 Ap '63
    Survey among unsuccessful applicants for the Ford
        Foundation film grants.   Film Comment 2-3:10 Sum '64
    Listing of films.   Film Culture 37:7 Sum '65

WILLIAMS, PAUL
    Wilson, J.   The revolutionary.   Sight & Sound 39-1:18
        Win '69/70
    Williams, P.   The making of Out of it.   Action 5-5:24
        S/O '70
    Dittlea, S.   Paul Williams' Dealing; a look at the grass
        on campus.   Show 2-6:46 Ag '71
    On the scene.   Playboy 19-1:220 Ja '72
    Interview; filmog; bibliog.   Dialogue On Film 6: entire
        issue '72
    McKay, M.   Interview.   Interview 1-10:25 n. d.

WILLIAMS, RICHARD
    Williams, R.   Animation and the little island.   Sight &
        Sound 27-6:309 Aut '58
    Cowie, P.   The face of '63--Great Britain.   Films &
        Filming 9-5:19 F '63
    Cruck, P.   The need to draw 80, 000 bug-eyed men; interview.   Film 40:16 Sum '64

Cowie, P. Interview. International Film G 2:167 '65
Portrait of an artist; filmog. International Film G 1:169
    '64

WILLIAMS, RON
    Williams, R. Images. American Cinematographer
        52-8:785 Ag '71

WILLIAMSON, D. C.
    Williamson, D. C. Dealing with the establishment.
        Films & Filming 8-2:13 N '61

WILLIS, JACK
    Willis, J. TV and the social documentary. Film Library
        Q 1-1:50 Win '67/68
    The filmmaker involved; address. Sightlines 3-4:3
        Mr/Ap '70
    Interview on Hard times in the country. Film Library Q
        4-2:23 Spg '71

WILSON, BEN
    Sketch. Motion Pic 9:110 Ap '15
    Hornblow, A. Jr. Interview. Motion Pic Classic 2:14
        My '16

WILSON, ELSIE JANE
    Denton, F. Lights! camera! quiet! ready! shoot!
        Photoplay 13-3:48 F '18

WILSON, RICHARD
    Wilson, R. Hoodlums: the myth or the reality. Films
        & Filming 5-9:10 Je '59
    Wilson, R. It's not quite all true. Sight & Sound
        39-4:188 Aut '70
    Higham, C. It's all true. Sight & Sound 40-1:55 Win
        '70/71
    Wilson, R. Reply to Higham's It's all true. Sight &
        Sound 40-1:55 Win '70/71

WINDUST, BERTAIGNE
    Biography. Current Biography '43
    Bertaigne Windust and J. L. Logan. Theatre Arts 31:31
        Ap '47

WINNER, MICHAEL
    Bean, R. The importance of being ... what's 'isname?;
        interview. Films & Filming 14-5:4 F '68

Spiers, D. Interview. Screen 10-3:5 My/Je '69
Norman, P. Believe it or not; they're still making
movies in Europe. Show 1-6:37 O '70
Winner, M. The transient revolution. Films & Filming
17-8:29 My '71
Castell, D. Making a film is like painting with money.
Films Illustrated 1-10:14 Ap '72
British cinema filmography. Film 65:10 Spg '72
Creative cornflakes. Films & Filming 18-9:12 Je '72

WIRTSCHAFTER, BUD
Schechner, R. Seventh street environment. Drama R
12:135 Spg '68
Wirtschafter, B. Cinema without walls. Filmmakers
Newsletter 4-5:26 Mr '71

WISBAR, FRANK
Obit. Screen World 19:241 '68

WISE, DAVID
Filmmaker. New Yorker 39:25 F 15 '64
Taylor, J. Interview. Film Culture 35:57 Win '64/65
Listing of films. Film Culture 37:7 Sum '65

WISE, ROBERT
Alpert, H. West side story. Dance 34:36 O '60
Talking about people. Film 32:6 Sum '62
Stark, S. Robert Wise; filmog. Films In Review 14-1:5
Ja '63
Sarris, A. Minor disappointments; filmog. Film Culture
28:41 Spg '63
Typhoons and taxes. Newsweek 67:98 My 9 '66
Should directors produce? Action 3-4:10 Jl/Ag '68
Special report--Orson Welles. Action 4-3:23 My/Je '69
What directors are saying. Action 5-2:16 Mr/Ap '70
Knight, A. Wise in Hollywood. Sat R 53:22 Ag 8 '70
Filmography. Films Illustrated 1-1:29 Jl '71
Pickard, R. The future ... a slight return. Films &
Filming 17-10:26 Jl '71
Wise, R. Impressions of Russia. Action 6-4:11 Jl/Ag
'71
American directors visit Moscow. Making Films 5-4:30
Ag '71
American Film Institute University advisory committee
seminar. Dialogue On Film 2-1:entire issue '72

## WISEMAN, FREDERICK
New producer. New Yorker 39:33 S 14 '63
Titicut follies. America 117:539 N 11 '67
Tempest in a snakepit. Newsweek 70:109 D 4 '67
Coles, R. Stripped bare at the follies. New Republic
    158:35 F 10 '68
Byron, C. Metropolitan follies. New York 3-4:60 Ja 26
    '70
Schickel, R. Frederick Wiseman's Hospital. Life 68:9
    F 6 '70
Interview. Film Library Q 3-3:5 Sum '70
McWilliams, D. E. Frederick Wiseman. Film Q
    24-1:17 Fall '70
Grahm, J. How far can you go; conversation. Con-
    tempora 1-4:30 O/N '70
Mamber, S. The new documentaries of Frederick Wise-
    man; interview. Cinema (BH) 6-1:33 '70
Graham, J. There are no simple solutions. Film
    Journal 1-1:44 Spg '71
Desilets, E. M. Titicut revisited. Film Library Q
    4-4:29 Spg '71
Fuller, R. Survive, survive, survive. Film Journal
    1-3/4:74 Fall/Win '72
Slavitt, D. R. Basic training, produced, directed and
    edited by Frederick Wiseman. Contempora 2-1:10
    F '72

## WISNIEWSKI, RAY
Listing of films. Film Culture 37:7 Sum '65

## WITHEY, CHESTER
Service, F. Interview. Motion Pic Classic 10:84 Ag '20

## WITNEY, WILLIAM
Malcomson, R. M. The sound serial. Views & Reviews
    3-1:13 Sum '71

## WOLF, KONRAD
Bean, R. The face of '63--Germany. Films & Filming
    9-9:41 Je '63

## WOOD, SAM
Biographical note; filmog. Movies & People 2:47 '40
Work of. Time 39:54 F 2 '42
Biography. Current Biography '43
Obit. Current Biography 10:58 N '49
    Current Biography Yearbook 1949:645 '50

N. Y.  Times p23 S 23 '49
Newsweek 34:60 O 3 '49
Screen World 1:235 '49
Time 54:65 O 3 '49

WORSLEY,  WALLACE  ASHLEY
Biography.   National Cylopaedia 33:439 '47

WORTH,  HOWARD
Smith, S. T.   Rage; interview.   Filmmakers Newsletter
5-9/10:24 Sum '72

WORTH,  SOL
Worth, S. & Adair, J.   Navajo filmmakers.   Filmmakers Newsletter 4-3:11 Ja '71
Jurors named anniversary awards.   Film Comment 2-2:50
n. d.

WRAY,  JOHN  GRIFFITH
Obit.   Current Biography '40

WREDE,  CASPER
British cinema filmography.   Film 65:10 Spg '72

WRIGHT,  BASIL
Wright, B.   The documentary dilemma. Hollywood Q
5-4:321 Sum '51
Basil Wright on the big screens.   Film 6:7 D '55
Wright, B.   Which is the way ahead?   Film 14:6 N/D
'57

WYATT,  RON
Wyatt Cattance productions.   Film 45:27 Spg '66

WYLER,  WILLIAM
Hogart, D.   His marriage.   Motion Pic 49:27 F '35
Biographical note; filmog.   Movies & People 2:47 '40
Direction by William Wyler.   Lions Roar 1-9:no p# My
'42
Director.   Time 39:72 Je 29 '42
Parsons, L. O.   Cosmopolitan's citation as one of the
best directors of the month.   Cosmop 122:100 Ja '47
Checklist of his films.   Theatre Arts 31:24 F '47
Isaacs, H. R.   Director with a passion and a craft.
Theatre Arts 31:20 F '47
Chandler, D.   Willy makes the stars tremble.   Colliers
125:26 F 4 '50

Griffith, R.  Wyler, Wellman and Huston.  Films In Review 1-1:1 F '50

Biography.  Current Biography 12:61 Ja '51

Same.  Current Biography Yearbook 1951:670 '52

The director and the public; a symposium.  Film Culture 1-2:15 Mr/Ap '55

The big screens.  Sight & Sound 24-4:209 Spg '55

Familiar subject.  Time 68:54 O 29 '56

Personality of the month.  Films & Filming 3-10:3 Jl '57

Reid, J. H.  A comparison of size.  Films & Filming 6-6:12 Mr '60

Reid, J. H.  A little larger than life.  Films & Filming 6-5:9 F '60

Zunser, J.  Wyler, westerns, Ben-Hur and Oscars. Cue 29-14:8 Ap 2 '60

Policeman, midwife, bastard.  Time 75:75 Je 27 '60

Adults' hour.  Newsweek 58:77 Ag 7 '61

Talk with the director.  Newsweek 59:101 Mr 12 '62

Sarris, A.  Fallen idols; filmog.  Film Culture 28:30 Spg '63

Brownlow, K.  The early days of William Wyler. Film 37:11 Aut '63

Heston, C.  Ben-Hur diaries.  Cinema (BH) 2-2:10 '64

Wyler's wiles.  Time 85:92 Je 18 '65

Interview at Cannes.  Cinema (BH) 2-6:39 Jl/Ag '65

Fixx, J. F.  Great Gallic volcano.  Sat R 48:16 D 25 '65

Heston, C.  Working with William Wyler.  Action 2-1:20 Ja/F '67

Hanson, C. L.  Filmography.  Cinema (BH) 3-5:29 Sum '67

Interview.  Cinema (BH) 3-5:23 Sum '67

Symbiosis continued.  Action 3-2:17 Mr/Ap '68

Should directors produce?  Action 3-4:10 Jl/Ag '68

What directors are saying.  Action 5-3:30 My/Je '70

Carey, G.  The lady and the director; Bette Davis and William Wyler.  Film Comment 6-3:18 Fall '70

Sarris, A.  Director of the month.  Show 1-6:14 O '70

Doeckel, K.  William Wyler; filmog.  Films In Review 22-8:468 O '71

Charlton Heston comments on Wyler.  Dialogue On Film 1:6 '72


WYNNE, BERT
    Obit.  Silent Pic 14:38 Spg '72

YATES, PETER
Lane, J. F. One way pendulum takes the lid off
suburbia. Films & Filming 11-2:7 N '64
Festival small but powerful. Hi Fi 16:MA15 Ag '66
Day, B. The suggestive experience; interview. Films &
Filming 15-11:4 Ag '69
What directors are saying. Action 4-5:32 S/O '69
What directors are saying. Action 5-1:28 Ja/F '70
What directors are saying. Action 5-4:30 Jl/Ag '70
Nolan, J. E. Films on TV; TV filmog. Films In Re-
view 21-10:631 D '70
Gow, G. Pressure; interview; filmog. Films & Filming
17-7:18 Ap '71

YOSHIDA, YOSHISHIGE
Biographical note. International Film G 8:193 '71

YOSHIMURA, KIMISABURO
Note. International Film G 2:35 '65

YOUNG, ROBERT
Cohen, S. B. Filmmakers of Nothing but a man; filmog.
Film Comment 3-2:8 Spg '65

YOUNG, TERENCE
Filmography. Film 14:8 N/D '57
British feature directors; an index to their work. Sight
& Sound 27-6:304 Aut '58
Sadism for the family; interview. Cinema (BH) 1-5:32
Ag/S '63
An underrated director. International Film G 1:51 '64
Lane, J. F. Young romantic. Films & Filming 13-4:58
F '67
British cinema filmography. Film 65:10 Spg '72

YOUNGERMAN, JOE
Windeler, R. Youngerman of the Director's guild of
America. Action 1-2:9 N/D '66

YUTKEVITCH, SERGEI
Yutkevitch, S. My way with Shakespeare. Films &
Filming 4-1:8 O '57
Yutkevitch, S. Cutting it to style. Films & Filming
8-6:10 Mr '62

ZADEK, PETER
  British cinema filmography.   Film 65:10 Spg '72

ZAFRANOVIC, LORDAN
  Biographical note.   International Film G 8:283 '71

ZAMPA, LUIGI
  Bluestone, G.   Luigi Zampa.   Film Q 12-2:9 Win '58

ZAMPI, MARIO
  British feature directors; an index to their work.   Sight
    & Sound 27-6:304 Aut '58
  Obit.   Film R p45 '64/65

ZAPPA, FRANK
  Manville, W. H.   Does this mother know best?   Sat
    Evening Post 241:56 Ja 13 '68
  Zapping with Zappa.   Newsweek 71:88 Je 3 '68
  Oracle has it all psyched out.   Life 64:82 Je 28 '68
  Medjuck, J.   Interview.   Take One 2-2:8 N/D '68
  Mephisto in Hollywood.   Time 94:46 O 31 '69
  Hit it, Zubin.   Time 95:72 Je 1 '70

ZAREMBER, SAM
  A still photographer turns filmmaker.   Making Films
    1-1:44 Mr '67

ZEBBA, SAM
  Zebba, S.   Casting and directing in primitive societies.
    Q Film Radio TV 11-2:154 Win '56

ZEFFIRELLI, FRANCO
  Corns, bunions and all.   Newsweek 57:58 My 22 '61
  Brien, A.   European portfolio.   Theatre Arts 46:62
    F '62
  Ardoin, J.   Zeffirelli.   Musical America 82:16 N '62
  Merkling, F.   Firebrand of Florence.   Opera News
    27:14 D 15 '62
  Revised standard Dane.   Time 82:38 D 27 '63
  New production of Verdi's Falstaff at the Met.   Time
    83:59 Mr 13 '64
  Final fugue.   Newsweek 63:94 Mr 16 '64
  Mayer, M.   High order of talent.   Opera News 28:6
    Mr 21 '64

Weaver, W.    Franco Zeffirelli; interview.    Hi Fi 14:30
    Mr '64

Lyon, N.    Second fame; good food.    Vogue 145:134 F 15
    '65

Stewart, R. S.    Vision of Franco Zeffirelli.    N. Y.
    Times Mag p10 S 4 '66

Make mingle with our tambourines; interview.    Opera
    News 31:33 S 17 '66

Freeman, J. W.    In the grand tradition.    Opera News
    31:40 S 17 '66

Tony and Cleo.    Newsweek 68:98 S 26 '66

Kolodin, I.    Barber's Antony, after Zeffirelli.    Sat R
    49:35 O 1 '66

Lane, J. F.    The taming of the shrew.    Films & Film-
    ing 13-1:50 O '66

Devlin, P.    I know my Romeo and Juliet.    Vogue 151:34
    Ap 1 '68

Wolf, W.    Shaking up Shakespeare.    Cue 37-38:15 S 21
    '68

Kael, P.    Current cinema.    New Yorker 44:209 O 19 '68

Kolodin, I.    Music to my ears.    Sat R 53:21 Ja 24 '70

Mayer, M.    Hey! Who pinched my libretto?    N. Y.
    Times Bio Ed Mr 19 '72

## ZEMAN, KAREL
Libuse, K.    Putting on a style.    Films & Filming
    7-9:35 Je '61

## ZETTERLING, MAI
Zetterling, M.    Some notes on acting.    Sight & Sound
    21-2:83 O/D '51

Wolf, W.    Mai Zetterling censures the censor.    Cue
    35-41:12 O 8 '66

Meeting with Mai Zetterling.    Cahiers (Eng) 6:63 D '66

Lerman, L.    International movie report.    Mademoiselle
    64:116 F '67

Pyros, J.    Notes on women directors.    Take One 3-2:7
    N/D '70

McGregor, C.    Mai is behind the camera now.    N. Y.
    Times Bio Ed Ap 30 '72

## ZILNIK, ZELIMIR
Biographical note.    International Film G 8:282 '71

## ZIMMERMAN, VERNON
Mekas, J.    Notes on the new American cinema.    Film
    Culture 24:6 Spg '62

Listing of films.   Film Culture 37:7 Sum '65

ZINNEMANN, FRED
He found what he wanted.   Lions Roar 1-8:no p# Ap '42
New faces among MGM directors too.   Lions Roar 1-11/
    12:no p# Jl/Ag '42
Directing a dog's life.   Lions Roar 2-2:no p# N '42
MGM's directors range from pioneers to newcomers.
    Lions Roar 3-4:no p# Jl '44
When Hitler was only a worm.   Lions Roar 3-4(sup):no
    p# Jl '44
Zinnemann, F.   Different perspective.   Sight & Sound
    17-67:113 Aut '48
Quick wonder.   New Yorker 26:17 Ag 19 '50
Morris, J.   Zinnemann's international family.   Parents
    26:32 Ja '51
Knight, A.   Fred Zinnemann.   Films In Review 2-1:21
    Ja '51
Zinnemann, F.   Choreography of a gunfight.   Sight &
    Sound 21-1:16 Jl/S '52
Samuels, G.   Director, Hollywood's leading man.   N.Y.
    Times Mag p22 O 26 '52
Biography.   Current Biography 14:58 Mr '53
    Same.   Current Biography Yearbook 1953:672 '53
Fred Zinnemann, Oscar winner.   Vogue 123:110 My 1  '54
Crist, J.   Movie maker.   Scholastic 67:6 N 17 '55
Knight, A.   Hook.   Sat R 40:23 Jl 27  '57
Wonderful things.   Newsweek 50:121 O 14 '57
Bachmann, G.   The impact of television on motion
    pictures; interview.   Film Culture 3-2(12):3 '57
Director's view; Nun's story.   America 101:469 Je 27 '59
Young, C.   The old dependables.   Film Q 13-1:2 Fall '59
Bob; a conversation.   Film 21:27 S/O '59
Zinnemann, F.   A conflict of conscience; interview.
    Films & Filming 6-3:7 D '59
Taylor, J. R.   Interview.   Sight & Sound 30-1:15 Win
    '60/61
Zinnemann, F.   From here to eternity; letter.   Films In
    Review 12-9:564 N '61
A discussion: personal creation in Hollywood: can it be
    done?   Film Q 15-3:16 Spg '62
Neyman, M.   Off the highway.   Sight & Sound 31-4:177
    Aut '62
Fenin, G.   The face of '63--United States.   Films &
    Filming 9-6:55 Mr '63
Sarris, A.   Fallen idols; filmog.   Film Culture 28:30
    Spg '63

Desert island films.   Films & Filming 9-11:11 Ag '63
The directors choose the best films.   Cinema (BH)
    1-5:14 Ag/S '63
Schickel, R.   Fred Zinnemann: quiet man on the set.
    Show 4-3:80 Mr '64
Quiet man on the set.   Show 4-7:80 Jl/Ag '64
Zinnemann talks back; interview.   Cinema (BH) 2-3:20
    O/N '64
Johnson, W.   Zinnemann pictures a modern dilemma.
    Senior Scholastic 85:28 S 30 '64
Zinnemann, F.   Revelations.   Films & Filming 10-12:5
    S '64
Zinnemann, F.   Montgomery Clift.   Sight & Sound
    35-4:204 Aut '66
Lerman, L.   International movie report.   Mademoiselle
    64:117 F '67
Reid, J. H.   A man for all movies.   Films & Filming
    13-8:5 My '67
Some questions answered.   Action 2-3:22 My/Je '67
Stanbrook, A.   A man for all movies.   Films & Filming
    13-9:11 Je '67
Biography.   British Book Year 1968:116 '68
Jeremiah.   The stars' stars; astrology.   Show 1-5:16
    My '70
Adler, D.   Zinnemann's fate.   Show 1-5:41 My '70

ZWARTJES, FRANS
    Biographical note.   International Film G 9:200 '72

# LIST OF PERIODICALS RESEARCHED

Action; Directors' Guild
  of America
AFI Report
After Dark; Magazine of
  Entertainment
Afterimage
America
American Artist
American Cinematographer
American City
American Federationist
American Heritage
American Home
American Imago
American Magazine
American Magazine of Art
American Mercury
American Photography
American Projectionist
American Record Guide
American Scandinavian
American Scholar
Americana Annual
Americas
Annals of the American
  Academy of Political and
  Social Science
Applause
Architectural Forum
Architecture
Arizona Highways
Art in America
Art News
Arts & Decoration
Asia, Journal of the
  American Asiatic
  Association

Athenaeum
Atlantic Monthly
Atlas
Audio Visual Guide
Audubon Magazine

Better Homes & Gardens
Black Oracle
Blue Book Magazine
Bookman, The
Bookman [London]
Brighton Film Review
British Book Year
Broadcasting
Business Week

Cahiers du Cinema [in
  English]
Camera
Canadian Bookman
Canadian Forum
Canadian Magazine
Castle of Frankenstein
Catholic World
Chemistry & Industry
Christian Century
Christian Science Monitor
  Magazine
Cinéaste
Cinefantastique
Cinema [Beverly Hills]
Cinema [Hollywood] (... for
  Discriminating Movie
  Goers)
Cinema [London]

Cinema Arts
Cinema Digest
Cinema Journal
Classic
Classic Film Collector
Collier's
Collier's Yearbook
Columbia Mirror
Commentary
Commonweal
Congressional Digest
Contempora
Contemporary Review
Coronet
Cosmopolitan
Craft Horizons
Creative Art
CTA
CTVD: Cinema--TV--Digest
Cue: the weekly ... guide
   to ... New York ...
Current Biography
Current Biography Yearbook
Current History
Current Opinion


Dance Magazine
Dancing Times
Delineator
Design
Dial, The
Dialogue on Film
Discovery
Discussion
Drama Review
Dramatic Mirror
Dunn's Review and Modern
   Industry


Ebony
Economist
Editor & Publisher
Educational Theatre Journal
8mm Collector
Electrical World
Encounter

Esquire
Etude
Evergreen Review
Everybody's Magazine
Exceptional Photoplays
Exhibitors' Herald
Experimental Cinema


Famous Monsters of Film-
   land
Feature Movie
Film
Film Comment
Film Culture
Film Fan Monthly
Film Heritage
Film Journal, The
Film Journal [Australia]
Film Library Quarterly
Film Players Herald &
   Movie Pictorial
Film Quarterly
Film Review
Film Society Review
Filmmakers Newsletter
Filmograph
Films and Filming
Films Illustrated
Films In Review
Finders Keepers; The Maga-
   zine of Esoteric Discover-
   ies
Flying
Focus! Chicago's Movie
   Journal
Focus on Film
For Monsters Only
Forbes
Fortnightly Review
Fortune
Forum
France Illustrated
Free World
Funnyworld


Golden Book Magazine

Good Housekeeping
Gore Creatures
Graphic
Green Book Magazine


Harper's Bazaar
Harper's Weekly; Harper's
    Monthly
Hearst's Magazine
High Fidelity
Holiday
Hollywood Quarterly
Horizon
Horn Book
Horticulture
House & Garden
House Beautiful
Hudson Review


Illustrated London News
Illustrated World
Independent
Independent Woman
International Film Annual
International Film Guide
Interview (Andy Warhol's
    Inter/view)

Japanese Fantasy Film
    Journal
Journal of Popular Film,
    The
Journal of the Optical
    Society
Journal of the Society of
    Motion Pictures and
    Television Engineers


Kenyon Review
Kinema


Ladies' Home Journal
Leslie's Weekly
Liberty

Library Journal
Life
Life and Letters
Lion's Roar
Literary Digest
Literary Review
Living Age
Living for Young Home-
    makers
London News
Look


Mademoiselle
Magazine of Art
Making Films in New York
Massachusetts Review
McCall's
McClure's Magazine
Mentor, The
Metropolitan Magazine
Mise-en-Scène
Modern Drama
Modern Photography
Monogram
Motion Picture
Motion Picture Classic
Motion Picture Supplement
Motor Trend
Movie
Movie Classic
Movie Pictorial
Movies and the People Who
    Make Them
Ms
Munsey's Magazine
Musical America
Musical Courier


Naborhood Theatre Review
Nation, The
Nation, The [London]
National Magazine
National Cylopaedia
National Geographic
National Review
Nation's Business

Nature Magazine
New Outlook
New Republic
New Statesman
New Statesman & Nation
New Theatre
New York
New York Clipper
New York Dramatic Mirror
New York Film Review
New York Herald Book
   Review
New York Times
New York Times Bio-
   graphical Edition
New York Times Book
   Review
New York Times Magazine
New Yorker
Newsweek
Nineteenth Century
North American
North American Review


On Film
One Act Play Magazine
Opera News
Outdoor Life
Outing Magazine
Outlook, The
Overland Monthly


Parents' Magazine
Partisan Review
Peabody Journal of
   Education
Photography
Photon
Photoplay
Photoplay Journal
Pictorial Review
Picture Play
Pictures & Picturegoer
Playboy
Plays and Players
Popular Mechanics

Popular Photography
Popular Science
Poetry
Print
Progressive Architecture
Publishers Weekly


Quandrum
Quarterly of Film, Radio,
   TV


Radio & TV News
Radio Guide
Ramparts Magazine
Reader's Digest
Redbook
Reporter
Review of Reviews
Rotarian


St. Nicholas
Saturday Evening Post
Saturday Review
Scandinavian Studies
Scholastic
School Arts
Science Digest
Science Newsletter
Scientific American
Screen: The Journal of the
   Society for Education in
   Film and Television
Screen Book
Screen Education Studies
Screen Facts
Screen Greats
Screen Legends
Screen World
Scribner's Magazine
Senior Scholastic
Seventeen
Sewanee Review
Show: The Magazine of
   Films and the Arts
Sight and Sound

Sightlines
Silent Picture, The
Silver Screen
Social Studies
Spectator
Spectator [London]
Sports Illustrated
Stage, The
Strand Magazine
Story World
Sunset
Survey

Take One
Television
TeleVision Guide
Theatre
Theatre Annual
Theatre Arts Magazine
Theatre Guild Magazine
Theatre World
Those Enduring Matinee
  Idols
Time
Todays Filmmaker
Todays Health
Town and Country
Travel
Travel and Camera
Tulane Drama Review
TV Guide
TV Personalities
Twentieth Century

U. N. Bulletin [U. N. Weekly
  Bulletin]
U. N. World
UNESCO Courier
Unifrance
U. S. Camera
U. S. News and World
  Report

Vanity Fair
Velvet Light Trap, The
Views & Reviews

Virginia Quarterly Review
Vision
Vital Speeches of the Day
Vogue


Week-End Review
Wilson Library Bulletin
Woman's Home Companion
Woman's Journal
Women & Film
World Review
World Theatre
World's Work
World's Work [London]
Writer


Yale French Studies
Yale Literary Magazine
Yale Review

## Appendix II

## KEY TO ABBREVIATIONS

| | |
|---|---|
| Ap | April |
| Ag | August |
| Aut | Autumn |
| D | December |
| F | February |
| Filmog. | Filmography |
| Ja | January |
| Je | June |
| Jl | July |
| Mr | March |
| My | May |
| N | November |
| n. d. | Not Dated; No Date |
| O | October |
| obit. | Obituary |
| p | Page |
| S | September |
| sec | Section |
| Spg | Spring |
| Sum | Summer |
| sup | Supplement |
| Win | Winter |